Strategic Brand Management

Strategic Brand Management

Third Edition

Richard **Rosenbaum-Elliott**
Larry **Percy**
Simon **Pervan**

OXFORD
UNIVERSITY PRESS

OXFORD
UNIVERSITY PRESS

Great Clarendon Street, Oxford, OX2 6DP,
United Kingdom

Oxford University Press is a department of the University of Oxford.
It furthers the University's objective of excellence in research, scholarship,
and education by publishing worldwide. Oxford is a registered trade mark of
Oxford University Press in the UK and in certain other countries

First edition 2007
Second edition 2011

Impression: 2

Published in the United States of America by Oxford University Press
198 Madison Avenue, New York, NY 10016, United States of America

British Library Cataloguing in Publication Data

Data available

Library of Congress Control Number: 2015933306

ISBN 978–0–19–870420–1

Printed in Great Britain by Bell & Bain Ltd., Glasgow

Contents

vii

New to this edition

- An international focus with many new examples from Asia, Australia, and Europe.
- Updated and extended coverage of online and technological changes to brand management strategies, including social media and internet communities.
- A range of new and updated case studies and examples illustrate significant developments in brand management practice since 2011.
- New key concept boxes allow the reader to recap and review the core theories and ideas set out at the beginning of each chapter.
- A new full-colour presentation enhances the reader's understanding of brand management theory and practice.

Preface

Creating a true brand is one of the most powerful things any company can do to enhance its market power.

(Financial Times)

Successful branding adds customer value and can provide protection from price competition and pressures towards commoditization. This involves complex processes of authenticity, reassurance, the development of meaning, the transformation of experience, and differentiation which eventually move from satisfying a basic human need for control and assurance to becoming a medium of social exchange and social structuration in advanced societies. The subject is now considered vitally import, since financial services, politicians, celebrities, and even religions come to be recognized as brands that can and should be managed.

The theoretical base for the book comes from the prominent research of the first author into brands and symbolic meaning, identity, and emotion; that of the second author into brands and advertising, as a leading academic and consultant to companies around the world; and the third author who, as co-editor in chief of Europe's leading consumer behaviour journal, works extensively with scholars and practitioners on research into contemporary brand settings. It also draws on the communication and positioning models covered in the companion text (*Strategic Advertising Management*) and therefore integrates brands and advertising in a unique fashion not covered elsewhere.

The third edition brings sharper focus to key concepts in brand management and highlights the integration of web-based technologies and market places like social media and online retailing. Electronically mediated environments are now too pervasive to be treated as 'new technology' and, as such, their impact is illustrated throughout the book with many new cases and updated examples provided.

The book takes a sociocultural approach which draws on contemporary sociology, cultural studies, anthropology, and social theory rather than relying on just the cognitive, information-processing approach to branding. We believe it moves the subject field forward in intellectual terms. However, the wide experience of the authors in consulting with industry and teaching on demanding MBA and executive development courses around the world means that these complex and exciting ideas are firmly grounded in managerial implications and applications.

How to use this book

Key concept list

Identify the important concepts addressed in each chapter using these bullet-pointed lists. This feature can also be used to plan and organize your revision.

Key Concepts

1 Measuring brand performance and the effectiveness of a brand's marketing communication is critical to effective brand managemen

2 There is an important difference between the strength and the nat brand equity.

3 To effectively measure brand equity one must understand how it is and developed.

4 A brand equity audit helps to uncover the elements of a brand and market that are likely to affect its equity.

Tables and figures

Develop your understanding through visual illustrations of key models and important data.

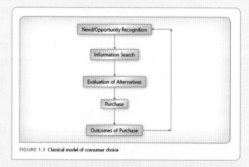

FIGURE 1.3 Classical model of consumer choice

Photographs

Refer to the full-colour photographs throughout the book which illustrate examples of brands or advertisements referenced in the text.

ENGINEERED FOR A LOWER IMPACT ON THE ENVIRONMENT
THE LOWEST CO2 EMISSION CAR RANGE IN EUROPE

Key concept boxes

Return to the core ideas set out at the beginning of each chapter and recap on key theories and concepts as you work through the text. This is also a useful tool for revision.

KEY CONCEPT

Brand building in mindspace

How does one build a brand in a mindspace? What we mean by this is that we hold different associations in our minds (you could visualize this as different places in your mind) as we become more committed to a brand. The model in Fig. 8.1 is presented as hierarchy, so a customer will go through each of the steps in a sequence. It is desirable that your customers are further up the chain because they are then likely to be more committed to you. The reality is that most brands have customer groups at each of these stages. It is the brand manager's task to move them up but also to be aware that some customers will move down, for example, if a crisis event occurs with the product or a new entrant manages to gain share of that mindspace. So, although presented as a sequence, the process is often iterative and brand managers must closely monitor the market to counter the competition to maintain customer positions at the top as well as move others up.

Chapter summaries

Review your understanding at the end of every chapter.

CHAPTER SUMMARY

In this chapter we have discussed how in postmodernity brands can become symbolic resources for the construction, communication, and maintenance of identity. Brands can acquire symbolic meaning in a variety of ways, but one of the most potent sources is advertising, particularly through narrative and the construction of socially shared meanings. We have seen that the symbolic consumption of brands can help establish and communicate some of the basic cultural categories, such as social status, gender, and age. Brands can acquire deep meaning through the socialization process and such brands can restore a sense of security. We suggest that mass-market brands can acquire individual meanings through ritual and personal interpretations of meaning.

Discussion questions

Reflect on what you have learned from each chapter and use these questions as a basis for class discussion and debate.

DISCUSSION QUESTIONS

1 What does it mean to be a postmodern consumer?
2 What is the difference between self-symbolism and social-symbolism and how does it relate to brands?
3 What is the difference between lived and mediated experience?
4 Explain the process of discursive elaboration in relation to a brand.
5 How important is the lived experience of using a brand compared with the influence of advertising?
6 What are the implications of postmodern fragmentation for brand strategy?
7 How might a brand acquire deep meaning?

xi

Case studies

Apply your understanding by analysing a range of real-world examples in more detail.

CASE STUDY

The cultural meaning of stationary! Where do we draw the line? The case of kikki.K and Smiggle

Introduction

Fashion. Stationery. Who would have thought that these two worlds–the former, synonymous with style, design and innovation and the latter, associated with utility, practicality and functionality–could come together? Yet, in spite of its apparent incompatibility, fashion and stationery is a match made in heaven.

The emergence of the fashion stationery product category can be traced back to 1996, when UK-based brand Paperchase introduced its range of stylish, design-led stationery. Its ascendance however can be attributed two Australian brands; kikki.K and Smiggle. With their innovative product designs and creative marketing, branding, and retail activities, kikki.K and Smiggle have transformed stationery into a fashion accessory; a statement of one's style, personality and individuality. In the process of turning the then dull stationery market on its head, kikki.K and Smiggle have created a cult-like following amongst both children and adults, and fuelled a sub-culture of 'stationery freaks'.

kikki. K

Further reading

Take your learning further with relevant supplementary reading, recommended by the authors.

FURTHER READING

• An excellent introduction to the sociology of consumption is Slater, D. (1997), *Consumer Culture and Modernity*, Cambridge: Polity Press.
• Seminal contributions to the theory of consumer society are contained in M. Lee (ed.) (2000), *The Consumer Society Reader*, Oxford: Blackwell.
• Leading-edge thinking about branding as a cultural process can be found in J. Schroeder and M. Salzer-Morling (eds) (2005), *Brand Culture*, London: Routledge.

How to use the Online Resource Centre

Visit www.oxfordtextbooks.co.uk/orc/elliott_percy3e/ to access supporting content for students and registered lecturers.

For students

Web exercises

Develop your research skills and put your knowledge to the test with exercises related to online articles and websites.

> **Chapter 04**
>
> Visit http://www.saabsunited.com/ a brand community for Saab enthusiasts. Read the posts and comments and try to identify examples of the four thematic categories of value creation in online brand communities, developed by Schau et al (2009) and outlined below. Are there any other themes that you can see emerging?
>
> 1. *social networking*, which includes welcoming, empathizing with, and governing each other;
>
> 2. *impression management*, the creation of favourable impressions of the brand through

Web links

Connect to relevant and reliable brand management resources using web links organized by chapter.

> **The Social Psychology of Brands: Emotion, Symbolism, Cultural Meaning**
>
> http://www.millwardbrown.com
> Millward Brown is a global research agency specializing in advertising, marketing communications, media and brand equity research. This site contains up to date "Insights"; case studies on leading brands and brand trends.
>
> http://www.yankelovich.com
> Daniel Yankelovich is considered by many as the founding father of public opinion research in the USA. This site provides case studies and expert opinion about branding and consumer research.

For registered lecturers

PowerPoint slides

Adapt PowerPoint slides for use in your lecture presentations. The slides can be easily customized to match your own teaching requirements, or can be used as hand-outs in class.

> **What is a brand?**
>
> • A brand is a label, designating ownership by a firm, which we experience, evaluate, have feeling towards, and build associations with to perceive value (Brakus, et al., 2009).
> • Brands only exist in the minds of customers.

Resource box

Access a variety of links to articles, books, YouTube videos, and other websites to support your teaching.

> **Chapter 02**
>
> 'Learning to Use Regret: Studies in the negative emotions and how to use them', *Kellogg Insight*: Focus on Research, based on the research of Neal J. Roese, Colleen Saffrey, and Amy Summerville. Availble at: http://insight.kellogg.northwestern.edu/index.php/Kellogg/article/learning_to_use_regret [posted May 2010].
>
> In this article, a study on regret is reported. The author of the study suggests that regret is not an unwanted emotion. Indeed many more people report that they benefit from feeling of regret rather than suffer as it provides the impetus for positive change. The article closes with an example of how to structure marketing messages and advertising to leverage the idea of regret and make consumers value a company or product more highly.

The Sociocultural Meaning of Brands

This section locates brands in relation to consumer behaviour and the growth of consumer culture, drawing on psychology, sociology, and anthropology.

Understanding the Social Psychology of Brands

1

Key Concepts

1 Brands exist in the mind of the market, so brand management is the management of perceptions.

2 Brands can be separated into those that are primarily functional and those that are primarily emotional.

3 We review the ways in which consumers make choices between brands and emphasize the key role played by involvement.

4 In low-involvement situations, top-of-mind awareness may be the single most important factor.

4

Introduction

A brand is a label, designating ownership by a firm, which we experience, evaluate, have feeling towards, and build associations with to perceive value (Brakus, *et al.*, 2009). In building brand value 'perception is more important than reality' (Duncan and Moriarty, 1998), and as brands only exist in the minds of customers the management of brands is all about the management of perceptions. The power of a brand to influence perceptions can transform the experience of using the product. Think about the computer on your desk, the toothpaste you use, the sunglasses you wear, the charity you choose to support—brands matter! In order to manage brands strategically we need to understand how perceptions are organized, how they influence behaviour, and how a brand can compete in the battle for 'mindspace' (Corstjens and Corstjens, 1995).

The history of brands

Brand-like marks have been in existence for thousands of years. Fig. 1.1 outlines a brief history of brands and their purpose. Evidence of brands, like labels or seals, can be traced back to prehistory and Bronze Age society (Wengrow, 2008). The early use of these kinds of brand was for administrative purposes. Initially signatures or marks were used to indicate ownership, place of origin, or jurisdiction. As society and trade became more complex and specialized they were used to indicate the content of containers and also the quality of the product; for example, to this day, hallmarks and watermarks are used to indicate the quality of metal and paper. Perhaps the most significant change in the use of branding, one that branding as we know it depends on, was how it was utilized in the separation of production from consumption. Goods were not used only to be consumed but also to extend into time and space as signifiers of authority, ownership, and status (Moor, 2007). The first examples of this were where nations who conquered new territory (and people) needed to leave their mark to remind their subjects who their new rulers were.

Branding as we know it today only really began in 1760, when the industrial revolution allowed rapid gains in packaging and printing innovation. This provided a systematic way for manufacturers to place their mark on a product (Moor, 2007); before then, manufacturers usually sold in bulk to retailers who then placed the product into their own, or unmarked, packaging. Now they had a means to differentiate their product from others and confer meaning via the images they used and promotional material that could be developed with these signs. The industrial revolution was also the first time supply began to consistently outstrip demand. Here as well the desire to brand resulted from the separation of production from consumption. Driven by the political ideology of industrial capitalism, the pursuit of profit through economic growth meant that all that was made was not guaranteed a sale. Branding had emerged as a key element of a product's value in an increasingly competitive market place.

The organizing framework for this book is constructed by the separation of the concept of the brand into a functional domain as a representation of what the product actually does for us and an emotional/symbolic domain as a representation of what the product means to us. See Fig. 1.2. In the functional domain, the basic brand attribute is a product that keeps its promises of performance; in essence what you see is what you get. Honda played with this notion in their advertising campaign, 'more reliable than life', when the Brio was

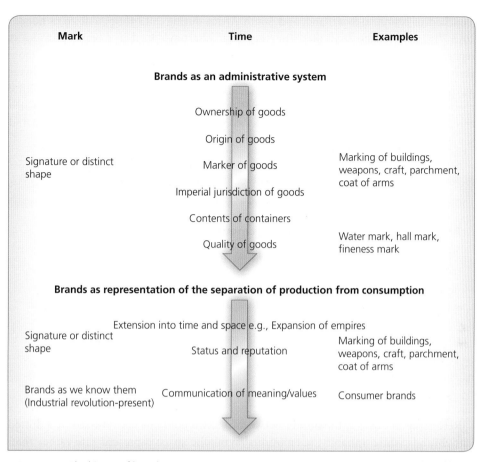

FIGURE 1.1 The history of brands

	Brand attributes	Consumer benefits
Involvement		
	Symbolic meaning	Social language of the brand Self-enhancement Self-positioning
Emotional realm	Personality Authenticity	Transformation of experience
	Reassurance	Safe choice
		Easy choice
Functional realm	Keeping promises of performance	Certainty in an uncertain world
		Replicability of satisfaction

FIGURE 1.2 The Social Psychology of the Brand

launched in Namibia, Swaziland, and South Africa during 2013 (http://ddb.co.za/honda/2013/7/29/more-reliable-than-life). The very basic consumer benefit a brand provides is replicability of simple satisfaction of a functional need, the solving of a problem. At a more abstract level we can say that it brings some certainty in an uncertain world and this delivers a prime benefit for the consumer: it makes choice easy, simplifying the world for us. Think about how unsettling it can be trying to negotiate a supermarket of unfamiliar brands whilst abroad. In our familiar environments we develop habitual behaviour, because once we find something that works, we often continue to buy it, not having to think or worry.

KEY CONCEPT

Brand management is the management of perceptions

Try and explain in a sentence what Red Bull means to you? Would the answer be a high caffeine sugary beverage? Unlikely. You would almost certainly ponder a while and try to articulate a feeling: daring, fear, excitement, or describe a person: risk taker, dangerous, free. Oh to be able to bottle these things, to manage them in the traditional sense, and to store them. We of course cannot do this, but what we can do is try to create a perception of our brand through careful management of communication to target audiences.

Returning to Fig. 1.2, the border between the two domains is expressed by a dotted line. Brands which inhabit the emotional/symbolic space represent safe rather than easy choices. The difference is due to increasing levels of risk, both functional and symbolic. As risk increases, the choice has to be more than just easy, consumers have to develop a trust relationship with the brand. As consumers become more involved with a purchase decision their choice becomes increasingly driven by emotional processes and so the consumer benefit of the brand becomes a safe choice. Safe in terms of all of the expectations that consumers have for the product, be it performance, excitement, style, or status. In Chapter 2 we will be examining emotion-driven choice and the development of trust in brands. It is this trust as a fundamental component of brand equity which is examined in Chapter 5. As consumers become still more involved with the brand, its symbolic meaning becomes of prime importance as it transforms their lived experiences and may become part of how they build and communicate their social and cultural identities. The symbolic meaning of a brand is discussed in Chapter 3 and the cultural communication process is discussed in Chapter 4. However, before we come to the specifics of brand meaning and how it is used by consumers, we need to locate brands in formal models of consumer behaviour.

Understanding consumer behaviour

The traditional approach to understanding consumer behaviour is as a sequence of stages through which the buyer moves, gathering information and evaluating competitive offerings before reaching a decision and acting upon it. This is an idealized

KEY CONCEPT

Functional and emotional brands

All brands have a functional element; the things that deliver core benefits, the nuts and bolts of the good or service. For example, the functional element of toothpaste is that it cleans your teeth, for an MP3 player it is sound quality. Some brands compete on their function, but unless the product is truly superior or demand exceeds supply this strategy is not sustainable. Most brands also need to generate an emotional response. Even low involvement brands such as toothpaste want to generate emotional responses associated with positive outcomes like familiarity, family well-being, or safety. Why? Because an emotional association is much harder for competitors to replicate or 'reverse engineer' and is, therefore, a more defendable position to hold.

model which has its origins as a cognitive psychological model of how a rational purchaser makes purchase choices and only rarely describes how people actually behave. See Fig. 1.3.

Fig. 1.3 shows the consumer moving through a series of psychological states and sequences of action before reaching a choice decision. It is an information-processing model which assumes that the consumer is sufficiently motivated to invest the mental and physical effort required to search out and process information. However, if we examine what we as consumers actually do through the various stages, we find wide divergence from the classical model.

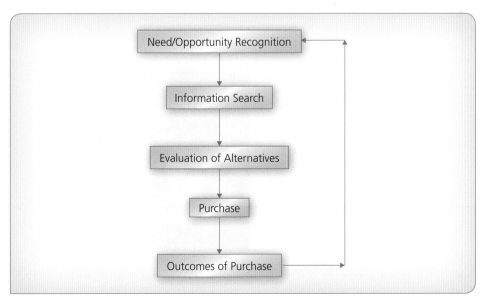

FIGURE 1.3 Classical model of consumer choice

Need/opportunity recognition

Consumers recognize a need or an opportunity for a product when they perceive an important gap between their current state and their ideal or desired state. Opportunity recognition occurs when life changes or when advertising prompts an upward change in expectations, for example you may desire a more expensive suit after a promotion or move from instant to espresso coffee as your tastes become more sophisticated. This represents much of the growth of consumer product and service markets. However, the level of motivation required to prompt a purchase may be at a much lower level than this suggests. For example, much consumption is driven by a desire to emulate other people, and this may often be at a subconscious level, thus the emphasis on a process initiated by conscious perception may be overstated. Also low levels of simple curiosity may be sufficient to prompt purchase.

Information search

Searching for information may involve an internal search of memory and/or an external search of the environment for information. For most consumers, for most products, an internal search of memory substitutes for an external search and awareness alone may be sufficient to effect choice. For instance, were you one of the many who wanted an Apple iPhone 6 or Google Nexus 6 before the specifications and reviews were available to consciously trigger a need? Studies of external information search and actual shopping behaviour for consumer durables have found wide differences between individuals' search behaviour (McColl Kennedy and Fetter, 2001; Guo 2001). Early research by Beatty and Smith (1987), indicated that just 25% of people visited four or more shops, while 37% bought at the one and only shop they visited; 32% only considered one brand while 16% considered four or more; 52% obtained no independent information, while 11% consulted two sources. Even for the purchase of new cars, more than 30% of people considered only one make of car and visited only one car dealer prior to purchase (Punj and Staelin, 1983). Even for expensive goods most of us only visit one shop, do not gather additional information from advertising, and generally process very little information.

Apple iPhone 6: Limited external search? © Mutlu Kurtbas / istockphoto.com

The internet has enabled us to seek information much more easily. Many industries have been fundamentally changed by this. For example, the travel industry is now dominated by online retailers, many of whom offer price comparison options across the full range of airlines rather than having contractual arrangements with just a few. Flight Centre in Australia, the largest bricks and mortar travel agency, had to quickly move to online services after the success of solely online competitors such as WebJet and Expedia, who make their money out of service and booking fees rather than airline commissions. Initially they offered only budget airline information online, but adjusted to the full suite when they realized customers, and not just the digital native 18–30 year olds, were comfortable searching for information for travel on the internet. Flight Centre have managed to maintain their physical stores by focusing on high service corporate accounts, niche travel destinations, and the growing cruise liner market. These are more complex offerings, which are more likely to require interpersonal interaction.

Evaluation of alternatives

In order to choose between competing brands consumers must decide which evaluative criteria will be used and employ some form of decision rule. The evaluative criteria (sometimes called choice criteria) are the product attributes, functional, symbolic, and emotional on which the relative performance of the competing alternatives will be compared. The decision rule is the strategy that is used to deal with the information available and arrive at a choice. However, consumers also use certain tangible attributes as surrogate indicators, or signals, of less tangible attributes. In particular, price and brand name are often used as surrogate indicators of quality and this appears to be a cultural universal (Dawar and Parker, 1994). Decision rules can be categorized as either compensatory or non-compensatory. Compensatory rules allow poor performance on one attribute to be offset by good performance on another attribute. For example, you may forgo a cheaper price for superior sound quality on your MP3 player. Non-compensatory decision rules are simpler strategies in which consumers use one single standard and eliminate those alternatives which do not measure up to it. For example, 'my sound system must play iPod technology'. Rules are developed by experience and stored in memory and can be retrieved when necessary; at other times consumers may construct rules as they go along, using fragments of rules stored in memory to make an on-the-spot choice (Payne *et al.*, 1992). For example, they may make a choice between two brands of instant coffee based partly on knowledge about the comparative prices, the colour of the packaging, and a vague memory of a taste preference.

It has become clear in recent years that our information-processing limitations greatly affect the way in which we make purchase decisions. In conjunction with the dominant perspective of humans as 'cognitive misers' who will always seek to reduce cognitive effort and will be content to merely satisfy rather than maximize their decision outcomes, the study of decision rules has moved towards the study of various simplifying decision heuristics or 'rules of thumb' used by consumers to reduce the cognitive effort of choice. It has been argued that some of these 'rules of thumb' are efficient and accurate, such as the equal weight rule which examines all of the attributes and all of the data but simplifies the process by ignoring the relative importance or probability of each attribute.

However, most 'rules of thumb' that we use seem to be either inaccurate strategies or to lead to severe and systematic bias when compared with the rational decision-making model of economic theory. For example, consumers often use simple counts of good or bad features or rely on rules such as 'buy the cheapest brand' or 'buy what my parents buy' or the simplest habit rule 'buy the brand I bought last time' (Hoyer, 1984). Perhaps the most common is when a consumer retrieves pre-formed evaluations from memory and the one with the highest level of overall liking is chosen. We shall consider this simple use of emotion to drive the choice process in Chapter 2. We use inferences based on experience of the market place to help cope with information. For example, it appears that many of us cannot handle the arithmetic needed to compare prices across different quantities, and instead use a 'market belief' such as that 'if an item is on price promotion then it must be a better buy' (Alpert, 1993). These consumer market beliefs incorporate such brand beliefs as 'own-label brands are just the same as brand leaders sold under a different label at a lower price', and 'all brands are basically the same', and shop beliefs such as 'the more sales assistants there are in a shop, the more expensive are its products', and 'larger shops offer better prices than small shops'.

Other inherent biases in our 'rules of thumb' are evident in three prominent judgement rules that we use: representativeness, availability, and anchoring. These are general in their applicability and seem to operate over a wide range of decision areas (Kahneman and Tversky, 1979). Representativeness refers to the tendency to judge the probability that an object belongs to a category based on how typical it appears to be of that category, ignoring the statistical probability. This has important implications for brands which are strongly associated with particular product categories and may explain the limited success of consumer brands such as Bic perfume and Virgin Cola. The availability rule refers to the tendency for an event to be judged more probable in terms of how easily we can bring it to mind. For example, the performance of products with unusual brand names is more likely to be judged as a failure than the same product performance with a less distinctive brand name (Folkes, 1988). A further judgemental bias is the 'framing effect', in which the way in which product attributes are framed with either a positive or a negative label will affect our evaluations. Consumers who were presented with minced beef that was labelled '75% lean' had much more favourable evaluations of the meat than when the beef was labelled '25% fat'. However, this effect was reduced after actually tasting the meat (Levin and Gaeth, 1988). Adding further complexity to our understanding of decision heuristics, research indicates that if the ad for meat had focused on a goal that its consumption helps us to achieve, for example, 'reduction in heart disease' as opposed to an attribute focus, for example, '75% fat free', consumers prefer negative framing. Thus the positively framed goal that 'having red meat in your diet will help you to reduce the risk of heart disease' is less effective than the negatively framed goal that 'if you don't eat red meat in your diet you risk the chance of increasing heart disease' (Pervan and Vocino, 2008).

Purchase

Two important aspects of the purchase stage are the extent to which the purchase is actually pre-planned, and the choice of outlet to buy from. There are a range of factors which will intervene between a formed purchase intention and actual purchase. In many instances a conscious purchase intention is not formulated prior to the purchase act (Jones *et al.*, 2003). In supermarket shopping, the displays of products can act as a surrogate shopping list and prompt a type of impulse purchase (Cobb and Hoyer, 1986). This would be more accurately termed a partly-planned purchase as, although no specific intention is formed, a general intention to purchase exists. True impulse purchasing involves a sudden strong urge to purchase with diminished concern for the consequences. A large US study of supermarket purchase decisions found that the majority of brand decisions are made in-store, with 83% of snack food choice being decided upon in the shop (Meyer, 1988).

Rather than a choice between brands, for many people and many types of product shops form the group of brands from which choice is made, and brands may only be chosen once the shop decision has been made. Where do you do your supermarket shopping? Aldi, Carrefour, Tesco, Alcampo, Sainsbury's may all be in the evoked set of possible stores. For many people shopping is a recreational activity, a pleasure-giving activity for a significant proportion of the population with browsing leading to many unplanned purchases (Elliott, 1994; Peck and Childers, 2005).

Impulse or unplanned purchasing is not only a brick and mortar phenomenon. Social media sites such as Facebook have developed apps that allow purchase of products without having to click outside of the site (Freeman *et al.* 2014). Prices and menu upgrades for convenience food are offered exclusively to Facebook users, providing a simple purchase option. Freeman *et al.* (2014) examined 27 food and drink brand Facebook pages and found, in addition to impulse purchasing, people who experienced strong positive emotions while viewing Facebook page content for food and beverage brands were 3.25 times more likely to recommend the brands and 2.5 times more likely to prefer the brands.

Outcomes of purchase

The essence of post-purchase evaluation is whether the consumer is satisfied or dissatisfied with the product. The major cognitive approach in this area is the Expectancy Disconfirmation Model (Szymanski and Henard, 2001), which points to the importance of prior expectation in determining how we will interpret experience with the product post-purchase. If we have low expectations then poor performance will not cause much dissatisfaction. If, however, we have high expectations then poor performance will result in high levels of dissatisfaction. The opposite is true for satisfaction, in that if we have low expectations and the product performs well then we will be satisfied. However, recent research has emphasized the extra role of emotional aspects in achieving satisfaction versus the purely instrumental aspects of dissatisfaction (Homburg *et al.*, 2005).

Although dissatisfaction with purchases is common, relatively few of us actually make complaints. Complaint behaviour seems to be determined largely by an individual's propensity to seek redress, with as few as one in 20 taking action (Chebat *et al.*, 2005). However, the internet has allowed us to make complaints with relatively little cost and these are often publically shared via social networking sites. Negative word-of-mouth about a brand is now a much more pressing issue for brand managers. In the past, a brand's image was controlled predominantly through top down communication to the customer. However, now publicity about a brand, particularly when negative, can spread like wildfire across the internet. When this occurs, its image may be shaped from the bottom up (van Noort and Willemsen 2011). Take the IPhone 6 as an example. Within days of its release customers were complaining that it began to bend after a prolonged time in the hip pocket. What may have been a few disgruntled customers 15 years ago became a global issue within hours.

Our ability to learn from the experience of purchasing and using products is subject to a number of limitations and cognitive biases. In particular, if not highly motivated, we may limit learning by relying on previously learned schema, which can often be derived from advertising. In general, it is suggested that our learning from experience can be managed, with market leaders having much to gain by impeding learning. Take mobile phone network providers, for example, do you fully understand the myriad of pricing plans like 'flexible boosters', or 'mix and match 500' offered by some of these brands? In a recent nationwide study in Australia involving over 500 participants (Harrison, McQuilken and Robertson 2011), consumers reported 'a broad frustration and disappointment with the way in which the telco sector communicated to them. Some simply felt that the sector relied on 'information overload' as part of its business model ... All participants experienced confusion as a result, amongst other factors, of the jargon used by telcos' (p.13). Whether by design or perhaps because of the sheer complexity of niche offerings, this service sector, as well as retail banking and health clubs, has been singled out for criticism because of confusing product offerings (McGovern and Moon, 2007). Ill-informed consumers in these industries have led to significant revenue gains through penalties, fees, and over/under use of agreed packages. The principal method used is to encourage ambiguity by avoiding direct comparisons, and by attempting to control the attribute agenda by suggesting belief structures or schema which consumers can use to interpret consumption experiences (Alba and Hutchinson, 1988). Importantly, this is not always a cynical attempt to squeeze more revenue from customers. For instance, some Share Funds are attempting to set the attribute agenda for investors by adopting the claim that they are ethical. Brands such as Standard Life UK Ethical and BT Wholesale Ethical Share Fund in Australia are having increasing success convincing customers that ethical investment is a key attribute on which to judge competitors.

Consumer involvement

The concept of involvement is pivotal in consumer psychology as it attempts to describe aspects of the relative personal relevance or importance that a product or brand has for an individual. Fundamentally, involvement can be seen as the motivation to search for information and to engage in systematic processing, and it is a motivational state which affects many of the key aspects of consumer behaviour such as decision making, responses to persuasion, and processing of advertisements. Although it should properly be understood as a continuum running from very low to very high, it is useful to refer to high versus low involvement as a structural aid in locating different individuals' subjective perceptions of the personal relevance of a product, a brand, a purchase decision, or an advertisement. There are a number of different definitions of involvement and several alternative measurement methods but there is some agreement that involvement is a function of three sources of importance: the consumer, the product, and the situation (Richins *et al.*, 1992). Individual differences in the characteristics of the consumer include self-concept, values, personal goals, and needs. Product characteristics which will affect the level of involvement include the price, how frequently it is purchased, the symbolic meanings associated with the product and their social visibility, the perceived risk of poor performance or potential for harm, and the length of time one will have to commit to the product once it is purchased. The situational variables include aspects of the purchase situation itself, such as the amount of time available; whether the purchase is made privately or in the presence of others; and, more importantly, aspects of the intended use situation such as whether the product is intended as a gift, or will be used in an important social situation. It must always be remembered that involvement is person/product/situation specific, and while we can classify products as high- or low-involvement for ease of application, no product is low-involvement for every person at all times. The key elements of this model of involvement are shown in Fig. 1.4.

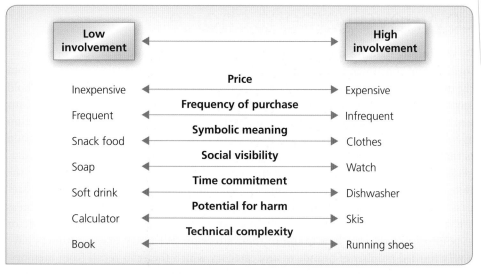

FIGURE 1.4 Factors influencing consumer involvement with products

The classical model of consumer decision making usually only applies to high-involvement products and/or when there are important situational factors. In these cases consumers may often seek extensive information prior to purchase. However, a qualification of the simple 'More involvement equals more information search' hypothesis is only true of functional products, those which satisfy by their actual performance like a lawnmower or home mortgage. Expressive or symbolic products, those which help us express our personality or self-concept are at once both highly involving and are purchased with little information search, as the psychosocial interpretation of these products is difficult to deconstruct into 'searchable' attributes as it is often particular to individuals—perhaps it is to be seen in the hat you will wear to a wedding or the tie to that important business meeting. This will be addressed when we consider emotion-driven choice in Chapter 2. But what do we know about how we make purchase choices when we are not involved with the product?

KEY CONCEPT

The importance of involvement

The more personally relevant we find something, the more involved we are. We can be involved with the product, a brand, a purchase decision, or an advertisement. Brand managers believe that the more involved a customer is with the brand the greater potential to build brand loyalty. This is because customers often engage in an extensive problem-solving process for high involvement brands and, if satisfied with their purchase, have greater certainty that is was the right choice. For the same reason (and if the customer is dissatisfied) they are likely to be more certain that they made the wrong decision and avoid the brand in the future.

Low-involvement choice

By combining data from a wide range of studies we can build a picture of the low-involvement consumer. It seems clear that consumers have very little knowledge about the differences between brands and perceive them as all being very similar. If they hold any beliefs about an individual brand then these are likely to be very weak, and thus easily changed. Avoidance of mental and physical effort seems to be the key motivation as consumers seek to be satisfied, not necessarily delighted. Perhaps the major criterion is that the choice be the one least likely to give them any problems. It has been suggested that for much of the time, consumers pay little or no conscious attention to the information environment, but rely on past behaviour as a guide. In most cases, awareness of a brand is a key predictor of purchase, in that brands in 'top-of-mind' awareness are the only ones consumers are likely to choose from, unless some situational factor at point-of-sale draws a new brand to their attention. We know that consumers have a very limited number of brands in any category which they can recall from memory, usually seven plus or minus two, and in low-involvement categories this figure is nearer to four plus or minus one. So building top-of-mind awareness is a crucial task for marketing communications in low-involvement categories. However, the major route to awareness is through past behaviour (Ehrenberg, 1974). You will recall that one of the factors that predicts that a product will be low-involvement is frequent purchasing, so that once a consumer has purchased a brand several times and found it reasonably satisfactory, they fall back on habit from then on. On the first purchase occasion, trial may be used as a low-risk method of evaluating the brand, before any judgements are formed about it. This model of low-involvement choice is shown in Fig. 1.5.

So far we have considered the extent to which we engage in mental effort in choosing a brand, that is the extent of information-processing that is carried out. But many products and services are not thought about coolly and rationally, so what happens when choice is under the control of emotional processes? We will be considering the combination of emotion and high involvement in the next chapter, but now let's look at the combination of low involvement and low levels of emotion.

KEY CONCEPT

Top-of-mind awareness

Top-of-mind awareness can be thought of as the first few brands that come to a customer's mind when they think of a product category. It is no good having a fantastic product, superior to competitors, if your brand does not even come to mind in a purchase situation. This is particularly important for low involvement purchase decisions, because the customer is often not motivated to seek out information about new brands. If your brand is not top-of-mind then it will not even be considered!

FIGURE 1.5 Low-involvement choice

Low-involvement choice and emotion

When consumers are not so involved with a product or service but it is still an area where judgement is largely driven by emotional factors, studies of the effects of emotion on judgement have shown that even slightly positive emotional states lead to less thought, less information seeking, less analytic reasoning, less attention to negative cues, and less attention to 'realism'. In this state consumers are seeking a mild sense of warmth, rather than hot emotion, and seeking to choose the brand which they simply feel best about. This feeling of warmth may derive from a number of factors. There is a large amount of experimental evidence that far from 'familiarity breeding contempt', mere exposure to a brand name over time can result in the development of a non-rational preference. Emotional responses can be used as a signal, in particular a basic emotional signal is that of rejection or dislike. The 'refusal of other tastes' may well be a fundamental process in that we first reject everything we dislike, and that what is left must be what we like. Also, emotional responses can carry information, in that we can consult our feelings for information for a choice decision: 'Well, how do I feel about it?' Because we are not so involved with the choice we may not be motivated to justify our choice with rational arguments, but some people still feel the need to seek out information that justifies their choice, although this may be a rather more passive operation than when choice is driven by emotion. This low emotion model of choice is shown in Fig. 1.6.

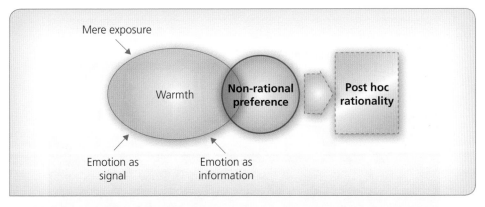

FIGURE 1.6 Low emotion choice

Brands and low-involvement choice

When people are not involved with a purchase, then the brand becomes an heuristic, or shortcut, for making choices and their mental resources are barely involved in processing information, rather, they learn passively by subconscious processing that places brands in their memory with little or no processing. It is this low-involvement processing that is 'the glue that holds the entire world of brands together' (Heath, 2000). Choice between brands is driven largely by simple associations between the brand and attributes or emotions usually created and sustained through advertising. Consumers will even construct causal inferences about a brand and its functional attributes which need have no basis in reality. The evidence suggests that meaningful brands can perhaps be built from meaningless differentiation on irrelevant attributes (Carpenter et al., 1994), and we will be developing the ways in which a low-involvement brand can be differentiated from the competition in Chapter 9.

But brand associations can also be constructed to emotional responses without the need for conscious awareness through the processes of conditioning and 'mere exposure'. Classical conditioning requires the repeated pairing over time between a brand and a positive emotional stimulus (e.g. a beautiful picture of a sunset or high profile celebrity) and eventually the brand alone will automatically evoke the pleasant emotional response (Shimp et al., 1991). Corona's 'from where you'd rather be' campaign uses this to great effect by framing small groups of friends sipping their refreshing beer within relaxing beachside locales, which always include a beautiful, warm-hued sunset. The tagline reinforces the link with the assertion that the product comes from an idyllic source. The mere exposure effect describes the situation where, after repeated exposure to a brand name in the absence of any other stimulus, mild positive emotional responses are eventually evoked (Bornstein, 1989). Both of these processes have been demonstrated to successfully influence brand choice, even against competitors with superior performance characteristics (Baker, 1999). We will be discussing how these emotional processes can be built into brand strategy in Chapter 9.

Corona: 'From where you'd rather be' campaign

CHAPTER SUMMARY

In this chapter we have demonstrated that perceptions of brands must be the focus of managerial action. We have reviewed what is known about how consumers make choice decisions between brands and identified the critical role played by levels of consumer involvement. We suggested that in conditions of low involvement, achieving top-of-mind awareness might be the primary management goal. We went on to explore how even low-involvement brands may be associated with low levels of emotion and non-rational preference.

DISCUSSION QUESTIONS

1 Why do we have brands?

2 Distinguish the concept of a brand in terms of it functional and emotional domain.

3 Discuss one other industry substantially impacted by the information search power of the internet.

4 To what extent do consumers make thoughtful, rational choices between brands?

5 Explain the bottom up effect that consumer can have in relation to purchase outcomes?

6 How can the classical conditioning method of learning be used to elicit an emotional response towards a brand?

7 What is the role of past behaviour in building brand awareness?

8 How can emotions be linked to low-involvement brands?

17

CASE STUDY

Tide—SuperMum

Tide is a popular brand of laundry detergent manufactured by Procter & Gamble. For over six decades, Tide has been a well-recognized laundry detergent, gaining dominance in many markets around the world and successfully beating competing brands in the detergent segment. Over the years, Tide has introduced many variants of laundry detergents, proving, as their slogan entails, that Tide 'knows fabric best'. Nonetheless, even the most successful brands are not immune from the often harsh dynamics of the market place. As Tide learned, a constant monitoring of the external business environment and responses to change are crucial survival techniques in consumer markets.

The problem started in 2006, across several Balkan countries (mainly Romania and Serbia) when Tide began to drastically lose market share to competitive offerings. Tide was facing a significant decline of volume shipments and a share loss of 2.5% between the fiscal years of 2004/05 and 2005/06 and reached an all-time share point low in 2006. This loss of market share was attributed to the aggressive growth of the economy detergent segment as opposed to the middle-priced detergent segment, where Tide was positioned as a major player. Within the economy detergent segment, Tide was facing strong competition and losing share to low-priced brands. For example, while Tide was losing market share in Romania, Dero (a detergent manufactured by Unilever) was enjoying a share growth of 3.5%. Likewise, during the same period of radical loss for Tide in Serbia, Merix (a detergent manufactured by Henkel) had grown by 3.8%. Furthermore, this intense competition imposed a threat on Tide's brand recognition resulting in consistently low levels of brand awareness (below the essential 50% awareness mark needed). Meanwhile, the position of the economy detergent segment was backed up and reinforced by the use of influential consumer messages emphasizing strong value and performance. This complicated matters further in such a critical period and aggressive market place.

This competitive environment called for a revision of marketing and communication strategies. Specifically, Tide was concerned with satisfying two major and crucial objectives:

1 Reversing Tide's declining volume sales and loss of market share, thereby reinforcing Tide's strong market position in Romania and Serbia.

2 Increasing unaided brand awareness and therefore increasing Tide's brand recognition within Romania and Serbia.

Tide was in a potentially life threatening situation, facing a real challenge; convincing consumers to spend more and purchase Tide, as opposed to other lower-priced detergents. Tide's survival in the Balkan market was dependent upon winning back those consumers stolen by the lures of the low-priced detergent competitors. So, how did Tide solve this dilemma?

Seeking to distinguish itself from the obvious functional benefits that competitors were marketing, Tide decided to use a strong emotional appeal to win back its customers' hearts. Playing on the emotional side of consumers is a fruitful strategy in an attempt to build brand affinity, create justifications for a higher price, and convince consumers to choose Tide as opposed to a competitor's product. To create a successful emotional appeal across Romania and Serbia, Tide recognized the importance of finding a common ground in which their target markets overlap. The first step in that direction was to learn more about Tide's broad market segment, which largely consisted of mothers (with middle incomes and children under the age of 18 years).

At first glance, Tide learned that its target woman obtained her personal and social realization from the love and appreciation she received from her husband and children. Further market research revealed intriguing insights about Tide's target woman: an emotional gap was discovered to exist between mother and child—and this is what Tide sought to take advantage of.

Tide discovered that while mothers go to great lengths to fulfil their caretaking duties for their families, they feel a lack of appreciation from their children. Specifically, mothers reported that their children rarely expressed thankfulness and almost certainly took their mothers for granted.

Briefly, on the surface, it seemed obvious that mothers want to do everything for their children. In-depth analysis, however, revealed that in addition to a mother's desire to fulfil her children's wishes, all mothers want to be recognized for their hard work and be viewed as a 'SuperMum' by their children. Hence, in an attempt to reconcile that emotional distance, Tide launched the 'SuperMum' campaign.

The idea of the campaign was simple and logical: A 'SuperMum' is naturally and continually striving for family harmony every day; and laundry is one means to that end. Tide was advertised as the laundry detergent that successfully fulfils that job, positioning itself as the obvious choice of laundry detergent for 'Super Mums'. Using that strategy, Tide believed they would be able to effectively communicate, unlike their competitors, that Tide enjoys an in-depth understanding of the 'SuperMum'.

The 'SuperMum' campaign was launched in Romania and Serbia for a period of five consecutive months (from 1 August 2006 to 31 December 2006). The total cost of the campaign's commercial communications was estimated to be between €10 million and €20 million. During the campaign, Tide ensured that its price and distribution remained steady. Furthermore, Tide avoided engaging in any form of national promotional activities. This was especially important to secure long-term loyalty as opposed to promoting short-term sales. In the meantime, Tide's competitors were pursuing heavy promotional strategies, higher budgets, and superior SOV (share of voice).

Tide's 'SuperMum' campaign was primarily intended for and mainly focused on TV as its medium to reach Balkan consumers. Print media and public relations events were used as secondary media to increase campaign awareness. TV was chosen as the major medium because of its popularity as a primary entertainment source among Tide's target audience. It was estimated that the average Balkan consumer viewed TV for four to five hours on a daily basis. Consequently, 99% of the 'SuperMum' campaign's media strategy was focused on TV, whilst only 1% was attributed to public relations events.

The major focus of the 'SuperMum' campaign was on the 'My mum is super' advertising, aimed at letting mothers know that children appreciate their hard work when they wash with Tide (even though they do not verbally express this). Since one of the key objectives of the 'SuperMum' campaign focused on increasing brand awareness, the advertising comprised two matching advertisements in the hopes of extending the scope of the brand reach. These advertisements were broadcast between family programmes and family viewing times, always being aired during the same programme break.

The two advertisements created for the campaign featured the same story, aired from two different perspectives; the baby's point of view was first shown followed by the mother's stance. To create a strongly emotional appeal, Tide focused on targeting the consumer's motherly side, using a cute pre-verbal baby with innocent expressions in its advertising. Specifically, a 30" ad copy was created focusing on the baby's perspective, mainly to create an emotional bond with the viewer, and a 15" ad copy was attributed to the mother's point of view and aimed to reassure the viewer of Tide's cleanliness from an expert 'Super Mum's' point of view.

In terms of public relations events, Tide organized special events under the 'SuperMum' concept across Romania and Serbia. The events consisted of children's contests: a drawing contest was organized under the theme 'My mum is super' which was intended to be appealing to the 'SuperMum' in everyone. The drawing contest influenced and created a larger awareness of further public relations and outdoor media.

The results of the 'SuperMum' campaign were remarkable, with Tide's volume index enjoying an increase of over 60% in both Romania and Serbia—the volume index for Romania increased by 69%, and for Serbia it increased by 67%. Tide was able to regain lost consumers and once again dominate the Balkan market.

To sum up, Tide has successfully proved that responding to changes in the external environment is crucial for brand survival. In the face of a downturn, Tide searched for a creative marketing strategy that provided them with a unique connection with their target audience. As opposed to competitors, Tide aimed for a strong emotional connection in a seemingly functional segment. Their approach helped the brand override mere functional benefits, exposing the brand's symbolic, emotional attributes and winning the hearts of its Balkan consumers.

Source: WARC, Euro-Effies, Bronze winner, 2007, Tide—SuperMum. Edited by Fajer Saleh Al-Mutawa

DISCUSSION QUESTIONS

1 Why did the use of an emotional appeal in advertising win back Tide's consumers? What does this say about consumer rationality in decision making?

2 If Tide's target consumer was male, how do you think Tide's campaign would have been executed? Would it be directed by an emotional or functional appeal? Why?

3 Why do you think Tide's competitors were not using emotional appeals? What are the advantages and disadvantages of Tide using an emotional advertising appeal?

4 Based on the information provided on Tide's target segment (and ignoring the launch of the 'SuperMum' campaign), propose a suitable marketing campaign for Tide.

FURTHER READING

- There is a vast amount of experimental evidence about the consumer decision-making process based on the cognitive information-processing model and a very comprehensive source is Franzen, G. and Bouwmen, M. (2001), *The Mental World of Brands*, Henley-on-Thames: WARC.

- A radical alternative to the cognitive model which instead emphasizes the primary role of behaviour and its ability to be used to mathematically model consumer choice is proposed by Ehrenberg, A. (1988), *Repeat-Buying*, Oxford: Oxford University Press.

- A comprehensive discussion of low-involvement processes is Heath, R. (2001), *The Hidden Power of Advertising: How Low Involvement Processing Influences the Way We Choose Brands*, Henley-on-Thames: Admap Publications.

REFERENCES

Alba, J. and Hutchinson, W. (1988), 'Dimensions of consumer expertise', *Journal of Consumer Research*, 13, 411–454.

Alpert, F. (1993), 'Consumer market beliefs and their managerial implications: an empirical examination', *Journal of Consumer Marketing*, 10, 2, 56–70.

Baker, W. (1999), 'When can affective conditioning and mere exposure directly influence brand choice?' *Journal of Advertising*, XXVIII, 4, 31–46.

Beatty, S. and Smith, S. (1987), 'External search effort: an investigation across several product categories', *Journal of Consumer Research*, 14, 83–95.

Bornstein, R. (1989), 'Exposure and affect: overview and meta-analysis of research, 1968–1987', *Psychological Bulletin*, 106, 259–89.

Brakus, J.J., Schmitt, B.H., and Zarantonello, L. (2009), 'Brand experience: What is it? How is it measured? Does it affect loyalty?', *Journal of Marketing*, May, 73, 52–68.

Carpenter, G., Glazer, R., and Nakamoto, K. (1994), 'Meaningful brands from meaningless differentiation: the dependence on irrelevant attributes', *Journal of Marketing Research*, XXXI, 339–50.

Chebat, J.-C., Davidow, M., and Codjovi, I. (2005), 'Silent voices: why some dissatisfied consumers fail to complain', *Journal of Service Research*, 7, 4, 328–42.

Cobb, C. and Hoyer, W. (1986), 'Planned versus impulse purchase behaviour', *Journal of Retailing*, 62, 384–409.

Corstjens, J. and Corstjens, M. (1995), *Store Wars: The battle for mindspace and shelfspace*, Chichester: John Wiley.

Dawar, N. and Parker, P. (1994), 'Marketing universals: consumers' use of brand name, price, physical appearance, and retailer reputation as signals of product quality', *Journal of Marketing*, 58, 81–95.

Duncan, T. and Moriarty, S. (1998), 'A communication-based marketing model for managing relationships', *Journal of Marketing*, 62, 1–13.

Ehrenberg, A. (1974), 'Repetitive advertising and the consumer', *Journal of Advertising Research*, 14, 2.

Elliott, R. (1994), 'Addictive consumption: function and fragmentation in postmodernity', *Journal of Consumer Policy*, 17, 159–79.

Freeman, B., Kelly, B., Baur, L.Chapman, K., Chapman, S., Gill, T., and King, L. (Forthcoming), 'Digital junk: food and beverage marketing on Facebook,' *American Journal of Public Health*.

Folkes, V.S. (1988), 'The availability heuristic and perceived risk', *Journal of Consumer Research*, 15, 13–23.

Guo, C. (2001), 'A review on consumer external search: amount and determinants', *Journal of Business and Psychology*, 15, 3, 505–19.

Harrison, P., McQuilken, L., and Robertson, N. (2011), 'Seeking straight answers: consumer decision-making in telecommunications', Deakin University and Australian Communications Consumer Action Network ACCAN: Sydney.

Heath, R. (2000), 'Low-involvement processing', *Admap*, March, 14–17.

Homburg, C., Koschate, N., and Hoyer, W.D. (2005), 'Do satisfied customers really pay more? A study of the relationship between customer satisfaction and willingness to pay', *Journal of Marketing*, April, 69, 84–96.

Hoyer, W. (1984), 'An examination of consumer decision making for a common repeat purchase product', *Journal of Consumer Research*, 17, 141–48.

Jones, M.A., Reynolds, K.E., Weun, S., and Beatty, S.E. (2003), 'The product-specific nature of impulse buying tendency', *Journal of Business Research*, 56, 505–11.

Kahneman, D. and Tversky, A. (1979), 'Prospect theory: an analysis of decision under risk', *Econometrica*, 47, 263–91.

Levin, I. and Gaeth, G. (1988), 'How consumers are affected by the framing of attribute information before and after consuming the product', *Journal of Consumer Research*, 15, 374–79.

McColl Kennedy, J.R. and Fetter, R.E., Jr., (2001), 'An empirical examination of the involvement to external search relationship in services marketing', *Journal of Services Marketing*, 15, 2, 82–98.

McGovern, G. and Moon, Y. (2007), 'Companies and the customers who hate them', *Harvard Business Review*, June, 78–84.

Meyer, M. (1988), 'Attention Shoppers!' *Marketing and Media Decisions*, 23, 67.

Moor, L. (2007) *The Rise of Brands*. Oxford: Berg.

Payne, J., Bettman, J., and Johnson, E. (1992), 'Behavioral decision research: a constructive processing perspective', *Annual Review of Psychology*, 4, 87–131.

Peck, J. and Childers, T.L. (2005), 'If I touch it I have to have it: individual and environmental influences on impulse purchasing', *Journal of Business Research*, 59, 765–9.

Pervan, S.J. and Vocino, A. (2008), 'Message framing: keeping practitioners in the picture', *Marketing Intelligence and Planning*, 26, 6, 634–48.

Punj, G. and Staelin, R. (1983), 'A model of consumer search behaviour for new automobiles', *Journal of Consumer Research*, 9, 366–80.

Richins, M., Bloch, P., and McQuarrie, E. (1992), 'How enduring and situational involvement combine to create involvement responses', *Journal of Consumer Psychology*, 1, 2, 143–53.

Shimp, T., Stuart, E., and Engel, R. (1991), 'A program of classical conditioning experiments testing variations in the conditioned stimulus and context', *Journal of Consumer Research*, 18, 1, 1–12.

Szymanski, D.M. and Henard, D.H. (2001), 'Customer satisfaction: a meta analysis of the empirical evidence', *Journal of the Academy of Marketing Science*, 29, 1, 16–35.

Wengrow, D. (2008), 'Prehistories of Commodity Branding', *Current Anthropology*, February, 1, 7–34.

van Noort, G. and Willemsen, L. M. (2011), 'Online Damage Control: The Effects of Proactive Versus Reactive Webcare Interventions in Consumer-generated and Brand-generated Platforms', *Journal of Interactive Marketing*, 26, 131–140.

 Test your understanding of this chapter and explore the subject further using our Online Resource Centre. Visit the Online Resource Centre at http://www.oxfordtextbooks.co.uk/orc/elliott-percy3e/

Emotion and Brands

2

Key Concepts

1 Emotions are social and cultural as well as psychological, so it is vital to understand the sociocultural environment in which a brand is marketed.

2 The symbolic meaning of consumption is prime motivation for emotion-driven choice.

3 Non-rational preferences involve holistic perception and non-verbal imagery.

4 People may justify an emotional choice by post hoc rationalization.

5 Trust is very important for reducing perceptions of purchase risk and involves a reliance on emotion.

6 Trust is most important for symbolic brands and involves consumer-brand intimacy.

7 The emotional significance of a brand will influence how much attention is paid to it.

8 It is possible to 'emotionalize' a product that has little rational connection with emotions.

Introduction

Have you ever walked away with a new item of clothing buzzing with the excitement of the find? Or do you remember the anxiety and, hopefully, relief at choosing the 'right' shoes to wear on your first day at a new school? In this chapter, we shall be dealing with the importance of emotions both to choosing brands and to evaluating and forming opinions about them. The predominant model of consumer choice process is based upon cognitive information processing, even though this cognitive framework has rarely managed to explain more than 20% of the variance in global evaluation measures of behaviour (Obermiller, 1990). Emotion informs cognitive processing, yet is too often ignored by those trying to understand consumer behaviour. But the consumption experience is replete with emotion, often of a high degree of intensity. In the area of impulse buying, consumers describe a compelling feeling that was 'thrilling', 'wild', 'a tingling sensation', 'a surge of energy', 'like turning up the excitement volume' and a study of the everyday consumer experiences of women yielded descriptions of making purchases in a 'dreamlike' way when they were 'captivated' by a product and gave an impression of an almost seamless flow of events unpunctuated by 'stopping to think'. In addition, emotion is a critical part of the consumer evaluation of brands. There are emotional associations linked to brands in memory, and these will influence how new information about a brand is processed, as well as shape judgements about it during purchase.

What is emotion?

To begin with, when considering emotion, a frequent source of confusion is the tendency to think about emotion and feelings as the same thing; they are not. Feelings are part of the emotional language that describe the point where a person becomes aware of the emotion (Bradley and Lang, 2000). Emotion is made up of a number of components, most often considered within the context of the so-called 'reaction triad' of psychological arousal, motor expression, and subjective feeling (Scherer, 2000). As Damasio (1999) has put it: 'The full human impact of emotions is only realized when they are sensed, when they become feeling, and when those feelings are felt. That is where they become known, with the assistance of consciousness. It is this aspect of emotions that concerns us.

Everyone experiences these 'feelings'. But the concept of emotion goes beyond this, and is perhaps best understood within the context of something called affect program theory (Griffiths, 1997). Affect is a term often used interchangeably with the feeling of emotion and, in its modern form, the affect program theory deals with what are generally considered the six basic, or primary, emotions following Ekman (1992): surprise, anger, fear, disgust, sadness, and joy. Known as affect program states, these have evolved within us since ancient times, and represent informed reflex responses that appear to be independent of cultural considerations. It is important to understand that, when one is dealing with a primary emotion, it will be the same for everyone. For example, in Italy, China, New Zealand, and Argentina emotions such as sadness or joy are felt the same way.

However, while primary emotions are a basic part of our being human, there are many others, for example embarrassment or guilt, that are to some extent acquired, and are triggered by things we have come to associate with that emotion through experience. These so-called secondary or social emotions (cf. Damasio, 1999, and others) are informed by cultural schemas and are part of social construction notions of emotion. Importantly, they are part of higher-order cognitive processes and they will differ across cultures and over time. For example, in the Nātyaśāstra, a medieval Hindu Sanskrit text, regarded as a seminal early work on 'The Emotions', amusement is defined in part as the 'contemptuous, indignant or derisive laughter at the faults and inferior status of others' (Shweder *et al.*, 2008, p. 411). The definition, clearly more bound by time than culture, bears little resemblance to modern day notions of amusement, which include more generalized ideas of being occupied in a pleasing or entertaining way.

In summary, we might think of emotion in two fundamental ways. First, there are the six primary emotions that comprise the affect program theory, and which are basic to all humans. These are triggered by a cognitive system that does not freely exchange information with other cognitive systems, and are therefore basically uncontrolled automatic responses of the nervous system. Secondly, there are all the other emotions, which are associated with the sociocultural environment, and are informed by experience. In this chapter, we are primarily concerned with the latter.

KEY CONCEPT

Emotions are social, cultural, and psychological

Emotions, such as fear and sadness, are psychological. People around the world feel and express them the same way. These are base emotions; we can think of them as part of our genetic makeup. But what about the emotions you may feel presenting to senior management or going out on a date? Perhaps embarrassment or anxiety. These are socially constructed (secondary); we learn to feel them through our experience of interaction with others. Our culture often informs our response to different social situations and therefore also impacts emotions. For example, if the presentation to senior management went poorly, an English person or Australian might feel disappointed or embarrassed while a person from China might feel shame—a less-often experienced emotion in Western cultures.

25

Emotion and consumer choice

Traditional models of consumer behaviour have assumed a hierarchy of effects in which cognitive activity is followed by emotional evaluation in the formation of an attitude, which ultimately results in behaviour. This assumes that cognition mediates emotion, meaning that through cognition emotion is brought about, while emotion mediates behaviour. Although the growing recognition of the existence of low-involvement purchasing has made much of the importance of emotional processing, producing such concepts as affect-referral and spontaneous attitude accessing, these were still assumed to be a result of previous cognitive processing which was stored in memory. A major challenge to this orthodoxy was made by Zajonc (1980), who proposed that emotion is not only a separate processing system which does not involve cognition, but also the primary influence on the development of preferences and sometimes actually precedes cognition. He defined some of the other characteristics of emotion as: inescapable; irrevocable; judgements which implicate the self; difficult to verbalize; and independent of cognition.

While this idea was seriously challenged by Lazarus (1982) at the time, the real issue according to Griffiths (1997) is the *degree* to which the information-processing system responsible for emotional response is independent of, or a part of, the same system that is involved in longer-term, cognitively driven, planned behaviour. There is no question that the system dealing with emotion in the brain (principally the prefrontal cortex and amygdala) can perceive and store information that does not reach conscious attention, yet it does engage the declarative memory system, which is where memories are drawn that can be consciously discussed and used to plan behaviour (Eichenbaum, 2002). However, whilst the declarative memory system is home to cognitive processing, a separate pathway seems to be involved with emotion (Yamasaki *et al.*, 2002). What all this means is that, while most decisions involve higher-order cognitive processing, some do not; and even higher-order cognitive processes may be mediated by unconscious emotional responses. The example shown of a print ad for John Deere tractors has none of the technical specifications one might expect for a complex machine. Instead, John Deere focuses on the emotions the owner may experience whilst in charge of one of their products.

An interesting example of a non-cognitive way of looking at the role of emotion in consumer choice is offered by Mittal's (1988) affect choice model. This model applies to the purchase of expressive products (products with symbolic meaning) like clothes, shoes, or perfume and suggests that emotion-based choice is holistic, self-focused, and not capable of being verbalized. Holistic choice means that consumers are unable to separate out the individual attributes or 'preferenda' but form an overall impression. For example, can you explain your preference for a perfume by breaking it down into specific attributes? Choice is self-focused in that emotional judgements of expressive products involve the judge directly. That a car is 'too flashy' reflects the values and personality of the judge more than any inherent property of the car. Emotional judgements are made almost instantaneously and reflect basic

YOUR NEW DEERE WILL INCITE JEALOUSY AMONG THE NEIGHBORS.
YOUR NEIGHBORS ARE MOUNTAIN LIONS.

They will beset upon you from all sides, but you will remain cool. You will tell your Deere to remain cool as well. "Be cool," you will say. The lions will creep closer. You will thoughtfully, calmly gun the engine until it drowns out your panicked shrieking with a mighty roar.
A mighty, American made, direct-injected diesel roar that says, "This is the sound a tractor makes." It will be heard. It will be feared. The kittens will scamper off to terrorize lesser creatures. You will pat your Deere affectionately.

Print advertisement for John Deere

subjective feelings which may not have verbal descriptors, and thus emotion relies much more on non-verbal channels of communication.

Another concept of 'extraordinary experience' has been used to describe a special class of unusual hedonic consumption which is intrinsically enjoyable and involves high levels of emotional intensity. A study of white-water river rafting demonstrated that despite the vivid recall of retrospective reports of the intensity of the emotional experience, participants did not appear to want to engage in very much cognitive recall as the magic was 'best preserved if the associated feelings and sensations are not examined too closely' (Arnould and Price, 1993).

Social perspectives on emotion

A major issue with the conceptualization of emotion used in much consumer research is that it refers to a personal and individual phenomenon, when in fact the many important aspects of emotion are social. This is reflected in the social constructivist models of emotion (Harré, 1986; Shweder, 1993). They posit that the meaning of emotion is generally constructed by social interaction leading to an understanding of accepted behaviour and value patterns. In this sense the meaning of emotions may vary between cultures and sub-cultures.

Advocates of social constructivist models do not deny that emotions can be generated as independent, 'psychobiological' reactions, but they consider this secondary to the meaning derived from the sociocultural context. Emotions are not simply internal events but are communicative acts addressed to specific audiences, and are thus partly defined according to conventional cultural representations.

Cross-cultural studies have shown that cultural differences in the conceptualization of the self can play a central role in shaping emotional experiences. For example, if you are from an Asian culture you may have a greater focus on the fundamental relatedness of individuals to each other, resulting in different experiences of such emotions as pride, guilt, and anger in comparison with Western peers who are more focused on individual and inner attributes (Markus and Kitayama, 1991). Thus the cultural context of consumption will lead to socially constructed emotional responses, under the direction of situational norms. Hochschild (1983) describes how we learn the local 'Feeling Rules' in a social situation so that our emotions are appropriate to local circumstances and meet the expectations of other people.

While primary emotions are fixed biologically and some secondary emotions can certainly be the result of individual emotional development, there is much evidence that pronounced social and cultural variations exist not only in the representation of secondary emotions but also in the ways in which we experience, express, and regulate them (Parkinson *et al.*, 2005). This is why it is so important to understand the sociocultural environment within which a brand is marketed. It will be that environment that informs the extent and manner in which emotions will influence both consumer decision making and brand evaluation.

Emotional response

While we have just seen how important the sociocultural context is to understanding and defining emotions and emotional responses, this does not mean that knowing the sociocultural context will make it easy to predict an emotional response. One way to approach understanding emotional response is to assume that emotions are grounded in mechanisms which are not voluntary and are under only limited human control. These principles, which have been consistently observed, have been framed as laws by Frijda (1988), who proposed 11 laws of emotional responding, four of which are crucially important in understanding the consumer.

The law of concern

Emotions arise in response to events that are important to our goals, motives, or concerns; for example, events which aid or inhibit a desire to be successful, liked, or virtuous. In this sense we continually interpret the situations we face through the values we hold dear and have a preference to experience things that reinforce these values. Thus hidden behind every emotion is a more or less enduring disposition to prefer certain states of the world. This is a key issue for understanding consumer emotions, as it is the law of concern which links our motivations and emotional responses and underpins consumer involvement and thus drives much consumption. A prime source of emotional involvement is the search for identity. In postmodern society the individual is threatened by a number of 'dilemmas of the self' (Giddens, 1991, p. 201): fragmentation, powerlessness, uncertainty, and a struggle against commodification. These dilemmas are driven by the 'looming threat of personal meaninglessness' as we endeavour to construct and maintain an identity which will remain stable despite a rapidly changing environment. Part of this dilemma is the fear that mass commodification will lead to a reduction in our choices as products are standardized. However, as consumers we are increasingly atuned to this phenomenon and have an unprecedented ability to communicate with different aspects of the market and to gain and process large amounts of information, all of which has led to a plurality of consumer choice. This means that what may be taken away with commodification is perhaps more than gained through consumer empowerment. For example consumers are increasingly asked to help design products, be it the flavour of Walkers Crisps or the colour of a pair of Nike shoes. Furthermore, using social media, consumer advocacy campaigns can be quickly and effectively launched. In 2013 for instance, within just nine days of a public announcement by whisky brand Maker's Mark that the alcohol content of their product had been reduced, the decision was reversed citing the widespread criticisms made by their customers on Facebook and Twitter. The company made an abrupt return to the original recipe after share prices took a hit and news sources picked up on the level of social outcry. In this way, consumers are offered resources which may be used creatively to achieve 'an ego-ideal which commands the respect of others and inspires self-love' (Gabriel and Lang, 1995, p. 98). Thus it is likely that goods which can be used as resources to construct and maintain identity will involve emotion-driven choice. The symbolic meaning of goods will be explored in Chapter 3.

The law of apparent reality

Emotions are elicited by events appraised as real, and their intensity varies according to the level of reality attributed. In this regard, 'knowing means less than seeing'. For example, organizations such as the Red Cross have more success showing potential donors an image of a single starving child than telling them that 1,000 have died. Vivid imagination also has the power of 'reality' and is capable of eliciting strong emotions;

in this respect 'feeling means more than knowing'. Recall how your own euphoria at securing tickets to a favoured rock band or football match often extends well beyond a rational assessment of either group's ability to entertain. Conversely, an individual sending five parcels around the world at the local post office is often a target of extreme annoyance from those waiting to buy a single local stamp. Again, there is no rational reason for this but that does not inhibit the reaction. Thus the law of apparent reality accounts for the weakness of reason as opposed to the strength of passion as it suggests that imagination and fantasy can overwhelm reason and that the consumer can create their own 'reality'.

The law of closure

Emotions tend to be closed to probabilities and likelihoods, and to be absolute in their judgements and have control over the action system. It may be that the cause of an emotion may be relatively minor, but the emotional response may not recognize this and be a total experience. When one is very angry the thing that happened is felt to be absolutely bad and the person involved is felt to be intrinsically bad too. Verbal expressions of emotion tend to reflect this absoluteness in quality and time: 'I could kill him' or 'I cannot live without her'. The absoluteness of feeling and thinking tends to be reflected in behaviour and to override other concerns. The law of closure may be considered the essential feature of emotion, in that it captures the involuntary nature of strong emotional impulses and urges. Desire for a product can be a totally overwhelming sensation which drives out all other aspects of the environment and entails complete absorption in the shopping experience.

The law of the lightest load

There is a tendency to view any situation in a way that minimizes negative emotional load. We tend to avoid and deny unpleasant knowledge and will seek to interpret a situation in a way which maximizes emotional gain. This suggests that emotion can drive our interpretation of a situation in such a way that we can make it more pleasing to us and that we are motivated to develop strategies of emotion management. In addition, we may be motivated to preserve a positive emotional state by using mood maintenance strategies, and to alleviate negative emotional states through strategies of mood repair. Mood repair has been found to be the prime motivation maintaining addictive consumption, in that the shopping experience is a very effective short-term solution to feelings of unhappiness and stress (Elliott, 1998). We will often engage in what has become colloquially known as retail therapy, buying that dress because we've had such a bad week or treating ourselves to chocolate after a stressful day. It is likely that mood repair is a major motivation underlying a broad range of compensatory consumption behaviour. Strategies of mood maintenance may include the common social behaviour of going out to dinner after a pleasant occasion and then going on after that for a drink.

So despite their cultural and sub-cultural variations, emotions may be law-like in their effect upon us. The law of apparent reality states that once events are subjectively perceived to be real, often through imagination and fantasy, then the emotional responses overwhelm objective evidence; and the law of closure proposes that emotions are blind to reason and that they 'know no probabilities . . . they do not weigh likelihoods' (Frijda, 1988). In this sense then, preferences really do direct inferences and emotion does dominate cognition (Zajonc, 1980).

Consumption and the symbolic meaning of goods

As soon as a product's ability to satisfy mere physical need is transcended, then we enter the realm of the symbolic meaning of goods. The functions of the symbolic meanings of products operate in two directions, outward in constructing the social world: *Social-Symbolism*, and inward towards constructing our self-identity: *Self-Symbolism*. This will be explored further in Chapter 3.

If consumers 'identify themselves by the formula: I am what I have and what I consume' and it is symbolic meaning that is used in the 'search for the meaning of existence' (Fromm, 1976, p. 36), then we can think of the extraction of symbolic meaning from consumption as a powerful motivational force. Symbolic interpretation is essentially non-rational improvization that does not obey the codes of language but operates at the unconscious level. A Jungian analysis goes even further and suggests that the full significance of a symbol cannot be grasped in purely intellectual terms; if it becomes fully definable in rational terms it is no longer a true symbol (Storr, 1973). This suggests that perhaps the function of emotion is to make up for the insufficiency of reason (O'Shaughnessy, 1992) and to help us carry out the vital task of symbolic interpretation so that we can effectively construct an identity and communicate it to others. Thus the symbolic meaning of consumption can be seen as a potent and perhaps prime motivation for emotion-driven choice. Take the advertisement for the premium clothing brand Gant. The models in the image are not even fully visible wearing the product. What is more important is the emotion conveyed by young lovers sharing a moment.

Gant: Symbolic meaning of goods. Reproduced with kind permission of Mikael Jansson / Trunk Archive.

KEY CONCEPT

The symbolic meaning of consumption

Some brands are purchased because they represent something special to us as individuals (self) or they convey something important to others about us (social). When we can't actually say what that is 'yet we just know' we call that symbolic. If we could communicate this important aspect of ourselves we wouldn't need the brand! Symbolic brands do the talking for us. They are used to define our very being and, as such, we are highly motivated (involved) when deciding on the brand choice.

A conceptual model of emotion-driven choice

We can now begin to construct a conceptual model of the process of emotion-driven choice as being motivated by the interpretation of symbolic meaning and the construction of self and social identity. The model is illustrated in Fig. 2.1. What the model shows is that symbolic consumptions occur out of non-rational preference. What we mean by this is that the product is purchased and used to express something about our individual or social selves that we cannot fully articulate. The true value of a symbolic product is that is does the talking for us, it says much more than we can express ourselves. However, we have a tendency to desire an explanation, to seek closure for these kinds of consumption decisions. As such we are

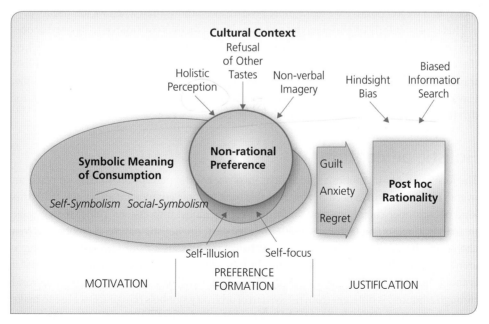

FIGURE 2.1 A model of emotion-driven choice

motivated to avoid feelings of guilt, anxiety, and regret regarding the purchase. What helps us to avoid feeling these emotions is the application of reason to the purchase, which occurs after the event: this is what is meant by post hoc rationalization. In this way, we convince ourselves that we didn't really make an emotion-based purchase––it was in fact well thought through. We are of course engaging in a degree of self-deception when we do this, but research has shown that those of us with the capacity for mild self-deception are generally more confident and happy (von Hippel and Trivers 2011)

Emotion and preference formation

Self-illusion

The law of apparent reality suggests that imagination and fantasy can overwhelm reason and that the consumer can create their own 'reality'. Campbell (1987) has suggested that modern consumption is active pleasure-seeking, often carried out in a state of 'self-illusory hedonism', characterized by daydreams where we can 'know something to be false but feel it to be true'. In this state of self-illusion, rational beliefs are suspended because they are not strong enough to prevent us enjoying ourselves. How else can we justify those new shoes when there are ten pairs already sitting in the closet?

Self-focus

Emotional judgements implicate the self, in that our assessment is more about us than it is about what is being assessed. When evaluating an item of clothing, we are more likely to be imagining how we would look in the clothing rather than features of the clothing itself. In addition, we may frequently use our own emotional state at the time of judgement as a piece of information in a 'How do I feel about it?' heuristic. Rather than computing a judgement on the basis of cognitive evaluation, we may instead rely on our present feelings to guide a judgement, such that if we feel positive we make more positive evaluations than when we feel negative.

This is particularly likely when the emotional judgement is considered to be overly complex, or if it is based on information processing, when there are time constraints and when there is little other information available. The observation of car company tag lines illustrates a market awareness of the importance of self-focus and self-illusion. For example, Haval informs their customers in Australia to 'Have it all'; BMW that it is 'Designed for driving pleasure'; whilst Volvo insists that it is 'For life'.

Holistic perception

The formation of an emotional judgement involves holistic perception, in that we reach an overall evaluation which need not be traceable back to some component attributes. With this kind of consumer choice, we tend to 'form sweeping global impressions' rather than engage in analytical reasoning (Schwarz, 1990). In large part, the holistic nature of emotion-driven choice may be a result of our inability to verbalize the reasons for our feelings: 'there simply aren't very effective verbal means to communicate why we like people and objects or what it is about them that we like' (Zajonc, 1980). The way in which we directly experience the world through emotions is different from the system of arbitrary symbols (language) we use to make verbal descriptions. Does the successful business person deconstruct for colleagues the meaning behind their €3,000 Armani suit or indeed the student their €20 Zara summer dress? With 'the articulation of our feelings through words we acquire a distance from them, so it is possible to act with respect to our emotions rather than expressing them directly' (Radley, 1988).

Non-verbal imagery

The communication of emotion relies heavily on non-verbal channels, especially facial expression which may have elements of pan-cultural universality (Ekman and Friesen, 1971). The 'vividness effect' evoked by pictures has much more effect on attitudes and behaviour than verbal reports of the same events (Fiske and Taylor, 1984). The iconicity of advertising images (the ability of an image to represent reality by partial similarity or by analogy) means that they can be 'soaked with meaning' by their association with a rich variety of emotions to which we are already attuned through our interactions with our social and natural environments (Messaris, 1997). Returning to car manufacturers, by way of example, many are attempting to reduce the perceived environmental impact of their latest models, by evoking powerful images of harmony in recent campaigns. These include cars floating effortlessly on balloons above the skyline, the reconstruction of trees and plants into the components of an automobile, and even putting an icon of endangered species protect, the panda bear, behind the wheel. Thus imagery can allude to many of our past experiences and cultural learning with a potency unavailable to the more restricted channel of language. Imagery interpretation processes are 'subconscious and private in nature' and have 'a latent content that does not appear in overt verbal reports' (Holbrook and Hirschman, 1982).

Fiat: Non-verbal imagery. Reproduced with kind permission of Fiat Chrysler Automobiles. Advertisement created by Marcel, Paris.

Refusal of other tastes

Bourdieu (1984) suggests that the basic element in the forming of preference may not be a positive emotional response but a negative one, not to choose that we like most but to reject those that we most dislike. This 'refusal of other tastes' is a powerful force: 'disgust provoked by horror or visceral intolerance (sick-making) of the tastes of others.' The rejection of other people's consumption lifestyles may be one of the strongest barriers between social classes, and is proposed as a fundamental factor in establishing and maintaining social class distinctions. So perhaps consumer choice may often follow from rejection of disliked alternatives, leaving those not rejected as the preferred option. This is particularly likely to be so in the case of goods which carry high levels of social-symbolic meaning. A number of prominent brands have benefited from our tendency to refuse as a form of preference. For example, Apple urging consumers to reject IBM as an Orwellian Big Brother, or Sony Mobile, which launched an advertising campaign in 2014 under the slogan: 'Don't settle for good. Demand great.'

Justification of emotion-driven choice

Post hoc rationalization

Zajonc and Markus (1982) have argued that decision research has consistently overestimated the role of cognition in choice because many people believe that they should act rationally and therefore report rational judgement activities that they did not actually use. This ever-present tendency for us to engage in post hoc rationalization is similar to the proposition that 'hedonic consumption acts are based not on what people know to be real but on what they desire reality to be' (Holbrook and Hirschman, 1982). In short, we are motivated to justify the choices we have already made.

Another form of post hoc rationalization is described by Zajonc (1980), who suggests that we form a preference first based on emotional response and then justify it to ourselves cognitively. It is proposed here that this process, if it occurs at all, is driven by attempts to cope with post-decisional and/or post-purchase feelings of guilt, anxiety, and regret.

KEY CONCEPT

Non-rational preferences and post hoc rationalization

A consumption decision made with little or no conscious thought, but rather because it feels right, is the result of non-rational preference. If asked why we made that decision we could not at that moment say exactly. Given some time, most of us will find the capacity to explain it in a more logical fashion. This is called post hoc rationalization. Brand managers need to be careful when interpreting the post hoc process for future brand strategy. This is because often our motivation to appear as rational decision makers to others is more important than the truth. Even though we may explain our purchase preference with apparent logical detail, the reason the purchase was non-rational in the first place was because we could not fully articulate why we prefer the brand.

Guilt, anxiety, and regret

The subjective emotional experiences of regret, remorse, and self-blame after purchase are facets of consumer guilt (Lascu, 1991). Unfortunately the whole area of post-purchase theory and research is 'still at an early stage' (Gardial *et al.*, 1994) and the role played by emotions has tended to focus on rather simplistic analyses of consumer satisfaction. Two exceptions are studies of impulse buying which have shown that many impulse buyers subsequently experienced feelings of anxiety and guilt (Rook, 1987), and that when asked about their mood following a recent impulse purchase just as many respondents said they were anxious and guilty (24%) as said they were feeling pleasure and excitement. Consumer guilt has been used in advertising through 'guilt appeals' which attempt to arouse feelings of guilt (or fear of such feelings) and then offer a guilt-reducing solution. Many social marketing organizations manage the process from guilt to redemption with what is known as 'the baby is sick, the baby is well' campaigns. Here, initial communication objectives are to highlight the problem, be it deforestation, blood bank reserves, poverty or the lack of donor action or charitable support (the baby is sick). Subsequent campaigns then aim to reassure people about the good their support has provided (the baby is well). Alternatively, advertising may attempt to diminish the importance of guilt by the promotion of a 'guiltless hedonism' (Lascu, 1991). Guilt is a culturally constructed emotion and varies according to the cultural location and the local feeling rules in relation to the self, society, and the interdependence of the two (Markus and Kitayama, 1991). Opinions differ as to whether there has been a general decrease in the occurrence of feelings of guilt in response to the consumption of luxury goods (Lunt and Livingstone, 1992) or in contrast, an increase in feelings of guilt associated with postmodernity (Giddens, 1991). At the moment there are insufficient data on the subject, but it seems likely that the global growth of consumer culture is associated with a reduction in feelings of guilt, anxiety, and regret and as a consequence in the frequency of post hoc rationalization.

Hindsight bias and biased information search

The theory of Motivated Choice (Kunda, 1990) proposes several mechanisms through which post hoc rationalization may affect judgement and choice. Building on evidence that in testing hypotheses people rely on a positive test strategy, that is they seek out instances which are consistent with their ideas rather than seeking instances which are inconsistent, it is proposed that a hypothesis-confirmation bias operates and we tend to search out evidence which supports our desired outcome, and will ignore or 'forget' evidence which might disconfirm our hypothesis or desired outcome. For example, for some time after buying high involvement products like an expensive camera, or computer, we have the tendency to process advertisements for the identical product seeking reinforcement for our decision. A second mechanism of hindsight bias is where we maintain a belief that events that happened were bound to happen. One of the advantages of shopping with a friend for clothes, for instance, is that we can blame one another if a poor choice is made perhaps joking that, 'I thought it looked good on the rack and you made me buy it anyway'. In both cases, the underlying mechanism seems to be resistant to the provision of 'rational' information and we will often make considerable efforts to defend our emotional judgements against contradictory arguments and go to great lengths to construct seemingly reasonable justifications for our conclusions.

The process of emotion-driven choice

When driven by emotion the process of choice is non-linear, in that non-rational preference is formed holistically and faster than cognitive processing, in fact, almost instantly. It may then be followed by attempts at post hoc rationalization. The formation of preference may be driven by the deriving of symbolic meaning for use by the individual in their project of identity construction, or it may be a negative drive emanating from a refusal of other tastes. Once the non-rational preference is formed it tends to drive out further rational evaluation as the emotional responses overwhelm objective evidence and dominate consumer behaviour.

The apparent absence of thoughtful decision making and unbiased reasoning when consumer choices are driven by emotion may not necessarily be detrimental. It may actually be beneficial, not least because unrealistically positive views of the self and the social environment are often very adaptive. There is evidence that actually thinking about the way we feel about a product preference may have disruptive effects leading to less optimal choices, and to being less satisfied with our choices (Wilson and Schooler, 1991).

Emotions and trust

'The ultimate goal of marketing is to generate an intense bond between the consumer and the brand, and the main ingredient of this bond is trust' (Hiscock, 2001), but trust is an elusive concept. A wide variety of conceptualizations, shown in Table 2.1, have resulted 'in a confusing potpourri of definitions applied to a host of units and level of analysis' (Shapiro, 1987).

TABLE 2.1 The conceptualization of trust

Author	Trust is . . .
Deutsch (1973)	. . . a person's willingness to be dependent on another party in the belief that the party will not intentionally disappoint them.
Bagozzi (1975)	. . . the degree of perceived validity in the statements or actions of one's partner in a relationship.
Dwyer and Oh (1987)	. . . a party's expectation that another desires coordination, will fulfil its obligations, and will pull its weight in the relationship.
Shapiro (1987)	. . . a social relationship in which principals invest resources, authority, or responsibility in another to act on their behalf for some uncertain future return.
Powell (1990)	. . . cooperation that emerges from mutual interests with behaviour standards that no individual can determine alone.
Ring and Van de Ven (1994)	. . . faith in the moral integrity or goodwill of others.
Gulati (1995)	. . . a type of expectation that alleviates the fear that one's partner will act opportunistically.
Gronroos (1996)	. . . cooperation or commitment to a mutual cause.

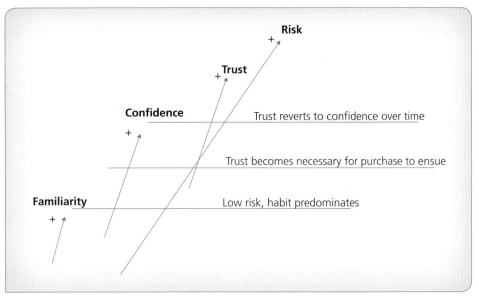

FIGURE 2.2 Theory of trust: cognitive and emotional perceptions

A sociological theory of trust has been proposed by Luhmann (1979), who argues that there are three modes of asserting expectations about the future based on personal experiences and cultural meaning systems: familiarity, confidence, and trust. Familiarity is a precondition of trust: 'Trust is only possible in a familiar world, it needs history as a reliable background' (p. 20). But trust is required only in situations of high perceived risk; at other times confidence or mere familiarity will suffice for action to ensue. 'One who trusts takes cognizance of the possibility of excessive harm arising from the selectivity of others' actions' and 'a fundamental condition of trust is that it must be possible for the partner to abuse the trust and that the partner must have a considerable interest in doing so' (Luhmann, 1979, p. 24).

In order to relate the active investment of trust to expectations about the future, Möllering (2001) argues that a further element is required to enable the proverbial 'leap of trust', and this is 'suspension'. Suspension is the mechanism of 'bracketing the unknowable', thus making expectations of the future 'momentarily certain'.

Translating this approach to consumer brands, when faced with purchase decisions involving low levels of perceived risk, familiarity (which is a binary division as things are either familiar or they are unfamiliar) will suffice for purchase. At higher levels of perceived risk, confidence is required and this is a mix of cognitive and emotional perceptions, largely based on experience. At high levels of perceived risk trust becomes necessary for purchase to occur and this involves emotional judgements rather than cognitions, and for a suspension of fear of the unknowable. With repetition over time risk perceptions reduce and trust reverts to confidence. This is illustrated graphically in Fig. 2.2.

Trust in human relationships

Psychological theory allows us to further model how trust in brands develops over time with experience, by analogy with the way that we develop trust within human relationships. Trust in people is seen to evolve out of past experiences and prior interaction and

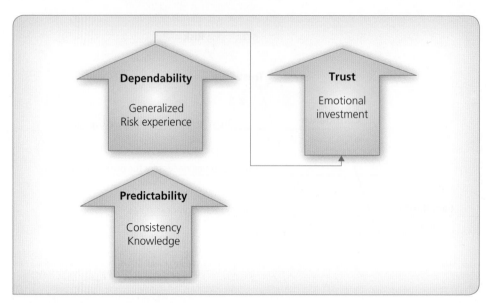

FIGURE 2.3 Hierarchy of emotional involvement

develops in stages moving from predictability, to dependability, to trust, and eventually sometimes to faith (Rempel *et al.*, 1985). This represents a hierarchy of emotional involvement which reaches trust when we make an emotional involvement in another person. The basic requirements for predictability are some experience of consistency of behaviour from which we can build a knowledge base. Dependability requires further experience and involves a move away from specific behaviours to a more generalized set of beliefs which are invested in the person and are therefore not readily available from others. This move is likely to depend heavily on the accumulation of evidence from a limited and diagnostic set of experiences involving risk and personal vulnerability. Trust requires a move from reliance on rational cognitions to reliance on emotion and sentiment and a developing intimacy which leads to an investment of emotion in the person. See Fig. 2.3.

A model of trust and confidence in brands

We can draw these models of social trust and human relationships together into an integrative model of trust and consumer brands. See Fig. 2.4.

We can see that the concept of trust is particularly relevant to symbolic brands, with high involvement due to high perceptions of purchase risk.

Functional brands, at the lowest level of perceived risk if they are familiar, provide an *easy choice* based on predictability and credibility. With increased risk, functional brands provide a *safe choice* through confidence which allows consumers to depend on them. Symbolic brands in markets with high perceived risk need to provide *trust*, which is achieved through developing perceptions of consumer–brand intimacy and emotional investment, and this will be discussed further in Chapter 8.

```
Risk
Perceptions
        +   │   Symbolic brands
            │   Intimacy  ⟶  Emotional Investment  ⟶  Trust
            │
            │   Functional brands
            │   Easy Choice  ⟶  Dependability  ⟶  Safe Choice
            │
            │   Functional brands
            │   Predictability  ⟶  Credibility  ⟶  Easy Choice
```

FIGURE 2.4 Brand trust and brand confidence

KEY CONCEPT

Trust and reliance on emotion for symbolic brands

Successful symbolic brands are trusted by customers. Symbolic brands are purchased out of a non-rational preference in which emotion plays a primary role. There is therefore an element of the unknown in why the preference is felt. This is why trust is important, because the brand requires a leap of faith from the customer, 'I like this brand, but I'm not completely sure why'. If the customer understands with certainty their preference then trust is replaced by expectation; these are safe and easy choices.

Emotional brand associations

Up to this point we have been concerned with the role of emotion as socially or culturally constructed, and its mediating effect upon choice and behaviour. Now we will address the role that emotional associations *with* brands plays in informing effective strategic planning. Everyone holds in non-declarative emotional memory—which is where unconscious responses occur from learning episodes often forgotten—emotional associations with memories. This means that we have emotional associations with brands that have grown out of our experiences with them, and they are linked in memory to those brands.

When a memory is recalled, all the component parts of that memory, including the emotional associations, are reunited. When we think about a brand, we will be drawing from memory not only its cognitive associations such as benefits or features, but also the emotional 'feelings' about the brand. Measuring the emotions associated with a brand provides the manager with a powerful tool for better understanding their brand because these emotional associations will inform how people process information about the brand.

We discussed earlier the idea that emotion is likely to be part of a neural system that is independent of those generally associated with higher-order cognitive processes. But as it happens, secondary emotions appear to be highly integrated with cognitive processes. Primarily, emotion is centred in the amygdala, which is an important part of the limbic system. It is here that the link to a higher-order cognitive process is made. The limbic system, while sometimes debated in the specific, is generally understood to be the controlling factor in processing both emotional and cognitive information. Within the limbic system, the hippocampus is concerned with cognitive processing and the amygdala with emotional processing.

Emotion, interacting with declarative memory (what we are conscious of), plays a role in motivating deliberate plans of action rather than triggering the rapid, reflex-like responses that proceed out of consciousness. They are likely to be integrated into cognitive processing that leads to more long-term planning or decisions. In a sense, this is consistent with the evolutionary neuropsychology idea that there is an adaptive value in having such emotional feelings because they can be important to long-term planning and explicit processing systems, especially where there are too many factors to be easily handled at a cognitive level (Rolls, 1999). So, even though emotions are not part of cognitive neural systems, they are nonetheless integrated into the cognitive processing of information. In a very real sense it is emotion that 'frames' conscious cognitive processing.

An interesting study using functional magnetic resonance imaging (fMRI) investigated the influence of implicit memory (i.e. unconscious, non-cognitive memory) on brand choice (Deppe *et al.*, 2005). What the authors found was an integration of previous emotional experience with a brand into ongoing decision processing. In fact, when someone made a choice of their favourite brand, it was characterized by reduced activation of the cognitive areas of the brain associated with working memory and reasoning and increased activation in areas involved in the processing of emotions. Later, in Chapter 5, we will be discussing another study using fMRI that shows when someone is choosing between Coke and Pepsi, and they know what they are drinking, those whose favourite brand is Coke are only using those areas of the brain associated with emotional memory when stating their preference. But when people do not know what they are drinking, only those areas of the brain involved with taste are active. There is no doubt that emotion is involved in brand choice.

While positive emotional memories will never override negative cognitive associations in brand choice decisions, in all other cases the emotion will provide a positive feeling as information about a brand is being processed, or when someone is thinking about it. As a result, the emotional significance of a brand will influence how much attention is paid to it, and how much someone will elaborate upon its significance. It also means that emotional associations with brands will determine what information is potentially available for recall when making brand choice decisions.

KEY CONCEPT

Emotional significance of a brand

Our emotions are powerful motivators. When we feel positively towards a brand we are not only more inclined to process (cognitively) information about it, but our positive mood means we are more likely to interpret the information positively. Further, we are more likely to ponder that information, associate it with other fond memories and, in doing so, develop more 'trigger points' in our minds that will allow us to recall or recognize the brand.

Fortunately, it is possible to measure the emotion associated with a brand (Percy *et al.*, 2004). With that information in hand, a manager is better able to address issues of positioning and marketing communication because the emotional associations with a brand will inform how people will process information about it. Consider the results of a study that measured the emotional associations with three shampoo brands shown in Table 2.2. The numbers in the table reflect the overall strength of the emotional associations (other data identified the specific emotions involved).

There are strong emotional associations with Sanex and Dove, but a negative emotional association with Head & Shoulders. But if we look at the strength of the emotional associations with each brand broken down between users versus non-users of each brand, we see something quite different (Table 2.3).

We see that *users* of Head & Shoulders, far from holding negative emotional associations with the brand, hold very strong positive feelings. On the other hand, the emotional strength for Sanex and Dove does not differ significantly between users and non-users. Strategically, this has critical implications. It suggests that Head & Shoulders may enjoy considerable brand loyalty amongst current users; however, attracting switchers to the brand will be very difficult until the negative associations held by non-users are changed. But with Sanex and Dove, because everyone holds positive feelings for these brands, loyalty may be diluted. This may not be problematic if the segment is large enough and consumers simply variety-seek between these two brands. However, brand managers must be aware that switching is much easier. This then presents them with the opportunity of gaining significant market share should they strengthen the emotional connection amongst users and, conversely, they risk losing significant market share should the competing brand do so.

TABLE 2.2 Emotional intensity measures for shampoo brands

Brand	Net strength
Dove	0.742
Head & Shoulders	−0.099
Sanex	1.281

TABLE 2.3 Emotional intensity measures for shampoo brands: users versus non-users

Brand	Net strength
Dove user	0.910
Dove non-user	0.832
Head & Shoulders user	2.650
Head & Shoulders non-user	−0.525
Sanex user	1.694
Sanex non-user	1.133

Implications for brand strategy

As emotion is socially constructed, we learn the feeling rules appropriate for our culture through the socialization process. One of the social roles of advertising is in educating consumers how to feel about products and services, and this is exemplified in the current move towards 'emotionalizing' many product categories. For example, instant coffee and luxury ice-cream have both been repositioned successfully as products with romantic/sexual connotations. This suggests that it is possible to 'emotionalize' products which have little rational connection with powerful emotions. This will be discussed in relation to symbolic brand strategy in Chapter 8. However, when marketing across borders, care must be taken to ensure that an emotional positioning strategy is culturally appropriate.

KEY CONCEPT

It is possible to 'emotionalize' a product

Most brand mangers want customers to have an emotional connection with their brands. This is because it is much harder for competitors to 'reverse engineer' an emotional response. It is easy enough to take an item of clothing and use the same fabric, colour, and design as a successful brand. However, what if that brand triggers emotions associated with sassy, urban counter culture? How is that reverse engineered? This is why so many brand managers spend a lot of time and money trying to engender an emotional response to even the most mundane products—toilet paper, toothpaste, and fabric softener. Clever associations with emotion-laden images and situations have shown this to be possible.

As emotion-driven choice is an almost instantaneous process, it is imperative for marketers to ensure that there are no impediments to immediate purchase. In some cultures, and with some product categories, it may be necessary to provide consumers with rational evidence to support their emotion-driven choice, either during or post-purchase. This will be discussed in relation to low-involvement brand strategy in Chapter 9.

As already noted, the emotional associations with a brand that we hold in memory will influence how we process information about that brand. Profiling the emotions linked to a brand versus competitors will help guide the development of more effective positioning and marketing communication programmes for that brand. The ability to measure these emotional associations also means managers can track changes in them, or their strength in response to marketing and communication programmes.

CHAPTER SUMMARY

In this chapter we have explored the complexity of emotions and how the symbolic meaning of consumption is fundamental to understanding the ability of brands to communicate social, psychological, and cultural messages. Trust is an emotional factor in brands and we have shown how it develops over time. It is possible to emotionalize a product or service that has little rational connection with emotions, and we explore these issues further in the next two chapters.

DISCUSSION QUESTIONS

1 What is the difference between an emotion and a feeling?

2 What assumptions have traditional consumer behaviour models made about the hierarchy of effects?

3 Why might the symbolic meaning of brands be a prime motivation for emotion-driven choice?

4 Discuss the implications for our consumption habits of the law of the lightest load.

5 How is the 'refusal of other tastes' involved in consumer choice?

6 How might brand marketers manage the post-purchase emotions of guilt, anxiety, and regret?

7 When do consumers need to trust a brand?

8 How do consumers build emotional associations with a brand?

CASE STUDY

Blowing up a storm

Planning redefined the role of this 80-year-old brand from providing control to encouraging release via a big emotional thought (a mass unclenching where people 'let it all out') that was inextricably linked to product usage.

Planned by: Angela Morris
Agency: JWT
Client: Kleenex

Summary

This is a story about how planning took an 80-year-old fmcg (fast moving consumer goods) superbrand and reinvigorated it to ensure success for the next 80 years. It's about breaking conventions and how you can build market share from a brand campaign with no product messaging. All it takes is a new type of thinking, and a willingness to turn everything on its head. The problem was that Kleenex was stalling—both in the UK and the USA. Our challenge was to grow share and change Kleenex from well known to loved. The planners led an overhaul of brand strategy. We reframed the target audience from buyer to user. And turned the brand promise from functional to emotional. Then we redefined the role of the brand—into the opposite of the role it had played since launch—Kleenex went from providing control to encouraging *release*. Finally, we created a new communication model, built on participation, with an integrated campaign including ATL, online, PR, and experiential media. Kleenex would both encourage and enable people to 'Let It Out'. Early results showed that brand share went up by almost three times the target and brand warmth and appeal generated by communications doubled.

Introduction

Kleenex was stalling, on both sides of the Atlantic. One of the most famous brands in the world, it had fought off competition for 80 years, but now was struggling in an increasingly commoditized market where own-label quality was often parity, and in some cases cost a staggering 80% less. No surprise then that brand share was plateauing and, although brand equity was still strong, that too was weakening. It seemed almost unbelievable. Kleenex is a superbrand. And JWT had helped build that success, having worked with Kimberly-Clark for 65 of those 80 years. But that was part of the problem. Kleenex had become so much part of the fabric of life that it had become the generic. So Kleenex was taken for granted; known and respected, but not loved. It wasn't enough. Our superbrand was vulnerable. In order to grow market share we needed to increase brand appeal and warmth.

A revised brand strategy

Our first job was to look again at the brand strategy. What could and should we be doing differently? Our team of three planners (from New York and London) led workshops and insight sessions, and we trawled through data for clues as to how the brand could be reinvigorated. The result? A new brand ambition and completely revamped brand blueprint. Two areas in particular were critical to the work that followed:

1 We reframed the target audience from buyer to user—we would target everyone with a nose. Because, we planners argued, if you are going to generate an emotional connection, you need a relationship with the user, not just the purchaser.

2 We changed the brand promise—upping the emotional reward. Kleenex would no longer simply make it better; Kleenex would make people *feel* better. This led to a new communications objective: to engage people in the brand emotionally—to make it known AND *loved*.

The thinking

We needed to find an engagement opportunity for Kleenex. One that allowed us to change the relationship with the brand. It was time to delve deep into the world of emotions. The modern world, we planners found, is increasingly emotion-provoking. Too little time, too much to do, too many people in the way. It's a recipe for emotion. And, sometimes, that emotion spills over. Even supposedly mild-mannered Britain is placed second in the world for frequency of road rage attacks! To help us understand this phenomenon better we commissioned surveys on both sides of the Atlantic and found that 70–80% of people think they should and could emote more—what's more, 77% of British men even considered crying in public to be socially acceptable.

This was good news surely? More emoting means increased tissue occasions. But it wasn't all good. For 80 years Kleenex had been positioned as being about control; the opposite of emoting. Kleenex's role was to be there at those moments when things got emotionally and physically messy, and to return you to a state of control and tearfree, snot-free, socially acceptable normality. That's what the product did; that's what the brand was built on.

We needed to find a way to reframe the role of the brand that was relevant to today. We kept looking, and we found that in practice, rather than emoting freely, people were still bottling it up. NHS prescriptions for anti-depressants doubled between 1975 and 1998. One in five Britons has had some form of counselling or psychotherapy according to The Future Foundation. An *Observer* poll revealed that 39% of British men said they did not believe men talked about their feelings enough. So for all of Gazza's sobbing, Diana-related outpourings of grief and weekly floods of tears on the X Factor, we still keep our emotions in check.

We had found an intention gap between attitudes and behaviour—72% of UK consumers thought that bottling it up was 'bad for your health', yet less than 20% had got it off their chest in the past 24 hours. US statistics were comparable. We wanted to dig a bit more, so we ran an internet study. This proved a revelation; there is a hierarchy of emotions people are prepared to emote. Everyone felt more comfortable than they used to expressing joy and excitement, but other more 'vulnerable' emotions (like fear, disappointment, sadness or pride, i.e. the ones most likely to lead to a tissue need) made them feel uncomfortable.

A planner light bulb went on at this point. Could this be the answer to a new emotional role for Kleenex? Could it simply be that people just need a little more encouragement to get over their discomfort about emoting, especially about the more taboo emotions?

What if Kleenex encouraged the very thing it was previously positioned to control? We felt sure we were on to something, so we ran some groups. The traditional role for Kleenex— functionally controlling the by-products of being human, so generating emotion (relief)—is in fact only one of the emotional opportunities for the brand. It's credible, but it's difficult to *own*. Because the functionality is generic, it is hard to connect the emotional resolution to your brand. However, we had uncovered a second emotional opportunity—*before* the tissue need, when people are bottling it up. The Kleenex role could be the exact opposite of its past— instead of control, it could stand for *release*. It could become a permissive brand, encouraging and inspiring people to act differently—to cry, shout, scream, and laugh when they want to. It could stand up for emoting, and fight against bottling it up. And it could be associated with that good feeling. We had found the Kleenex cause, one that people would love the brand for and one that fitted the emergent, but still fledgling, trend (evident in outgoing expressives, bloggers, and social networkers) of emoting or 'putting yourself out there'.

The communications strategy

So, we could credibly be part of this new world, with an emotional role very different from Kleenex's past. But the problem was only half solved. How did we communicate this? We knew we couldn't just create 'push' messaging old-world style. We needed to break category norms and talk in a new language—one that would have consumer pull. The planners decided Kleenex should start something akin to a movement, one that would encourage people to emote and would grow exponentially as people joined in. To achieve this, the planning team created a new communications model:

The three connection platforms would be actioned simultaneously to enable people to immediately respond and become participants:

1 *Ignite*—to get the idea out there and to encourage people to release.

2 *Inform*—to raise awareness of the importance of emoting and generating a debate.

3 *Involve*—to enable people to participate, to join those happy people who emote.

The creative brief

Our brief was to create a rallying cry that encouraged people to unclench and release that emotion. One that would strike a chord that felt *real*. And one that tapped into how people relate to, comment on, and involve themselves in communications messaging today. This was to be executed with a range of communications in the three areas of the model including online, experiential, and in store. We asked the creatives to make it as *participatory* as possible. Even the static stuff. And they did.

The creative work

The rallying cry JWT created was simple but visceral: *Let It Out*. It felt good. And big. And right. But would it work? Could Kleenex credibly give people permission to let it out? First we wrote a manifesto, calling on people to 'say goodbye to the stiff upper lip'. The creatives had an idea about using real people emoting in our communication. The planners were keen that this must come across as genuine; what could we do to reassure us it would feel *real*? The answer the creatives suggested was a live film test. We went into the street, set up a sofa, a sympathetic looking 'listener' and a box of Kleenex and filmed what happened. What would it take for people to let it out? Turns out all you really need is a good listener and a box of Kleenex tissues. People wanted to let it out. And they let it out in all kinds of ways—crying, laughing, ranting, cheering. This test film became our Let It Out anthem. It also became the demo for the eventual TV launch spot, filmed entirely with real people stopping in the street to let it out. But this was about more than TV, we had the rest of the model to think of:

1 *Ignite*—we had the 60-second launch TV spot plus cut downs, but we also created online advertising, idents, and point of sale (POS). We even had 'before and after' interactive print, which allowed the reader to lift a flap to change the expression from bottled up to emoting.

2 *Inform*—we hired a social anthropologist as a way of generating PR and debate. By explaining the psychological importance of letting it out, she lent credibility to the movement. Coming from a mature fmcg brand like Kleenex, a communications campaign with this approach generated phenomenal interest and coverage.

3 *Involve*—the backbone of this was www.letitout.com where you could upload your own stories, read others, find out the 'back stories' behind the TV spot and the people in it, and see reports about the emotional state of the nation. We also went to where consumers were already blogging—MSN Spaces. In the real world we arranged a sofa tour to give people the chance to let it out on the soon-to-be-famous blue sofa (from the TV advertising). We also got the campaign onto the airwaves, and set up radio partnerships and micro sites. Listeners were encouraged to ring or write in and let it out. We released the TV sound track single as the campaign broke and used music PR to promote it. Lastly, we put the ad on youtube.com to invite comment and encourage word of mouth discussion.

Did it work?

People loved it. They enjoyed the anthemic TV advertising, loved the music, went to the website and MSN site, called the radio stations, blogged about it, and generally let it out.

Kimberly-Clark received passionate messages of support and others raved about it on youtube. com. The TV soundtrack charted and the US TV station VH1 spoofed the film with a hilarious, but bloody, ending!

Early results for the UK showed that our key metric, value share, was up 2.6% by the end of March (the target for end of 2007 was a 1% increase) and volume was up with the first Q1 year-on-year growth in three years. Advertising tracking for the brand film easily outdid norms (set by Millward Brown):

- Recognition 68% (vs. 49% norm).
- Enjoyment 77% (vs. 55% norm).
- More likely to use 51% (vs. 36% norm).

And the TV advertising outshone the performance of previous Kleenex TV advertising:

- Made Kleenex seem much more appealing; 46% (vs. 22%).
- Is a warm and caring brand; 61% (vs. 32%).

Conclusion

What did we planners learn through this work? That even the 'most mundane of products' can be turned around and brought kicking and screaming into today's consumers' hearts, minds, and inboxes. That fmcg brands can successfully build market share through a brand campaign that doesn't for one second mention product or functionality. And that consumers can be persuaded to engage and participate with brands in commodity markets. All it takes is a new type of thinking, and a willingness to turn everything and anything on its head.

With thanks to the full planner team for their invaluable contributions—Ted Florea and David Baker.

DISCUSSION QUESTIONS

1 What did the findings of researchers at JWT tell us about social perspectives on emotions?

2 When driven by emotion the process of choice is non-linear. Explain this statement in relation to the objectives of the 'Let it Out' campaign.

3 What hurdles will JWT have faced in relation to the emotional associations consumers already had with memories of the Kleenex brand?

4 An important strategic implication for emotion-driven choice is that sometimes there is a need to educate consumers how to feel about products and services. Discuss how JWT managed this for Kleenex.

5 Using a major competitor familiar to you, profile the emotions linked to that brand. What implications might this have for the future positioning of Kleenex?

FURTHER READING

- An examination of the different aspect of emotion and its role in human behaviour is provided by Lewis, M., Haviland-Jones J. M., and Feldman Barrett L. (eds) (2008) *Handbook of Emotions*, New York: Guilford Press.

- A review of the role of emotion in a wide range of information-processing activities is provided by Chaudhuri, A. (2006), *Emotion and Reason in Consumer Behaviour*, Oxford: Butterworth-Heinemann.

- The psychology of emotion is explored in detail by Strongman, K. (2003), *Psychology of Emotion: From Everyday Life to Theory*, London: John Wiley.

- The evidence that reason and emotion are closely linked is argued from a solid base in neuroscientific research by Damasio, A. (2006), *Descartes' Error: Emotion, Reason and the Human Brain*, London: Penguin.

REFERENCES

Arnould, E. and Price, L. (1993), 'River magic: extraordinary experience and the extended service encounter', *Journal of Consumer Research*, 20, 24–45.

Bagozzi, R. (1975), 'Marketing as exchange', *Journal of Marketing*, 39, 4, 32–40.

Bourdieu, P. (1984), *Distinction: A Social Critique of the Judgement of Taste* (R. Nice, trans.), London: Routledge.

Bradley, M.M. and Lang, P.J. (2000), 'Measuring emotion: behaviour, feeling, and physiology', in R.D. Lane and L. Nalel (eds), *Cognitive Neuroscience of Emotion*, Oxford: Oxford University Press, 242–76.

Campbell, C. (1987), *The Romantic Ethic and the Spirit of Modern Consumerism*, Oxford: Blackwell.

Damasio, A. (1999), *The Feeling of What Happens*, New York: Harcourt.

Deppe, M., Scheindt, W., Kugel, H., Plassman, H., and Kenning, P. (2005), 'Nonlinear responses within the medial prefrontal cortex reveal where specific implicit information influences economic decision making', *Journal of Neuroimaging*, 15, 171–82.

Deutsch, M. (1973), *The Resolution of Conflict: Constructive and Destructive Processes*, New Haven: Yale University Press.

Dwyer, F.R. and Oh, S. (1987), 'Output sector munificence effects on the internal political economy of marketing channels', *Journal of Marketing Research*, 4, 347–58.

Eichenbaum, H. (2002), *The Cognitive Neuroscience of Memory*, Oxford: Oxford University Press.

Ekman, P. (1992), 'Facial expressions of emotion: new findings, new questions', *Psychological Science*, 3, 1, 34–8.

Ekman, P. and Friesen, W.V. (1971), 'Constants across cultures in the face and emotion', *Journal of Personality and Social Psychology*, 17, 124–9.

Elliott, R. (1998), 'A model of emotion-driven choice', *Journal of Marketing Management*, 14, 1–3, 95–108.

Fiske, S. and Taylor, S. (1984), *Social Cognition*, New York: Random House.

Frijda, N. (1988), 'The laws of emotion', *American Psychologist*, 43, 5, 349–58.

Fromm, E. (1976), *To Have Or To Be*, London: Routledge and Kegan Paul.

Gabriel, Y. and Lang, T. (1995), *The Unmanageable Consumer: Contemporary Consumption and Its Fragmentations*, London: Sage.

Gardial, S., Clemons, S., Woodruff, B., and Burns, M. (1994), 'Comparing consumers' recall of prepurchase and postpurchase product evaluation experiences', *Journal of Consumer Research*, 20, 548–60.

Giddens, A. (1991), *Modernity and Self-Identity: Self and Society in the Late Modern Age*, Cambridge: Polity Press.

Griffiths, P.E. (1997), *What Emotions Really Are*, Chicago: The University of Chicago Press.

Gronroos, C. (1996), 'Relationship marketing: strategic and tactical implications', *Management Decision*, 34, 3, 5–15.

Gulati, R. (1995), 'Does familiarity breed trust? The implications of repeated ties for contractual choice in alliances', *Academy of Management Journal*, 38, 1, 85–112.

Harré, R. (ed.) (1986), *The Social Construction of Emotions*, Oxford: Basil Blackwell.

Hiscock, J. (2001), 'Most trusted brands', *Marketing*, March, 32–3.

Hochschild, A.R. (1983), *The Managed Heart: Commercialization of Human Feeling*, Berkeley: University of California Press.

Holbrook, M. and Hirschman, E. (1982), 'The experiential aspects of consumption: consumer fantasies, feelings, and fun', *Journal of Consumer Research*, 9, 132–40.

Kunda, Z. (1990), 'The case for motivated reasoning', *Psychological Bulletin*, 108, 480–98.

Lascu, D. (1991), 'Consumer guilt: examining the potential of a new marketing construct', *Advances in Consumer Research*, 18, 290–5.

Lazarus, R.S. (1982), 'Thoughts on the relation between emotion and cognition', *American Psychologist*, 37, 1019–24.

Luhmann, N. (1979), *Trust and Power*, Chichester: John Wiley & Sons.

Lunt, P. and Livingstone, S. (1992), *Mass Consumption and Personal Identity*, Milton Keynes: Open University Press.

Markus, H. and Kitayama, S. (1991), 'Culture and the self: implications for cognition, emotion, and motivation', *Psychological Review*, 98, 2, 224–53.

Messaris, P. (1997), *Visual Persuasion: The Role of Images in Advertising*, Thousand Oaks: Sage Publications.

Mittal, B. (1988), 'The role of affective choice mode in the consumer purchase of expressive products', *Journal of Economic Psychology*, 9, 499–524.

Möllering, G. (2001), 'The nature of trust: from Georg Simmel to a theory of expectation, interpretation and suspension', *Sociology*, 35, 2, 403–20.

Obermiller, C. (1990), 'Feelings about feeling state research: a search for harmony', *Advances in Consumer Research*, 17, 590–3.

O'Shaughnessy, J. (1992), *Explaining Buyer Behavior: Central Concepts and Philosphy of Science Issues*, New York: Oxford University Press.

Parkinson, B., Fisher, A.H., and Manstead, A.S.R. (2005), *Emotions in Social Relations*, New York: Psychology Press.

Percy, L., Hansen, F., and Randrup, R. (2004), 'How to measure brand emotion', *Admap*, November, 32–4.

Powell, W.W. (1990), 'Neither market nor hierarchy: network forms of organizations', *Research in Organizational Behavior*, 12, 295–336.

Radley, A. (1988), 'The social form of feeling', *British Journal of Social Psychology*, 27, 5–18.

Rempel, J., Holmes, J., and Zanna, M. (1985), 'Trust in close relationships', *Journal of Personality and Social Psychology*, 49, 1, 95–112.

Ring, P.S. and Van de Ven, A. (1994), 'Development processes of cooperative interorganizational relationships', *Academy of Management Review*, 19, 90–118.

Rolls, E.T. (1999), *The Brain and Emotion*, Oxford: Oxford University Press.

Rook, D. (1987) 'The buying impulse', *Journal of Consumer Research*, 14, 189–99.

Scherer, K.R. (2000), 'Psychological models of emotion', in J.C. Borod, (ed.), *The*

49

Neuropsychology of Emotions, New York: Oxford University Press, pp. 139–62.

Schwarz, N. (1990), 'Feelings as information', in E.T. Higgins and R. Sorrentino (eds), *Handbook of Motivation and Cognition: Foundations of Social Behavior*, Vol. 2, New York: Guilford Press.

Shapiro, S.P. (1987), 'The social control of impersonal trust', *American Journal of Sociology*, 93, 623–58.

Shweder, R.A., (1993), 'The cultural psychology of emotions', in M. Lewis and J.M. Haviland (eds), *Handbook of Emotions*, New York: Guilford Press, pp. 417–34.

Shweder, R.A., Haidt, J., Horton, R., and Joseph, C. (2008) 'The cultural psychology of the emotions: ancient and renewed', in M. Lewis, J.M. Haviland-Jones, and L. Feldman Barrett (eds) *Handbook of Emotions*, New York: Guilford Press, pp. 409–27.

Storr, A. (1973), *Jung*, London: Fontana.

Von Hippel, W., and Trivers, R. (2011). 'The evolution and psychology of self-deception', *Behavioral and Brain Sciences* 34 (1), 1–56.

Wilson, T.D. and Schooler, J.W. (1991), 'Thinking too much: introspection can reduce the quality of preferences and decisions', *Journal of Personality and Social Psychology*, 60, 2, 181–92.

Yamasaki, H., Labor, K., and McCathy, G. (2002), 'Dissociable prefrontal brain systems for attention and emotion', *Proceedings of the National Academy of Sciences USA*, 99, 11447–51.

Zajonc, R. (1980), 'Feeling and thinking: preferences need no inferences', *American Psychologist*, 35, 151–75.

Zajonc, R. and Markus, H. (1982), 'Affective and cognitive factors in preferences', *Journal of Consumer Research*, 9, 2, 123–32.

Test your understanding of this chapter and explore the subject further using our Online Resource Centre. Visit the Online Resource Centre at http://www.oxfordtextbooks.co.uk/orc/elliott-percy3e/

The Symbolic Meaning of Brands

3

Key Concepts

1 Brands can be used as symbolic resources for the construction and maintenance of identity/identities.

2 Advertising can build symbolic meaning through narratives.

3 Brands can help establish and communicate some fundamental cultural categories.

4 Brands can also be used to counter some of the threats to identity posed by postmodernity. 后现代性

5 Brands can acquire deep meaning through the socialization process.

Introduction

Do you name your car, or identify as a 'Mac user?' Have you ever talked about ads whilst out with friends? Contemporary social theory has begun to focus on consumption as playing a central role in the way in which the social world is constructed and developments in post-structural anthropology have led to a renewed interest in the relationship between society and material culture, essentially the way in which we use the things we produce to give meaning to our lives. These trends can be subsumed into the development of postmodern theories of consumer culture which focus on aspects of cultural practice in the construction of consumer society rather than just on consumption itself. The implications for the marketing of brands under conditions of postmodernity are that many assumptions about the consumer and consumption require fundamental reassessment.

The postmodern consumer and symbolic meaning

Central to postmodernism is the recognition that the consumer does not make consumption choices solely from products' utilities, that is what they actually do, but also from their symbolic meanings, that is, what they communicate. The functions of the symbolic meanings of brands operate in two directions, outward in constructing the social world: *Social-Symbolism*, and inward towards constructing our self-identity: *Self-Symbolism*. The social-symbolic meanings of brands can be used to communicate to other people the kind of person we wish to be seen as. For example, an ad for Seiko watches says very plainly 'It's not your shoes, it's not your tie, it's not your car, it's your watch that says most about who you are'. Similarly, an ad for Baldessanini men's fragrance from Hugo Boss says 'Separates the men from the boys'. More subtly, and with a touch of postmodern irony, Volkswagen ran a TV campaign for the Golf in the UK which showed a series of vignettes where a man showed off a large gold watch with the subtitle 'I'm loaded', a man sat at pavement café reading a serious book with the subtitle 'I'm an intellectual', a skinhead was seen with a ferocious dog with the subtitle saying 'I'm hard'. The final scene was a young man in jeans and a t-shirt getting into a Golf with the subtitle 'I'm just going down the shops'. The sign off was 'VW Golf, a car not a label'. The self-symbolic meaning of brands is what their usage communicates to us about who we are or want to be. As consumption plays a central role in supplying meanings and values for the creation and maintenance of the personal and social world, which is one definition of what constitutes a consumer society, so advertising is recognized as one of the major sources of these symbolic meanings. These cultural meanings are transferred to brands and it is brands which are often used as symbolic resources for the construction and maintenance of identity.

This semiotic perspective of products as symbols (which is explored in more detail in Chapter 4) raises difficult questions about the location of cultural meaning. The term symbol itself can relate to the brand that carries meaning or to the meaning it carries, and the interpretation of meaning is a complex mix of what is contained in the representation of the brand and what the individual brings to the representation. Symbolism can be analysed semiotically by examination of the system of signs and what they signify, however,

KEY CONCEPT

Brands and the construction and maintenance of identities

Many of the brands we use in everyday life have no particular relevance to our identity. The computer or sticky tape dispenser on your office desk, the tiles or roofing iron on your house. But stop to think about the brands that do matter and you may be quite surprised. That top you are wearing, the watch on your wrist, the school you have sent your children to, or even the stationary your child takes to school. Brands have become very important signifiers of our personal and social identities. They can even help us 'shape shift' a little. For example, the suit you are wearing to corporate lunch versus the outfit your wear to a band on Saturday night with friends.

it is impossible to make sense of the system of signs as a whole because one sign leads to another without there ever being anything 'real' outside the system. All meaning is socially constructed and there is no essential external reference point, so ultimately 'There is nothing outside the text' (Derrida, 1977). To complicate matters further, symbols are typically interpreted in an improvised and non-rational manner that does not obey the codes of language but operates at the subconscious level. We don't think too hard about them otherwise symbols lose their 'symbolism' so to speak. What this suggests is that there is a very high likelihood that the symbolism which you interpret in a brand may differ from that which an organization has endeavoured to craft. As we discuss in Chapter 4, the meaning of a brand may even be appropriated to serve someone's own sub-cultural purposes.

Consumption of the symbolic meaning of products is a social process that helps make visible and stable the basic categories of a culture which are under constant change, and consumption choices 'become a vital source of the culture of the moment' (Douglas and Isherwood, 1978). The meanings of consumer goods are grounded in their social context and the demand for goods derives more from their role in cultural practices than from the satisfaction of simple human needs. Consumer goods, therefore, are more than just objects of economic exchange, 'they are goods to think with, goods to speak with' (Fiske, 1989) and are an important part of the symbols and signs which we use to locate ourselves in our society. Consumption as a cultural practice is one way of participating in social life and may be an important element in cementing social relationships, whilst the whole system of consumption is an expression of the existing social structure through a seductive process which pushes the purchasing impulse until it reaches the 'limits of economic potential' (Baudrillard, 1988). Baudrillard further suggests that consumption is a necessary part of the political economy as the capitalist system, which prevails in most countries of the world, is predicated on continual economic growth and, as such, relies on our desire to consume.

It is within this social context that the individual uses consumer goods and the consumption process as the materials with which to construct and maintain an identity, form relationships, and frame psychological events. Access to social media has provided new avenues for this process. For example Facebook's (FB) capacity to aid in consumer self-disclosure makes it particularly relevant to identity construction. It is thought that we devote 30–40% of speech output to informing others of our own subjective experiences (Tamir and Mitchell, 2012). In a study across five experiments Tamir and Mitchell show that disclosing information is intrinsically rewarding and that people were even willing to forgo money to talk about themselves. From a brand perspective, the importance of FB lies in its capacity for consumer self-disclosure, i.e. to communicate how they interact with brands. Researchers have observed that social networking sites generate much more self-disclosure and personal questions than face to face conversations (Tidwell and Walther, 2002). With more than 1 billion registered users (Facebook, 2012), and an enormous number of brand-focused sites (Waters et al., 2009), the unique advantage FB has over other social networking sites is that it tends to draw people offline (friends and family in existing networks) into the online environment (Ross et al., 2009). Thus we need to understand the ecology of a brand, which means how it integrates with the wider social and cultural experiences of the consumer. We will discuss brand ecology further in Chapter 8.

The postmodern consumer and identity

The self is conceptualized in postmodern consumer culture not as a given product of a social system nor as a fixed entity which we can simply adopt, but as something we actively create, partially through consumption. As consumers we exercise free will to form images of who and what we want to be, although, paradoxically, 'free will' is directed by values which are probably also a social product. Thompson (1995, p. 210) describes the self as a *symbolic project*, which the individual must actively construct out of the available symbolic materials, materials which 'the individual weaves into a coherent account of who he or she is, a narrative of self-identity.'

The individual visualizes her/his self according to their imagined possibilities of the self. Markus and Nurius (1986) suggest that 'an individual is free to create any variety of possible selves, yet the pool of possible selves derives from the categories made salient by the individual's particular sociocultural and historical context and from the models, images, and symbols provided by the media and by the individual's immediate social experiences.' Thus the nature of the self-concept is complex: we may possess a variety of actual selves (or roles) and a variety of possible or ideal selves. Think about how you present yourself at work and how this compares with the way you present yourself to family at a Christmas lunch or to friends when going to a movie. If we possess a multiplicity of role identities, how can these multiple selves coexist in harmony? How does each identity develop? And how do we express each self in a particular social situation? We live in a symbol-rich environment and the meaning attached to any situation or object is determined by the interpretation of these symbols. Through the socialization process we learn not only to agree on the shared meanings of some symbols but also to develop individual symbolic interpretations of our own. We use these symbolic meanings to construct, maintain, and express each of our multiple identities. Perhaps your confident and successful self wears Manolo Blahnik Classics for work, your dependable, caring self wears Birkenstock Clogs at Christmas lunch and your self-effacing but stylish self wears Ted Baker Pumps to the movies with friends. Here lies enormous potential for brands to offer an identity or self-image that we can buy into by adopting the brand as being symbolic of ourselves, saying something that we want to be associated with.

Narrative identity theory suggests that in order to make time human and socially shared, we require a narrative identity for our self, that is, we make sense of ourselves and our lives by the stories we can (or cannot) tell (Escalas, 2004). Thus we come to know ourselves by the narratives we construct to situate ourselves in time and place. This task can be greatly aided by symbolic resources; the main one articulated by Ricoeur (1977) is literature, which gives structure and meaning to the complexity and confusion of life by providing a causal model for the individual by linking disparate life events into a coherent sequence. However, advertising can also be used as a symbolic resource for the construction of narratives to give sense to our life history and personal situation. For example, in 2014 Barclays launched an advertising campaign that was formulated around the promotion of its youth employment programme, 'LifeSkills', by featuring several 30-second narratives of young people speaking directly to camera about personal hindrances that they were able to overcome by participating in the programme.

Advertising can build symbolic meaning through narratives

Narrative, or storytelling, is a way we have made sense of objects or 'things' for thousands of years. Storytelling is considered fundamental to human development. We are social beings and relating an object to social interaction is critical to our understanding of it. Brand managers can help customers makes sense of their brands by providing the impetus for a story, even a whole story, in their advertising. Hugely successful advertising campaigns have been based around appealing characters facing everyday life situations. Sometimes these stories take on a life of their own like the social media interaction on Twitter and Facebook between the Old Spice guy and his legions of fans.

The development of individual self-identity is inseparable from the parallel development of collective social identity, and this problematic relationship has been described as the *internal–external dialectic of identification* by Jenkins (1996), who maintains that self-identity must be validated through social interaction and that the self is embedded in social practices. This means that there is always a social dimension to a brand; an individual may love a brand's image, but will want his/her important others to like it too. This is particularly true of adolescents who are actively building their identity in relation to their peer group and are very sensitive to peer group approval or disapproval. Australian surf brand Billabong's rose to fame on the back of the counter culture mystique of the surfing community. Its fall from grace has coincided with surf culture persona becoming a mainstay of Australian society and is in-part blamed on the fact that the young men who bought the brand in 1970s and 1980s are still wearing it and are now the not-so-cool parents of children who don't want to look anything like them. Endeavours to create our self-identity often involve the consumption of products, services, and media and there is always a tension between the meanings we construct for ourselves and those we are exposed to socially, and this dialectical tension requires active negotiation of meaning. Dittmar (1992) comments that 'material possessions have a profound symbolic significance for their owners, as well as for other people and the symbolic meanings of our belongings are an integral feature of expressing our own identity and perceiving the identity of others.' The key point here is that not only do we interpret the symbolic meanings of other people's possessions but at the same time they are interpreting ours in a complex process of symbolic meaning construction and communication. Although McCracken (1988) suggests that ritual is the prime means for the transfer of symbolic meaning from goods to the person, the complex social practices of consumer culture extend far beyond the concept of the ritualistic, and entail a reciprocal, dialectical relationship between the individual and her/his cultural milieu.

Identity and self-symbolic consumption

All voluntary consumption carries, either consciously, subconsciously, or unconsciously symbolic meanings; if we have choices to consume, we will consume things that hold particular symbolic meanings. These meanings may be idiosyncratic or widely shared with other people. For example, using recycled envelopes may symbolize 'I care for the environment', going to classical concerts may symbolize 'I am cultured', while supporting gay rights may signify 'I am open-minded', or buying unbranded detergent may mean 'I am a clever consumer'.

A considerable literature suggests that we are what we consume, since possessions are viewed as major parts of our extended self (Belk, 1988). Csikszentmihalyi and Rochberg-Halton (1981) suggest that the consumer invests 'psychic energy' such as effort, time, and attention in an object. This energy and its products are regarded as a part of the self because they have grown or emerged from the self. To an extent then, our possessions are as much a part of us as our limbs or our ideas. The symbolic meanings of our possessions may portray essences of our individuality, or reflect our desirable connections with others (Kleine et al., 1995), and symbolic consumption helps us to categorize ourselves in society, to ease our self-transitions and to achieve our sense of continuity and eventually preparation for death. How people dispose of their possessions through wills and direct gifts is an important part of preparing to die, and the symbolic meaning of a gift from a now-dead relative lives on in many of our homes with items of pure sentimental value.

Possessions can also be part of a process of symbolic self-completion, where those of us who perceive ourselves as lacking a personal quality attempt to fill this gap using symbolic resources (Wicklund and Gollwitzer, 1982). This offers huge potential for brands as we may not be able to actually achieve our desired image, say as a thrusting successful manager, but we can buy part of the image through using and displaying brands that we believe to have the appropriate symbolic meaning, for example the pairing of a bottle of Veuve Clicquot and a Cohiba cigar.

Although we learn and develop consumption symbols through socialization processes and exposures to mass media (e.g., advertising), it does not mean that everybody who possesses the same product bought it for the same symbolic meaning. A product may carry a varied range of meanings since the creation of meaning is not deterministic and unidirectional, and each of us may ascribe different and inconsistent cultural meanings to a product depending on the extent to which we share the collective imagination. This means that we can get the symbolism wrong, that is we can misjudge the meaning of a brand, especially in the area of culturally significant goods where taste is an arbiter of appropriateness. For example, a clearly branded polo shirt may carry a symbolic meaning of success for one sub-cultural group or social class, but signify a lack of taste to another.

Lived versus mediated experience

The symbolic resources available to us for the construction of the self can be distinguished as being either lived experiences or mediated experiences. Lived experience refers to the practical activities and face to face encounters in our everyday lives. It is situated, immediate, and is largely non-reflexive, in that we take it for granted as 'reality'. Mediated experience is an outcome of a mass-communication culture and the consumption of media products and involves the ability to experience events which are spatially and temporally distant from the practical context of daily life. It is recontextualized experience, in that it allows the experience of events that transpire far away, and will vary widely in its relevance to the self. Perhaps you consider yourself an aficionado of alternative music. In constructing the self as a serious music lover, you may go to gigs regularly, attend Glastonbury festival, and talk with friends about your favourite bands, all of which are lived experiences. However, you may also read the *NME* or *Rolling Stone* magazines, regularly watch MTV, and listen to Radio 1, and these are mediated experiences. We can draw selectively on mediated experience and interlace it with lived experience to construct the self. The life history and social situation of individuals will vary between those at one end of the continuum who value only lived experience and have little contact with mediated forms, and others at the opposite end of the continuum for whom mediated experience has become central to the project of the self. However, central to postmodern consumer culture is a growing range of opportunities for the use of mediated experiences in the project of the self, countless narratives of self-formation, countless visions of the world such that we may be encountering 'symbolic overload' (Thompson, 1995, p. 216). This means that the battle for mindspace is not only about levels of brand awareness but also about competing visions and narratives of identity that are offered to the market. We will discuss this further in Chapter 8.

Symbolic meaning, advertising, and brands

Advertising is recognized as one of the most potent sources of valued symbolic meanings. As a part of a cultural system, advertising is viewed as a guideline to map out all aspects of the consumer's existence; on the other hand, all aspects of the consumer's existence are also guidelines to map out advertising creativity. In the first instance, advertising agencies draw on their knowledge of consumers to construct their ads; consumers then interpret these ads based on their own lived and mediated experiences. The relationship between advertising and the consumer is dialectical: advertising not only helps in creating, modifying, and transforming cultural meanings for the consumer (Lannon and Cooper, 1983), but also represents cultural meanings taken from the consumer's world view and invested into the advertised product. This dialectical relationship drives a cyclical flow of symbolic meanings derived from culture and transferred into the semiotic world of advertising, then interpreted and used by consumers to internally construct their self-concept and externally construct their social world. Take the ad for SUPERGA, an Italian casual footwear brand. One intention of the visual is clear; paring the Fiat Bambino with the shoe emphatically stamps the brand as Italian. The creative content of the ad is therefore led by consumer perceptions that this positioning is positive for the brand; Italian shoes are 'cool'. However, further meaning may be read. The shoe may be seen as stylish by association, or perhaps hard wearing or even quirky. In addition the ad may amuse you, encouraging you to mention it to a friend over coffee and in doing so discuss the publication you were reading and when and where you saw it. This may itself say something about you as a person. Thus the ad becomes so much more than a pitch to sell. Developed initially in response to how an advertising agency felt the brand contributed to cultural meaning, it might then be used by consumers to reinforce even reinterpret their own sense of self. 'Finally as part of the external construction of an individual's life world the meaning returns back to its original starting point, the mass of flowing meanings that represents culture' (Ritson and Elliott, 1995). Thus, advertising is both a means to transfer or create meanings into culture and a cultural product itself.

SUPERGA: The dialectical relationship between advertising and the consumer

Although advertisers aim to create particular meanings for their brands in advertising, meanings interpreted by the consumer may be varied and diverse. There is growing recognition that we are an active and participating audience (Mick and Buhl, 1992). However, we may attend only to certain messages and interpret or make sense of the meanings according to our personal perception and our social knowledge. The meaning of a particular advertisement is not given within the advertisement itself, for as Anderson and Meyer (1988) point out: 'meaning is not delivered in the communication process, rather it is constructed within it.' But the meaning that we construct from advertising is viscous in nature, it is not firm and finalized but liable to change, and signification through the media is likely to be much less potent than signification through actual behavioural experience (Elliott et al., 1993). Certainly, there is considerable empirical evidence that attitudes formed through direct experience are stronger, more accessible, held more confidently, and are more predictive of behaviour than those derived from mediated experience through advertising (e.g. Fazio and Zanna, 1978). Thus lived experience with a brand, through purchase and usage over the life cycle, will tend to dominate the mediated experience of advertising, and both forms of experience will be validated through social interaction, particularly for brands with a social-symbolic positioning.

Identity and social-symbolic consumption

The creation of meanings does not just consist of a negotiation process between advertising content, the brand, and the consumer simply during the period of exposure to the advertisement. Since advertising is a form of mass communication, its meanings also emerge in interpersonal communication among ourselves and may later become socially shared meaning.

The issues of cultural meaning and interactive advertising can be integrated by a model of advertising literacy (Ritson and Elliott, 1995, and see Fig. 3.1).

Modelled within the framework of contemporary literacy studies, advertising literacy is comprised not only of the skills to be able to understand and transfer meaning from an advertisement but also of the ability to use that meaning within the social context of the life world, a person's lived as opposed to mediated experiences. This is a practices and events model, which shows that literacy must consider the interpretive skills (practices) that the audience brings to an advertisement, but must also look at the ways in which advertising is involved in social interactions (events) and the uses to which the meaning is put in social life subsequent to the advertising exposure. Advertising literacy becomes a significant factor employed by many consumers, especially teenagers, to locate and relocate their social groups and their identities within those groups, because advertising literacy is used by group members to evaluate each other (Ritson and Elliott, 1999). The process of *discursive elaboration* involves the social consumption of advertising meanings, as they are described, discussed, argued about, laughed at. Advertisements become 'tokens in young people's system of social exchange' (Willis, 1990, p. 57); they are a form of cultural capital for teenagers, to be invested in carefully to gain dividends in terms of social status and self-esteem. Willis (1990) notes that young people are increasingly involved with advertisements and proposes that part of this increased interest in advertising stems

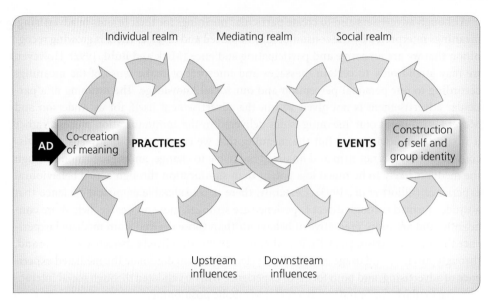

Individual realm   Mediating realm   Social realm

AD → Co-creation of meaning   PRACTICES   EVENTS   Construction of self and group identity

Upstream influences   Downstream influences

FIGURE 3.1 A model of advertising literacy

from the ability of advertisers to utilize the latest fashions in order to make advertisements aesthetically pleasing as a product independent of the advertised item. He also describes young people deriving 'symbolic pleasure' from the advertisements and in particular they are appreciative of the 'active role' they are expected to play in understanding the advertisements.

Buttle (1991) describes several studies which show that advertising is used in some situations as a means of initiating social interactions. Social media campaigns like Domino's Tweet for Cheap Pizza, which ran in 2014, sought to control and encourage this. Domino's reduced the price of a featured pizza according to how many people tweeted in time for lunch. With the promotion running from between the hours of 9am and 11am customers brought the price down from £15.99 to £7.74. In addition O'Donohoe (1994) notes that advertisements are also used on a social level in peer relationships. Generally advertisements were seen by her respondents as being facilitators to conversation. Diamond *et al.* (2009) investigated the American Doll brand which includes dolls from nine different historical periods and a number of ethnicities, each with their own story and accessories. In understanding how consumers interpret the brand they identified a 'mesh of interwoven experiences . . . some engineered by marketers, others improvised by stakeholders' like intergenerational relatives who pass on their own stories about the times the dolls represent (p. 132). Until meanings from mediated experiences of advertising have been subjected to discursive elaboration in a social context and interwoven with behavioural significations derived from lived experience with the brand, they remain viscous, liable to be rejected, or just forgotten. Only after this discursive elaboration can symbolic meanings be fully concretized and become what Eco (1979, p. 14) calls 'realized text'.

The process of the consumption of the mediated experience of brand advertising, the lived experience of the purchase and usage of brands and the two realms of self-symbolism and social-symbolism is illustrated in Fig. 3.2.

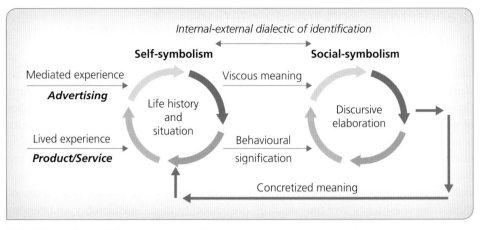

FIGURE 3.2 The symbolic project of the self

Some implications for brand strategy

As consumers we use brands as resources for the symbolic construction of the self, both social identity and self-identity. The symbolic consumption of brands can help to establish and communicate some of the fundamental cultural categories such as social status, gender, age, and such vital cultural values as family, tradition, and authenticity. In order for the meaning of brands to become fully concrete, the mediated meaning derived from advertising and promotion must be negotiated with the lived experience of purchase and usage, and particularly for brands with social-symbolic positioning strategies these meanings must be validated through discursive elaboration in a social context: they must be authenticated by the social or peer group. But brands can also be used to counter some of the threats to the self posed by postmodernity, such as fragmentation, loss of meaning, and loss of individuality.

KEY CONCEPT

Brands and fundamental cultural categories

Cultural categories represent ways we can think about and identify culture. They can take many forms, for example use of artefacts like songs, pictures or stories. Or they could be attitudes, for example attitude toward power, religion, politics, and social class. Others are purely descriptive, such as gender profile, ethnicity, and age. Brands can help to authenticate many of those categories, for example the consumption of Guinness on St Patrick's Day by many of Irish heritage. Sometimes the most unusual products hold special significance. People from the South Pacific islands view canned corn beef as a very important food item, often referred to in the islands as 'helapi', named after Hellaby's, the most popular New Zealand based brand owned by Heinz-Watties. Canned corn beef is particularly important at weddings and funerals. Other examples appear less directly tied to culture, but nevertheless help to reinforce important categories, for instance the symbolism of Western values a MacDonald's restaurant may have to many travellers.

Brands, trust, and fragmentation

As highlighted in the previous chapter, one of the prime features of the postmodern experience is fragmentation, where the inherited self-identity of history, from family and traditional hierarchical positions, is no longer a stable, secure fact but requires active construction: 'A self-identity has to be created and more or less continually reordered against the backdrop of shifting experiences of day-to-day life and the fragmenting tendencies of modern institutions' (Giddens, 1991, p. 198). This construction of self and identity is achieved partly through developing coherent narratives about ourselves and partly through finding opportunities for the investment of trust in institutions other than the traditional ones such as the church. Brands offer consistency in an ever-changing world and this reassurance is a vital element in their added value. As in human social relationships, from consistency over time develops predictability, then dependability, and eventually trust in the brand (Gurviez, 1996). Again discussed in Chapter 2, in large part, trust in a brand evolves from the delivery of consistent benefits over time, that is from lived experience which carries behavioural signification by practical experience of using the brand. However, the meaning derived from the mediated experience of advertising can enhance our experience and give a narrative coherence to it by giving words to thoughts we 'know but can only speak of incompletely' (Polanyi, 1967). In the following tagline, Volkswagen have perfectly captured the ability of the brand to replace other less reliable relationships: 'If only everything in life was as reliable as a Volkswagen.' We will discuss this opportunity for developing brand mythologies in Chapter 8.

KEY CONCEPT

Brands countering the threats to identity posed by postmodernity

There was a time, in the first sixty or so years of the 20th century, when we were relatively sure of our identities. Cultural institutions like religion and community groups were strong, population mobility meant people weren't exposed in any real way to different ethnic groups, and media was still dominated by print, radio, and then TV. In essence we lived in relatively controlled environments. What's more, up until around the 1960s we were quite happy for brand managers to tell us how to live our lives. TV and persuasive advertising was all new! In the 60s and 70s, counterculture movements emerged as a result of a feeling that we were being too controlled and that we were losing our identity as individuals—as sovereign consumers. This was exasperated by a proliferation of advertising offering pathways to different identities and emerging new media options. Furthermore, dominant cultural institutions were losing primacy as we became more culturally mixed as a society. This was representative of postmodernity. Holt (2002) explains that conversely, although there was a backlash against 'bossy brands' as other sense making institutions crumbled or got lost in the crowd, we have become *more*, not less, reliant on brands as identity signposts. However, we no longer wanted them to tell us how to live our lives. Instead we have begun to 'use' them to present a steady identity position. As such, brands are now increasingly relied upon to construct a stable identity for ourselves.

Brands and deep meaning

Brands can acquire deep meaning for consumers by their involvement in the socialization process of growing up, and from then on brands can evoke profound feelings of nostalgia and provide comfort from insecurity. Olsen (1995) has explored the history of brand use, brand loyalty, and intergenerational transfer in families with a recent history of emigration. She found that certain moments in our lives become powerful memories, interconnecting brand, people, and places and that 'family brands become part of the tool chest in strategies for survival during critical life passages'. Consumers bought brands that evoked memories of their grandparents, often through the smell which instantly returned them to the time and place of their childhood. Holbrook and Schindler (1994) have suggested that there is a 'sensitive period effect' for products, where early childhood and, particularly, adolescence are periods when we are most likely to develop preferences. Brands that we have a lived experience with during sensitive periods may acquire a depth of meaning unattainable by brands at later stages in our lives. If we have frequent sensual experience, particularly relating to smell with brands during childhood, then at later stages of our lives we may use them in nostalgic activity, and/or to restore a sense of security. Again, behavioural signification through lived experience with a brand seems by far the most potent source of meaning, but advertising can provide a narrative structure for concretizing these emotional meanings. Unilever's long running 'Monkey and Al' campaign for PG Tips tea provides UK consumers with a narrative identity that encapsulates both nostalgic reverie and current life situations. We will discuss the use of nostalgia as a brand strategy in Chapter 8.

KEY CONCEPT

Brands and deep meaning

How many of you use the same cookbooks or washing powder you had growing up? Or buy the same sweets on long road trips your parents bought for you? Even the most innocuous of brands can acquire deep meaning when we associate them with our socialization process.

This doesn't stop at childhood. You may have a favourite restaurant you visit because it represents a special time with your partner (or avoid for the same reason). You may have a brand of work clothing that you return to in high pressure situations because you have worn it when you have been successful in the past. It helped you navigate the rules and norms (socialize) of the corporate environment. Whenever a brand becomes associated with positive or negative experiences in your navigation of the different social setting you face, it has the potential to gain deep meaning.

The adolescent sensitive period is captured by Levi's 'Originals never fit' campaign with their provision of both self-symbolic and social-symbolic meaning through heavy advertising support which is validated in a virtuous circle by discursive elaboration by teenagers who know and value the meanings depicted in the advertising and discuss them with their friends (Auty and Elliott, 1998).

The ubiquity of brands in developed capitalist societies is such that we live in a rich 'brandscape' (Sherry, 1987) from which we must select a personal 'brandspace' in which to live. In large part, the creation of personal brandspace will be achieved through the creation of deep meaning and the development of trust, but brands can also facilitate the development of personal involvement by the encouragement of the meaning transfer processes of personal ritual and social interaction. McCracken (1988) identifies four ritual activities which transfer meaning from consumer goods to the individual: exchange, possession, grooming, and divestment rituals. Each ritual presents an opportunity for the individual to affirm, assign, or revise the meanings derived from the mediated experience of advertising and construct an individual meaning for themselves. By suggesting brand rituals through engagement in 'Brandfests', Jeep have provided their consumers with ways to make one person's Jeep different from other people's. We will discuss this use of brand communities as a brand strategy in Chapter 8.

At a social, sub-cultural level, Ritson and Elliott (1997) have described how the elusive audience of Generation X may be encouraged to actively interpret advertising by using deliberately 'weak' texts which encourage 'strong' reading. This openness relates to a lack of specific narrative direction and explicit meaning context. Instead these 'open' ads feature the product and simply evoke a positive general response to the ad from the consumer, by using music or imagery for example. The consumer views the deliberately 'open' ad and, because it lacks any strong intended meaning, is empowered to perform a very strong reading of it. As a result the consumer derives a very personal interpretation of the ad's meaning related to their own individual life situation and history. At this point, in need of the social confirmation all Xers crave, the consumer discusses the meaning of the ad with others who share the same basic interpretation of advertising. Thus an advertising literacy event occurs and the individuals form an interpretative community, not purely by demographic or psychographic factors but by their shared interpretation of the meaning of the advertisement. The use of 'open' ads is explored further in the discussion of neo-tribes in Chapter 8.

In postmodern consumer culture, individuals are engaged in a constant task of negotiating meanings from lived and mediated experience as they endeavour to construct and maintain their identity. As part of the resources for this task they utilize the symbolic

Levi's: Mass-market brands—individual meanings

meanings of consumer goods, and through an understanding of the dynamics of the process of identity construction, opportunities can be identified for brands to play an important role in the symbolic project of the self.

CHAPTER SUMMARY

In this chapter we have discussed how in postmodernity brands can become symbolic resources for the construction, communication, and maintenance of identity. Brands can acquire symbolic meaning in a variety of ways, but one of the most potent sources is advertising, particularly through narrative and the construction of socially shared meanings. We have seen that the symbolic consumption of brands can help establish and communicate some of the basic cultural categories, such as social status, gender, and age. Brands can acquire deep meaning through the socialization process and such brands can restore a sense of security. We suggest that mass-market brands can acquire individual meanings through ritual and personal interpretations of meaning.

DISCUSSION QUESTIONS

1 What does it mean to be a postmodern consumer?

2 What is the difference between self-symbolism and social-symbolism and how does it relate to brands?

3 What is the difference between lived and mediated experience?

4 Explain the process of discursive elaboration in relation to a brand.

5 How important is the lived experience of using a brand compared with the influence of advertising?

6 What are the implications of postmodern fragmentation for brand strategy?

7 How might a brand acquire deep meaning?

CASE STUDY

Chobani Australia: Bringing soul to a category dominated by science

During 2013, Chobani—a fairly new brand within the fiercely competitive and price-driven Australian yoghurt marketplace—was tasked with driving up household penetration exponentially. With very little total brand awareness and a considerably larger price than the category average, the challenge stimulated the development of an innovative marketing strategy. This small brand had huge ambitions that it set out to reach by rapidly outpacing the competition in terms of consumer engagement within social media channels.

When Chobani quietly entered the Australian yoghurt category in 2011, the aim was to be a 'step-up' yoghurt that not only captured share from the mainstream and no-frills tiers below, but also from the brands in the super-premium tier above, such as Jalna. At the time, mainstream brands, such as Yoplait and Danone, held the lion's share of shelf space with national retail giants Coles and Woolworths. The no-frills private-label brands, such as Coles Simply and Woolworths Select, were quickly gaining traction though.

In order to become the fastest growing brand within the category, their marketing strategy had to take several challenges into consideration. Firstly, the top selling brands all had much higher total brand awareness than Chobani. Secondly, discounting was ubiquitous throughout the category and Chobani was more costly than the average price per kilogram. Thirdly, after witnessing the phenomenal success achieved by Chobani within the United States through their release of single-serve Greek-style yoghurt, many Australian brands readily released offerings that essentially copied those of Chobani once it entered the market.

This highly competitive market prompted the decision to push the performance of the brand up by raising brand awareness through the creation of memorable positioning. Marketing insight revealed that the yoghurt category was dominated by rational messaging; whereby each brand competed for their share of the yoghurt category with scientific facts, such as the amount of probiotics or cultures, so as to emphasize the health benefits of yoghurt consumption. In this way, the whole category benefitted from a 'health halo' and the overall size of the market continued to increase. Chobani could have followed suit and competed with the established brands purely based upon the health contents of their product line (Chobani contains no preservatives and a higher amount of protein than any other brand available). However, strategic thinking led the brand towards a unique approach that resulted from their analysis of Australian social media chatter.

Through listening to social media users, the discovery was made that health enthusiasts, fitness professionals, and foodies were united by two commonalities: a passion for food and an urge to 'out-interest' each other. Further social insight indicated that people love to share photos of new culinary discoveries and unique creations, and if it was healthy that was a plus, but not a must. To social media users, food is not only about function; it's about fun; it's about family and friends; it's a way to express individuality. This recognition revealed that, when it comes to social media, one of the competition's greatest strengths—the ability to promote brand awareness via rational messaging—was actually a social marketing weakness, because rational messaging doesn't give users anything intriguing to talk about; such conversations have a limited lifespan.

In light of this, Chobani strategized to connect with their audience by using terms that social media users understood and by replacing the science of yoghurt with some soul. At the heart of the brand, there were three core values that would also drive consumers to share with one another. Firstly, the Chobani community—staff and consumers—had a real passion for good authentic food. Secondly, they had an appreciation for quality and real ingredients that were creatively brought together. Thirdly, they considered food to be as much about enjoyment, entertainment, and real fun as it is about consumption. The values of real people, real creations, and real fun formed the guiding pillars of their 'Go real' global brand identity. To appeal to an Australian audience, one characterized by laid-back larrikinisms, irreverence, and a happy-go-lucky disposition, the tone of the campaign was aligned with these prevalent personality traits.

Chobani's social creative team focused on three channels—Facebook, Instagram, and Twitter—to activate their social strategy. Given the brand's low awareness in the market, the campaign first sought to improve brand awareness with memorable positioning. To spread the message of 'real fun', simple but creative brand content that aimed to put a smile on Facebook viewers' faces was interwoven with special occasions such as Star Wars Day, UFO Day, and

World Environment Day. These content pieces had no media spend allocated yet they still managed to harvest incredible results, as seen later in the case study.

Next on the agenda was the pillar of 'real people'. With the supermarket shelves holding in excess of 20 brands, a vastly unique approach was implemented. Born from the creative vision of the typical 'sad' office fridge—the familiar empty fridge or one that holds uninspiring and neglected ingredients like old, wilting vegetables and expired milk—Chobani offered to turn 'sad' office fridges into 'happy' ones, by stocking them full of real, delicious Chobani yoghurt. Followers on Instagram were asked to upload a photo of their own 'sad' office fridge to get the Cho mobile vans (distribution vehicles) to come and cheer (fill) it up. A small budget was spent on the campaign but it essentially created new distribution channels for the brand and it reached offices in every major state and territory of Australia.

Lastly, the 'real creations' element of the strategy was brought to life through regular content uploaded to their Facebook page that displayed Chobani's versatility and usefulness in a number of recipes, including reposting photos of creations shared by fans. This content proved to be so successful that it continues to be a regular feature on the page; fans consistently seek to recreate the visuals shared on the site.

In terms of real results, after only one month, activity on the Chobani Facebook page jumped by 209% to an engagement level of 4.3%, which is over 700% more than the average brand engagement rate (0.53%) for fast moving consumer goods. In comparing this engagement rate to a monthly external analysis of Australia's branded engagement pages (compiled by SocialBakers), Chobani became the third most engaged page in Australia during March, and the second most engaged page during April and May. Riding on this initial wave of success, the latter half of the year also proved to be fruitful for their social creative team; Chobani reached the number one position for most engaged page in Australia during September. To put this degree of achievement into context, SocialBakers measures all attainable brand pages in Australia and most of the top performing pages are from established brands that benefit from high recognition and awareness. This includes such iconic Australian brands as Weet-Bix, Vegemite, and Dick Smith Foods.

Other externally obtained data showed that the brand began experiencing extraordinary uplifts across the social sphere. Despite the fact that only a small portion of the brand's marketing budget was spent in social, Chobani managed to capture on average 66% share of voice in social, effectively stealing share of voice from the major brands. Yoplait, Ski, Danone and Vaalia were reduced to 14% in total share of voice in social media outlets. In addition, the objective to grow their Facebook community to 5,000 fans by December 2013 was more than satisfied as Chobani managed to grow the page to over 16,000 fans, 264% above target.

The effects that these social media outcomes had upon the business were tremendous. Not only did the uplift in penetration from social media directly translate into incremental sales that were several times higher than the target, but it also contributed a similar level of effect as TV (which received a far higher media budget). The campaign delivered an exceptional return on investment (9.22 for every dollar spent) and this small challenger brand managed to raise both unaided and prompted awareness. Chobani also made social media the most cost efficient driver of awareness, and against all odds, it became the fastest growing brand in the Australian yoghurt category.

Source: WARC, Warc Prize for Social Strategy 2014, Chobani Australia: Bringing Soul to a category dominated by science. Edited by Suni J. Mydock III

DISCUSSION QUESTIONS

1 The focus of the symbolic meanings of yoghurt consumption changed from product-attribute focus (i.e. health benefits) to an emotion-attribute focus (i.e. interesting and fun creations). How did the change improve Chobani's sales?

2 How did Chobani apply socially shared meanings around the three core values of real people, real creations and real fun, to establish the symbolic identity of the brand?

3 Was it possible that Chobani, as a mass-market brand, could deliver individual meanings in its advertising of real fun?

4 To what extent is 'go real' a viable brand strategy for other product categories and other cultures?

FURTHER READING

- The first major writer on marketing as a symbolic activity was Sid Levy and his collected work is a rich resource for thought: Rook, D. (ed.) (1999), *Brands, Consumers, Symbols, & Research: Sidney J. Levy on Marketing,* London: Sage.

- Helga Dittmar's excellent book extends many of the ideas is this chapter: Dittmar, H. (1992) *The Social Psychology of Material Possessions: To Have is to Be*, Hemel Hempstead: Harvester Wheatsheaf.

- Narrative and the construction of identity through cultural consumption is discussed at length in Mackay, H. (1997) *Consumption and Everyday Life*, London: Sage.

REFERENCES

Anderson, J. and Meyer, T. (1988), *Mediated Communication: A Social Action Perspective*, London: Sage.

Auty, S. and Elliott, R. (1998), 'Fashion involvement, self-monitoring and the meaning of brands', *Journal of Product and Brand Management*, 7, 2&3, 109–23.

Baudrillard, J. (1988), 'Consumer society', in M. Poster (ed.), *Jean Baudrillard: Selected Writings*, Cambridge: Polity Press.

Belk, R. (1988), 'Possessions and the extended self', *Journal of Consumer Research*, 15 (September) 139–68.

Buttle, F. (1991), 'What people do with advertising', *International Journal of Advertising*, 10, 95–110.

Csikszentmihalyi, M. and Rochberg-Halton, E. (1981), *The Meaning of Things: Domestic symbols and the self*. Cambridge: Cambridge University Press.

Derrida, J. (1977), *Of Grammatology* (trans. G. Spivak), Baltimore: Johns Hopkins University Press.

Diamond, N., Sherry, J. F., Jr., Muñiz, A. M., Jr., McGrath, M. A., Kozinets, R. V., and Borghini, S. (2009), 'American Girl and the brand gestalt: Closing the loop on sociocultural branding research', *Journal of Marketing*, May, 73, 118–34.

Dittmar, H. (1992), *The Social Psychology of Material Possessions: To Have is to Be*, Hemel Hempstead: Harvester Wheatsheaf.

Douglas, M. and Isherwood, B. (1978), *The World of Goods: Towards an Anthropology of Consumption*, London, Allen Lane.

Eco, U. (1979), *The Role of the Reader: Explorations in the Semiotics of Texts*, London: Hutchinson.

Elliott, R., Eccles, S., and Hodgson, M. (1993), 'Re-coding gender representations: Women, cleaning products, and advertising's "New Man"', *International Journal of Research in Marketing*, 10, 311–24.

Escalas, J. E. (2004), 'Narrative processing: Building consumer connections to brands', *Journal of Consumer Psychology*, 14, 1&2, 168–80.

Facebook (2012) *Facebook.com*. Retrieved February 14, 2012, from http://www.facebook.com/press/info.php?statistics

Fazio, R. and Zanna, M. (1978), 'On the predictive validity of attitudes: The role of direct experience and confidence', *Journal of Personality*, 46, 228–43.

Fiske, J. (1989), *Reading the Popular*, Boston: Unwin Hyman.

Giddens, A. (1991), *Modernity and Self-Identity: Self and Society in the Late Modern Age*, Cambridge: Polity Press.

Gurviez, P. (1996), 'The trust concept in the brand-consumer relationship', in J. Beracs *et al.* (eds), *Marketing for an Expanding Europe. Proceedings of the 25th Annual Conference of the European Marketing Academy*, Budapest: Budapest University of Economic Sciences, 559–74.

Holbrook, M. and Schindler, R. (1994), 'Age, sex, and attitude towards the past as predictors of consumers' aesthetic tastes for cultural products', *Journal of Marketing Research*, 31, 412–22.

Holt, D. B. (2002), 'Why do Brands Cause Trouble? A Dialectical Theory of Consumer Culture and Branding', *Journal of Consumer Research*, 29, 1, 70–90.

Jenkins, R. (1996), *Social Identity*, London: Routledge.

Kleine, S.S., Kleine, R.E., III, and Allen, C.T. (1995), 'How is a possession "Me" or "Not Me?" Characterizing types and antecedent of material possession attachment', *Journal of Consumer Research*, 22, 327–43.

Lannon, J. and Cooper, P. (1983), 'Humanistic advertising: A holistic cultural perspective', *International Journal of Advertising*, 2, 195–213.

McCracken, G. (1988), *Culture and Consumption: New Approaches to the Symbolic Character of Consumer Goods and Activities*, Bloomington: Indiana University Press.

Markus, H. and Nurius, P. (1986), 'Possible selves', *American Psychologist*, 41, 9, 954–69.

Mick, D. G. and Buhl, C. (1992), 'A meaning-based model of advertising experiences', *Journal of Consumer Research*, 19, 317–38.

O'Donohoe, S. (1994), 'Advertising uses and gratifications', *European Journal of Marketing*, 28, 8/9, 52–75.

Olsen, B. (1995), 'Brand loyalty and consumption patterns: The lineage factor', in J. Sherry (ed.), *Contemporary Marketing and Consumer Behavior: An Anthropological Sourcebook*, Thousand Oaks, CA: Sage Publications.

Polanyi, M. (1967), *The Tacit Dimension*, London: Routledge & Kegan Paul.

Ricoeur, P. (1977), *The Rule of Metaphor: Multi-disciplinary Studies of the Creation of Meaning in Language* (trans. R. Czery), London: Routledge and Kegan Paul.

Ritson, M. and Elliott, R. (1995), 'A model of advertising literacy: the praxiology and co-creation of advertising meaning', in M. Bergadaa *et al.* (eds), *Marketing Today and for the 21st Century: Proceedings of the 24th Annual Conference of the European Marketing Academy*, ESSEC. Cergy-Pontoise—France: Imprimerie Basuyau.

Ritson, M. and Elliott, R. (1997), 'Marketing to Generation X: Strategies for communicating with "Advertising's Lost Generation"', *Proceedings of the AMA Special Conference: New and Evolving Paradigms: The Emerging Future of Marketing*, Dublin: AMA.

Ritson, M. and Elliott, R. (1999), 'The social uses of advertising: An ethnographic study of adolescent advertising audiences', *Journal of Consumer Research*, 26, 3, 260–77.

Ross, C., Orr, E. S., Sisic, M., Arseneault, J. M., Simmering, M. G., and Orr, R. R. (2009), 'Personality and motivations associated with Facebook use', *Computers in Human Behavior*, 25, 2, 578–86.

Sherry, J. F. (1987), 'Advertising as a cultural system', in J. Umiker-Sebeok (ed.), *Marketing and Semiotics: New Directions in the Study of Signs for Sales*, Berlin: Mouton de Gruyter, 441–62.

Tamir, D. I. and Mitchell, J. P. (2012), 'Disclosing information about the self is intrinsically rewarding', *Proceedings of the National Academy of Sciences*, 109, 21, 8038–43.

Thompson, J. B. (1995), *The Media and Modernity: A Social Theory of the Media*, Cambridge: Polity Press.

Tidwell, L. C., and Walther, J. B. (2002), 'Computer-mediated communication effects on disclosure, impressions, and interpersonal evaluations', *Human Communication Research*, 28, 317–48.

Waters, R. D., Burnett, E., Lamm, A. and Lucas, J. (2009), 'Engaging stakeholders through social networking: How nonprofit organisations are using Facebook', *Public Relations Review*, 35, 2, 102–6.

Westbrook, R. A. (1987), 'Product/consumption-based affective responses and postpurchase processes', *Journal of Marketing Research*, 24, 3, 258–70.

Wicklund, R. A. and Gollwitzer, P. M. (1982), *Symbolic Self-Completion*, Hillsdale, NJ: Lawrence Erlbaum.

Willis, P. (1990), *Common Culture: Symbolic Work at Play in the Everyday Cultures of the Young*, Milton Keynes: Open University Press.

Test your understanding of this chapter and explore the subject further using our Online Resource Centre. Visit the Online Resource Centre at http://www.oxfordtextbooks.co.uk/orc/elliott-percy3e/

Cultural Meaning Systems and Brands

4

Key Concepts

1 Semiotics are sign systems that operate according to specific cultural rules that link signs to meaning.

2 Consumers may think of brands as being like a person and having a brand personality.

3 Consumers may also think of a brand as being like a personal friend and having a relationship with them.

4 Products and consumption practices can be used in order to differentiate between social groups within a culture.

5 Products and consumption practices can also be used in order to integrate social groups and maintain social relationships.

6 Neo-tribes and sub-cultures may use the consumption of symbolic brands to develop and communicate their identity.

7 Sub-cultures may adopt and then hijack a famous brand image for their own purposes.

8 Aikido brands use the fame and image of a brand against itself.

Introduction

We live in a symbol-rich environment, where we must construct meaning from a plethora of images. Within this cultural space, brands play an important role in the ways in which we communicate to each other the fundamental meaning categories of age, gender, social groupings, and social hierarchy. It is the meaning of brands that gives them their added value and these brand meanings are partly added by the producers (McCracken, 1993). In this chapter we will explore how brands can be used as signalling systems to create and send meanings of social differentiation and social integration; but first we need to understand the basic analytical tools of semiotics, the science of signs.

Semiotics and brand meanings

A crucial distinction in the semiotic analysis of signs is between the signifier and the signified. The signifier—for instance a brand name—has no meaning in its own right, but must acquire meaning through associations with other pre-existing meanings until it comes to signify some concept or idea. The signifier is a denotative communication, a simple statement of fact, the signified is a connotative communication, which generates personal associations, overtones, and feel, and can be literally any meaning that can be associated with the signifier, in most cases through advertising and packaging. Luedicke *et al.* (2010) describe how a single brand can have vastly different connotations because of brand-mediated moral conflict. Their focus was on the Hummer sports utility vehicle, which, at the time the study was conducted, was considered a niche market success but has since suffered in the market place with General Motors announcing in 2010 its intention to sell or shut down the brand. As the authors describe, the mythology around this brand was built though media portrayals of its forerunner, the robust HUMVEE military vehicle, which was used extensively to depict to the American public a sweeping victory in Operation Desert Storm. They found that the same brand signifiers, military styling, large size, and a luxury price tag, led to dramatically different connotations. On the one hand Hummer devotees interpreted an American frontier spirit within the brand, seeing it as synonymous with the right to personal liberty and freedom of the individual. Conversely, Hummer protagonists saw the brand as wasteful of natural resources, contributing to climate change, and endangering the lives of pedestrians and other drivers whilst its military significations were interpreted by some as an uncomfortable indicator of American imperialism. What marketers need to do is to understand the systems of meaning or communication codes operative in a particular cultural situation. Codes are sets of unspoken rules and conventions that structure sign systems and link signs to meaning (Lawes, 2002). An illustration of the semiotic analysis process can be gained from a study of the advertising for beer brands (Harvey and Evans, 2001). From detailed study of TV and print ads, the advertising for two major brands in the UK were analysed in terms of codes deployed, codes challenged or explicitly broken, and the overall profile of codes used by each brand. The resulting semiotic analysis is illustrated in Fig. 4.1.

The researchers then went on to analyse major beer brand advertising from six major markets worldwide and identified 26 key codes which mapped into seven clusters of which three sample codes are illustrated in Fig. 4.2.

Carling Black Label	Stella Artois

• Key codes
  – heritage, roots, masculinity, sports
 	
• Brand codes
  – nationalism, tabloid attitude
 	
• Substantiators
  – Football sponsorship, popularity
	• Key codes
	  – parody, humour, heritage
	
	• Brand codes
	  – France/French language, music, cinematic references
	
	• Substantiators
	  – Premium price
	  – 'Reassuringly expensive'

FIGURE 4.1 Semiotic analysis of UK beer ads

Source: Harvey and Evans (2001)

Cosmopolitan style	Alternative humour	Totem of the tribe
Modern city life • Style bars • Bright lights, big city • Market savvy	Self-deprecating humour • Twist in the tale	Bonding focal points • Dances, music • Teams • Couples, family
Western (v. local) lifestyle • Western music • Western attitude	Irony, cynicism • Defining style clans • Sub-cultures	Nation and icons • Flags • Music • Humour • Funny foreigners
Beautiful people • Style • Confidence, self-ssurance • Narcissism	Parody • Making fun of mainstream • Humour and 'serious' genres • Reinterpreting other brands and equities	Looking alike • Uniforms • Animal allegories • Lizards, frogs

FIGURE 4.2 International language of beer advertising—signifiers for three sample codes

Source: Adapted from Harvey and Evans (2001)

This analysis enabled the clients to feel that they had a good grasp, in an international context, of how beer advertising communicates and the underlying propositions competitor brands were conveying to consumers. This enabled them to develop new advertising propositions as part of brand strategy planning.

A different approach to semiotic analysis has been used to explore the meaning of special, irreplaceable possessions (Grayson and Shulman, 2000). Based on the principle of indexicality, a relationship can exist between a sign and an object based on a factual connection beyond just psychological perceptions and shared meanings. Do you still have a soft toy or similar gift given to you at graduation, perhaps a children's book signed by your grandparent, or ticket stub from your first live concert? In this study, consumers demonstrated a semiotic linkage between their special possessions and their personal history. The possessions served as physical evidence, 'indices' of a special relationship with people, places, and events. This verification function underlay connections with a wide range of possessions which had been 'contaminated' by real experiences and could therefore remind people of their past. More than 85% of the irreplaceable possessions in the study were in fact mass-produced, but nonetheless, consumers could invest them with a semiotic meaning of authenticity which enabled them to distinguish between objects which on the face of it looked identical.

KEY CONCEPT

Semiotics are sign systems that operate according to specific cultural rules that link signs to meaning.

When we think about brands and semiotics what is important to understand is that the product (goods or service) is the actual object in the world and that the brand name of the product is just one sign that tells us something about it. However, it doesn't do this on its own, but in association with other signs, e.g. the use of colour, music, and language. How we interpret these signs depends on cultural rules and codes. For example, purple signifies royalty in Thailand but it is more commonly associated with romance and luxury in the UK or US. A thumbs up sign in Australia signifies 'I want to hitch a ride', but it means 'I'm ok' if you are scuba diving. So you can see how the same sign can have many interpretations depending on the culture or situation, i.e. signs are embedded with codes that as brand managers we need to be aware of. Sometimes these codes do not remain static and the meaning of the same sign in the same culture can change. Returning to Australia, the national flag is understandably used as a symbol of national pride and is displayed with many brands. Yet, after the Cronulla Riots (race based clashes between youths) of 2005, where many protagonists were draped in Aussie flags it came to signify negative connotations of nationalism.

Personal meanings

Two major approaches to the person–brand relationship have been based on metaphors: the brand-as-a-person metaphor and the brand-as-a-friend metaphor.

Brand personality: the brand-as-a-person

The idea that we may think of a brand as if it had some of the characteristics of a person has a long history. The basic approach is that human personality traits come to be associated with a brand directly through the real people that consumers associate with a brand, such as their typical users, celebrity endorsers or a chief executive, such as Richard Branson and the Virgin brand. Personality traits can also become associated with a brand indirectly through a wide range of features such as brand name, symbol, advertising stylistics, price, and distribution channel (Aaker, 1997). It has also been argued that brand personality includes demographic categories such as gender, age, and class (Levy, 1959). Recent approaches have taken the route of transferring personality concepts and measurement techniques from human psychology to brands and Aaker (1997) demonstrated that five major factors summarized the traits that consumers attributed to a wide range of brands: sincerity, excitement, competence, sophistication, and ruggedness.

Subsequent work has shown that personal meanings of brands are partly socially constructed and that they also vary across cultures. It has been suggested that through a process of 'linguistic sedimentation', words that describe human personality are extremely functional in the development and maintenance of social relations and they become a vital part of the vocabulary of everyday life which we learn through socialization into social and cultural groups (Caprara *et al.*, 1998). As we tend to perceive other people on the basis of the characteristics they display in social situations, then the same argument applies to brands and their use in particular situations, so that personal meanings also have to be negotiated as social meanings (Ligas and Cotte, 1999). Indeed it has been shown that there are important boundary conditions for the generalizability of Aaker's (1997) brand personality framework to individual brands and that it works best when applied to aggregated data across diverse product categories (Austin *et al.*, 2003). When applied across different cultures, the five factors of brand personality have to be revised. In Japan and Spain, only three of the factors transferred from the USA (Aaker *et al.*, 2001), and similar results were found in Russia (Supphellen and Grønhaug, 2003).

75

KEY CONCEPT

Consumers may think of brands as being like a person and having a brand personality.

We don't mean you would take your favourite brand out for dinner or necessarily have a conversation with it/him/her, although I'm sure some of you do. Brands can be thought of like people though in the sense that we imbue them with human-like characteristics, for example we may personify them with our descriptions or think of them as having personality. Is Samsung the 'new kid on the block' in terms of handheld devices? Is clothing brand American Apparel sexy and confrontational or Monki caring and environmentally conscious? Brands like these have benefited enormously from human-like associations.

Brand relationships: the brand-as-a-friend

An increasingly prominent approach to metaphorical thinking has been the idea that a consumer can form something similar to an interpersonal relationship with brands.

Fournier (1998) describes how some consumers move beyond simply ascribing human-like personality traits to brands and form meaningful human-like relationships. She suggests that brands can form viable partners in a relationship, playing a number of roles. Consumer–brand relationships differ in their quality, and the strength of the relationship can be evaluated according to the nature and depth of the bond using a 'brand relationship quality scale'. The theory is that brand relationships which are high on such factors as intimacy, commitment, and love will exhibit high degrees of enduring loyalty and we will tolerate and forgive the brand for lapses. Subsequent research suggests a complexity to these relationships warranting further investigation. Aaker *et al.* (2004) showed that brands perceived as sincere by consumers were punished more when a transgression occurred, compared to brands perceived as exciting. This occurred despite sincere brands enjoying a deeper kind of relationship, akin to personal friendship, whilst 'exciting brands evinced a trajectory characteristic of short-lived flings' (p. 1). Sincere brands which transgressed seemed to hurt loyal consumers who were made to question the premise on which they had developed their loyalty, finding it difficult to come to terms with the situation even when reparation was made. Conversely, exciting brands in their rollercoaster relationship with consumers did not surprise when transgressing and their efforts to recover were interpreted as genuine and insightful and actually served to strengthen rather than weaken the relationship. Building on this study, Swaminathan *et al.* (2009) examined consumer attachment style and found that consumers who were anxious and concerned about their self-worth were more likely to discriminate between brands based on their personality, using them to signal their ideal self-concept to others. Specifically, anxious types who liked to interact and engage in intimate relationships preferred sincere brands whilst those who were less trusting and emotionally connected with others preferred exciting brands.

More recently the metaphor 'brand as loved' has emerged. Batra, Ahuvia, & Bagozzi (2012) developed a prototype conceptualization of consumer brand love. Given the complexity of the construct, and the tendency to extrapolate interpersonal notions of love to brands, the prototype engaged additional dimensions to reflect integration of the loved brand into the consumer's current and future identity. Unlike classical definitions, prototypes include more than the phenomenon itself by incorporating its antecedents and outcomes. This enables a more holistic understanding of love in relation to brands and includes fuzzy notions of brands that are loved, not loved, and kind-of-loved. Table 4.1 outlines the dimensions Batra *et al.* (2012) identified. Their study suggests that Brand Love encourages positive word of mouth, loyalty, and resistance to negative information.

Evidence in practice includes Saatchi and Saatchi's Lovemarks.com and the Social Bakers BrandLove app. The Lovemarks site allows consumers to eulogize favourite brands as well as read those of others. Lovemark brands are considered by Saatchi as those which can 'reach your heart as well as your mind, creating an intimate, emotional connection that you just can't live without' (Lovemarks.com, 2010). The BrandLove app gathers user generated data from over eight million social media profiles across Facebook, Twitter, YouTube, Linkedin, Instagram, Google + and VK. Consumers are able to use the tool to express their 'love, or not' for brands using an Android or Apple based app which feeds directly into their preferred social media platform.

Although the concept of a human-like relationship with a brand opens up some fascinating possibilities for brand strategy, as yet there is little published evidence of the existence of relationships involving love and passion and the predicted beneficial outcomes occurring. One experimental study in Korea found that subjects scoring a brand high on

TABLE 4.1 Prototype conceptualization of Consumer Brand love—adapted from Batra, Ahuvia, & Bagozzi (2012, p.13)

Dimension	Explanation
passion driven behaviours	reflecting strong desires to use it, to invest resources into it, and a history of having done so;
self-brand integration	including a brand's ability to express the consumers' actual and desired identities, its ability to connect to life's deeper meanings and provide intrinsic rewards, and frequent thoughts about it;
positive emotional connection	broader than just positive feelings, including a sense of positive attachment and having an intuitive feeling of 'rightness'
anticipated separation distress	if the brand were to go away
long-term relationship	which includes predicting extensive future use and a long-term commitment to it
positive attitude valence	
attitudes strongly held	with high certainty and confidence

relationship quality indicated that they would be more likely to accept a brand extension (Park *et al.*, 2002). Children used interpersonal relationship metaphors when asked to talk about the brands in their lives (Mindy, 2002). Similarly, towards the other end of the age spectrum, women at the mid-life stage appear to relate brands to a number of life themes, especially comfort and security (Olsen, 1999).

Another finding which has important implications for using brand–consumer relationships in brand strategy is some experimental evidence that men and women may relate to

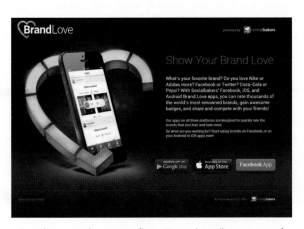

BrandLove app homepage [http://www.brandloveapp.com/]

brands in a different way. It seems possible that men distinguish brands that are close to them in terms of their own actions towards the brand and are less likely to see it as an active partner in the relationship, while women more easily interpret a brand which is close to them as an active interacting partner and as such are more likely to personify its signals (Monga, 2002).

The emergence of metaphors like the brand as loved companion is perhaps in part explained by postmodernity, introduced in Chapter 3, where consumers use brands to search for individual and social meaning in an increasingly fragmented environment. The right brand may develop hyper importance in this world. But before leaving the brand-as-friend metaphor, it is worth remembering that it is only a metaphor. A brand is an inanimate object and cannot think and feel, and just because, when asked, a consumer can talk about brands in terms of personalities, this does not entail any form of reciprocal interpersonal relationship (Bengtsson, 2003). However, it does seem possible that we can form some kind of emotional attachment to a brand based on meanings in our life in which the brand is implicated and this can be part of building a brand over time.

Nostalgia 懷舊

When a brand is associated with sensitive periods in our lives, then enduring preferences may be formed (Holbrook and Schindler, 1994). At the heart of this form of brand relationship is the concept of nostalgia: 'a preference towards experiences associated with objects that were more common when one was younger' (Holbrook and Schindler, 2003). A key aspect of the nostalgic sentiment is that it attaches to products at certain times in the lifespan, particularly the sensitive periods of adolescence and early adulthood. At the most person-centred level, sensory experiences, smell and taste, connect people with pleasurable incidents in their past which can be recalled in great detail. But we also recall not just pleasurable incidents but more complex experiences, especially friendships and loved ones: a product can provide a material representation of human affection. In January 2010, Tangerine Confectionary, a company based in Blackpool in the UK, announced a deal to send over three million Sherbet Fountains and 70,000 cases of Taverner's Proper Sweets for distribution throughout Australian supermarkets. The UK expatriate population in Australia was seen as being responsible for the demand, wanting to introduce their children and grandchildren to a much loved brand from their own childhoods. The power of nostalgic bonding between a brand, a person, and their past life events offers some intriguing opportunities for developing symbolic brand strategy and this will be explored further later.

We shall return to a consideration of semiotic codes and personal meanings and their possibilities for brand strategy in Chapter 8, but now we turn to cultural meaning systems and how they function in society.

Sherbet Fountain: nostalgic sentiment

Social differentiation and social integration

Consumption practices are involved in processes of both differentiating between social groups, for example between classes and genders, and creating new social groupings such as brand communities. These two broad categories of meaning can be utilized as the basis of alternative brand strategies and this will be discussed in Chapter 8.

Social differentiation

But let us start by considering the traditional areas of the use of goods to differentiate between people, starting with the concept of conspicuous consumption (Veblen, 1899). Veblen argued that it was a basic fact of human society that people need to display their social status, and that the consumption of goods could be used to maintain a position of social prestige. In order to demonstrate a separation between the upper and lower classes, it was necessary to accord most status to the consumption of goods that had little or no functional value, a conspicuous waste of time and money. Thus consumer goods can be seen as signifiers of advantage in a competition for social status: symbolic brands become status symbols. Conspicuous consumption is part of a process of emulation: 'Goods are able to mark status because they are part of the lifestyle of a high status group. Consequently, lower status social climbers lay claim to higher status by emulating that lifestyle, by buying those goods, consuming after the fashion of the higher orders, 'aping' their manners, style, etiquette and so on' (Slater, 1997, p. 156). Importantly, the process of emulation is dynamic, as the higher-status groups attempt to maintain distinctions between themselves and the lower-status groups by changing their lifestyle and consumption patterns. This is a 'trickle-down' theory about social change and the crucial role played by fashion.

For Veblen (1899, p. 168), the very public nature of clothing makes it an ideal site for displaying status, especially by demonstrating that fashionable clothing is not actually functional: 'in an inclement climate . . . to go ill clad in order to appear well-dressed.' Fashion in clothing can be seen as expressing the tensions between the oppositions of class, gender, and wealth and as an essential element in the maintenance of social divisions (Davis, 1992). So branded fashions are symbolic markers of a wide range of cultural categories and are used to communicate identity among an ever-greater number of fragmented social groupings. A key issue in understanding the marketing of branded fashions is the concept of exclusivity. By carefully limiting access to the brand both by price and by supply, the value of the brand is maintained at both the status-marking level and at the identity-marking level (Park *et al.*, 1986). We shall return to how fashion can be a vital element in developing symbolic brand strategies in Chapter 8.

The theory of conspicuous consumption was based on assumptions about the relative distribution of wealth: economic capital; but a significant development more appropriate to consumer culture in developed economies is the concept of 'cultural capital' based on differences in taste and style. Bourdieu (1984) suggests that in contemporary Western societies, where there is much less strict hierarchical division between social classes and much more equality in terms of wealth, distinction between social groups is maintained through structures of taste. In the act of consumption we both exercise and display our taste or style, and taste is not an individual preference but is socially structured into hierarchies of taste (Slater, 1997). Do you regularly purchase or the Kerrits or Hunter brand? If so, the chances are you that come from at least an upper middle class background or certainly aspire to be seen as such. Both position themselves as prestige outdoor clothing brands. Kerrits equestrian clothing range includes specialty fox hunting attire, whilst the Chelsea range of Hunter wellies (gumboots) will cost you around £90. The choice of opera rather than soap opera communicates a great deal about a consumer's educational and class background, income, and social aspirations. Thus brand choice, particularly for cultural products, displays an unconscious knowledge of the legitimacy of various lifestyles, and this is usually conditioned by social class.

Holt (1998) showed that differences in cultural capital, based on class position, structure both patterns of taste and consumption practices in American mass culture. Jee Han *et al.* (2010) have developed this further in relation to the consumption of luxury goods. They provide a taxonomy of four groups—patricians, parvenus, poseurs, and proletarians—based on wealth and need for status. Patricians use quiet signals of status by paying a premium for inconspicuous brands. They are more interested in associating with each other than disassociating from other classes. Luxury brands like Baume & Mercier (watches) or Edward Green (shoes) may attract this group. Parvenus are also wealthy but do not have the ability to interpret subtle signs, they crave status and use overt signals to convey this. Unlike patricians their primary motivation is to disassociate with other classes. High profile luxury brands like Louis Vuitton and Rolex are favoured by this group. Poseurs have a high need for status but low wealth; they are therefore prone to consuming counterfeit versions of the patricians' favoured luxury goods. Finally proletarians have a low need for status and low wealth and are not concerned with signalling status using luxury goods. Thus the choice between certain brands may be seen as demonstrating relative amounts of cultural capital and thus individual choice will be partly determined by historical social background rather than recent marketing activity. The implications of cultural capital for brand strategy will be discussed in Chapter 8.

The final manifestation of social differentiation through consumption is that of gender. Gender is a major social category which we use in marking distinctions between people, and it is widely used in marketing practice, for example market segmentation and advertising management. Many products and services are gender-associated, and much consumption behaviour is also gendered. Basic judgement processes between brands show gender differences, and perceptions of the symbolic meaning of brands are gendered (Elliott, 1994). There is also considerable evidence that men and women interpret the same advertising executions in very different ways (Elliott *et al.*, 1995), and because gender is a cultural construct, gender differentiation may be very marked in traditional cultures (Costa, 1994). But gender roles are changing rapidly, and in this developing cultural space there is the potential for brands to use gender identity as a social differentiation brand strategy for women and men; and as a social integration brand strategy, especially for non-heterosexuals (Kates, 2000).

Products and consumption practices can be used in order to differentiate between social groups within a culture and maintain social relationships.

Brands, as with pictures, can say a thousand words. That is very useful when you don't like to repeat yourself or when what you are saying may be a little uncomfortable for others to hear. I earn more money than you; I'm more successful than you; I'm a more serious supporter of my football team than you. The list goes on. All can be conveyed through consumption of brands, be it luxury cars, suits or shoes, football shirts and season passes. We are not complete masters of our destiny when trying to identify with a social group. We rely on the consumption and recognition of others. If, for example, everyone started to purchase a brand then it may lose its differentiating meaning. Or an undesirable group (from the point of view of the incumbent consumers) may begin to purchase the brand. Luxury brand Burberry famously experienced this in the early to mid-2000s when perceived lower class, delinquent youth in the UK, known by outsiders to the group as Chavs, increasingly used the brand as one of their social symbols.

Social integration

The communication value of brands can be thought of as fundamentally integrative, in that knowledge of consumption codes and attendance at consumption events are essential to being included as part of a social group (Slater, 1997). The meanings of goods can be used within everyday consumption practices to make and maintain social relationships (Douglas and Isherwood, 1979). Brands are involved in construction, maintenance, and membership communication through brand communities, neo-tribes, and sub-cultures.

Brand communities

The seminal study of Muniz and O'Guinn (2001) defined a brand community as a non-geographical community based on a set of structured relations between admirers of a brand. They demonstrated that three brands—Ford Bronco, Macintosh, and Saab—had groups of consumers who shared not just ownership of the brand but three traditional markers of community: shared consciousness, rituals and traditions, and a sense of moral responsibility. Shared consciousness relates to the perception among individuals that 'we sort of know one another' even if they have never actually met. This triangular relationship between a consumer, another consumer, and the brand is a central facet of a brand community. There is also a sense of brand users being different from other people, and this extends into the concept of legitimacy which differentiates between true members of the community and more marginal consumers who might buy the brand but for the 'wrong' reasons. The wrong reasons are usually revealed by failing to truly appreciate the culture, history, and rituals and traditions of the community. At the extreme, shared consciousness involves oppositional brand loyalty, that is the community derives much of its cohesion from opposition to rival brands. For example, members of the Macintosh brand community used their overt opposition to Microsoft as a source of unity. Rituals and traditions typically centred on shared consumption experiences with the brand. For example, members of the Saab brand community would always flash their headlights or wave at other Saab drivers they encountered on the road. The sense of a shared moral responsibility involves a sense of duty to other community members and is demonstrated in integrating new members into the community and in assisting members in the 'proper' use of the brand.

A broader perspective on brand community is to focus not on a triangular relationship but on a customer-centric model which involves a customer's relationship with the actual product, and with marketing agents and institutions as well as other customers (McAlexander *et al.*, 2002). This puts the focus on the customer's experiences rather than on the brand around which that experience revolves. In particular, the attendance at 'brandfests' where customers meet at events hosted by the brand, for example in the case of Jeep: Jeep Jamborees and Camp Jeeps were related to the development not only of brand community but a resultant brand loyalty. Brand tracking data indicates that Jeep's community-building efforts through brandfests resulted in significantly increased repurchase rates among participants. A key implication here is that a brand owner can invest in building a community around their brand as a primary brand strategy which may result in long-term brand loyalty.

Encouraging value-creating practices among participants appears key to the development of effective brand communities. Schau *et al.* (2009, pp. 34–5) examined nine diverse brand communities and identified 12 elements of value creation under four thematic categories including:

1. *social networking*, which includes welcoming, empathizing with, and governing each other;

2. *impression management*, the creation of favourable impressions of the brand through evangelizing and justification;

3. *community engagement*, for instance staking, which involves specifying particular domains of interest within the community; milestoning, the communication of standout brand experiences like receipt of a new model or accessory; badging whereby a signifier is created to commemorate a milestone perhaps a certificate or ranking within the community; and documenting, sharing the story with others and constructing a narrative of brand engagement;

4. *brand use*, which relates to customizing and enhancing the use of the brand and includes grooming, consumer driven suggestions for product care; customizing, the creation of additional product features and accessories by the community; and commoditizing, ensuring the availability of customized resources and advocating for the availability of key resources to the community from the manufacturer.

These practices highlight the importance of the co-creation of brand meaning between customers and the firm (Vargo and Lusch, 2004) and they are further discussed in Chapter 10.

Neo-tribes

A more temporary and fragmented form of social grouping is that based on the metaphor of tribal communities arranged around consumption. Cova and Cova (2001) argue that neo-tribes are inherently unstable, small-scale, and involve 'shared experience, the same emotion, a common passion', but unlike a brand community the tribe is characterized by a 'volatility of belonging', which means that homogeneity of behaviour and adherence to formal rules is not expected. A tribe is defined as a network of different persons, in terms of age, sex, and income who are linked by a common emotion. In fact, individuals can belong to more than one neo-tribe and can vary dramatically in the extent of their tribal affiliation. A study of in-line roller skaters demonstrated that neo-tribes are a fuzzy concept, a shifting aggregation of emotionally bonded people in an open system that use consumption as but one sign of tribal identity, which can vary from devotees, through participants at events, to mere sympathizers, from skating fanatics to occasional amateurs. But whatever the depth of their affiliation with the tribe, they still consume not only branded skates but also symbolic brands such as tribal magazines and tribal T-shirts. Similarly Goulding *et al.* (2009, p. 770) examining clubbing in the UK, showed how participants shared a common desire to escape the mundane and seek an 'environment of seemingly unfettered restorative pleasure' through the consumption of particular music and dance, the organization of space, and the effects of the drug ecstasy.

Sub-cultures

A more stable and structural social grouping is that of the sub-culture. Sub-cultures related to consumption are predominantly based on geography, age, ethnicity, and class.

Class-based sub-cultures have traditionally been located within a framework of social resistance and reaction against dominant hierarchies of control. Historically this perspective has been used to explain the emergence of such sub-cultures as the 'Teddy Boys', Punk Rockers, and Hippies. Most of the studies of sub-culture identify social class and particularly the powerlessness of the working class as the main catalyst for the developments of these sub-cultures (Goulding *et al.*, 2002).

However, increasingly, sub-cultural spaces are becoming sites of creativity and self-expression for both male and female participants from all social backgrounds. There is a plethora of sub-cultures which exhibit tendencies of style and behaviours which characterize the consumption of music, fashion, and symbolic experiences which exist in modern society. Sub-cultural activity is important for the construction and expression of identity, rather than cells of resistance against dominant orders. It is also important to recognize that sub-cultural choices are also consumer choices involving fashion, leisure, and a wealth of accessories, which speak symbolically to members of the group.

Thornton (1995) draws attention to the importance of 'authenticity' in the performance of identity in what she calls 'taste cultures', where people can develop 'sub-cultural capital' through authentic displays of 'cool'. The vital role played by authentic performance was identified in Nancarrow *et al.*'s (2002) study of 'style leaders' which analysed 'cool' as requiring the bodily expression of 'ironic detachment'. In becoming members of a sub-culture we need to develop competence in the performance of appropriate cultural codes. The boundaries of a sub-cultural world are 'transgressed and rendered visible through 'overperformance' of appropriate behaviour' (Horton, 2003). If an aspiring member of a sub-culture becomes aware of their inability to perform authentically, aware of their ignorance of their cultural codes, then self-consciousness and discomfort emerge.

Goffman (1969) uses a dramaturgical metaphor to discuss the performance of identity, what he calls 'face work'. The body plays a crucial part in a competent performance, constantly signalling to others and reading the signals of other sub-cultural members. Thus authentic performance is both the transmission and reception of culturally appropriate actions. He maintains that the performer must believe in the action, must believe in the part being played. In order for the performance to be interpreted as authentic, the performer himself/herself should believe the performance is authentic. Failure to believe in the performance is what Sartre (1956) meant by 'bad faith', using the example of a café waiter who acted the part but did not perform it authentically, a form of self-deception.

In a study of style sub-cultures and the consumption of fashion brands and music, Elliott and Davies (2005) demonstrate the importance of the performance of identity, how authenticity can be recognized, and how consumers learn how 'to get it right' as they move from being novices to respected members of the sub-culture. They found that authenticity of performance played a vital role in building sub-cultural capital and facilitating membership of micro-cultures and their associated brand communities of music and fashion.

Beverland and Farrelly (2010, p. 853) offer a different perspective, contending that the nature of authenticity depends on our goals. Countering the assumption that authenticity is not possible where 'standards of what is real and what is fake are lacking', they claim that different personal goals and standards allow consumers to find authenticity in brands and events that others may find fake. For example, the desire to feel in control explained a surfer's rejection of some brands seen as important signifiers for that sub-culture whilst still considering themselves an authentic part of that scene.

KEY CONCEPT

Neo-tribes and sub-cultures may use the consumption of symbolic brands to develop and communicate their identity.

Neo-tribes are characterized by people linked by a common emotion. As with brand communities, they are often centred around consumption. Unlike brand communities a single brand is not the be all and end all. In contrast, one or more brands, as well as other behaviours and practices, help to bring the tribe together. Take rock climbers as an example. Brands such as La Sportiva and Mad Rock are prominent and signal the seriousness of the tribe member, but they form only part of a broader emotional commitment to climbing. This commitment, and signalling of tribe membership may, with the support of other symbolic brands, also include an attitude of environmental awareness, love of the outdoors, and the desire to thrill seek.

Sub-cultures and appropriation of brand meanings

The ability of brands to help sub-cultures develop and express their identities has been demonstrated in a number of studies. Holt (2002) shows how the practice of 'creative resistance' enables some postmodern consumers to act as 'citizen-artists' in adopting the brand meanings they choose in acts of personal sovereignty. Brands are used as one form of expressive culture, similar to film, TV, or music, that can be used in their identity projects.

A more active sub-cultural activity is to adopt the imagery of a famous brand, and then use it to build an alternative identity to that originally associated with the brand. Political campaigns use branding strategies to carefully craft a specific portrayal of a candidate, but in 2008 Shepard Fairey—a contemporary street artist and graphic designer—appropriated a copyright protected image of presidential candidate Barack Obama, and rebranded it into what became an iconic image of hope. The ensuing series of stickers and posters were not directly affiliated with the Obama campaign, nor did the campaign assist in the popularization of the illustration. Instead, much of its popularity can be attributed to the graffiti subculture tagging the nation with over 350,000 'HOPE' posters. To democratic Americans, and minority groups in particular, the image became synonymous with a belief in their ability to effectuate change through voting for Obama. Fairey has since set up OBEY clothing using the iconic 'HOPE' portrait as well as other famous propaganda images to ironic effect.

Aikido brands 合氣道

Aikido is a Japanese martial art involving some throws and joint locks that are derived from Jujitsu and some throws and other techniques derived from Kenjutsu. Aikido focuses not on punching or kicking opponents, but rather on using their own energy to gain control of them or to throw them away from you. A classic Aikido brand that uses the fame and image strength of a brand against itself is Mecca Cola.

Mecca Cola was launched in France in late 2002, designed to exploit anti-American sentiment around the world. The aim is to make Mecca Cola the soft drink of choice for Muslims: 'It is about combating America's imperialism and Zionism by providing a substitute for American goods and increasing the blockade of countries boycotting American goods' (Mathlouthi, 2003). The bottles bear the slogan 'No more drinking stupid, drink

Sub-cultural appropriation: Obama 'HOPE' image © Juli Hansen / Shutterstock.com

with commitment' and promise that 10% of the profits go to Palestinian charities and 10% to European NGOs working for world peace. There are two similar Islamic colas: ZamZam Cola in the Middle East and Qibla Cola in the UK. Qibla Cola also promises that 10% of its profits will go to the Muslim charity Islamic Aid. The founder of Qibla Cola said: 'Muslims are increasingly questioning the role some major multinationals play in our societies. Why should the money of the oppressed go to the oppressors?' (Parveen, 2003).

Some brands use opportunistic Aikido techniques. For example, when *oneAustralia* famously broke in half and sank (while racing *Team New Zealand* in the 35th America's Cup Yacht Race) the next day, in the national broadsheet, *The New Zealand Herald*, Lion Nathan ran a full page ad for its flagship brand Steinlager beer. The ad featured a photograph of *oneAustralia* sinking, with the Fosters logo, flagship brand of Australian rival Carlton United Breweries, on the sail just visible above the waves. The headline ran, 'Only one thing goes down quicker than an ice cold Steinlager'.

KEY CONCEPT

Aikido brands use the fame and image of a brand against itself.

As the iPhone 6Plus was launched so too was #Bendgate. It became apparent that the phone actually bent when it had been in a pocket of prolonged period of time, though not by design. Within days Kit Kat had tweeted an image of a broken Kit Kat with accompanying tag 'We don't bend, we #break.' Dockers had tweeted 'Avoid #bendgate with our hidden security side pocket. Smart phone, meet the #SmartestKhakis ever made.' Further ignominy has ensued with the major phone brands jumping on board. The first to do so was LG with this tweet 'Our phone doesn't bend, it flexes... on purpose. #bendgate'. Samsung was also unable to resist releasing a YouTube video showing the three point bend test, which simulates their device being sat on repeatedly, with no ill effect.

CHAPTER SUMMARY

In this chapter we have explored some of the ways in which brands can help communicate a variety of cultural meanings, and how these can be categorized as fundamentally concerned with either social differentiation or social integration. We have also suggested that powerful brands may expect to have their brand hijacked by anti-capitalists and other sub-cultural groups and their brand awareness and meanings used against them by Aikido brands.

DISCUSSION QUESTIONS

1 Explain the difference between signifier and signified in relation to a brand.

2 Is it possible to love a brand?

3 Explain the difference between social integration and social differentiation using brands.

4 How does the concept of cultural capital explain our consumption behaviour?

5 Has social media changed the nature of the relationships we can have with brands?

6 What makes a neo-tribe different from traditional ideas of a tribe?

7 How does 'bad faith' relate to the consumption of brands?

8 How does an Aikido brand use a famous brand's image?

CASE STUDY

The cultural meaning of stationary! Where do we draw the line? The case of kikki.K and Smiggle

Introduction

Fashion. Stationery. Who would have thought that these two worlds–the former, synonymous with style, design, and innovation, and the latter, associated with utility, practicality, and functionality–could come together? Yet, in spite of its apparent incompatibility, fashion and stationery is a match made in heaven.

The emergence of the fashion stationery product category can be traced back to 1996, when UK-based brand Paperchase introduced its range of stylish, design-led stationery. Its ascendance however can be attributed to two Australian brands: kikki.K and Smiggle. With their innovative product designs and creative marketing, branding, and retail activities, kikki.K and Smiggle have transformed stationery into a fashion accessory; a statement of one's style, personality, and individuality. In the process of turning the then dull stationery market on its head, kikki.K and Smiggle have created a cult-like following amongst both children and adults, and fuelled a sub-culture of 'stationery freaks'.

kikki. K

It is 3am. Swedish-born Kristina Karlson is wide awake in her Melbourne apartment. As she tosses and turns, she ponders the direction in which her career is heading. Frustrated with her restlessness, her partner, Paul Lacy encourages her to make a list of what is important to her, to be used to guide her career decisions. This was on Kristina's list:

- To do something she was passionate about
- That would allow her to keep in contact with her friends and family in Sweden
- Whatever it was had to be design related
- And would result in her own business
- It also would generate an income of $500 a week

Armed with her list, Kristina, an avid stationery lover and a stickler for organization, set out to set up her home office. As she embarked on this pursuit, she quickly realized that the stationery market–in Australia at least–was boring, and very much price driven. The stationery she came across had no design or style aspect. Nor were they inspirational, like those she was used to from her home country. If she selected from the available options, her home office would appear to consist of stationery borrowed (or perhaps stolen) from the workplace–a far cry from the beautiful sanctuary where passion-is-nurtured-and-creative-ideas-spawned image she had in her mind. There marked the beginnings of the brand now known as kikki.K.

Upon conducting some initial focus groups, Kristina found a gap in the market. There were others out there, who, just like her, adored stationery and had trouble finding gorgeous stationery. Her market research efforts also identified a business opportunity. There was a growing number of people working from home. This trend was in part due to organizations becoming increasingly open to the notion of flexible workplace arrangements and an increasing number of home-based businesses. Kristina found her calling: to bring order and beauty to the world with stationery inspired by the Swedish design philosophy of simplicity, form, and function.

In the world that is cluttered and chaotic, kikki.K's clever use of simple, clean lines in the design of its core products and broad range of colour coordinated pens, journals, folders, boxes, message boards, ring binders, staplers, tape dispensers, waste paper bins, magazine holders, letter trays, soy wax candles, homeware, and kitchenware conveys a sense of being calm and in control. To further support customers in their missions to create (and maintain) an inspiring, beautiful, and clutter-free home office, kikki.K's also offers group and one-on-one organization workshops. Since its introduction, these workshops have proved to be very popular, catering to approximately 50 participants per month. Kikki.K has also very successfully developed an 'inspiration' range–which consists of a series of journals and tools to assist in consumers in goal-setting, purposeful living, finding happiness, expressing gratitude, and getting healthy.

Subscribing to the view that stationery should be the fashion accessory to complement any outfit and convey one's sense of style and individuality, the kikki.K product range is purposefully designed with an element of seasonality. The stylish nature of kikki.K stationery has not gone unnoticed by the fashion and design industry. Kikki.K stationery is a regular feature in fashion and design magazines. In fact, Vogue magazine was one of the first to publish an article about the kikki.K's fashionable and sophisticated product range. To further cement its link to the world of fashion, kikki.K officially sponsors various high profile fashion events, such as the L'Oreal Melbourne Fashion Festival.

With the use of clean and clear lines and professionally displayed merchandize, the layout and design of kikki.K boutiques and pop up stores appears more like a fashion clothing retailer than a stationery store. From time to time, the retail window will feature paper-based prototypes of clothing fashion designs–which are a fashion statement in and of themselves. Kikki.K also boasts its very own concept boutique–the 'White Store', which offers a limited edition collection of merchandize in, as its name implies, the colour white. Plans for a 'Black Store' are underway.

Known for being home to all things stationery and home office organization, kikki.K has managed to garner a cult-like following amongst its target market of home-based workers and business owners. The kikki.K brand has also succeeded in appealing to sub-groups of interior designers, architects, and advertising and marketing professionals who genuinely appreciate the design effort that has gone into creating the kikki.K brand and its merchandize. To maintain a connection and further strengthen the emotional bond it has with its fans, kikki.K has developed a very strong and active presence on social media. In addition to creating an official kikki.K blog and using Twitter and Facebook to engage with its customers, kikki.K features regularly on Pinterest and Instagram. Kikki.K has also recently launched a new initiative, 'CREATE with kikki.k', which gives its customers the opportunity to customize calendars, books, notepads, journals, boxes, and gifts.

Kristina has well and truly achieved her personal mission. A sense of order and beauty do indeed exude from kikki.K's product offerings as well as its marketing, branding, and retail activities. It is not surprising that in a little over 10 years, kikki.K has grown to be an internationally recognized brand with over 100 retail boutiques across Australia, New Zealand, and Singapore, over 120 stockist worldwide, an online store which delivers fashionable stationery across the globe, and plans underway to establish kikki.K boutiques in Paris, Hong Kong, London, Stockholm, Copenhagen, New York, Tokyo, and expand market reach to Canada and the Middle East.

Smiggle

Not long after kikki.K's entrance into the fashion stationery market, Smiggle was born. While Smiggle is also a fashion stationery retailer, its brand concept is markedly different from kikki.K's. Instead of competing for market share in the fashion conscious adult world of home-based workers, business owners, interior designers, architects, and advertising and marketing professionals, its founders, Stephen Meurs and Peter Pausewang found an untapped niche: children.

Using bright, loud colours and quirkily-designed stationery, Smiggle stationery stands out amongst the crowd. With its value-driven pricing strategy and strategically located retail outlets (in shopping malls and in high streets near public and private schools), Smiggle stationery swiftly penetrated its target market. In Australia, where most schools have strict guidelines on uniform, hair styles, and personal appearance, Smiggle stationery–imagine a lime green alligator stapler or sky blue elephant-shaped tape dispenser or a scented lollypop eraser–quickly became a sensation in schools. Smiggle became *the* fashion item used by students to express their sense of individuality.

Smiggle's success may also be attributed to its ability to tap into the collector within each child. With newly designed products released every fortnight and new quirky characters released on a monthly basis, children are seduced into spending their pocket money (or their parents') collecting the entire product range and having a complete set. In fact, a simple YouTube search of the brand reveals several home-made videos of children displaying their Smiggle collections. Not surprisingly, some products within the collection may never make it to school–just in case it gets lost or stolen. Smiggle's success may also be attributed to the peer-pressure phenomenon where students only purchase Smiggle merchandize mainly because their friends have it. Naturally, as parents do not want their children stick out or to miss out, they end up purchasing Smiggle merchandize.

Regardless of the reasons behind Smiggle's success, its espoused brand values, which centre on fun, positivity, creativity, and value-for-money, are evident across not only their colourful and quirky product range, but also their marketing, branding, and retail activities. In fact, all Smiggle customer touch-points are purposefully designed to fuel the creative spirit and with the intention to make its customers smile and giggle (hence the name, Smiggle). For example, with its bright lights, boldly coloured, and oddly shaped merchandize–all arranged in colour-coded fashion–and its cheerful, down-to-earth sales team, Smiggle retail outlets have a Willy Wonka-come-Dylan's Candy Bar feel to them. And, while traditional retail shops tell children 'Do Not Touch', at Smiggle, children are encouraged to touch, play, and be creative. Smiggle's high energy and upbeat brand personality and its commitment to being a fun, creative, and playful outlet for individual expression is also reflected in several of their design programs and competitions. In these programs, Smiggle engages with and encourages university design students to turn their creative ideas into marketable business projects. Smiggle often sponsors design competitions, with the winning designs re-produced as a limited-edition product range and sold in stores. Smiggle also regularly collaborates with different emerging artists to design new products.

In its short time in the marketplace, Smiggle has grown to be an internationally recognized brand with over 157 stores across Australia, New Zealand, and Singapore. It has just entered into the UK market, and there are plans to expand into South Korea, China, Japan, Indonesia, and Malaysia. Smiggle has also managed to generate a loyal fan base, so much so that fans have started to call themselves 'Smigglers'. To maintain and strengthen its relationship with its fan base, Smiggle has developed a very content-rich website, maintains a blog, and has an active presence across a variety of social media platforms, including Twitter, YouTube, and Facebook. It is interesting to note that Smiggle's Facebook page has more than 300,000 fans from across the globe–even in countries where Smiggle merchandize is not retailed; thus demonstrating a high level awareness of the brand internationally. Smiggle has also very recently launched its first official app: Bob and the Smiggle Colour Lab–a puzzle game available via iTunes.

To further resonate with its tech conscious fans, Smiggle launched its Colour Crews customer relationship management program. The Colour Crews program is designed to get Smigglers participating in creative activities, challenges, riddles, brain teasers, and cryptic questions, engaging with other Smigglers, and to creatively blend consumers' online and offline brand experiences. For example, to complete certain Colour Crew activities, Smigglers are redirected to the Smiggle website, its Facebook page, or its physical store. In so doing, Smiggle not only generates an on-going conversation with its fan base, it also creates a sense of community amongst Smigglers. To date, Smiggle has managed to accumulate 150,000 Colour Crew members. And, since the introduction of the Colour Crew program, Smiggle has experienced a marked increase in online sales and a 1000% increase in its Facebook fan base.

With its cheerful spirit, Smiggle has, without a doubt, come to be a brand loved by children and parents alike. With its distinctively bright colours, funky characters, quirky product designs, and its fun-filled creative activities, Smiggle stationery injects fun into the learning experience and lets kids express their individuality. Smiggle has also made what used to be an arduous task–the annual mission of shopping for school supplies–into an enjoyable one. And, given the love children seem to have for Smiggle products, it is regularly used as a reward for good behaviour; by far a better alternative to chocolates and lollies. The biggest drawcard for both children and parents however, is perhaps what the Smiggle brand represents: positivity, creativity, and happiness.

Conclusion

In the age of smart phones, laptops, and digital note taking devices, it was assumed that the stationery industry would meet the same fate as the publishing, video rental, and music industry. However, if kikki.K's and Smiggle's success is anything to go by, the stationery industry is well and truly alive. In fact, there has been a renaissance–what used to be a low involvement, low commitment purchase decision based on cost and functionality is now a highly emotional one based on style, design and personality.

Case Written by Dr Jo En Yap | Lecturer, Marketing
Faculty of Business and Law, Swinburne Business School | Department of Marketing, Tourism and Social Impact
Swinburne University of Technology

CASE QUESTIONS

1. kikki.K and Smiggle are very successful brands that have clearly differentiated themselves and communicated their uniqueness to their target markets. Based on your understanding of the brand-as-a-person metaphor, discuss the personality characteristics associated with each brand.

2. Do you think kikki.K and Smiggle have successfully developed relationships with their customers? What is the nature of the relationship?

3. Discuss how kikki.K and Smiggle facilitates and contributes to social differentiation and social integration.

4. What value creating practices have kikki.K and Smiggle employed to develop their respective brand communities?

5. Discuss the socio-cultural factors giving rise to the fashion stationery industry.

FURTHER READING

- An excellent introduction to the sociology of consumption is Slater, D. (1997), *Consumer Culture and Modernity*, Cambridge: Polity Press.

- Seminal contributions to the theory of consumer society are contained in M. Lee (ed.) (2000), *The Consumer Society Reader*, Oxford: Blackwell.

- Leading-edge thinking about branding as a cultural process can be found in J. Schroeder and M. Salzer-Morling (eds) (2005), *Brand Culture*, London: Routledge.

REFERENCES

Aaker, J. (1997), 'Dimensions of brand personality', *Journal of Marketing Research*, XXXIV, 347–56.

Aaker, J., Benet-Martinez, J., and Garolera, J. (2001), 'Consumption symbols as carriers of culture: A study of Japanese and Spanish brand personality constructs', *Journal of Personality and Social Psychology*, 81, 3, 492–508.

Aaker, J., Fournier, S., and Brasel, S. A. (2004), 'When good brands do bad', *Journal of Consumer Research*, 31, 1, 1–15.

Austin, J., Siguaw, J., and Mattila, A. (2003), 'A re-examination of the generalizability of the Aaker brand personality measurement framework', *Journal of Strategic Marketing*, 11, 2, 77–93.

Batra, R., Ahuvia, A., & Bagozzi, R. P. (2012). Brand love. Journal of Marketing, 76 (2), 1–16

Bengtsson, A. (2003), 'Towards a critique of brand relationships', *Advances in Consumer Research*, 30, 154–8.

Beverland, M.B. and Farrelly F.J. (2010), 'The quest for authenticity in consumption: Consumers' purposive choice of authentic cues to shape experienced outcomes', *Journal of Consumer Research*, 36, 5, 838–56.

Bourdieu, P. (1984), *Distinction: A Social Critique of the Judgement of Taste*, London: Routledge.

Caprara, G., Barbaranelli, C., and Guido, G. (1998), 'Personality as metaphor: extension of the psycholexical hypothesis and the five factor model to brand and product personality description', *European Advances in Consumer Research*, 3, 61–9.

Costa, J. (ed.) (1994), *Gender Issues and Consumer Behavior*, London: Sage.

Cova, B. and Cova, V. (2001), 'Tribal aspects of postmodern consumption: The case of French in-line roller skaters', *Journal of Consumer Behaviour*, 1, 1, 67–76.

Davis, F. (1992), *Fashion, Culture and Identity*, Chicago: University of Chicago Press.

Douglas, M. and Isherwood, B. (1979), *The World of Goods: Towards an Anthropology of Consumption*, London: Allen Lane.

Elliott, R. (1994), 'Exploring the symbolic meaning of brands', *British Journal of Management*, 5, Special Issue, 13–19.

Elliott, R., and Davies, A. (2005), 'Symbolic brands and authenticity of identity performance', in J. Schroeder and M. Salzer-Morling (eds), *Brand Culture*, London: Routledge.

Elliott, R., Jones, A., Benfield, A., and Barlow, M. (1995), 'Overt sexuality in advertising: A discourse analysis of gendered responses', *Journal of Consumer Policy*, 18, 2, 71–92.

Fournier, S. (1998), 'Consumers and their brands: Developing relationship theory in consumer research', *Journal of Consumer Research*, 24, 4, 343–73.

Goffman, E. (1969), *The Presentation of Self in Everyday Life*, London: Allen Lane.

Goulding, C., Shankar, A., and Elliott, R. (2002), 'Working weeks, rave weekends: Identity fragmentation and the emergence of new communities', *Consumption, Markets, and Culture*, 5, 4, 261–84.

Goulding, C., Shankar, A., and Elliott, R. (2009), 'The marketplace management of illicit pleasure', *Journal of Consumer Research*, 35, 5, 759–71.

Grayson, K. and Shulman, D. (2000), 'Indexicality and the verification function of irreplaceable possessions', *Journal of Consumer Research*, 27, June, 17–30.

Harvey, M. and Evans, M. (2001), 'Decoding competitive propositions: A semiotic alternative to traditional advertising research', *International Journal of Market Research*, 43, 1, 171–87.

Holbrook, M. and Schindler, R. (1994), 'Age, sex and attitude towards the past as predictors of consumers' aesthetic tastes for cultural products', *Journal of Marketing Research*, XXXI, 412–22.

Holbrook, M. and Schindler, R. (2003), 'Nostalgic bonding: Exploring the role of nostalgia in the consumption experience', *Journal of Consumer Behaviour*, 3, 2, 102–7.

Holt, D. (1998), 'Does cultural capital structure American consumption?' *Journal of Consumer Research*, 25, 1, 1–25.

Holt, D. (2002), 'Why do brands cause trouble? A dialectical theory of consumer culture and branding', *Journal of Consumer Research*, 29, 1, 70–90.

Horton, D. (2003), 'Green distinctions: The performance of identity among environmental activists', *The Sociological Review*, 51, 2, 64–77.

Jee Han, Y., Nunes, J., and Drèze, X. (2010), 'Signaling status with luxury goods: The role of brand prominence', *Journal of Marketing*, July, 74, 15–30.

Kates, S. (2000), 'Out of the closet and out on the streets: Gay men and their brand relationships', *Psychology and Marketing*, 17, 6, 493–504.

Lawes, R. (2002), 'Demystifying semiotics: Some key questions answered', *International Journal of Market Research*, 44, 3, 251–64.

Levy, S. (1959), 'Symbols for sale', *Harvard Business Review*, 37, 4, 117–24.

Ligas, M. and Cotte, J. (1999), 'The process of negotiating brand meaning: A symbolic interactionist perspective', *Advances in Consumer Research*, 26, 609–14.

Lovemarks.com (2010), 'The future beyond brands', http://www.lovemarks.com. Last accessed 29 July 2010.

Luedicke, M.K., Thompson C.J., and Giesler, M. (2010), 'Consumer identity work as moral protagonism: How myth and ideology animate a brand-mediated moral conflict', *Journal of Consumer Research*, 36, 6 (in press, published online at http://www.journals.uchicago.edu).

McAlexander, J., Schouten, J., and Koenig, H. (2002), 'Building brand community', *Journal of Marketing*, 66, 38–54.

McCracken, G. (1993), 'The value of the brand: An anthropological perspective', in D. Aaker and A. Biel (eds), *Brand Equity and Advertising*, Hillsdale: Lawrence Erlbaum.

Mathlouthi, T. (2003), Interviewed on BBC World News/BBC News Online, 8 January 2003, available at http://news.bbc.co.uk/2/hi/middle_east/2640259.stm, last accessed 8 September 2010.

Mindy, J. (2002), 'Children's relationships with brands: "true love" or "one-night stand"?' *Psychology and Marketing*, 19, 4, 369–81.

Monga, A (2002), 'Brand as relationship partner: Gender differences in perspective', *Advances in Consumer Research*, 29, 36–41.

Muñiz, A. and O'Guinn, T. (2001), 'Brand communities', *Journal of Consumer Research*, March, 27, 412–32.

Nancarrow, C., Nancarrow, P., and Page, J. (2002), 'An analysis of the concept of cool and its marketing implications', *Journal of Consumer Behaviour*, 1, 4, 311–22.

Olsen, B. (1999), 'Exploring women's brand relationships and enduring themes at mid-life', *Advances in Consumer Research*, 26, 615–20.

Park, J., Kim, K., and Kim, J. (2002), 'Acceptance of brand extensions: Interactive influence of product category similarity, typicality of claimed benefits, and brand relationship quality', *Advances in Consumer Research*, 29, 190–202.

Park, W., Jaworski, B., and MacInnis, D. (1986), 'Strategic brand concept-image management', *Journal of Marketing*, 50, 135–45.

Parveen, Z. (2003), Interviewed on Islam-Online. net/English/news/2003–02.

Ritson, M., Elliott, R., and Eccles, S. (1996), 'Reframing IKEA: commodity-signs, consumer creativity and the social/self dialectic', *Advances in Consumer Research*, 23, 127–31.

Sartre, J.-P. (1956/2003), *Being and Nothingness: An Essay on Phenomenological Ontology*, London: Routledge.

Schau, H.J., Muñiz, A.M., and Arnould, E.J. (2009), 'How brand community practices create value', *Journal of Marketing*, 73, 5, 30–51.

Slater, D. (1997), *Consumer Culture and Modernity*, Cambridge: Polity Press.

Supphellen, M. and Grønhaug, K. (2003), 'Building foreign brand personalities in Russia: The moderating effect of consumer ethnocentrism', *International Journal of Advertising*, 22, 203–26.

Swaminathan, V., Stilley, K.M., Ahluwalia, R. (2009), 'When brand personality matters: The moderating role of attachment styles', *Journal of Consumer Research*, April, 35, 985–1001.

Thornton, S. (1995), *Club Cultures: Music, Media and Subcultural Capital*, Cambridge: Polity Press.

Vargo, S.L and Lusch, R.F. (2004), 'Evolving to a new dominant logic for marketing', *Journal of Marketing*, 68, 1, 1–17.

Veblen, T. (1899/1979), *The Theory of the Leisure Class*, New York: Kelly.

Brand Equity and Brand Building

This section introduces the concept of brand equity and how to build brands through marketing communication, with detailed consideration of consumer research methods for tracking brand performance and measuring brand equity.

5

Brand Equity

Key Concepts

1 Brand equity has both a financial and a consumer aspect.

2 Brand equity, from a financial perspective, considers the importance of brands in terms of their asset value to a company.

3 Brand equity from a consumer perspective results from awareness of a brand leading to brand knowledge and a positive attitude towards the brand, resulting in loyalty to the brand.

4 Brand attitude plays the most important role in building brand equity.

Introduction

In the last chapter, it was pointed out how brands can be used as signalling systems in order to create and send social meaning, and that it is the meaning of brands that give them added value. In this chapter we are going to take a closer look at this notion of added value. Since the late 1980s marketers have talked about this idea of added value in terms of something they called brand equity. But what is meant by the term 'brand equity' is anything but clear. Nevertheless, there is a general consensus, and we shall be exploring it, why it is important, and how to build and sustain a positive brand equity.

Name value

Before turning our attention to the concept of brand equity, it would be a good idea to consider the general idea of how a particular name, and that name alone, may be associated in memory with specific value. Thinking about areas of life outside of the realm of products and services, there are many places where a 'name' makes all the difference in the world. For example, when we are not well, it is one thing for a friend to suggest a cure, quite another a doctor. We recognize the added credibility associated with the 'name' doctor when it comes to ailments. There is a definite added value to a doctor's recommendation.

In Chapter 3 we looked specifically at the symbolic meaning of brands. The idea of 'brand equity' is closely linked with this because in many ways the symbolic significance of a brand is reflected in attitudes toward that brand which informs its equity. Following the emergence of *Homo sapiens*, in what Donald (1991) has described as the 'mythic' stage in the development of human culture and cognition, which was characterized by the use of complex language skills and narrative thought, came the capacity for the use of symbols. This use of symbols has been described as of defining importance to human culture (White, 1949), and dates from the Neolithic (or agricultural) Revolution and the inception of sedentism. It was at this time that material goods came to have symbolic importance, and when certain material goods came to be associated with high value (Renfrew, 2007).

Have you ever been in a museum or art gallery and found yourself looking at a painting with which you were not familiar? How does your opinion of that painting differ if you learn it is the work of a familiar 'great master' artist versus if you see that it is by an unknown artist, one you have never heard of? Even when someone does not like a painting, they tend to think better of it if they learn it is by a master. In these situations, it is the name value that makes a difference. In fact, the name value in a case like this can also have very real financial value.

In 1968, a group of eminent art historians were charged with the task of examining Rembrandt's oeuvre, with the goal of compiling a definitive catalogue of his paintings. It was called the Rembrandt Research Project, and it was to go on for over 30 years. The art historians involved travelled the world to examine over 600 paintings reputed to be by the hand of Rembrandt. Many proved to be overly optimistic attributions. In their examination of 280 paintings just from the period 1625–42, only 146, a little over half, were considered to be autograph works (i.e. actually by the hand of Rembrandt). Many of the paintings no longer attributed to him were found in the collections of many of the world's greatest museums.

The value of the paintings no longer considered to be autograph works dropped dramatically. It was not unusual for paintings that had been valued at well over £2 million to suddenly be re-valued at less than £100,000. The point here is that the actual painting itself, the image on the canvas, did not change. It was exactly the same painting originally acquired by the collection. But the perceived value was in the *name* Rembrandt.

Brand equity and the value of Rembrandt is not the only thing affected by a change in attribution. When people are told a work of art is an 'authentic' Rembrandt vs. a copy by another hand, different areas of the brain are active while *viewing* the painting (Kemp, 2014). While the expected activator in the lateral visual cortex areas corresponding to regions sensitive to face and object recognition occurred regardless of what people were told, being told that an authentic Rembrandt was not an original resulted in activation in the frontopolar cortex and right precuneus, as opposed to the orbitofrontal cortex when told the painting they were viewing was authentic. Interestingly, the orbitofrontal cortex is an area of the brain that has been associated with reward and monetary gain.

This idea of name value is at the heart of what is known as brand equity. There is a value to a brand over and above the intrinsic value of the product itself. Just as with a de-attributed Rembrandt, the product itself, the painting, had one value; but with the name Rembrandt attached to the painting, significant added value was created.

This is, of course, why companies jealously guard their brand names. Perhaps one of the best brand names in the world is Budweiser. But that name has been contested over the years by the Czech brewer Budjejovicky Budvar. Their claim goes back to the Austro-Hungarian Empire, when Budweis was the name of a Bohemian city famous for its beer (restored after the 1st world war to its Czech name Budejovice). But in a 2013 court ruling by Italy's Supreme Court, AB InBev lost the rights to use the name Budweiser in Italy (Carney and Esterl, 2013).

This dispute complicated AB InBev's hope of making Budweiser a global brand. In a number of major European countries, including France and Russia, they already used 'Bud' on the label rather than Budweiser. Recently, they even stopped marketing the beer in Germany, where it had used the name Anheuser-Busch Bud. However, in 2014 AB InBev solved the problem by purchasing the Czech brewery (Rouser, 2014).

Defining brand equity

Marketers have always understood the idea that brand names add value to a product, but it was not until the late 1980s that this notion began to figure in the actual asset value of a company. Kapferer (1998) has suggested that this change came about during the massive wave of mergers and acquisitions among large companies with well-known brands that occurred in the 1980s. Those spearheading these transactions were looking beyond the traditional sense of asset value and net income to include 'goodwill'. They were interested in a company's brand portfolio because of the power of these brands in the market. Even if accepted accounting procedure did not permit considering the added value of a brand name on the balance sheet, it was nonetheless being factored into the net value of the firm.

Out of all this activity the term brand equity was born. Unfortunately, there were almost as many definitions of brand equity as there were people using the term. Fig. 5.1 lists just a few definitions offered by marketing executives at the time. While they each take a somewhat different specific view, they all are describing how a brand name provides added

- Brand equity can be thought of as the additional cash flow achieved by associating a brand with the underlying product or service (Alexander Biel)[1]
- Brand equity is the difference between the value of the brand to the consumer and the value of the product without that branding (Josh McQueen)[2]
- Brand equity is the measurable financial value in transactions that accrues to a product or service from successful programmes and activities related to branding (J. Walker Smith)[2]
- Brand equity to me in its simplest definition is the value of worth that resides in a particular brand name, trademark or product. It is not one single thing but a composite . . . it is all the elements created by marketing, advertising, research, and production, that over the years have made the product or service what it is in consumers' minds today (John Pagano)[3]
- One expert might say it is the residual equity that remains after you compare the blind and identified versions of the same product (Richard Chay)[3]

[1] ARF Researching the Power of Brands Workshop, 12–13 February 1992.
[2] ARF Brand Equity Workshop, 5 February 1991.
[3] ARF Brand Equity Workshop, 22–23 February 1990.

FIGURE 5.1 Brand equity definitions from marketing executives

value to a product. In the end, they seem to see this added value either in financial terms, or in how consumers perceive the brand.

In Fig. 5.2 we have several definitions of brand equity that were offered by academics in 1980 at an MSI (Marketing Science Institute) conference called to address the issue. Although the language may be more 'academic', it is clear that both marketing executives and academics define brand equity in much the same way. Both groups see it in terms of either financial considerations or consumer perceptions of a brand.

Some people at the time defined brand equity in terms of both financial consider-ations and consumer perceptions of the brand. Moran (1991), a marketing executive much involved with the strategic importance of brand equity in the 1990s, defined it this way in 1991: 'I believe the concept of brand equity to be that any given brand name, itself, has particular meaning and value to its consumers and to its direct customers, the distributive trade, which affects the future earning potential of the product or products which are sold under that name.' In the same year, in his book *Managing Brand Equity* (arguably the first book to deal with the subject seriously), Aaker (1991) defined brand equity as: 'A set of brand assets and liabilities linked to a brand, its name and symbol,

- Specific attribute beliefs and global evaluative beliefs consumers have learned to associate with the brand name (John and Loken)[1]
- Net value of brand image (i.e. mental inventory which people hold for a brand); brand image is specific associations with brand and overall attitudes towards brand in memory, as perceived by decision makers (Aaker and Keller)[1]
- The incremental cash flows which accure to a branded product over and above the cash flows which would result from the sale of a product (Simon and Sullivan)[1]
- The added value with which a given brand endows a product. A product is something that offers a functional benefit (e.g. toothpaste, a life insurance policy, or a car). A brand is name, symbol design or mark that enhances the value of a product beyond its functional purpose (Faquhar)[2]

[1] MSI working paper presented at 1990 Marketing Science Institute Conference on brand equity.
[2] Marketing Research, 1, September, 24–33 (1989).

FIGURE 5.2 Brand equity definitions from academics

that add to or subtract from the value provided by a product or service to a firm and/or to that firm's customers.'

But by looking at all these definitions of brand equity, are we really closer to *understanding* it? Any number of ways have been proposed to measure brand equity, but they are as varied as the definitions. In the early 1990s Sattler (1994) looked at 49 different studies of brand equity that had been conducted in Europe and the USA and found in them at least 26 different ways of measuring it! How to measure brand equity will be discussed in Chapter 7, but this incredible lack of consensus reflects the rather unsettled state of just what constituted brand equity (a situation not much changed today).

In a very real sense, understanding brand equity must come from the consumer's point of view because that is what ultimately will affect brand success. It is the consumer's sense of added value that will lead to a preference for a particular brand. Financial consequences of brand equity will follow from the consumer's perception of added value. But before considering more carefully how consumers come to understand this added value for a brand, the financial consequences to a company of a positive brand equity will be addressed.

KEY CONCEPT

Brand equity has both a financial and a consumer aspect.

The concept of brand equity has consequences for both consumers and companies. For companies, the equity of its brands, and even the company itself as a 'brand', will have financial implications. For consumers, perceived brand equity provides an indication of value.

Financially-based brand equity

Strong brands have become an important part of the asset value of a company. Prior to 1980, when large companies were acquired or merged, the ratio of the price paid to the firm's earnings was generally in the area of about eight to one. After 1980, multiples of 20 or more times earnings were not unusual (Aaker, 1991). Why was this? While there are always special circumstances in some cases, at the heart of things was an increasing realization of the importance of strong brand names to a company's long-term *financial* success.

Gone was the notion that only traditional assets in bricks and mortar, patents, or R&D had value. Brand names were increasingly seen as one of a company's most important assets. In earlier times a firm interested in acquiring a beer marketer would be thinking in terms of a brewery; now they want to acquire names like Molsen or Bass. Even if a company is not doing well financially, it could still be an attractive merger or acquisition target if it has strong brands. Kapferer (1998) has put it very well in describing such situations: 'Balance sheets reflect bad management decisions in the past, whereas the brand is a potential source of future profits.'

For financial analysts, a key consideration when looking at companies with strong brands is that they present less risk. Strong brands generally remain strong, and this assumes the likelihood of a solid income stream. This strong income stream reflects the interaction of several factors. With a strong market share usually comes relatively higher price points, coupled with lower price elasticity relative to competitors. This leads to better margins and a higher return on investment. Poor management can be corrected; significantly increasing market share for a weak brand is much more difficult.

Well-known brands are much more likely to enjoy good distribution, which helps maintain high market share. For fmcgs (fast moving consumer goods), where the competition for shelf space is fierce, strong brands have the advantage. Because of strong consumer demand, distributors and retailers will be inclined to carry the brand. For less frequently purchased products, especially industrial products, wholesalers and distributors will again be keen to associate with a strong brand because they know it will sell.

Summarizing all this, strong brands, brands with a strong positive brand equity, are generally brands with a highly loyal core of consumers; and high market share as a result. Of course, there are exceptions where a brand may have a highly loyal customer base, but a low market share (e.g. niche brands). Regardless, strong brand loyalty leads to a number of advantages in marketing the brand that help sustain its position, and contribute to its financial value. With a high degree of brand loyalty, a company can generally expect sales to remain stable and strong over time. Because of continuing consumer demand, a strong brand will be more attractive to the trade, leading to good levels of distribution. This in itself will help maintain higher market share.

Having high brand loyalty means a company can generally charge a relatively high price for its product and maintain higher margins than its competitors in the category. It also means price elasticity is low (the brand will be less sensitive to competitive price reductions, especially competitor promotions). All this helps generate a high net profit and ROI (return on investment) for the company, as we see in Fig. 5.3.

In addition, there are many other areas where having a strong brand name will help contribute to building and maintaining higher profits. For example, a strong brand discourages new competitors from entering the market. It also means less risk when introducing line extensions, or extending the brand name into new product categories (areas that will be covered in Chapter 11). Additionally, a strong brand has internal resonance, and can lead to becoming an 'employer brand' and improved employee relationships (as discussed in Chapter 10). How strong brands contribute to financial value is listed in Fig. 5.4.

There is no question that the financial value of a brand reflects its brand equity, and some people even define brand equity in terms of financial value. But, we would argue that the financial value of a brand is the *result* of brand equity (among other things, of course) and not the definition of brand equity. Rather, a positive brand equity provides value to a company by enhancing such things as marketing programmes, brand loyalty, price and

| High loyalty | ⇒ | STRONG BRANDS | ⇒ | • Trade acceptance
• Higher price points
• Higher margins
• Low price elasticity | ⇒ | GREATER PROFITABILITY |

FIGURE 5.3 How strong brands generate greater profitability

- High brand loyalty sustains future sales
- Greater trade cooperation and support, minimizing the need for trade incentives
- Sustainable higher price points
- Higher margins vs. competitors
- Low price elasticity
- Barrier to new competitors
- Less risk for line and product extensions

FIGURE 5.4 Strong brand contributions to financial value

margins, and trade leverage, and by providing a platform for brand extensions. In our view, as mentioned above, brand equity must be considered in terms of the consumer's response to the brand, and this is reflected in their overall attitude towards it.

KEY CONCEPT

Brand equity, from a financial perspective, considers the importance of brands in terms of their asset value to a company.

In financial terms, strong brands with high positive brand equity, will be more likely to enjoy larger market share and generate greater profit. This in turn makes the brand a strong asset for the company. And while this is important, it must be remembered that the financial value follows from consumer response to the brand.

Consumer-based brand equity

If brand equity is something that adds value to a brand, how is that reflected in consumer perceptions of the brand? In the last chapter, for example, we discussed how the perceived social meaning of brands adds value. Aaker (1991) talks about how brands bring value to the consumer by reducing risk, and offers eight functions of a brand that create value for a consumer (things like the ability to easily identify the product, an assurance of consistency, and quality). Franzen (1999) looks at a brand's value to the consumer in terms of something he calls 'mental brand equity', described in terms of awareness, perception, and attitude, and also 'behavioural brand equity' that accounts for various aspects of purchase behaviour. He goes on to describe brand equity as a set of assets and liabilities that he groups into four categories: brand awareness, brand associations, perceived quality, and brand loyalty.

While the words may be different, the ideas expressed here are basically the same. What they have in common is a sense that brand equity springs from a consumer awareness of the brand that triggers associations in memory that are linked to the brand. Over time, this positive brand attitude takes on strong emotional associations that extend well beyond simply 'liking' the brand. At its most positive, brand equity is much like what Hall (1959) has described as a 'formal system'. In their lives, people look for rules to govern certain aspects of their behaviour so that it is not necessary to make decisions continuously about everything they do. One knows when a formal system is being challenged because there is no readily available rational response. Everyone has experienced as a child asking their parents why they can't do something, or why certain things are as they are, and received a frustrated 'because' as the answer. A formal system has been challenged. There is no ready reason, it just is not done, or just is that way.

This sounds very much like what is involved with brand equity. A loyal user of a brand just 'knows' it is better. When loyal Coke drinkers are asked why they prefer it to Pepsi, they may offer some reason like it 'tastes better'. But if it is pointed out that they failed to prefer it in a blind taste test, and are again asked why they prefer it over Pepsi when they cannot tell the difference in taste, the response is often a frustrated 'because'. They just know they like it better. The favourable brand attitude built over time by the acceptance of perceived benefits for the brand, and loyal brand behaviour, has resulted in a strong positive brand equity: a preference for the brand that goes beyond any objective consideration of the product. In fact, a fascinating neuroimagery study demonstrated just that.

A taste test between Coke and Pepsi was conducted among drinkers of both brands in order to determine preferences in various pairings of the two colas, in both blind and branded conditions. Many studies over the years have shown that even for regular drinkers of the brand, in blind taste tests preference is random. The interesting aspect of this experiment was that the tasting and preference judgements were carried out during functional magnetic resonance imaging (fMRI). In other words, when people were tasting the colas and picking a favourite, fMRI equipment was measuring the activity occurring in the brain (McClure *et al.*, 2004).

When people did not know what they were tasting, so that preference was based solely on sensory information (the objective characteristics of the product), only the ventromedial prefrontal cortex areas of the brain were active, that area of the brain dealing with sensory evaluation (essentially sweetness in this case). But when there was brand knowledge, at least in the case of Coke, for regular drinkers of Coke the hippocampus, dorsolateral prefrontal cortex (DLPFC), and midbrain were also active. Both the hippocampus and DLPFC are known to be involved in modifying behaviour based upon emotion and affect. In fact, it has been suggested that DLPFC is necessary for employing affective information in biasing behaviour.

What this means is that when taste preferences are based solely upon sensory information, when people do not know what they are drinking, only that part of the brain that deals with sensory information is utilized. But when there is brand knowledge (at least in the case of Coke in this study), additional areas of the brain are activated, modifying the strictly objective evaluation. These additionally activated areas are those that deal with emotion and affect, and are seen to influence preference decisions. How people 'feel' about a brand does indeed bias their preference for it, leading to decisions based upon much more than the objective characteristics of a product.

Brand equity from the consumer's perspective may be summarized as follows: (1) awareness of a brand leads to (2) learning and the formation of attitudes about that brand, which will be influenced by emotional associations, which result in (3) preferences for that brand, building brand loyalty. Each of these components of brand equity from the consumer's perspective are discussed next.

KEY CONCEPT

Brand equity from a consumer perspective results from awareness of a brand leading to brand knowledge and a positive attitude towards the brand, resulting in brand loyalty.

Brand equity does not just happen, but is the result of consumer understanding and experience with a brand. It begins with becoming familiar with a brand, a 'feeling' about it. This provides the beginning of knowledge about it, and a tentative attitude toward it. As familiarity and experience with the brand grows, if it is positive, attitude toward the brand strengthens, resulting in a strong brand equity, which in its turn leads to brand loyalty.

Brand awareness

The first component to consider is awareness of the brand itself. It may seem obvious that people must be aware of a brand in order to prefer it, but its importance to brand equity goes beyond this. In a study among business managers, in which they were asked to identify those things they believe provide a substantial competitive advantage, name recognition was the third most frequently mentioned consideration. Strong brand awareness can indeed provide a significant competitive advantage. Think of centrally positioned brands that quite literally define a product category: Xerox, Kleenex, Hoover, or Levi's (Rossiter and Percy, 1997).

The power of strong brand awareness comes from the sense of familiarity it brings. As Schacter (2001) has pointed out, familiarity involves a primitive sense of knowing without the need for specific details. This is a real asset for a brand, because in terms of memory, when attention is divided someone is *much* less likely to recall specific details of an experience, but there is little or no effect upon a sense of familiarity. As a result, when shopping, someone is more likely to 'remember' familiar brands than, say, the details of a new brand, or to remember the details of an advert trying to persuade them to switch to another brand.

Aaker (1998) has suggested that in addition to a feeling of familiarity, strong brand awareness also suggests a 'presence, commitment, and substance for the brand'. He points out that this can be especially important for buyers of high-priced products, including expensive business-to-business purchases. In a sense, this is really the result of familiarity with the brand. If someone is aware of a brand, there must be a good reason for it. One is unlikely to be aware of 'minor' or less important brands.

In the end, brand awareness is essential for *intentional* brand purchases. If someone is buying a product and is not concerned about brands, for that person, in that product category there is no such thing as brand equity in the sense we are considering it. This is true even though the brand might be familiar to that person, and even considered a 'good' brand. If that knowledge and feeling do not inform the purchase decision, it is little use to the brand (Zajonc, 1968).

Brand awareness for a purchase may take two forms: recognition or recall (Rossiter and Percy, 1997). Recognition brand awareness reflects the ability to recognize a brand at the point-of-purchase in enough detail to facilitate purchase, something that is needed for most fmcgs. For other purchase or usage decisions, a brand name must be recalled from memory once the need for the product is recognized, such as needing to remember a specific restaurant to go to when deciding to eat out. But for either of these forms of brand awareness to facilitate purchase, the brand must be *salient*. That means it is associated in memory with the consumer's set of preferred brands to meet a particular need, and is likely to come to mind when the need for such a product occurs (Ehrenberg *et al.*, 1997). We shall be looking more closely at brand awareness in the next chapter, where we will be considering its role as a communication objective in marketing communication for building brands.

When brand awareness is considered as an asset in terms of brand equity, it is really being considered in terms of brand salience. The brand is familiar, and linked in memory with those situations where such a product would be needed; and the more salient the brand, the more likely it will be the chosen or preferred brand when a purchase decision is made. The importance of brand salience to a brand's success has been illustrated by an analysis of an 11-year tracking study of the effect advertising has on brand awareness, brand attitude, and market share for rental cars. What was found is that market share was primarily influenced by increasing brand salience (Miller and Berry, 1998).

Brand attitude

People who think about brands and what they mean to consumers often talk in terms of things like 'value', 'perceived quality', and 'image'. What this all comes down to is brand attitude, the associations in memory linked to the brand. In the end, this is what brand equity is all about. As already noted, with brand awareness comes the beginning of knowledge about the brand, learning occurs, and salience for the brand builds. Over time, associations are built and attitudes are formed. With a strong, positive brand attitude, key preference and loyalty for the brand results. The key here is a strong, positive brand attitude (Fig. 5.5). The nature of these brand associations that underlie brand attitude will be dealt with next.

Brand associations in memory must be strong, positive, and unique to the brand in order to build a brand attitude that leads to strong brand equity. These associations are a result of any and all communication about a brand to the consumer. This is usually thought about in terms of marketing communication (everything from the package, product placement, and event marketing to traditional advertising and promotion) and we will be dealing with this in the next chapter. However, it also includes such things as word-of-mouth and experience with the product, as well as more indirect means of communication such as a brand's distribution channels, its parent company, and the environment in which it is used. Every aspect of the relationship between a brand and the consumer contributes to learning that leads to the associations in memory that constitute brand attitude.

FIGURE 5.5 Brand awareness, salience, and attitude leading to brand loyalty

KEY CONCEPT

Brand attitude plays the most important role in building brand equity.

At the heart of brand equity is brand attitude. This is a function of all the things known about the brand weighted by how important these things are to someone. The more a brand is seen as strong in terms of those characteristics of the product that are seen as important, the more positive the consumer's attitude will be toward that brand: and the more positive the brand attitude, the stronger the perceived brand equity.

A short review of some descriptions of these brand associations found in the brand management literature will provide a useful starting point. Keller (2008) discussed brand associations under a broader heading of Brand Image, and sees them in terms of what he calls 'attributes', 'benefits', and 'attitudes'. Before going any further, it is important to understand that different authors often use the same terms to mean slightly different things. For example, we would argue that attitudes include an assessment of benefits, which in turn could include or be built upon attributes. It is important not to become too closely focused on terms, but to consider the concepts being discussed by various scholars in the field as they look at the idea of brand associations.

When Keller talks about attributes, he makes a distinction between what he calls product-related attributes and non-product-related attributes. Product-related attributes are the objective characteristics of a brand, such as specific ingredients (e.g. '100% certified organic') or qualities such that they may be specifically measured or discussed (e.g. 'Nationwide over 150 approved installers'). This is in fact how the current authors (Percy and Rosenbaum-Elliott, 2012) define attributes (in their role as a potential benefit). Keller's non-product-related attributes are described as things that do not directly affect product performance, such things as price, imagery, and feelings. He defines benefits as the personal value and meaning consumers attach to a brand's attributes, and are seen as either functional, symbolic, or experiential. Finally, attitudes are the consumer's overall evaluation of a brand, the typical consumer behaviour definition.

Franzen (1999) discusses what we are talking about as brand associations in terms of 'mental brand equity', one of his three components of brand equity (the others are behavioural brand equity, an area which is considered later; and financial-economic brand equity, a subject already discussed). Three of his characteristics of mental brand equity may be seen in terms of brand associations in memory: product meaning, which deals with a consumer's perceptions of the functional aspects of a product; symbolic meaning, or 'brand personality', which reflects values important to consumers and which differentiates the brand from competitors; and perceived quality.

Aaker (1998), like Keller (2008), talks about this in terms of brand associations, which he broadly defines as anything that is directly or indirectly linked to the brand in memory. He discusses product attributes and consumer brands and details such associations as: organizational, where the focus is more on corporate than product attributes; brand personality, where the brand-as-person is used as a metaphor; symbols to represent the brand; emotional benefits; and something he calls 'self-expressive' benefits, where the brand offers a way for personal expression by the consumer.

In considering these various ways of looking at brand association in memory, what conclusions might be drawn? Although these authors may appear to be describing brand associations in brand equity from different viewpoints, actually there is a reasonable similarity in their views. A careful review suggests that brand associations in memory are seen basically in terms of the objective and subjective characteristics of a product.

Brands have attributes that may be either product or non-product specific, but which are objective characteristics of the brand. This reflects a person's specific knowledge about a brand in memory, and may or may not be seen as a benefit. For example someone may know that a snack brand is 'sugar-free', or that a watch is 'Swiss-made', each are attributes of the product. These associations in memory form part of their knowledge about the brand. If 'sugar-free' or 'Swiss-made' is important to them when making a snack or watch brand choice, these attributes will be seen as a benefit and contribute to a positive brand attitude, which will help build a strong brand equity. If they are not important, that knowledge about the brand will not be seen as a benefit, and will not contribute to a positive brand attitude.

On the other hand, brands may also be seen in a number of subjective ways, reflecting perceptions of the brand's 'personality' or symbolic meaning. These too may or may not be considered benefits by the consumer, but they constitute a person's assumptions about a brand in memory. Both knowledge and assumptions are brought to bear when a person sees or thinks about a brand, during what neuropsychologists call *top-down processing*. On the other hand, a person could see a brand in the store, recognize it, and purchase it almost reflexively without 'thinking' (along the lines of what Howard (1977) long ago talked about as 'routinized response behaviour'). This would be analogous to what neuropsychologists call *bottom-up processing*, where no real 'thinking' or cognitive activity is involved. But when you think about a brand choice, all of someone's knowledge and assumptions about the brand will become involved. Usually, this has been summarized in what is considered brand attitude, so a choice decision can be made quickly and easily.

In effect, what people like Keller, Franzen, and Aaker are doing when they detail various brand associations is to try and describe how knowledge and assumptions about brands might be organized. While useful, it does not help in understanding *how* these brand associations are likely to be involved in actually making a brand choice. Another way of looking at this objective versus subjective distinction in brand associations is in terms of the functional versus emotional domains introduced in Chapter 1. Recall that the functional domain deals with basic consumer benefits that reflect a brand's ability to perform as promised. This requires positive associations in memory related to product attributes, as well as with product quality. When choices are not easy and more trust in a brand is needed, emotional associations become more important. While there are emotional associations with all memories, the involvement of emotional associations with particular memories increases when these memories deal with more socially or personally relevant experiences, those with more symbolic meanings.

How does this distinction help in understanding how brand associations influence brand choice decisions better than a simple objective versus subjective distinction? This important distinction between functional and emotional domains takes things one step further, because it better reflects how the mind deals with processing information when making brand decisions. In the early chapters of this book we looked at the emotional, social, and cultural meaning of brands, and how this reflects trust in a brand, and also helps transform how a person experiences life and projects social and cultural identities. All of this meaning is informed by non-declarative emotional memory (NDEM), which is located in the amygdala, out of consciousness.

What seems to happen is that when a person experiences something—a brand in this case—what is known about it (their knowledge and assumptions), is called into working memory *along with* any emotional associations with that experience. In the functional realm, brand choices are easy because of a simple trust in the brand. There are no emotional complications because the NDEM associations with that brand reflect a fundamental emotion of comfort. Someone sees a brand, 'knows' it is one they like, perhaps even remembers a benefit, and 'feels' comfortable with it.

In the emotional realm, a brand must do more, so more is involved. More will have gone into the formation of brand attitude, and potentially many NDEMs will be associated with various aspects of the brand in memory. And the more difficult the choice, the more involving, the more *emotional* associations are likely to be involved. The wider array of knowledge and assumptions stored in declarative memory (that part of memory that contains what we 'know we know', what we are conscious of), reflecting more complicated brand meaning, enter working memory when someone is confronted with a more difficult brand choice, along with NDEMs. A person imagines how they will *feel* if they choose a particular brand, what it might say about them, or perhaps simply that they need not be afraid of spending so much money on it. This process is illustrated in Fig. 5.6.

In summary then, the many different ways of looking at brand associations reflect the basic distinction between the objective and subjective characteristics of a product that go into building brand attitude. They form the foundation of one's knowledge and assumptions about brands, and are used in making brand evaluations. This is enough when dealing with easy decisions where only negative motivations are involved, the need to solve or avoid a simple problem, and where the role of emotion is relatively minor. But when brand choice involves positive motivations, where personal or social rewards are sought in using a product, or when there are serious consequences attending a bad brand choice decision, emotion is much more involved in making brand evaluations. Thinking about brand associations as reflecting objective versus subjective product characteristics, but within either

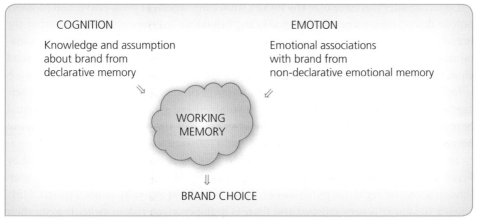

FIGURE 5.6 Interaction of cognition and emotion in making brand choices

a functional or emotional domain, provides a good way of understanding the role brand associations play in forming brand attitude, leading to a strong brand equity.

As a person learns about brands, over time a summary judgement is made about the brand. They like it, hate it, love it, or don't really care much about it. This judgement is the result of many things; in fact, all those things Keller, Franzen, Aaker, and others talk about, and much more. It reflects a person's knowledge and assumptions about a brand, and their emotional associations with it. This summary judgement is basically what we have been talking about as brand attitude. People do not start from scratch every time they evaluate a brand, recalling everything they have learned and experienced about the brand. Rather, they rely upon already formed attitudes; attitudes that reflect *trust* in the brand.

Why? Because it reflects a person's evaluations of a brand over time. For brand loyal consumers (considered in the next section) and for simple brand choice decisions, an over-all brand attitude is enough to make a decision. But for more involved choices in the emotional realm, other aspects of a brand's meaning will also be involved in working memory as a brand choice decision is made. But overall brand attitude will still *frame* the decision. Changing brand attitude is very difficult because of everything that goes into forming it in the first place; and in the end, this is why a favourable brand attitude is at the core of a strong brand equity.

Brand loyalty

A strong positive brand equity is also marked by strong loyalty to the brand. In effect, it is a *consequence* of the brand equity, just as was noted for financial value. The building of a strong positive brand attitude generally leads to a preference for the brand, and over time a loyalty towards it. Basically, brand loyal consumers have a reluctance to switch brands. As Franzen (1999) has put it, loyal brand users have a 'high degree of bonding with the brand and do not show much of an urge to switch'.

This 'bonding' he speaks of is a part of brand equity. But brand loyalty does not necessarily need to be a *function* of brand equity, even if it contributes to it. Brand loyalty may simply be out of habit; or it may be that the cost of switching to another brand is too high. Sometimes, it is simply not worth the effort. But when loyalty to a brand results from a genuine preference for it, it contributes to brand equity; and when it transcends rational preference (as seen, for example, in the cola taste test discussed earlier in the chapter), it becomes sustained by brand equity.

Let us consider this issue of brand loyalty from a management perspective, and consider how to determine whether or not loyal brand behaviour may be accounted as part of the brand's asset value. If brand loyalty is the result of habituation, it may or may not be a sustainable asset. Such purchases will usually fall into the functional realm because the brand choice is easy and there is general satisfaction with the product. The brand manager's job is to see that satisfaction is maintained, in terms of product performance as well as perception. To the extent that satisfaction is maintained and switching minimized, habitual brand purchase may be factored into the asset value of the brand, and hence a part of brand equity. But care must be taken to maintain satisfaction.

The role of perceived risk in switching when looking at brand loyalty is illustrated by Percy and Rosenbaum-Elliott (2012) in their Loyalty Model (Fig. 5.7). As shown, even though someone regularly purchases or uses a brand, their loyalty is not assured. Only when a consumer is very satisfied and there is high perceived risk in switching can their

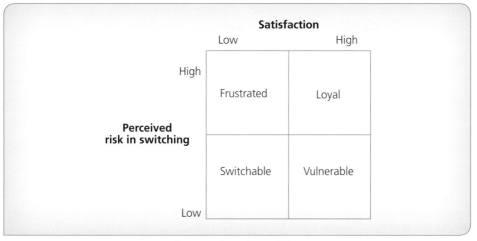

FIGURE 5.7 Percy and Rosenbaum-Elliott Brand Loyalty Model

Source: Percy and Rosenbaum-Elliott (2012)

loyalty be assured. Even someone very satisfied could be lured away if the barriers to switching are low.

This is especially true for low-involvement purchase decisions, as is the case with most fmcgs. Think about a snack brand you really like, and buy all the time. What if you learned about a new brand entering the market that was very similar to your favourite, and when shopping you saw a special display for the new brand? It is being offered at a special introductory price that was about half the price of your favourite brand. Would you be tempted to try it? There is almost no risk involved in buying. It is very inexpensive, and if you don't like it as well as your favourite, you have not lost very much.

What this example illustrates is that even very satisfied consumers may be vulnerable if the cost of switching is low. In this case, the brand manager for your favourite snack might want to run a promotion of some kind just prior to the introduction of the new brand to encourage loyal customers to 'stock up'. This is something called a *loading promotion*, and in effect takes people out of the market during the new brand's introduction, minimizing the likelihood of customers trying the new brand at its lower, introductory price.

Another model that takes into account the fact that brand loyalty involves more than just purchase behaviour is the so-called Conversion Model suggested by Hofmeyr (1990). It recognizes, as does the Percy and Rosenbaum-Elliott Loyalty Model, that it is the attitudinal component of brand loyalty that is the key to its role in a brand's equity. The Conversion Model looks at brand loyalty in terms of commitment to the brand in the case of users, and availability (i.e. openness to trying) among non-users (see Fig. 5.8). Users are seen as either 'secure' or 'vulnerable', and non-users are either open to possible trial or unavailable. Within the context of brand equity, secure users are a part of a brand's assets, but vulnerable users are unlikely to attach positive equity to the brand. Non-users open to a brand will have at least a positive brand attitude, even if not strong, and thus the potential for building brand equity. Those 'unavailable' are not likely to hold attitudes towards the brand that offer any potential for building brand equity.

In an interesting study using the Conversion Model to segment category users, people who are more committed to a brand reflecting a positive brand equity respond to

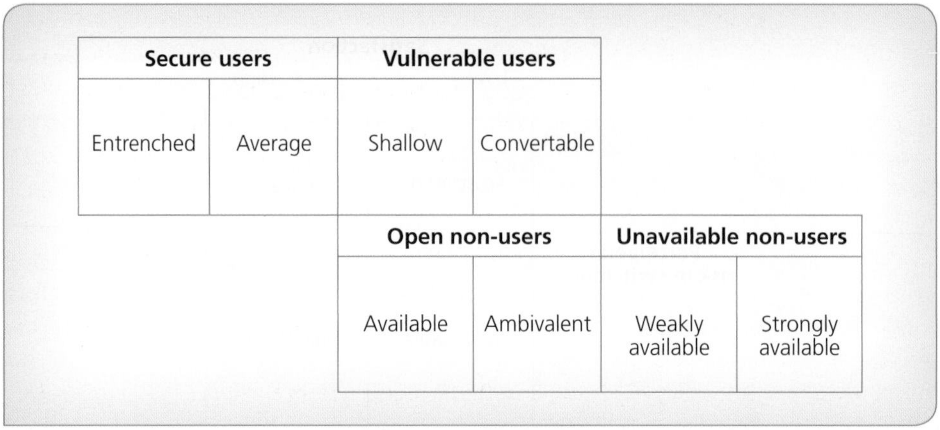

Secure users		Vulnerable users			
Entrenched	Average	Shallow	Convertable		

		Open non-users		Unavailable non-users	
		Available	Ambivalent	Weakly available	Strongly available

FIGURE 5.8 Hofmeyr Conversion Model for mature fmcg markets

advertising for the brand in a significantly more positive way. The results of the study are important for any product where the purchase decision is driven by positive motives, and in the emotional realm, where 'liking' advertising is critical to its effectiveness. It was found that those committed to a brand are two to three times more likely to 'like' a brand's advertising versus those classified as vulnerable. Additionally, non-users open to a brand are significantly more likely to find the brand's advertising 'likeable' than those unavailable (Rice and Bennett, 1998).

The management implications for building brand equity are clear. Among 'vulnerable' brand users, the task of building positive brand attitude will be difficult. Their general lack of commitment to the brand seems to lead to less interest in and 'liking' of marketing communication aimed at building positive brand attitude. This is certainly what might be expected from the results of neuropsychological studies. Without being able to communicate effectively with less committed consumers, it will be difficult to build a positive brand attitude, at least for those brand purchase decisions involving positive motivations within the emotional realm. And this, as already discussed, will make it unlikely that brand equity will develop.

This is another example of why it is so important to understand the *attitudes* of consumers, not simply whether they are regular purchasers of a brand. In this case, those not committed to a brand, even though they are users, will not perceive much equity in the brand, and will be less inclined to be positively influenced. This does not mean, of course, that it is impossible to build positive brand attitude and equity, and with it increased commitment to the brand, only that it will not be easy. Again the important thing is to realize that it is the brand equity that leads to brand loyalty; and just because someone regularly uses a brand does not mean that their behaviour is sustained by a positive brand equity.

When strong positive brand equity leads to brand loyalty it results in significant competitive advantages; and these advantages tend to last over time because of that loyalty. Perhaps the most important competitive advantage is that when a brand enjoys a large core of loyal consumers it significantly reduces marketing costs. Sustaining positive brand attitude is much easier, and less costly, than building brand attitude. Repeat purchase objectives are less costly than trial objectives. And, with strong brand loyalty there is less need for promotion.

Strong brand loyalty can also form a barrier to new brands entering a category. To be successful, a new competitor must gain substantial share from existing brands in the category. This requires getting current category users to consider switching (or at least trying) the new brand. The stronger a brand's equity, the higher their brand loyalty and the more difficult this will be. Aaker (1998) makes an interesting point within this context. He reminds the manager that for brand loyalty to actually be a barrier to new entry in a category, the potential competitor must fully understand that there is in fact high brand loyalty, not just behaviourally, but *attitudinally*. If there is a feeling that the brand loyalty is soft, that users are vulnerable in terms of satisfaction or commitment, it will not be seen as much of a barrier. Aaker suggests that a brand with substantial strong brand loyalty makes certain the market knows it.

Finally, strong brand loyalty leads to better leverage within the trade. When distributors and retailers know that a brand enjoys strong customer loyalty, they know the product will move out of their warehouses and off their shelves. They will also understand that there is a strong consumer demand for the brand, and that if they do not handle it, they will lose customers.

Corporate brand equity

It is important to remember that companies and corporations are also 'brands' with their own equity. As Keller (2000) has put it, corporate brand equity is the 'differential response by consumers, customers, employees, other firms, or any relevant constituency to the words, actions, communications, products, or services provided by an identified corporate brand entity'. In other words, corporate brand equity results from the associations in memory informed by how it is represented and communicated to its various audiences.

A corporate brand is a function of corporate meaning (Dowling, 2001), the relationship between corporate identity, corporate image, and corporate reputation. It is this relationship that provides the function for building corporate brand equity.

It may seem at first glance that corporate identity, image, and reputation must be pretty much the same thing, but they are not. Dowling (2001) has offered definitions that make the differences between them clear. He sees corporate identity as 'the symbols and nomenclature an organization uses to identify itself to people'. This would include such things as the McDonald's golden arches, the initials BP, the Nike 'swoosh', and Burger King's long-running slogan (for 40 years until changed in 2014) 'Have it your way'.

Corporate image is described as 'the global evaluation (comprised of a set of beliefs and feelings) a person has about an organization'. While everyone is unlikely to hold the same beliefs and feelings about a company, with consistent positioning and marketing communication over time a general consensus should emerge. For example, most people are likely to see the image of Volvo as concerned with making 'safe' automobiles.

Corporate reputation is described by Dowling as 'the attributed values (such as authenticity, honesty, responsibility, and integrity) evoked from the person's corporate image'. Again, there can certainly be differences in the assessment of values among different people, and this can be especially true for multinational companies because of the ways in which values can be culturally driven. We will have more to say about corporate reputation in Chapter 12.

Just as marketers understand that strong brand equity will add financial value to the company (as just discussed), more and more companies are building corporate brands as a strategic marketing tool in order to improve overall financial performance (Hatch and Schultz, 2001). And just as with any brand, this will require consistency in every message it delivers.

To be a successful corporate brand, the image projected to all of its various audiences must not only be an accurate representation of the company, but also be consistent with its own overall corporate strategy. Additionally, not only must a company efficiently communicate with its external audiences, the 'message' must be internalized by the organization, and communicated through all of its contacts with those outside of the organization. This means everyone for shareholders to consumers to vendors to the trade (Percy, 2014).

Just as with product brand equity, a corporate brand equity will result in its various audiences and stakeholders holding a more favourable attitude toward the company, which in its turn leads to more favourable responses to all of its corporate communication, beyond any purely objective reading of the message. A strong corporate brand equity will result from achieving awareness and salience for the company and the establishment of positive attitudes toward it. That means ensuring that beliefs about the company must be linked in memory to appropriate values held by its constituent audiences. This goes a step beyond what is needed for building positive brand equity for products, but the brand equity in the company's products will help reinforce corporate image, and as a result help inform corporate brand equity.

Still, corporate brand equity is *not* the same as the brand equity of the company's products, even when the corporate name is the brand name or used as in a source or endorser branding strategy (something we will be dealing with in Chapter 11). The brand equity of a company's products will of course be one of the building blocks of the corporate brand equity, but as we have seen, corporate meaning involves more than just perceptions of the company's products. We will be returning to the subject of corporate brands in Chapter 12.

The central role of brand equity in the management of brands

The reason so much attention has been given to the idea of brand equity here and in the next two chapters is that it is perhaps *the* central construct in the strategic management of brands. In earlier chapters we looked at the sociocultural meaning of brands, and much of this informs brand equity. In later chapters we will be dealing more directly with the managing of brands, among other things looking at the important difference between functional and symbolic brands. This too is tied to the idea of brand equity. Many of these relationships are shown in Figure 5.9.

At the top of the figure, a number of the considerations that go into making up a brand's 'image' are highlighted, and how this relates to functional and symbolic brands. Brand salience (i.e. how 'top-of-mind' a brand is when a need or desire for that type of product occurs) and ease of choice contribute to a brand's image, particularly functional brands. The importance and relevance of a brand, and the beliefs associated with it that tend to differentiate it from other brands, also contribute to a brand's image. These factors are especially important to functional brands, as we shall see in Chapter 8.

But they are also important to symbolic brands, especially in building trust. Here relevance will reflect a feeling that a brand is personally appropriate. Emotional considerations,

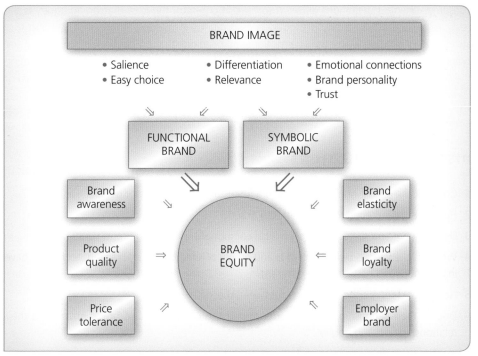

FIGURE 5.9 A synthetic model of brand equity

while an important part of the image for all brands, is especially important for symbolic brands. Much of this was covered in Chapter 2. A brand's image will effect management strategy for both functional and symbolic brands, and this will be a reflection of brand equity.

Many other aspects of a brand will also be reflected in a brand's equity. Brand awareness is critical to brand equity, and as we shall see in Chapter 7 may be used as an indicator of brand equity strength. Product quality will inform brand equity, as will price tolerance and elasticity. Brand loyalty, as we have discussed, is directly related to brand equity. Strong brands, brands with strong equity, can lead to what has become known as 'employer brands', where the fact that a brand has a strong positive equity helps attract and retain employees.

As this should make clear, brand equity is at the heart of understanding and managing brands, and Fig. 5.9 provides an overview of these indicators and consequences of brand equity that inform strategic brand management.

CHAPTER SUMMARY

In this chapter the rather amorphous idea of brand equity has been explored. We began by looking at how a name has the ability to provide value beyond the objective characteristics of an object, and noted that this concept is at the heart of brand equity. It was seen that there are many definitions of brand equity, all of which address this notion of 'added value', some in terms of financial considerations, but most from a consumer's perspective. These consumer-oriented definitions all seem to have in common the idea that brand equity is the result of awareness for a brand triggering associations in memory linked to it, leading to a strong brand attitude with positive emotional associations that go beyond merely 'liking' the brand. Many aspects of brands and their links to brand equity were introduced, illustrating the centrality of brand equity to effective strategic brand management, along with the idea of companies and corporations as 'brands'.

DISCUSSION QUESTIONS

1 Contrast the role of brand equity from a financial versus consumer perspective.

2 How does brand equity 'add value' to a brand?

3 Discuss what you see as the most critical component of a strong brand equity.

4 What do the various definitions of brand equity offered by Aaker, Franzen, and Keller have in common; and how are they different?

5 How important are the differences between these definitions?

6 Discuss the relationship between and among the components of brand image and their relationship to brand equity.

7 In what ways do companies and corporations function as 'brands'?

8 What is the difference between brand equity and corporate brand equity?

CASE STUDY

Evergood coffee

Norway is a country of few brands. One of the main exceptions to this rule is Evergood coffee, which can look back on 36 years of steadily rising popularity and market share, and always at a profit. In the course of these years there have been Cannes Lions and several Clio golds. Most important though: to be part of Norwegian marketing history.

• Over the past 32 years, Evergood Coffee has invested NOK 138 million in advertising, to create a revenue stream exceeding NOK 5 billion.

• In the past 5 years alone, the profit on this investment has been NOK 195 million, building a 'hidden value' of NOK 300 million in brand equity along the way.

• The brand is by far the most preferred in the market as a whole, but also amongst the customers of the two chains that never even carried the brand.

The Norwegian market for ground coffee

The Scandinavians are indeed heavy drinkers of coffee. The most common type of coffee by far is ground roast, constituting more than 90% of coffee consumed. With such a high consumption there should be no surprise that this market is hotly contested with several nationally distributed brands that all invest heavily in marketing and distribution. Approximately

34,000 tons of coffee are sold annually in Norway; 85% of this volume is sold through grocery stores.

In our case, Evergood is distributed in only half of the Norwegian grocery stores, the reason being that Joh. Johannson, the owner of the brand, has also been the majority shareholder in Norgesgruppen since 1991. Therefore, the three competing groups (Rema, ICA, and Coop) are reluctant to sell a brand that is owned by their biggest grocery competitor. Only the ICA group sells Evergood due to the strong preference that the brand enjoys, but it has raised the price since 1992, and as a result given it 'less favourable' placement in the shops to milk its popularity. Altogether Evergood has a market coverage of 57%.

The marketing strategy for Evergood

Right from the start it was decided that the strategy of being 'slightly more expensive because taste matters' should be the guiding star for all marketing actions. Evergood was never intended to be a big brand. Instead it was meant to be a small and profitable brand. This resulted in a brand with an unusual consistency—never discount—always the same strategy.

1. The product: The blend was a quality selection, including a small percentage of the most exclusive quality offered on the commodities exchange, the Kenya Blue Mountain quality. Extra care was taken so that the taste should not differ from season to season, or year to year (thus the name Evergood). This made it the first brand with a consistent product strategy.

2. The price: Evergood should be 'slightly more expensive'; it was never to be discounted. Even though consumers will find 'specials' on the marque, this is only because the trade has cut their margins to attract more customers. From the coffee house of Joh. Johannson the product has never been discounted! (UK readers should note that coupons are forbidden in Norway, so price reductions are given in store and available to everyone when offered.)

3. The distribution: Being the first to aim for a national brand, Evergood rapidly increased distribution to a point where it peaked at 60%. Owing to the integration of the retail trade over the past years it has fallen out of grace with major chains that would rather sell other brands or even own brands, so market coverage has taken a slight dip.

4. The promotion: This is what makes this case especially interesting: without coupons and with very limited use of other promotions, the Evergood brand has been the product of good old-fashioned mass communication such as commercials and print advertising. This combined with the fact that the mass communication has had a national reach, but only 62% market coverage, has created an ideal testing ground for a 'split run' situation to control the effect of the advertising.

In 1976, Evergood started below Friele—its main competitor—in preference but passed it after a couple of years, and has maintained a steady lead. It is an interesting fact that every time Evergood has faced stiffer competition, the consumer response has been new levels of preference, and as a result it has remained the most popular coffee brand, even amongst customers of chains that have never carried the brand.

The owners of Evergood believe in advertising and outspent their competitors up till 2002. It seems very likely that this is the main explanation for Evergood's remarkable ability to hold on to its preference in the population while being under attack from both Friele and three-quarters of the distribution. However, in the last year Friele has, for the first time, been the best-selling brand, probably due to increasing advertising spending and better market coverage.

What kind of values has the Evergood advertising created?

In addition to market share and profits, there has been a substantial build-up of 'hidden values' in brand equity for Evergood coffee. There are several ways to estimate brand equity. None of the methods can claim superiority, and the fact is that when a brand is up for sale one can usually apply several methods. The most common methods seem to be:

- *Estimated net value of the communications investment corrected for inflation*: This method is characterized by overestimating the value of young brands with heavy advertising investments. In Evergood's case it is the opposite that is true, since it has been advertised for more than 30 years. With this method the brand's value is estimated at NOK 300 million.

- *The conversion model*: This method is characterized by trying to convert a given budget to results in the form of awareness, trial, penetration, frequency, and market share. The calculations are done backwards from market share to awareness, that is: how much must you gain at every level to obtain a certain market share? To achieve results at Evergood's level, we can estimate the cost and thus the value at NOK 140 million. To this an insurance premium must be added in case one doesn't achieve sufficient distribution or fails the positioning. In total a sum of NOK 250 million seems realistic.[1] The insurance premium constitutes the brand's estimated result over three years.

- *Indirect value assessment*: This is more of an economist's method. One estimates the brand's contribution to the profits over the years the brand is expected to 'live' (normally restricted to 10 years). This is discounted via a cash flow analysis corrected for the risk in these years. The sum of the cash flow plus the estimated value of the brand at the end of the period will be the value of the brand. With this method we estimate the value of Evergood to be NOK 240 million.

- *The royalty method*: This method is based on estimating a royalty fee had the corporation leased the brand to a competitor for say a 10-year period. The royalty fee is mostly estimated from a percentage of turnover and is calculated for the period the leasing runs (normally 10 years). With this method we arrived at NOK 350 million for the value of Evergood.

From these estimates one could argue that the brand equity value of Evergood is close to NOK 300 million, which translates to £300 million since the UK has 16 times more inhabitants than Norway.

Conclusion

Brand equity is an estimation of the 'hidden value' in brands, and consists of two dimensions: the qualitative element of psychological values and the quantitative dimension consisting of economical values.

We think we have proved beyond reasonable doubt that the main influence in creating these values in this case has been the advertising since:

- Evergood has almost the same high preference amongst its loyal consumers as the consumers in chains that never stocked Evergood. Hence one cannot argue that this preference is a result of seeing the brand in store or experiencing it.

[1]The calculation is based on an investment requirement of NOK 40 mill per annum in three years to achieve 90% robust awareness, 60% trial and 30% preference-share.

- Evergood sustains its market growth even though it has suffered significantly in distribution and priority versus its main competitor Friele, due to its continuous investment in advertising.

Source: WARC, IPA, Effectiveness Awards 2004, Evergood Coffee—The Norwegian coffee that has been slightly more expensive for 36 years. Edited by Natalia Yannopoulou

DISCUSSION QUESTIONS

1 Critically evaluate the three brand equity approaches discussed in the case.

2 Would you characterize Evergood as a brand trusted by the consumers and why?

3 How could Evergood—the most preferred brand—become the best-selling coffee brand again?

4 How could Evergood capitalize on its brand equity in order to plan its future brand strategy?

FURTHER READING

- Lopo Rego, Matthew Billett, and Neil Morgan's article of 2009 'Consumer-based brand equity and firm risk', *Journal of Marketing*, 73 (6) offers an interesting discussion of how consumer-based brand equity can help inform a company's risk management strategy.

- In their 2010 article 'The sound of brands', *Journal of Marketing*, 74 (4), Jennifer Argo, Monica Popa, and Malcolm Smith discuss how the linguistic characteristics of brand names along with specific sound repetitions can affect brand evaluation.

- In Julie Macintosh's (2014) *Dethroning the King*, Hoboken, New Jersey: John Wily & Sons, she recounts the history of Anheuser-Busch and how the economic downturn lead to its collapse and hostile take-over by global brewing giant InBev in 2008, mirroring today's ongoing corporate troubles in many ways.

- Stephen Brown, Pierre McDonaugh, and Clifford J. Schultz, II (2013) in their article 'Titanic: consuming the myths and meanings of an ambiguous brand', *Journal of Consumer Research* Vol 40 (4), 595-614, talk about how ambiguity is an influential factor in why certain myths are meaningful for consumers, arguing that ambiguity in its multifaceted forms is integral to outstanding branding and consumer memory making.

REFERENCES

Aaker, D.A. (1991), *Managing Brand Equity*, New York: Free Press.

Aaker, D.A. (1998), *Strategic Market Management*, 5th edn, New York: John Wiley & Sons.

Aaker, D.A. and Keller, K. (1990), 'Extending brand equity: the impact of fit and multiple extensions on perceptions of the brand and future extensions', *MSI Working Paper*.

Biel, A.L. (1992), 'How brand image drives brand equity', *ARF Researching the Power of Brands Workshop*, 12–13 February.

Carney, S. and Esterl, M (2013), 'In Italy, sadder Budweiser: AB InBev switches to "Bud"', *Wall Street Journal*, 9 October, B-2.

Chay, R.F. (1990), 'Managing brand equity for a product consumers can't buy', *ARF Brand Equity Workshop*, 22–23 February.

Donald, M. (1991) *Origins of the Modern Mind: Three Stages in the Evolution of Culture and Cognition*, Cambridge, Mass.: Harvard University Press.

Dowling, G. (2001) *Creating Corporate Reputations*, Oxford: Oxford University Press.

Ehrenberg, A., Barnard, N., and Scriver, J. (1997), 'Differentiation salience', *Journal of Advertising Research*, November/December, 37, 7–14.

Farquhar, P. (1989), 'Managing brand equity', *Marketing Research*, September, 1, 24–33.

Franzen, G. (1999), *Brands and Advertising: How Advertising Effectiveness Influences Brand Equity*, Henley-on-Thames, UK: Admap Publications.

Hall, E.T. (1959), *The Silent Language*, New York: Doubleday & Co.

Hatch, M. J. and Schultz, M. (2001), 'Are the strategic stars aligned for your corporate brand?', *Harvard Business Review*, 129–34.

Hofmeyr, J. (1990), 'Conversion model—a new foundation for strategic planning in marketing', 3rd EMAC/ESOMAR Symposium, New Ways in Marketing Research, Athens.

Howard, J. A. (1977), *Consumer Behaviour: Application of Theory*, New York: McGraw-Hill.

John, D. and Loken, B. (1990), 'Diluting brand equity: the negative impact of brand extensions', *MSI Working Paper*.

Kapferer, J. N. (1998), *Strategic Brand Management*, 2nd edn, London: Kogan Page.

Keller, K. L. (2000), 'Building and managing corporate brand equity', in M. Schultz, M. J. Hatch, and M. H. Larsen (eds), *The Expressive Organization*, Oxford: Oxford University Press, 115–37.

Keller, K.L. (2008), *Strategic Brand Management* 3rd edn, Upper Saddle River, NJ: Prentice Hall.

Kemp, M. (2014), 'Connoisseurs and scientists both rely on ways of seeing', *The Art Newspaper*, 257, 49.

McClure, S. M., Li, J., Tomlin, D., Cypert, K. S., Montague, L. M., and Montague, P. R. (2004), 'Neural correlates of behavioural preference for culturally familiar drinks', *Neuron*, 44, 379–87.

McQueen, J. (1991), 'Leveraging the power of emotion in building brand equity', *ARF Brand Equity Workshop*, 5 February.

Miller, S. and Berry, L. (1998), 'Brand salience versus brand image: two theories of advertising effectiveness', *Journal of Advertising Research*, September/October, 38, 77–82.

Moran. W. T. (1991), 'The search for the golden fleece: actionable brand equity measurement', *ARF 3rd Annual Advertising and Promotion Workshop*, 5–6 February.

Pagano, J. (1990), 'Definition of brand equity: trademark, product, or both?', *ARF Brand Equity Workshop*, 22 February.

Percy, L. (2014), *Strategic Integrated Marketing Communication*, 2nd edn, Oxford: Routledge.

Percy, L. and Rosenbaum-Elliott, R. (2012), *Strategic Advertising Management*, 4th edn, Oxford: Oxford University Press.

Renfrew, C. (2007), *Prehistory, the Making of the Human Mind*, London: Weiderfield & Nicolson.

Rice, B. and Bennett, R. (1998), 'The relationship between brand usage and advertising tracking measurements: international findings', *Journal of Advertising Research*, May/June, 38, 58–66.

Rouser, L. (2014), 'InBev buys Czech brewery amid Budweiser name feud', *Wall Street Journal*, 3 July, B-2.

Rossiter, J. R. and Percy, L. (1997), *Advertising Communication and Promotion Management*, New York: McGraw-Hill.

Sattler, H. (1994), 'Der Wert von Marken', Research Paper No 341, Institut für Betriebswirtschaftslehre, Kiel University.

Schacter, D. L. (2001), *The Seven Sins of Memory*, New York: Houghton Mifflin.

White, L. A. (1949), *The Science of Culture: A Study of Man and Civilization*. New York: Grove.

Zajonc, R. B. (1968), 'Attitudinal effects of mere exposure', *Journal of Personality and Social Psychology Monographs*, 9, 2, part 2, 1–27.

Test your understanding of this chapter and explore the subject further using our Online Resource Centre. Visit the Online Resource Centre at http://www.oxfordtextbooks.co.uk/orc/elliott-percy3e/

121

6

Building Brands through Marketing Communication

Key Concepts

1 'Advertising' includes any message where the primary communication objective is brand awareness and brand attitude, *regardless* of the media used.

2 Effective positioning requires selecting the optimum benefit and correct benefit focus.

3 Benefit selection should be based upon importance to the target audience, perceived ability to deliver, and doing so uniquely or better than competitors.

4 Brand awareness will be either recognition or recall based, depending upon how the brand decision is made.

5 Involvement in purchase decisions is a function of risk, defined in either fiscal or psychological terms.

6 Brand purchase decisions will be driven by either negative motives, where a problem is to be solved or avoided, or positive motives, where a reward is sought from the product.

7 Both involvement and motivation are critical to communication strategy for building brand attitude.

8 Consideration of new media and other non-traditional media options for delivering a brand's message should be part of communication planning.

9 Digital media, especially social media, are providing more ways of directly targeting consumers.

Introduction

In the last chapter we saw that from a consumer's perspective brand equity follows from awareness of the brand, leading to learning something about it and the establishment of an attitude towards the brand, informed by emotional associations with that learning. When this is positive, it leads to loyalty to that brand. Establishing a strong positive brand equity is what is necessary for building strong brands, and this follows from effective marketing communication. In fact, it could be argued that without marketing communication, there would be no brand. With this statement we are taking a very broad view of marketing communication, but in essence we are saying that without some form of marketing communication it is unlikely that anyone will become aware of a brand, let alone learn anything about it.

When one thinks about brands and marketing communication, especially within a brand equity context, it is usually in terms of advertising. It is advertising, or perhaps more correctly advertising-like messages, that build awareness of a brand and contribute to a positive attitude toward the brand. This, over time, establishes brand equity.

> ## KEY CONCEPT
>
> **'Advertising' includes any message where the primary communication objective is brand awareness and brand attitude, *regardless* of the media used.**
>
> When most people think about advertising they are thinking about commercials on TV and adverts in magazines; or more and more annoying interruptions on the Internet or social media. But advertising is any message where the objective is to raise awareness of the brand and help build positive attitudes towards it. It does not matter how the message is delivered.

What do we mean by 'advertising-like' messages? Looking broadly at marketing communication, there are really only two basic types of messages: those that are meant to contribute to building long-term brand equity and those meant to stimulate immediate action. Advertising-like messages are the former, promotion messages the latter. In fact, this strategic distinction is embodied in the Latin root of the words advertising and promotion: *advertere*, to turn toward and *promovere*, to move ahead. This is why when talking about marketing communication in building brand meaning and equity we are almost always talking about 'advertising'; that is, messages meant to contribute to building and sustaining brand awareness and positive brand attitude, leading to a strong brand equity. Of course, managers do use marketing communication tactically with promotion, and the planning and strategic management of all this is what integrated marketing communication (IMC) is all about (Percy, 2014). And, as Prentice (1977) pointed out years ago, with something he called 'consumer franchise building' promotions, a promotion's message must also help build positive brand attitude, as well as contribute to long-term brand equity (Mela *et al.*, 1997). But in this chapter, we will only be considering advertising.

In this respect, it must be kept in mind that 'advertising' is *any message* where the primary objective is to build and sustain brand awareness and brand attitude, *regardless* of how that message is delivered. Managers must think more broadly than just traditional mass media. This is a *strategic* consideration, and the manager should be looking for any effective way to reinforce brand awareness and build positive brand attitude (i.e. to 'advertise'). This means potentially using anything from packaging, retail store atmosphere, trade shows, endorsements, even the side of delivery trucks, in addition to more traditional 'advertising' media such as television, radio, posters, magazines, and newspapers, along with digital media. For example, in 2013 when Pepsi began a concentrated effort to unify their 'look', they made changes to align it across all aspects of their marketing communication, from in-store marketing and coolers to trucks and packaging (Zmuda, 2013). All of these comprise what is often referred to as *contact points* (Donaghey and Williamson, 2003).

A manager's primary concern here must be with the long-term health of a brand, and it is within this context that we will be discussing marketing communication in this chapter. First we will be looking at the role of advertising-like messages in strategic brand management, how to develop effective brand positioning for marketing communication, and communication strategies for building brand awareness and positive brand attitude. We will then review several important options, beyond traditional advertising media, that are available to the manager for delivering a brand's message.

The nature of brands and marketing communication

The original meaning of the word 'brand' seems to derive from an Old Norse word *brandr*, which meant 'to burn' (Interbrand Group, 1992). Yet in the etymology of the word, this idea of branding as a 'permanent mark deliberately made with a hot iron' now takes second place to 'goods of particular name or trade mark' (*NSOED*, 1990). But does this really describe what is understood as a brand? The American Marketing Association describes a brand as a 'name, term, sign, symbol, or design, or a combination of them intended to identify the goods and services of one seller or group of sellers and differentiate them from those of competitors'.

The American Marketing Association (AMA) definition concerns the *reason* for a brand: to enable a person to identify one alternative from a competitor. All this is true, but a brand must be a *label* in the true sense of that word: something 'attached to an object to give information about it' (*NSOED*, 1990). The information about a brand in very large measure comes from its marketing communication, and as we have suggested it could be argued that without advertising there would be no brands. This is because in the main it is marketing communication in some form that raises awareness of a brand, and gives it 'meaning'. This meaning is informed by brand attitude and learning from marketing communication, which in its turn builds brand equity.

When thinking of brands, most people usually think of products they buy: Coke, Cadbury, Ford, Hoover, Persil, Mars. But just about anything can be 'branded'. Products, services, corporations, retail stores, cities, organizations, even individuals can be seen as 'brands'. Remember, a brand name is meant to embody information about something, information that represents an added value, differentiating it in a marked way from alternatives. A brand name is meant to trigger in memory positive associations with that brand. Politicians, hospitals, entertainers, football clubs, corporations, they all want their name, their *brand*, to mean something very specifically to their market. It is how they wish to be seen, and how they wish to be distinguished from competitive alternatives. Two strategic elements are essential to establishing and maintaining the desired meaning of a brand: an effective positioning and brand attitude strategy.

Positioning

Why do some people shop at 'better' stores when they can buy identical (brand name) products for much less at a discount store? Clearly, price is not the most important consideration in their shopping decisions. They are looking for something else, but how do they know where to find it? They rely upon their knowledge or experience of different retail stores to direct them to stores where they expect to find what they want. This *image* or understanding of the store in their mind is cued by or communicated by the store name, the *brand*. In marketing a retail store, one may want people to feel it always offers the lowest price, or the widest variety of merchandise, or the most enjoyable shopping experience; just as with any product, where a marketer is looking to differentiate or distinguish it from competitors. This is known as *positioning*, and it is the critical first step in developing marketing communication for a brand.

Before going on, an important distinction must be made. Brand positioning occurs at two levels. In the marketing plan, an overall positioning for the brand will be established. Is this a price brand or a luxury brand? Will it be marketed to a wide audience or a particular niche? Such positioning questions establish the target market for a brand. Once these general positioning parameters are established, a more defined positioning, designed to optimize particular benefits of the brand relative to competitors must be developed. It is this more refined positioning that is needed for a brand's marketing communication, and this is what we will be dealing with in this chapter.

Brand attitude

The idea of a brand as a label is really the key. A brand provides *information*, and that information comes from marketing communication. Think about a brand you know. What comes to mind when you think about it? No doubt a great deal more than the fact that it is a particular type of product. Perhaps you were thinking about how much you like it, that it is well known, or that it is 'one of the best'. All these thoughts reflect brand attitude. The attitude you hold towards a brand reflects everything you know about a particular product and what it means to you. It provides a convenient summary of your feelings, knowledge, and experience with the brand as we discussed in the last chapter. It means you do not need to spend a great deal of time 'researching' a product each time you are considering a purchase. Your evaluation of the product is immediately reconstructed from memory, cued by the brand name. In many ways, building and ensuring a continuing positive brand attitude is what strategic brand management is all about, and this is largely accomplished with advertising or some other form of marketing communication.

The effect of a positive brand attitude leads to *brand equity*, as we saw in the last chapter, and this brand equity represents an *added value* to a product in the consumer's mind, enhancing the overall value of that product well beyond its merely functional purpose. In trying to understand what the relationship between a brand and marketing communication is all about, it will pay to briefly consider a few questions. Think about chocolate for a minute. Basically, chocolate is chocolate. Or is it? Are some *brands* better than others? Why? What about washing powder? They all get the job done, and use the same basic ingredients. Or do you think some do a better job than others? What about toothpaste, or vodka, or underwear? Where do the differences among brands in these product categories come from? How much of the difference is 'real' versus perceived? Why do you prefer one brand over another, especially if, when looked at with a coldly objective eye, there is very little, if any, actual difference in the products? Answers to these questions reflect brand attitude built through marketing communication.

This underscores that to a large extent a brand is not a tangible thing at all, but rather the sum of what someone knows, thinks, and feels about a particular product. In a very real sense, brands only exist in the minds of consumers, but that does not make them any less real. It is the job of a brand manager to effectively manage how consumers see their brand versus competitive alternatives, and they do this with marketing communication.

Marketing communications strategy

There is a great deal involved in the development and execution of a strategic marketing communication plan. Using the overall marketing plan as a base, there are five essential steps: identifying the target audience; gaining an understanding of how that target audience goes about making decisions in the category (important for identifying the level of involvement in the decision and the motivation driving it that is critical for brand attitude strategy, as we shall see); establishing the positioning for the brand within the communication; setting the communication objectives; and setting media strategy (Percy and Rosenbaum-Elliott, 2012). For our purposes here, we will only be dealing with positioning and the two communication objectives of brand awareness and brand attitude because they are at the heart of establishing and maintaining brand meaning, and building a strong brand equity.

Positioning brands in communication

The idea of 'brand positioning' can mean many things. It could refer to where a brand is seen in a category relative to its competitors; it could refer to the benefits or 'images' associated with a brand. Kotler has defined it in terms of enabling a brand to occupy a 'distinct and valued place' in the mind of the target consumer (Kotler, 2003). All these meanings are important and must be considered when thinking about how to specifically position a brand when talking about it in advertising and other marketing communications. This is usually summarized in a positioning statement that addresses the benefits a brand offers a specific target audience in order to satisfy a particular need.

To begin, we need to understand two basic types of positioning: central versus differentiated positioning. A *centrally positioned* brand must deliver all the main benefits generally associated with the product category. This means that a centrally positioned brand may be described as the 'best brand in the category' and it would be believable because people see it as offering all the main benefits they are looking for in that type of product. Centrally positioned brands are generally category leaders, and they do not need to continually list their benefits. For example, a category leader might simply position itself as 'the best'. Of course, people must believe this. A central positioning can also work if a brand is seen as doing as good a job as the category leader, especially if it is lower priced.

All other brands should adopt a *differential* positioning, where one looks for an important benefit that consumers believe the brand offers, and does a better job than other brands. This is where the correct positioning strategy is so important, and that will be addressed in the rest of this section.

Brand positioning may be thought of as a 'supercommunication' effect that tells the potential customer what the brand is, who it is for, and what it offers. This reflects the relationship between brand positioning and the two core communication effects of brand awareness and brand attitude, which are discussed later in the chapter. Because brand awareness and brand attitude are always objectives for a brand's marketing communication, they provide the foundation for a general model of brand positioning (Fig. 6.1). In this general model, two questions are asked? What is it, and what does it offer? The answer to the first question, 'what is it?' refers to the link we want to establish in memory between a brand and the need, and what brand awareness is all about. When the need for a product occurs, we want our brand to come to mind. The answer to the question, 'what does it offer?' reflects the link we want to establish in memory between a brand and its primary benefit. As we shall see below, effective positioning requires selecting a benefit for the brand that will optimize the likelihood of building a strong, positive brand attitude.

Strong brand awareness (for almost any brand) must be generated and sustained with marketing communication. It is marketing communication, and advertising in particular, that builds and maintains *brand salience*. It is not enough for a brand to be recognized. If it is to be successful, a brand must occupy a 'salient' position within the target audience's consideration set. In fact, the strength of a brand's salience is one indicator of the brand's equity. (A useful measure of this is the ratio of top-of-mind recall to total recall among competitive brands in a category, which will be discussed in Chapter 7.)

The target audience for a brand should *immediately* understand that the advertising is talking to them. A brand must be positioned in its marketing communication in such a way that when the need for such a product occurs, that brand comes to mind. Then, the brand must be linked to a benefit that provides a motivating reason to consider it (the global benefit of 'best' in the case of a centrally positioned brand). It is this link between

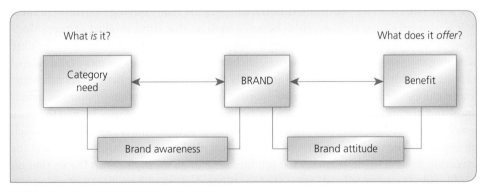

FIGURE 6.1 General model of brand positioning

the brand and benefit that lies at the root of building positive brand attitude, which in its turn builds positive brand equity.

> ## KEY CONCEPT
>
> ### Effective positioning requires selecting the optimum benefit and correct benefit focus.
>
> While the marketing plan will have positioned a brand generally, the positioning must be fine-tuned for its marketing communication. A benefit must be selected that will position the brand more favourably in the target's mind compared with the competition. And, it is important to talk about the benefit in a way that is consistent with the motivation that drives brand choice in that category.

Benefits and positioning

Benefits play a central role in effective positioning for marketing communication. But as already suggested, benefits are related to brand attitude, and brand attitude is what drives purchase motive. 'I love Cadbury' is an *attitude* about Cadbury that connects the brand in the consumer's mind with a likely reason to buy: sensory gratification. Where does this brand attitude come from? It is the result of one or more beliefs about the *specific benefits* that Cadbury is seen to offer. Effective communication strategy requires an understanding of what that belief structure is, and how it builds brand attitude. One might think of this as an overall summary judgement about a brand, and it follows the most widely used model of attitude, the expectancy-value model, which we will discuss below in the section on benefit selection.

Within the overall positioning that results from this understanding of how benefits and their importance build brand attitude, the manager must determine what the benefit emphasis and focus should be, which we take up in the section 'Benefit Focus'. But it is important first to remember that purchase motive is really the *underlying* basis of why a benefit is seen as important. Purchase motives are the fundamental 'energizers' of buyer behaviour. As a result, an effective positioning must reflect the correct motive, the one associated with why consumers in the category are *really* buying *particular* brands.

It is also important to distinguish between motives that drive product category decisions rather than brand decisions. People may buy lower calorie foods because they are watching their weight (a negative motive), but buy particular brands for more taste-related reasons (a positive motive). This is an absolutely critical distinction. Benefits such as being low in calories or fat relate to negative motives like problem-solution or problem-avoidance, and are unlikely to drive *specific brand* purchases. Someone may be looking for a lower calorie product, but probably *not* at the expense of taste. The reason that this is such an important point is that positive motives suggest marketing communication where the execution itself actually becomes the product benefit, as we shall see in the section on brand attitude strategies later in this chapter. When dealing with positive motives a truly unique execution is required where the brand owns the 'feeling' created by the advertising for the brand. On the other hand, when dealing with negative motives, the benefit is in the information provided.

Benefit selection

The benefits that a brand emphasizes in marketing communication should be selected according to three major considerations: importance, delivery, and uniqueness (Percy and Rosenbaum-Elliott, 2012). *Importance* refers to the relevance of the benefit to the underlying motivation. A benefit assumes importance *only if* it is instrumental in helping meet the consumer's purchase motivation. *Delivery* refers to a brand's perceived ability to provide the benefit. *Uniqueness* refers to a brand's perceived ability to deliver on the benefit relatively better than other brands. As Boulding *et al.* (1994) have pointed out, this uniqueness must be seen in the message about the benefit. What one is looking for are one or two benefits, relevant to the underlying motive, that can produce a perceived difference between alternative brands. These benefits should then be emphasized in a brand's marketing communication.

A note in passing. We are talking about *perceived* delivery and uniqueness. Just because a brand may not now be thought to provide benefits that could optimize purchase against important motives does not mean this perception cannot be created (unless, of course, it stretches the consumer's understanding of the brand, which is one reason why it is necessary to fully understand current brand attitude).

How can this idea of importance, delivery, and uniqueness be used to actually come up with the best benefits to use in a brand's positioning? One arrives at an optimum benefit selection by utilizing the assumptions of the expectancy-value model of attitude (Fishbein and Ajzen, 1975). The model assumes that a person's attitude towards something (A_o) is the sum of everything they know about it (b_i) weighted by how important each of those things are to them (a_i). The connection with the three benefit selection considerations is implied by the a_i and b_i components of the model. The importance of a benefit in brand selection is represented by a_i, and the belief that a particular brand can deliver the benefit is represented by b_i. Mathematically, this is expressed as:

$$A_o = \sum_{i=1}^{n} a_i b_i$$

Where A_o = attitude towards an object
a_i = importance of belief, and
b_i = belief about the object

An example here should help us see how this model works in terms of positioning. Suppose someone was looking to buy a new car, perhaps after receiving a promotion with a big increase in salary. Some of the things they might be considering in making a choice are: safety, value, mileage, power, stylishness, exciting envy. Obviously, this does not represent everything you might consider, but it will serve for our example. In order to determine which benefit (or benefits) is likely to be driving their consideration of a new car, one would need to know how important each of these considerations is to them, and whether or not they feel a particular automobile delivers that benefit.

Look at Table 6.1. Here is a hypothetical example of how the market might see Volvo versus BMW in terms of the six potential benefits we are considering. The importance weights represent how important the market considers each characteristic when making

TABLE 6.1 Comparative expectancy-value model of attitude for Volvo versus BMW

	Importance weight (a_i)	Beliefs (b_i)	
		Volvo	BMW
Safe	3	3	1
Value	1	1	0
Mileage	0	1	0
Stylish	3	0	3
Powerful	1	1	1
Exciting envy	1	0	3
$A_o = \sum_{i=1}^{n} a_i b_i$		11	16

a new car choice: if it is considered essential, it is weighted a 3; a 1 if considered desirable, but not essential; and if it is important, but not as important as the other characteristics, it receives a weight of 0. (This is not an arbitrary weighting scheme, but reflects relative importance weights.) The beliefs that Volvo or BMW deliver on the potential benefits are represented as: definitely deliver rates a 3, does an acceptable job receives a value of 1, and if it is not seen to deliver the benefit, a 0.

Looking at the summary attitude scores, Volvo is an 11 and BMW a 16. So what do these scores mean? According to the expectancy-value model, multiplying the importance weight by the belief score for each potential benefit, and adding them up, provides a sense

BMW © Boykov / Shutterstock.com

Volvo © Steve Lagreca / Shutterstock.com

of the *relative* strength of attitudes towards Volvo versus BMW. What these scores tell us is that people hold a more favourable attitude towards BMW than towards Volvo. Looking at why, the key difference is driven by perceptions of 'style'.

The two most important benefits (remember this is only a hypothetical example) are 'safety' and 'style'. Volvo definitely delivers on safety, while BMW is seen as doing an acceptable job. But in terms of 'style', BMW definitely delivers while Volvo doesn't at all. If you were the brand manager for Volvo, what would you do? The best course would be to try and change this perception. If people could be persuaded that Volvo did even an acceptable job in terms of 'style', overall attitudes would increase to a much more competitive level with BMW (14 versus BMW's 16 compared with the current 11 versus 16).

This example should illustrate how the idea of finding important benefits, related to the underlying motives driving choice, that the brand can deliver, is tied directly to people's attitudes towards the brand. That is why this is so important to positioning. One is looking for the one or two benefits most likely to positively affect brand attitude. The idea of uniqueness is related to trying to come up with benefits that the brand can be seen as delivering *better* than other brands. In this example, Volvo uniquely delivers 'safe' while BMW uniquely delivers on 'style' and 'exciting envy'. Because Volvo's overall attitude is lower than BMW's (again, in this example, not necessarily in the 'real world'), it must position itself against BMW's strength in order to find parity because of the importance of 'style' to people, while *maintaining* its unique position in terms of 'safe'.

Finding the best benefits to emphasize in positioning a brand is critical to its success, and using something like the expectancy-value model offers a powerful tool for identifying such benefits in terms of the three important criteria: importance, delivery, uniqueness. This can be done by doing research among the target audience to identify those things that are important in making choices, and how competitive alternatives rate in terms of delivering on them. With the results of the research in hand, it will be possible to evaluate potential benefits for emphasis in a brand's communication positioning in terms of:

- building or reinforcing a unique position in terms of important benefits;
- taking advantage of a competitor's weakness on an important benefit;
- emphasizing important benefits the brand delivers better than its major competitors;
- increasing the importance of a benefit the brand delivers better than its competitors (if it is not already considered 'essential');
- minimizing the importance of benefits the brand does not deliver as well as its competitors.

KEY CONCEPT

Benefit selection should be based upon importance to the target audience, perceived ability to deliver it, and doing so uniquely or better than the competition.

In selecting the brand benefit to use in marketing communication the manager is looking for something the target sees as essential, or at least desirable, in a product like it. The target audience must also believe that the brand can deliver the benefit, or has the potential to, and that it can do it better than other brands.

Benefit focus

The overall positioning of a brand basically chooses a location for the brand in the consumer's mind. The benefit selection analysis helps decide which benefit(s) to emphasize. After that, the manager must decide how to focus upon the benefit selected in the execution of marketing communications.

Up to now the term 'benefit' has been used in a rather general way. We have considered a benefit as any potential positive or negative reinforcer for a brand, in line with our definition of brand attitude as representing the overall delivery on the underlying motivation. It is important to remember that motivation is really the *underlying basis* of the benefits associated with a brand. Motivation is, after all, the fundamental 'energizer' of buyer behaviour. These same motives also energize the usage of products. A correct answer to the question of why buyers in the category are *really* buying particular *brands* reflects this underlying motivation. Again, this is why it is so important to explore this issue in qualitative research, which we will be looking at in the next chapter. Unfortunately, most benefits tend to be motivationally ambiguous.

As we discussed earlier, it is important to address the motivation underlying the brand decision in marketing communication, not the category decision. They can be different as we saw. Looking at other examples, people may buy casual footwear because it is comfortable (a negative motive), but buy particular brands for more 'style' related reasons (a positive motive). Benefits like comfort or low price relate to negative motives, and would not resonate with someone choosing a brand for style. As a result, they are less relevant to brand equity. Yes, someone may be looking for a good price in the category, but *probably not at* the expense of 'style'. You can't 'prove' you have a more 'stylish' or popular shoe, but you can make people *believe* you do.

Now we will consider benefits in more detail, distinguishing between attributes, benefits as subjective characteristics, and as emotions (a distinction made by Percy and Rosenbaum-Elliott, 2012). Thinking about the underlying motive as 'why the consumer wants a brand', benefits may be expressed in terms of:

- *attributes*, objective components of the product;
- *characteristics*, the subjective claims made about the product; or
- *emotions*, the feelings associated with the product.

A brand, for example, may offer attributes that the consumer may or may not think of as a benefit. Subjective claims in their turn may have various emotional consequences or antecedents, depending upon the underlying motive.

All marketing communication presents or implies a 'benefit' as either an attribute, subjective characteristic, or emotion as defined above. The key to *effective* communication is using the appropriate benefit *focus* (Rossiter and Percy, 2000). At this point it must seem that things are overly complicated, but this really is a powerful way of 'fine-tuning' a positioning, and not nearly as confusing as it may appear.

Throughout this discussion of positioning, mention has been made of the importance of the underlying motives that are associated with why people make particular choices. A brand's marketing communication, to be effective, must be consistent with this underlying motive. This will be dealt with more in the next section when we look at brand attitude strategies. But to understand the importance of getting the benefit focus right, it is necessary to relate it to whether a decision is positively or negatively motivated. When motives are positive, a brand's advertising and other marketing communication must address the target audience's 'feelings' in some way: for example 'I want to feel sexy', or 'I want to really impress her'. On the other hand, when motives are negative, information of some kind must be offered in order to address a problem: for example 'How can I get these stains out?', or 'What's the best investment for retirement?'

A brand's positioning, as presented in its marketing communication, must reflect this fundamental distinction between positive and negative motivations. The way this is done is through the benefit *focus*. When the motive is positive, the benefit focus should bear the *emotional consequences* of the benefit, and when the motive is negative, the benefit focus should be *directly* on the benefit. How is this done?

When dealing with a positive motivation, the focus should either be on an *emotional* benefit alone or be on the *emotion* that results from a *subjective characteristic of the benefit*. Suppose you are a brand manager at Mars and you are trying to reposition Bounty bars. You could focus entirely on an emotional benefit like 'Pure Pleasure', or use a subjective characteristic like 'Taste of the Tropics' to support an emotion, such as: 'With Bounty's taste of the tropics you will experience pure pleasure.' We are *not* suggesting this would actually be the creative used (we wisely leave that sort of thing to creative experts), but *strategically* this line illustrates how for the positive motive driving candy bar brand choice (sensory gratification) one can focus on either an emotional benefit alone or an emotional benefit resulting from a subjective characteristic of a brand.

On the other hand, when dealing with a negative motivation, the focus should generally be on either an *attribute* of the brand in support of a *subjective characteristic of the brand*, or a *negative emotion* that is resolved or eliminated because of a subjective characteristic attributed to the brand. The brand manager for Anthisan Plus sting relief spray would be dealing with a negative problem-solution motive. One benefit focus option would be to utilize an attribute of the product like 'anaesthetic' to support a subjective characteristic like 'fast relief': 'Our anaesthetic action means fast relief.' Another option would be to resolve a negative emotion such as *annoyance* at how long it takes for relief after applying most sting relief products with the *fast relief* of Anthisan Plus: 'No more annoying wait for relief from insect bites with the fast relief of Anthisan Plus.' Again, these are *strategic*, not creative examples, but they should illustrate how to focus on the benefit when dealing with negative motivations.

Of course, how you creatively execute the benefit focus in the advert is critical. One way of looking at this, especially when dealing with negative motivations, is something that has been referred to as 'framing'. According to Aaker (2013), framing defines a subcategory (or possibly a category) and shapes how the brand choice is discussed, providing a perspective and vocabulary. Supporting metaphors (for example) and the specific words used are key to framing. For example, it has been found that benefits expressed positively have more impact than if they are expressed negatively. It is better to say '75% lean' (positive) than (negative) 'only 25% fat' (Levin and Gaeth, 1988). The benefit is the same, the framing is different.

Which benefit focus to use within the options available for a positive or negative motivation will depend upon the specific benefit structure involved, and what is known about the strength of the various aspects of the potential benefit in positively effecting brand choice. This, of course, is addressed during the benefit selection process.

Positioning statement

We have looked at the important relationship between the brand and why people need it, the key to effective brand awareness. We have discussed the need to establish a link between the brand and its benefit, providing a motivating reason to consider the brand. We have seen how to optimize benefit selection by looking at its importance to the target audience, how well the brand is seen to deliver the benefit and where it can do it uniquely, and we have learned how to focus on that benefit in the brand's marketing communication. These steps are summarized in Table 6.2. Now the manager is ready to write a positioning statement.

In its simplest form, a positioning statement follows a format similar to: [brand name] is the brand for (target audience) that satisfies (category need) by offering (benefit). This may be refined somewhat as follows:

TABLE 6.2 Steps for positioning a brand in marketing communications

Step 1:	Relate the brand to a category need for effective brand awareness.
Step 2:	Relate the brand to an overall benefit to build positive brand attitude.
Step 3:	Select a specific benefit in terms of its importance, delivery, and uniqueness.
Step 4:	Correctly focus upon the benefit relative to the appropriate motivation driving behaviour in the category.

For the target audience, the brand

satisfies why people need it;

by providing a motivating reason to consider it;

emphasizing in its advertising an optimum benefit;

with a focus consistent with the motivation driving behaviour in the category.

Returning to the hypothetical example for repositioning Volvo discussed earlier, a positioning statement might read as follows: 'For people looking for an upmarket automobile, Volvo provides a sense of pride in ownership and its advertising should emphasize "style" as a subjective characteristic supporting an emotion benefit focus.' A more detailed discussion of the positioning statement may be found in Rossiter and Bellman (2005).

Now it is time to look at how to develop the best marketing communication strategy to deliver a brand's positioning.

Brand communication strategy

We have seen how a brand is a 'label' for something that helps someone identify a particular product, and is associated in memory with what is known and felt about it. That knowledge and those feelings help define a brand's 'equity', which is built and nurtured by how it is presented in marketing communication, how it is *positioned*. We have also seen that how a brand is positioned in its advertising and other marketing communication relates directly to the two universal communication objectives, brand awareness and brand attitude.

Positioning establishes the link in the consumer's mind between the brand and category need, and why the consumer wants the product. When a need for the product occurs, managers want their brand to come to mind. This is what brand awareness is all about. But how can a company ensure it is their brand that comes to mind and not a competitor's? Positioning also establishes the link in memory between a brand and what it offers, its benefit(s). But how can this be done? Answering these two questions is what brand communication strategy is all about.

Brand awareness strategy

Brand awareness and its critical link to brand equity was discussed in the last chapter, especially its contribution to a sense of brand familiarity. When someone goes shopping, they are likely to buy a brand with which they are familiar. But how did they settle on that particular brand? Did they see it on the shelf, or did they specifically ask for it? Or, did they go to the store with that brand in mind? Were they also familiar with other brands that they did not buy? How familiar? How many? A number of very important principles about brand awareness are suggested by these questions.

Consider these last questions for a moment, the ones dealing with brand familiarity. If someone is to name all the brands of pain relievers they can think of, how many are likely to come immediately to mind? Most people will think of one or two, possibly three, but not more. Yet as they consider the questions, additional brands are likely to come to mind. This difference between what is immediately thought of and those that come to mind later reflects something called *salience*. Brands that immediately come to mind are said to be

TABLE 6.3 Brand awareness strategy

Recognition brand awareness	When the purchase decision is made at the point of purchase, where the need for the product is stimulated by seeing the brand.
Recall brand awareness	When the brand name must be remembered (or recalled) once the need for the product occurs.

salient. People are generally aware of a lot more brands than are salient at any one time. A company really doesn't care that much if someone knows about their brand if it is not salient. For a brand to be purchased, almost always it must be one that comes to mind immediately. This is why getting the link between the brand and the category need correct in positioning is so important, and forms the basis for brand awareness strategy in marketing communication. It is this link that establishes salience for the brand in memory.

The other questions posed above reflect the ways brand awareness works, depending upon how someone actually makes a purchase in a brand's category, that were introduced in the last chapter. In many situations (almost all fmcg), people choose a brand after it is 'recognized' at the point of purchase. In other situations, they must 'recall' the brand they want in order to ask for it. And in yet other situations, they may think about wanting a particular brand before shopping, then be reminded of it when it is recognized in the store; or recall it when they get to the store so they can ask for it. These situations define the two fundamental types of brand awareness strategy: recognition and recall (Table 6.3).

Recognition brand awareness

If you stop to think about it, people spend very little time thinking about most of the things they buy: toothpaste, snacks, detergent, pain relievers, soft drinks, washing powder. These are all products purchased as a result of something John Howard (the father of the study of consumer behaviour) called *routinized response behaviour* (Howard, 1977). Someone sees the product in a store and decides they want it or are reminded that they need it.

When the purchase decision for a brand is made like this, the appropriate brand awareness communication objective is *recognition* brand awareness. Basically, this means visual iconic learning (Rossiter and Percy, 1988). In such cases a brand's advertising must present the brand as it will be seen at the point of purchase. In most cases this means it will be necessary to clearly feature the package in all advertising for the brand. It also means that when recognition is the brand awareness communication objective, radio should not be used in the media mix since obviously the package cannot be 'seen' as it will appear in the store. An exception to this rule would be if recognition of the brand occurred from *hearing* the brand name. This would be the case with such things as insurance or financial services companies, or in fact any product that is marketed via telemarketing. When called on the telephone it would be necessary for you to recognize the brand name if you were to seriously give it any consideration.

Recall brand awareness

While most of the things bought in stores occasion recognition brand awareness, there are many situations where the consumer must remember the brand name in order to ask for the product. For example, when a waitress in a restaurant asks what kind of beer a customer would like, they must recall the brand they want from memory. In fact, before they arrived at the restaurant they had to recall the restaurant name from memory. They decided they wanted to eat out, and considered what they were in the mood for (category need). That need was associated with or linked in memory to a salient set of restaurants, and they picked one from that 'considered set'. It is very unlikely they decided to go out to eat, then drove around until they recognized a restaurant where they would like to eat.

In situations like this where someone must pull the brand name from memory in order to make the purchase (or utilize the service), *recall* brand awareness is the appropriate brand awareness communication objective. This depends upon verbal paired-associated learning (Lee and Ang, 2003). When recall is the brand awareness communication objective, advertising for the brand should repeat the brand name as often as practical, but *always* linked to the category need. Repetition is important because associative learning is more difficult in a cluttered environment (Kent and Allen, 1993). In fact, the association should be need first, then brand. The advertising sets up the need, then provides the brand to satisfy the need. This is what helps establish the appropriate links in memory between the need and the brand so that when the need occurs in 'real life', the brand will come to mind.

This linkage is critical if the brand is to be successful. Unfortunately, many brand names in and of themselves do little to help consumers associate the name with the category need. As a result, brand names are subject to what neuropsychologists call 'blocking', that all-too-familiar experience of recognizing someone but not being able to remember their name (cf. Schacter, 2001). The information is in memory, and in fact retrieval cues may even be in place that would be expected to trigger recall, but the name remains tantalizingly out of reach when needed. The reason people often have trouble remembering someone's name is that names are difficult to retrieve from memory because they tend to be isolated from conceptual knowledge. After all, what *is* a Rosenbaum-Elliott or a Percy or a Pervan? Without a strong association in memory with something specific that is linked to the effort to remember a name, it will be hard to recall.

Just like proper names, brand names may be 'blocked', especially if they are not well integrated with a specific category need. There must be immediate associations in memory between the need and brand if it is to be recalled when that need occurs, and it is advertising's job to build and sustain that association. Another potential problem, if the links in memory are not strong, is that competitive brands with stronger associations will more likely be recalled, blocking recall of our brand. This is why it is so important to create a *unique* identity for a brand in its advertising and other marketing communication in order to avoid potential confusion in memory with other brands. This is especially true when a brand is not the market leader.

Brand recognition and recall

What if the manager is not sure if the purchase decision is driven by recognition or recall? Or what if in some situations recognition drives purchase and sometimes recall drives purchase? If someone goes to the shops for a bottle of gin, they are likely to 'recognize' the brand they want and purchase it. But if they are in a restaurant and ask for a gin and tonic, what if the waitress asks what brand of gin they would like? It would be necessary to recall the desired brand from memory. When someone is not sure, or if both types of decision-making situations are likely, the brand's advertising must take *both* recognition and recall brand awareness communication objectives into account. This means that a clear indication of the package as it will be seen at the point of purchase must be present, as well as a strong need–brand link established.

> ## KEY CONCEPT
>
> **Brand awareness will be either recognition or recall, depending upon how the brand decision is made.**
>
> There are two distinctly different types of brand awareness, based upon how purchase decisions are made. If the decision is made at the point of purchase when seeing (recognizing) the brand reminds the target of a need for it, this is recognition awareness. When a need brings the brand to mind, that is recall awareness. This distinction is important because it reflects different ways in which the brain deals with satisfying a need and creative tactics must account for this difference.

Brand attitude strategy

Brand attitude was discussed briefly in the section on positioning, and in the previous chapter. It is brand attitude that forms and sustains brand equity, and it is marketing communication, especially advertising-like messages, that help form brand attitude. In the discussion of positioning it was pointed out that brand attitude follows from the link between the brand and the benefits associated with it, and that effective positioning identifies what benefit(s) to include in advertising, along with what the focus should be. But simply identifying what benefits to talk about in marketing communication is only the first step in formulating a communication strategy for brand attitude.

There are two fundamental considerations that must be taken into account when developing a brand attitude strategy: involvement and motivation (Table 6.4). These two criteria go to the heart of how and why people make product choices, and as a result must guide how managers approach marketing communication for their brand. These issues are discussed in some depth in our *Strategic Advertising Management* text (Percy and Rosenbaum-Elliott, 2012), but they deserve some explanation here. The issue of

TABLE 6.4 Brand attitude strategy

Involvement	The degree of 'risk' (fiscal or psychological) associated with the purchase decision, whether low or high, determines whether the message must be accepted or believed (high involvement) or only a tentatively positive attitude created (low involvement).
Motivation	Understanding the motivation during the purchase decision, whether it is positive or negative, determines how to focus upon the brand's benefit.

involvement is important because it influences what is needed to successfully process a message. Motivation is critical because it dictates how the benefit must be treated in the execution of a brand's message. Obviously, the better the execution, the more likely it will be processed, and the more effective the brand's marketing communication will be in building and sustaining a strong brand equity.

Involvement

Involvement reflects the degree of *risk* perceived by people when deciding whether to buy or use a product or service (cf. Nelson, 1970). This perceived risk can be seen in terms of either psychological risk or fiscal risk, but in either case is specifically associated with the target audience. For most of us, buying casual clothes is a relatively low-involvement decision. They do not cost a lot of money, and we generally dress to please ourselves. Not so, however, with young teenagers. For them, a great deal is at stake, making the choice of casual dress a high-involvement decision. They would not be caught dead wearing something of which their peers did not approve. This suggests that the level of involvement in a product decision will be very much a function of how the target audience looks at the purchase.

The reason why it is so critical to be concerned about involvement in terms of advertising and brand attitude strategy is that it affects the degree of acceptance or believability required in the message. When dealing with low-involvement situations, when the target audience sees little or no risk in the purchase, it is not really necessary to completely accept the message as true. If a person thinks it *might* be true, something Maloney (1962) called 'curious disbelief', they will form a *tentatively* positive brand attitude. They can try the product, based upon this tentative belief, because if it turns out not to be true, they haven't lost much. But if it was true, and they did like the product, then a more permanent positive brand attitude will begin to develop. But when the target audience feels there is some risk in the purchase decision, they need to be certain of their choice before they make the purchase. With high-involvement decisions, the target audience must believe the message and accept it as true. This helps them form a positive brand attitude *prior* to actually making a purchase. As one might imagine, how one deals with the creative content of advertising will differ significantly depending upon whether one is dealing with a perceived low- or high-involvement purchase decision.

KEY CONCEPT

Involvement in purchase decisions is a function of risk, defined in either fiscal or psychological terms.

It is important to know if a brand's target audience thinks there is risk involved in the purchase of the brand. If there is no perceived risk, either fiscal or psychological, in buying the brand, this would be considered low involvement and it would not be necessary to convince the target with marketing communication, only make them curious about it. If a mistake is made and they do not like the brand, nothing much has been lost. But if there is a perceived risk in the purchase, this is a high-involvement decision and the claims made must be accepted as true before purchase to guard against making a mistake.

Motivation

Psychologists suggest that all human behaviour is the result of a particular motivation. While they may argue about what those motivations specifically are, there is general agreement that there are only a handful of different motivations involved. And again, while not all psychologists are in total agreement (some psychologists feel all motives are negatively oriented, that everything we do is to more-or-less 'solve' a problem in one way or another), most consider that some motives are positively originated and others negatively originated. This is the view that we take. While early thinking about motivation centred only on drive reduction, *both* drive reduction and drive increase are involved in behaviour (Wickelgren, 1977; Warr *et al.*, 1983).

The reason why it is so important to understand what motivates people to purchase or use a product or service for brand attitude communication strategy is that if the advertisers do not know *why* the consumer wants it they will not be able to effectively relate benefits to the brand. This point was made in the last section in talking about benefit focus in positioning. When dealing with negatively motivated behaviour, messages must focus directly on the benefit. But when behaviour is positively motivated, the message must deal with the emotional consequences of the benefit.

KEY CONCEPT

Brand purchase decisions will be driven by either negative motives, where a problem is to be solved or avoided, or positive motives, where a reward is sought from the product.

It is important to understand the underlying motivation driving brand purchase decisions because it will dictate creative tactics. With negative motivations the message should focus on the benefit positioning directly, but with positive motivations the benefit is indirectly communicated through the execution itself, arousing an emotional response which becomes the benefit.

When considering negatively motivated behaviour, it is important to understand that this does not mean negative in the sense of being 'bad'. Negative motives generally deal with behaviour that is meant to solve or avoid a problem. A homemaker has a counter full of dirty dishes (problem) and needs washing-up liquid to get them clean (solution); or a father is worried about what will happen to his young family if he has an accident and can't work (problem), so he buys insurance (avoidance).

Positive motives generally involve seeking personal satisfaction or social approval. A person sees some pastries in a bakery window and buys some to enjoy (sensory gratification), or they buy a fancy new outdoor grill to impress their neighbours (social approval). Whether the motivation driving the behaviour of the target audience is positive or negative, it is important that advertising is consistent with the underlying motivation. And as we have seen, an important way of ensuring this is by using the correct benefit focus in the creative execution.

The Rossiter–Percy grid

Recognizing the importance of involvement and motivation in the development of effective brand attitude communication strategy, these two considerations have been used to define the brand attitude quadrants of the Rossiter–Percy grid (1997). Basically this grid provides a structure for identifying the appropriate creative tactics to be used in effecting positive brand attitude with advertising and other marketing communication, as well as the appropriate brand awareness creative tactics. It may be thought of, then, as four basic brand attitude strategy quadrants, for each of which an appropriate brand awareness strategy must be considered. This is important because *both* brand awareness and brand attitude strategy must be considered *together* for all advertising.

We have already talked about the basic differences between the creative tactics needed for recognition versus recall brand awareness: clearly show the package as it will be seen at the point of purchase for recognition brand awareness, and provide a clear need–brand link for recall brand awareness.

Brand attitude strategies will reflect one of the four quadrants occasioned by combinations of involvement and motivation with the purchase decision. These brand attitude strategic quadrants are shown in Fig. 6.2. Notice that they label strategies for dealing with negatively originating motivations 'informational', and those dealing with positively originating motivations 'transformational'. These labels reflect the *general* goal of brand communication for negatively motivated behaviour to provide information to help solve or avoid the problem at hand, and for positively motivated behaviour to 'transform' your mood from a neutral or dull state to a more positive feeling resulting from enjoying a product or gaining social approval from purchasing it.

Before discussing the specific creative tactics suggested by the brand attitude communication strategy quadrants in the grid, we should point out that others in the past have proposed various 'grids' to help explain or identify types of marketing communication. Perhaps the best-known example is the so-called FCB grid introduced back in the 1960s. Despite many problems with this early formulation, many textbooks and marketing practitioners continue to refer to it. This is unfortunate, for there are serious problems with the ideas upon which it is built (Rossiter *et al.*, 1991).

The real strength of the Rossiter–Percy grid is that it helps focus the manager's thinking about a brand in terms of how its target audience makes choices in the category. What type of brand awareness is most likely? What is the perceived risk or involvement in the

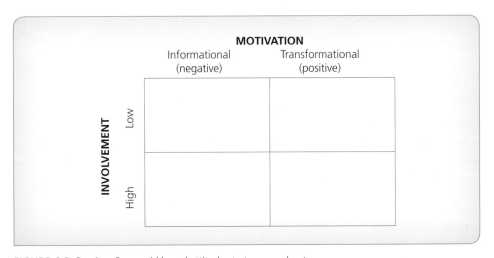

FIGURE 6.2 Rossiter–Percy grid brand attitude strategy quadrants

purchase or use of the brand? What motivates people to purchase products or services in the brand's category? Answers to these questions alert the manager to specific creative tactics that are likely to maximize the processing and positive response to the brand's advertising. We will now look at the four brand attitude strategy quadrants and see how they dictate significantly different creative tactics.

When dealing with low-involvement informational strategies, where there is little perceived risk in purchase and the motivation is negative, a wide variety of creative options are open. This is actually the easiest brand advertising to deal with, primarily because one does not need to convince the target audience, as pointed out when we talked about involvement. Remember Maloney's notion of curious disbelief? In fact, the target audience does not even need to like the advertising. The key is that the advertising provides some information, perhaps even exaggerated, to encourage the target audience to think the brand just might solve or help avoid a problem, so why not give it a try? It does not matter that the attempt to persuade is so obvious, because there is so little risk in trying (Wood and Quinn, 2003).

At the high-involvement level, when dealing with negative motives, there is a significant difference in creative tactics. Here the target audience *must be convinced* by what you say in the advertising. While in and of itself the message may not be enough to convince someone to purchase now, it must be believable, contributing to the building of a positive brand attitude. In order to ensure that a message will be believable, the benefit claims made must be consistent with how people currently think about a brand, its competitors, and the category in general. Otherwise, it leaves open the likelihood the target audience will consciously counter-argue the message (Gilbert, 1991). These tactics are summarized in Table 6.5.

When the underlying motivation driving category behaviour is positive, when dealing with transformational brand attitude strategies, the key to effective creative execution is *emotional authenticity*. This holds regardless of involvement. The target audience must identify with the advertising, and must like it. It is not unusual for the 'feeling' one gets from the advertising to become the actual brand benefit. In effect there must be increased arousal while processing the advert (Baumgartner *et al.*, 1997).

In one of the best examples of how this can work, the *taste* of beer is often more likely to be found in its advertising than in the bottle (at least in the US market). A study by one of the authors looked at taste evaluations for six then-currently marketed beer brands in the USA. In one test people knew what they were drinking, but in a second group the drinkers did not

TABLE 6.5 Brand attitude creative tactics

Low Involvement/ Informational	Provide one or two clear benefits, even exaggeration of the benefit.
High Involvement/ Informational	Provide believable information about the brand that is consistent with the target audience's existing attitudes, be careful not to over-claim.
Low Involvement/ Transformational	Key is the perceived emotional authenticity of the execution, and the target audience must like it.
High Involvement/ Transformational	Emotional authenticity is critical, and the target audience must personally identify with the feeling created.

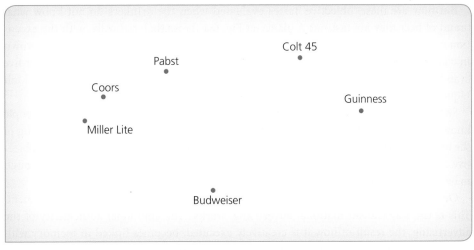

FIGURE 6.3 Taste perceptions of six beer brands where brand is known

know what they were drinking. The results of their taste evaluations were 'mapped' (using a multivariate statistical analysis which positions the brands in relation to how similarly they are evaluated, in our case in terms of taste), and the results are illustrated in Figs 6.3 and 6.4.

Fig. 6.3 shows the results of the relationships between the six brands studied in terms of how similarly or differently beer drinkers evaluated the taste of each when they knew what they were drinking. What was found is that on one side of the 'space', Coors and Miller Lite mapped rather close to each other, indicating that the beer drinkers felt they were rather similar in taste. In fact, Miller Lite is a lower calorie beer, and Coors tends to have a reputation as a 'mild' beer. Both are marketed as premium beers. In the middle of the space we find Budweiser and Pabst, each seen as tasting quite different from Coors and Miller Lite, but also different from each other. Budweiser is marketed as a premium beer, Pabst as a regular beer. Towards the right of the space we find first Colt 45, then Guinness Stout. Colt 45 is a malt liquor, and Guinness is, well, Guinness.

What does this 'map' tell us about how beer drinkers in the USA evaluate the taste of these six brands? It seems that running left to right is a 'strength' dimension, with a vertical dimension more-or-less dividing what are seen as more premium beers from the one regular beer, Pabst. Coors and Miller Lite are milder tasting beers, Budweiser and Pabst somewhat stronger, with Colt 45 stronger tasting yet, and Guinness the strongest or heaviest of all.

FIGURE 6.4 Taste perceptions of six beer brands where brand is not known

But how are these 'objective' tastes evaluated when the drinkers do not know what brand of beer they are tasting? A glance at Fig. 6.4 shows that, basically, with the exception of Guinness (which of course is not only a heavier tasting beer but also dark brown in colour), these drinkers could not distinguish between the taste of any of the other five brands. And remember, these ranged from the lower calorie Miller Lite to Colt 45 Malt Liquor, which has over three times the alcoholic content of the other brands.

So where does the 'taste' of these beer brands come from? The advertising. When people know what they are drinking, they judge the taste in terms of the general positioning of the brands in their advertising. When they do not know what they are drinking, the objective characteristics of the brands (with the exception of Guinness) are not different enough to be distinguished.

One can see from this example how *advertising* can actually become a brand's benefit. This is the way transformational advertising 'works'. The emotional authenticity of the advertising, the result of how it is creatively executed, becomes linked in memory with the brand. With low-involvement decisions, when the brand is recognized at the point of purchase, the feelings from the advertising are re-experienced, and that becomes reason enough to consider the brand. With high-involvement transformational strategies, the only real difference is that the target audience must *personally identify* with the experience conveyed by the advertising. This is what convinces them (remember, accepting the message as true is needed with high-involvement decisions) that they too will experience these same positive feelings, helping to build positive brand attitude, leading to purchase or use of the product or service. In fact, it has been argued that such emotional responses are a necessary precursor to subsequent top-down cognitive justifications for such decisions (Dijksterhuis *et al.*, 2005). These tactics are summarized in Table 6.5.

KEY CONCEPT

Both involvement and motivation are critical to communication strategy for building brand attitude.

Involvement and motivation are critical to marketing communication strategy because each, in their own way, inform the creative tactics needed to optimize the likelihood a message will be processed and effective. The Rossiter and Percy Grid utilizes these dimensions in identifying the appropriate creative tactics for each combination of involvement and motivation.

Building brands with non-traditional media

When most people think about a brand's marketing communication, they are generally thinking of traditional advertising in mass media. While that continues to be the primary source of messages about most brands, especially consumer package goods and services, there are of course many other ways of delivering a brand's message. We refer the reader elsewhere for the role of traditional media such as radio and television, newspaper, magazines, and outdoor in delivering brand messages that follows naturally from our discussion up to this point (e.g. Percy and Rosenbaum-Elliott, 2012). However, since it is also important for managers to consider more than just traditional media, we will briefly consider some of the more important non-traditional media. First, we will look at digital media, and then review a few other non-traditional media options available to a manager for building a brand.

An important point to keep in mind as we discuss these and other options is that everything we have been talking about up to this point applies to these non-traditional media. Regardless of how a brand's message is delivered, it must be well positioned and correctly address brand awareness and brand attitude. And critically, the actual message and execution must be consistent with everything else that is being communicated about the brand.

This is really what IMC (integrated marketing communication) is all about. It is the ability to plan and select appropriate media options to optimize the delivery of a consistent brand message (Percy, 2014). The same positioning must be used in all media, and the execution must have a consistent look and feel. The key benefit associated with the brand in a print advert or television commercial must be the same as that used on the Internet (and that includes the brand's website), at trade shows, in PR material, and even in personal selling. This is what ensures that all of a brand's marketing communication is working together in building the brand and its equity.

KEY CONCEPT

Considerations of digital media and other non-traditional media options for delivering a brand's message should be part of communication planning.

In developing a marketing communication plan, all options that are consistent with processing requirements of the brand attitude strategy should be considered. This should include not only digital media such as the Internet and social media, but also things like packaging, sponsorships, marketing public relations, and even the sides of delivery trucks. This does not mean they will necessarily be used, but the manager should always look beyond traditional media for opportunities to deliver the brand's message effectively.

Digital media

In this section we will be looking at what had become known as 'new media', but is now referred to as digital media. And although we will be addressing new media, it is important to remember that not only are applications of digital media being incorporated into more traditional media, it is turning to traditional media to market itself. For example, there are single-advertiser issues of magazines that are delivered electronically, and there are adverts with microchips embedded in them allowing sound.

Additionally, web companies are now spending serious money on television adverts to help build brand awareness. As an example, TripAdvisor used largely digital advertising and social media for 13 years, but in 2013 invested US$30 million on television advertising to help drive up their awareness. Other websites too are investing heavily in television advertising to take advantage of its strength in building brand awareness. Zillow Inc., one of the US's most popular websites for real estate, apartments, and mortgages, spent between US$30 and US$40 million on television advertising in 2013 after research showed that 88% of their market had never heard of them (Vrancia, 2013).

Today there are elaborate online campaigns that join a brand's message with high-tech entertainment. One example has been described by Vrancia (2005), where someone opens an email presenting a fictional newspaper with a headline reading: 'Another slaying at Datadyne HQ.' A link then sends you to a video of an autopsy, where the camera pans down to a tag on the toe of the body with the name of the person who opened the email. A Microsoft Xbox video game is then advertised, along with an invitation to send the link to a friend. If the link is forwarded, the sender's telephone rings and a message from the advertised video game's heroine reports, 'The job is done.' An email then arrives from the heroine with a picture of another dead body, this time with the friend's name on the toe tag.

There can be no question that there has been a tremendous surge in digital media options for marketing communication. And, as you read this, things may have already moved well beyond what we are writing about, just as much of what we are dealing with would not have been part of a textbook written 5 or 10 years ago. However, despite increasing shares of media budgets being directed to digital media, to date there is no real evidence that it is effective. There is some anecdotal evidence, but this rush by marketers to digital media may be nothing more than a fear of being left behind. Don Schultz (2010) put this notion well when he said 'The question, though, is are all these heady measures of new media a sign of a gold-rush of new-and-improved advertising and marketing opportunities or simply fool's gold?'

But this growth in digital media does *not* mean that the role of advertising too must be changing. It is not, period. The role of advertising is, and always has been, to drive awareness of a brand, build positive affect for the brand, to drive sales, or to charge a higher price for the brand than consumers would be willing to pay in the absence of it (Rossiter and Percy, 2013).

And while there is no question that technology is changing the ways in which people communicate and the ways in which marketers are able to communicate with their target audiences, it is important to remember that the fundamental principles of communication that underlie our earlier discussions of positioning and communication strategy are *not* changing. How messages are delivered may change, but how the mind processes information does not. What we have been talking about in terms of the best way to create marketing communication to build and sustain brand equity is based upon how the mind works. Regardless of the medium, messages are still comprised of text, audio, and/or video.

KEY CONCEPT

Digital media, especially social media, are providing more ways of directly targeting consumers.

One of the strengths of digital media such as the Internet and mobile phones is the ability to more closely identify members of a brand's target audience. This follows from its ability to gather information at the individual level from users of digital media.

Internet

Global Internet advertising spending in 2010 was some US$63 billion, an over three-fold increase from 2005. Overall, Internet advertising in 2010 accounted for about 14 percent of total advertising spending worldwide. Online advertising is estimated to grow to as much as US$150 billion by the year 2015 (Guth, 2005). Yet even though the Internet is vast, almost all of the money spent on Internet advertising goes to the top 50 web companies, with most going to Yahoo, Google, AOL, and MSN. As with all media, this reflects their greater size and correspondingly larger number of visitors to their sites. For example, in December of 2010 the number of daily visits to Google was reported at 197.7 million, 183.5 million at Yahoo, and 180 million at AOL (ComScore, 2011). Something with the potential to slow their growth, however, is the possible effect of a 2003 EU law that requires non-EU companies to collect value-added taxes on fees for Internet services. Also, they would need to collect VAT for product downloads such as music, videos, and software by Internet users.

Some of the ways marketers are using the Internet to deliver online adverts include online video where listeners can respond to an advert by clicking on a box at a radio station's website that directs them to the advertised brand's website; by including messages in online video games; and by creating entertainment programming that weaves product endorsements into the storyline. Streaming video is also being used to offer mini-movies created by a marketer where their brand is prominently featured. These mini-movies are often produced by well-known producers and directors, using well-known actors (Silberer and Englehardt, 2005). As a result, they often create a strong 'buzz' for the brand. A good example is BMW, who have a separate site to their home page, BMWfilms.com, for just that purpose (Iezzi, 2010).

Small computer programmes that enable people to incorporate professional-looking content into their personal webpage or on their computer, called *widgets*, are considered by many marketers to be the source of the next generation of Internet advertising. A brand can sponsor a widget as a way to incorporate adverts into someone's webpage. For example, Reebok created a widget that enabled users to display customized RBK shoes for people to critique (Steel, 2006). Widgets are seen as a better approach than banner adverts and less annoying than intrusive videos.

Internet and online marketing companies are getting much better at targeting adverts to specific groups of users. Some, like Yahoo and Microsoft, monitor and analyse user search habits through something called 'behaviour targeting' to better target messages (Delaney and Steel, 2007). But this has raised important questions about privacy because most tracking devices (such as 'cookies') are installed on someone's computer without their knowledge or permission. This is even done by some marketers without the knowledge of the website. The issue has caught the attention of government regulators, but there has been an ongoing controversy over what to do about it. An EU regulation requiring websites to offer users the option of refusing the instillation of 'cookies' is considered unworkable (Sonne and Miller, 2010).

In addition to regulatory concerns, marketers must also be concerned about the extent to which they are able to maintain control over their brand's message on the Internet, and especially with social media. Marketers are able to exercise tight control over their message with traditional media, with one exception, marketing public relations. But, even there the marketer has some involvement. With digital media, however, a user cannot even be certain the message is coming from the brand, and not something that has come to be known as 'word of mouse'. This potential for unauthorized brand messages poses a very real problem in marketing a brand.

Social media

Towards the end of the first decade of the twenty-first century, social media such as Facebook, blogs, Twitter, and YouTube began to seriously attract the attention of brand marketers. In 2010 more than 2 billion people per day visited YouTube, in the US one in ten adults who use the Internet were also Twitter users, and Facebook had over 500 million active users (Gangadharbatla, 2012). Social marketing is now used by marketing and sales, research and development, customer-service, and other departments in many companies (Patel, 2010). And as with IMC, it is essential that all of the departments within a company using social media work together. There are even social-only advertising agencies.

There are many definitions of social marketing, but perhaps the most widely used is the one proposed by Andreas and Haenlein (2010). They define social marketing as 'a group of Internet-based applications that build on the ideological and technological foundation of Web 2.0, and allow the creation and execution of user-generated content'. This user-generated content can be a real problem for marketers because there is no gatekeeper of that content. Exacerbating this is the incredible speed with which a brand can be damaged, even by a single individual who in seconds can tell a hundred of their 'friends' about their concerns with a brand, which then travels exponentially to potentially millions of people (Iezzi, 2010).

The other side of this coin is 'sponsored content', an area that has attracted the attention of many marketers. Basically, this is brand advertising disguised as stories or videos created to subtly promote a brand. To work best, the content should be shared on social media, but it must be shown on the right network of sites. Although a small category, it was nevertheless one of the fastest growing advertising media segments in 2013 with spending of around US$19 billion (Launder, 2013). However, as with product placement in more traditional sources such as television and movies, the use of sponsored content raises the same ethical questions.

A more positive variation on this is where participants are involved in providing content for a brand. Brands from Coach to Lululeman search social media for photographs of people 'modelling' their fashions and accessories, and create links to their own websites or collect the pictures in galleries. Some, like Modcloth.com and Lululeman ask their customers directly to upload pictures to their site. The hope is that real-people pictures will help connect relationships with customers and keep them on the website longer (Binkley, 2013).

Major multinational marketers such as Procter & Gamble and Unilever have made major commitments to social media. In 2010, marketers began to use Facebook more as a marketing tool, trying to channel the networking power of the media, rather than using it simply as a place to host content that had been on the brands' websites. How successful this has been is not clear (at least at this writing, a necessary caveat with all digital media). For example, in early 2010 the 200,000 fans of P&G's Pampers on Facebook were dwarfed by the 1.5 million monthly visitors to Pampers.com. On the other hand, Coke's 5 million Facebook fans represented a far higher number than the 300,000 visitors to the website (Neff, 2010). L'Oréal for a number of years has been heavily involved in digital media, and in the autumn of 2013 introduced Em, their first brand to be marketed almost totally through social media and e-commerce (Neff, 2013).

However, along with the potential upside to using social media in brand marketing, there are very real problems for the manager to consider, well beyond those discussed above. For example, a small number of people can create the impression that a far wider group of consumers is involved. But of more consequence, cyber criminals and pranksters confuse consumers by creating false profiles in a brand's name. Blog entries on social networks are repositioned and the links they contain replaced with ones to different sites where consumers may be scammed or re-directed to other ventures or products. Also, discussion boards on brand websites can be infiltrated with posts of malicious content (Needleman, 2009).

Few, if any social media are making money now. They are looking to advertising revenue for survival. But unlike traditional media where the presence of advertising is more-or-less expected, social users are not happy about the intrusion of advertising. Yet they are not willing to pay to use social media (Nielson, 2010). And for advertisers, there is really no evidence that social media is effective for advertising. We alluded to this issue earlier. As Schultz (2010) has put it, marketers seem to feel a certain 'need' to use social media regardless of any evidence that it works because of the 'boxcar number of participants or fear of being left behind'. The extremely popular 'Subservient Chicken' promotion from Burger King, described as a 'watershed in the new era of interactive creativity' by Iezzi (2010) nevertheless does not seem to have had much of an effect, if any, on sales (Ries, 2011).

While social media is more and more a part of brand marketing, issues of control and effectiveness remain.

Table 6.6 outlines some of the digital media options we have been discussing.

Mobile marketing

In the UK, the Mobile Marketing Association (2005) defined mobile marketing as: 'The use of the mobile medium as the communications and entertainment channel between a brand and an end-user. Mobile marketing is the only personal channel enabling spontaneous, direct, interactive and/or target communications, anytime, anyplace.'

The use of banner adverts on mobile phones occurred as early as the year 2000 on the Pacific Rim, but was slow to catch on in Europe and the USA because of fear on the part of marketers that it would alienate customers. But by the mid-2000s, major mobile phone networks in the USA and Europe had begun to include advertising on their wireless information and entertainment service (Yuan and Bryan-Low, 2006).

TABLE 6.6 Digital media options

Internet	Brand websites Online video Target adverts
Mobile	Target adverts Specific apps
Social Media	Twitter Facebook YouTube Blogs

Rapidly improving mobile phone technology is making mobile advertising more attractive to marketers as they become, in effect, small computers with data connections and colour screens. Early mobile phones were not designed for downloading. As mobile devices added capabilities, spurred by the introduction of the iPhone, so too did app stores, permitting consumers to buy specific content. This attracted the attention of traditional magazine publishers, who saw it as an opportunity to provide digital editions of their publications, addressing a demand from marketers for apps where their advertising could appear. This need not be a copy of the print edition, but apps with specialized content. A leader here is Rodale, who offer workout apps, Men's Health and Women's Health apps, and variations such as the free Women's Health Best Foods for Women, and for US$4.99, Eat This, Not That, an extension of their book of the same name (Ives, 2010).

You can deliver coupons on mobile phones via display adverts in text messages, although there can be problems with redemption if the retailer cannot read the mobile barcodes. Surprisingly, outdoor advertising has become the second fastest growing form of mobile advertising, behind the Internet. Billboards and posters now have the ability to 'beam' information to cell phones. It is also possible to target messages based upon where the user is with their phone, enabling highly localized content or offers.

According to some projections, spending on mobile advertising is expected to exceed US$10.8 billion by 2016 (Advertising Age, 2012). The majority of this is expected to be spent on search advertising, followed by display and video. But just as we discussed with social media, people find mobile advertising more annoying than advertising in traditional media, and there are real questions about its ability to tightly target messages, as well as the ability to control the message environment and the timing of the exposure.

Mobile applications for smart phones and other mobile devices, when well integrated with a brand's overall communication strategy, offer marketers a good way to create 'buzz' for their brand, enabling consumers to connect with the brand while on-the-go (Sullivan, 2010). In addition, mobile usage is certainly growing. In fact, in the US more time is now spent with mobile devices than with print media (Advertising Age, 2012).

Additional non-traditional media

As mentioned earlier, when talking about brands and marketing communication, more often than not one is thinking about advertising. For most brands, at least brands marketed to consumers, traditional advertising delivered through mass media is likely to be the primary way the brand communicates with its target audience, along with an increasing use of digital media. But there are many other options, including the annual report. This should be much more than simply a presentation of facts and figures. It should communicate what the company and its brand(s) are all about. Austria Solar, a solar energy company managed this brilliantly in their 2012 annual report. Indoors it was a completely blank white book, but outdoors, the sun's rays interacted with specially treated paper to reveal the content of the report. This was a way to dramatically convey the company's mission in a way that ensured attention for the brand (Diaz, 2013).

Several other non-traditional media options are discussed below.

Packaging

An important, but all too often overlooked, part of a brand's marketing communication is the package. In fact, for many consumer products, the package provides an ongoing communication opportunity, a continuing reminder of the brand name and reinforcement of the primary benefit. Many products, such as toothpaste, shampoo, pain relievers, and household cleaners, are used *from the package*. In a very real way, a package is operating as post-purchase advertising. As Rossiter and Bellman (2005) have put it in their definition of packaging, it may be thought of as 'take-away or leave-behind' communication vehicles.

However, even though a study of brand managers found that they feel a package has the ability to attract attention and provide expression of the brand's image (Chareonlarp, 1997), its role is still often underestimated (Southgate, 1994). But given its potential, packaging is an area that deserves careful consideration by managers; and needs to be considered as part of the brand's marketing communication programme.

Sponsorships and event marketing

Another opportunity for delivering a brand's message is through sponsorships and event marketing. Sponsorships involve a brand providing support for an organization, cause, or individual (e.g. an athlete). While a brand can sponsor anything, most sponsorships worldwide involve sports (Meenaghan, 1998), with the Olympics providing perhaps the most sponsorships. Event marketing is basically the same as sponsorship, except it is limited to a single event rather than an ongoing relationship.

Sponsorships and event marketing offer the manager an opportunity for a brand to be presented within a positive environment where it can be associated in memory with favourable attitudes towards the sponsored activity or individual. But to be effective, there should be a clear link between the brand's primary benefit and what is sponsored.

Trade shows and fairs

Along with personal selling (considered later), trade shows and fairs play a major role in business-to-business and industrial marketing, often the only means of marketing communication for the brand. It has been estimated that industrial marketers spend between 20% and 25% of their communication budget on trade shows and fairs (Gopalakrishna and Williams, 1992). Almost every product category or industry has trade shows.

Because of the opportunity for personal interaction, trade shows and fairs offer a brand the chance to demonstrate use, which may be difficult or impossible to do in more traditional media. It also provides a brand with the opportunity to be in touch with nearly all its current or potential trade outlets. While most managers define effectiveness for trade shows as lead generation that results in sales, there are many 'non-sales' aspects valued by managers as well (Shipley *et al.*, 1993).

Marketing public relations

Public relations can play an important role in the marketing of a brand, although most PR practitioners do not like to see themselves as involved with marketing: they see themselves in a broader role of building the overall image or reputation of the company. Nevertheless, in the mid-1990s, 70% of PR activity was linked to marketing, and this lead Thomas Harris to introduce the term *marketing public relations* (Harris, 1993). He specifically described it as 'the process of planning, executing, and evaluating programmes that encourage purchase and consumer satisfaction through credible communication of information and impressions that identify companies and their products with the needs, wants, concerns, and interests of consumers.'

This idea has obvious implications for brands using source or endorser branding strategies. Any effort by PR to enhance the image of the parent company will help enhance its role as an endorser or source. But as we have seen with all of the other options discussed, it is essential that any MPR actively reflects the overall positioning of the brand, and be coordinated with the brand's other marketing communication. Even with such coordination, however, a potential problem with MPR is the lack of control over the message that is actually delivered by others as a result of the MPR activity.

Personal selling

Like trade shows and fairs, personal selling is a key part of business-to-business and industrial marketing communication, but it is also a significant part of many consumer oriented brands' marketing communication programmes (e.g. via telemarketing or high-end retail sales). It differs from other forms of marketing communication for a brand in that the message goes directly from the brand to a specific individual in the target audience, providing an opportunity for interaction and adjustment of the message to individual concerns. This two-way interaction, of course, is its key advantage. Nevertheless, the message must remain on strategy, and be consistent with the overall marketing communication programme.

This can be a problem for brand management when dealing with a sales force that is not a part of the marketing department, especially with consumer packaged goods companies; and when brand management and the sales force have separate budgets. With packaged goods companies, in effect retailers are the 'brand' for the sales force (Dewsharp and Jobber, 2000). In such cases the focus will be on the trade rather than the consumer. Still, the message must be consistent with the overall marketing communications strategy.

These additional options to traditional media for delivering a brand's message that we have been reviewing are summarized in Table 6.7.

TABLE 6.7 Alternative options to traditional media for delivering a brand's message

Alternative options	
Packaging	Offers an opportunity to reinforce the brand's key benefit and can be an ongoing reminder for many products that are used directly from the package.
Sponsorships and event marketing	Enables the brand to be seen in a favourable environment or linked to a well-known individual where the positive attitude associated with them is transferred to the brand.
Trade shows and fairs	Provides an opportunity for personal interaction, and the ability to demonstrate the product.
Marketing public relations	Helps enhance brand or corporate image through credible 'outside' communication.
Personal selling	Opportunity for two-way interaction, and the ability to modify and adjust the message to fit the specific needs of the customer.

CHAPTER SUMMARY

In this chapter we examined how marketing communication builds brands, and how advertising in particular helps define a brand for consumers. We looked at how to best position a brand versus its competition, utilizing benefits that are important to the consumer and that the brand can be seen as believably delivering, and ideally better than other brands. Based upon that positioning, a communication strategy is built around the correct focus upon the benefit, consistent with the motivation driving behaviour in the category.

We saw how brand awareness and brand attitude are critical communication objectives for all marketing communication, and how the correct use follows from the positioning. Brand awareness was seen as either recognition or recall based, depending upon whether in most purchase situations the consumer sees the brand and is reminded of a need, or whether the brand must be recalled when a need occurs. Brand attitude strategy was seen as depending upon the level of involvement people have in the purchase decision, defined in terms of risk, and the underlying motivation that drives purchase behaviour in a category.

Finally, we looked at the growing role of digital media in brand communication, and reviewed important non-traditional media options available to the manager as part of a brand's marketing communication programme.

DISCUSSION QUESTIONS

1 How does a brand name communicate information about that brand?

2 Identify two or three centrally positioned brands, and discuss what makes them so.

3 Discuss how to differentiate a brand in its positioning, with particular emphasis on benefit selection.

4 How is benefit selection related to brand attitude?

5 Why is it so important to get the benefit focus correct in advertising?

6 Discuss the importance of understanding the motivation driving category behaviour to positioning and communication strategy.

7 Identify two or three brands you feel involve recognition brand awareness, and two or three brands recall, and discuss why.

8 What are the roles of involvement and motivation in brand attitude strategy?

9 Identify two or three brands for each of the four quadrants of the Rossiter–Percy grid, and discuss why they belong there.

10 How does the role of digital media differ from that of traditional media?

11 What problems might social media pose for brands?

12 Discuss ways in which non-traditional media, other than new media, may be used as part of a brand's marketing communication programme, providing examples.

CASE STUDY

Andrex: sold on a pup

If a league table of great British brands were to be compiled, Andrex would be there in the premier division, richly deserving its status as a 'superbrand'. However, it must be said that intuitively it is strange that a brand of toilet paper should be in a position to achieve this accolade. The esteem in which this brand is held by consumers does not seem to fit with the esteem of the product and its function! Our assertion in this case history is that this effect is due in a major part to a Labrador puppy, who has appeared consistently in Andrex's TV advertising since 1972.

Andrex's success

Andrex is by far the biggest and fastest selling brand in its market, and has been since the early 1960s when soft toilet tissue became the norm. No other brand has since then ever held a share in this market of over 12%. In the period since the puppy advertising began in 1972, Andrex has increased its Nielsen volume share from under 5% to over 30%.

Currently Andrex, even though it is the most expensive product available, is the UK's second biggest brand by value, as it sells 1.5 million rolls every day. It also has very loyal buyers, as one-third of Andrex buyers never buy any other brand. In addition, Andrex is significantly preferred by consumers in blind product tests, a fact that shows the product's 'added value', that is, the value attributed to a brand over and above its functional attributes. Bearing in mind the nature of the product, the size of this 'added value' is exceptional.

Puppy advertising

Toilet paper is inherently a low-interest, low-anxiety product. For this reason it was felt at the outset that if advertising were to work effectively for Andrex it needed to create its own interest. A primary requirement for advertising this brand would be that it should generate high awareness, and get noticed. It was also felt that it was an equally important requirement in this case that the advertising be liked. And the puppy, which first appeared in 1972, has been central to both these requirements. However, the exceptional value of the puppy is really in the way that he has developed over the years and, as a result, achieved valuable consistency, while remaining relevant to successive generations of toilet tissue buyers. In addition to his role in demonstrating the product's softness, strength, and length, he has become inextricably linked with the brand, and a metaphor for everything people love about Andrex.

Hence, Andrex advertising is not only exceptionally noticed, it is also exceptionally popular. Millward Brown has found Andrex advertising to be one of the most exceptionally liked campaigns it has ever tracked, with over 85% of respondents saying that they enjoy the advertising (the second highest endorsement of all time on this dimension). The combination of this exceptionally high likeability and the exceptionally high Awareness Index is unmatched by any other brand.

Growing loyalty

The profile of Andrex users is very similar to that of the general population (as would be expected with nearly half the country's households buying the product), but the profile of its most loyal users tends to be older, probably because of its premium price. Therefore, it is important that non-users of Andrex hold the brand in high esteem, since they must continually be recruited to usership.

Possible threats

As in most grocery markets, Andrex faced the considerable threat of the rise in retailers' own brands. But their growth has been contained by Andrex's market share and policy of continuous advertising. Also the spectacularly fast growth of 'green' issues affected the whole market and, for the first time in its brand history, Andrex was facing an emotional threat. But, in spite of the fact that recycling has consistently been the biggest issue for consumers in this market, Andrex is always seen as a more environmentally friendly brand than even its competitor Kleenex, which offers a recycled variant. And by running advertisements to explain that the parent company is a major planter of trees, Andrex started to take volume away from recycled products. Lastly, as a premium-priced product, a recession might be expected to affect Andrex adversely: when money is tight, buying cheaper toilet tissue would seem an easy sacrifice to make. However, the indications are that Andrex suffers far less than one might expect.

Econometric modelling

In 1974, Scott appointed O'Herlihy Associates (OHAL) to devise modelling for the Andrex brand. The objective was to find out more about what was influencing the brand's performance, and thus to help management make future decisions on budget allocation. OHAL, through a greater understanding of the relationship between advertising and sales by the model, supported the view that the puppy campaign is the key to the success of the brand. Currently it is estimated that in any one period, advertising accounts directly for between four and five share points of Andrex's 30% volume share: that is, Andrex's share would drop by this amount if advertising stopped for a 12-month period.

Eliminating other factors

In order to further support our assertion that the puppy advertising has contributed so significantly to the exceptional performance of the Andrex brand, it is necessary to briefly isolate and eliminate other factors which, it could be argued, could have made an equally significant or greater contribution.

- *Distribution:* all the major brands in this market (Andrex, Kleenex, own-label) enjoy near-universal distribution and Andrex is far and away the fastest selling brand in the market on this basis.

- *Promotions:* promotions on Andrex can be divided into those which give extra value to the consumer (extra sheets, money off, etc.) and those designed to reward loyalty (collecting tokens for toy puppies, etc.). It is clearly unlikely that the strong performance of the brand in this period was fuelled by value-giving promotions.

- *Product quality:* has undoubtedly been fundamental to Andrex's success. In order, however, to isolate the effect of advertising, it is necessary to demonstrate that while actual quality is important, consumers' perceptions of Andrex quality exceed the reality.

- *Packaging:* preference alone could not account for the outstanding performance of the brand since 1972. Moreover, in a recent test, when asked what in particular people liked about Andrex, under 1% mentioned Andrex's packaging as a particular 'like'.

- *Product innovation:* Andrex has rarely been the first brand to innovate.

Conclusion

The Andrex puppy campaign began in 1972 and is a classic example of the best of British advertising. It is exceptionally well known and probably the best-loved campaign aimed at a housewife target. The real benefits of the advertising to Scott are the following:

- Toilet paper has not become a commodity market and Scott was able to sustain a premium price for a premium product.
- Andrex is the 'gold standard' toilet paper, as it is seen by housewives to dominate its competitors on all quality dimensions.
- While Andrex is not environmentally 'unfriendly', its 'green' credentials are more complex and harder to grasp than for recycled products. However, the great respect for Andrex, built through advertising, has given it the benefit of the doubt among most housewives and it has been able to retain share against the growth of recycled brands.
- Throughout the nearly four decades of puppy advertising more and more Andrex users have switched to buying just this one brand. The move is two-fold. Some people have become more loyal and new users have joined them.
- Econometric modelling has shown that advertising has a strong positive influence on Andrex's sales.

Andrex is an exceptional brand. Andrex puppy advertising is, according to all available measures, equally exceptional in its performance, and this case history, we hope, demonstrates what effective advertising can achieve for a product as dull as loo paper. For Scott Worldwide, the parent company of Scott Ltd, proof of their belief in the power of the puppy is shown in the fact that he has been 'exported' to Italy and Spain to advertise their premium product in these markets (Scottex).

Source: WARC, IPA, Advertising Effectiveness Awards 1992, Andrex: Sold on a Pup. Edited by Natalia Yannopoulou.

DISCUSSION QUESTIONS

1 By using the expectancy-value model, comment on the benefits selected by Scott in order to position Andrex.

2 How do you think routinized response behaviour applies in Andrex's case?

3 Do you think that Andrex has developed an effective positioning statement? Will it help Andrex face the challenges of the future?

4 Imagine being Andrex's main competitor. What steps will you take in order to position yourself as the most preferred brand within the market?

FURTHER READING

- A more detailed look at brands and marketing communication within the broader context of IMC (Integrated Marketing Communication) may be found in Larry Percy's 2014 book *Strategic Integrated Marketing Communications*, 2nd Edition. Oxford: Routledge.

- While new media providers have invested heavily in improving targeting for advertisers, target acceptance rates are low and declining. Jan H. Schumann, Florran van Wangenheim and Nicole Groene (2014) in their article 'Target online advertising: User reciprocity appears to increase acceptance,' *Journal of Marketing*, Vol. 78 (Jan), 59–75, present research that suggests ways for advertisers to meet this challenge.

- Debora V. Thompson and Prashant Malaviya (2013), in their article 'Consumer-generated ads: does awareness of advertising co-creation help or hurt persuasion?' show that publicizing the fact that adverts are consumer-generated can undermine message persuasiveness, especially in social media.

REFERENCES

Aaker, D. (2013), 'From positioning to framing', *Marketing News*, Jan, 22–23.

Advertising Age (2012 Mobile Fact Pack, 6.

Andreas, K. and Haenlein, M. (2010), 'Users of the world unite! the challenges and opportunities of social media', *Business Horizons*, 53, 1, 59–68.

Baumgartner, H., Sujan, M., and Padgett, D. (1997), 'Patterns of effective reactions to advertisements: the integration of moment-to-moment responses into overall judgements', *Journal of Marketing Research*, 34, 2, 214–32.

Binkley, C. (2013), 'More brands want you to model their clothes', *The Wall Street Journal*, 16 May, D6.

Boulding, W., Lee, E., and Staelin, R. (1994), 'Mastering the mix: do advertising, promotion and sales force activities lead to differentiation?' *Journal of Marketing Research*, 31, 2, 159–72.

Chareonlarp, S. (1997), 'An investigation of the representation of brand image through packaging', MSC Marketing Management Dissertation, Astor Business School, Astor University, Birmingham.

ComScore (2011), US panel data reported in *Advertising Age*, 28 February.

Delaney, K. J. and Steel, E. (2007), 'Are skins, bugs, or tickets the holy grail of Web advertising?', *The Wall Street Journal*, 13 August, B-1.

Dewsharp, B. and Jobber, D. (2000), 'The sales–marketing interface in consumer packaged-goods companies: a conceptual framework', *Journal of Personal Selling & Sales Management*, 20, 2, 109–19.

Diaz, A-C. (2013), 'How the usually dry annual report has become brands' secret marketing weapon', *Advertising Age*, 28 January, 11.

Dijksterhuis, A., Aarts, H., and Smith, P. K. (2005), 'The power of the subliminal: on subliminal persuasion and other potential applications', in R. Hassin, J. Uleman, and J. Bargh (eds), *The New Unconscious*, New York: Oxford University Press.

Donaghey, B. and Williamson, M. (2003), 'Thinking through "through-the-line" ', *Admap*, April, 24–6.

Fishbein, M. and Ajzen, I. (1975), *Belief, Attitude, Intention, and Behavior*, Reading, MA: Addison-Wesley Publishing.

Gangadharbatla, H. (2012), 'Social media and advertising', In S. Rogers, E. Thorsen (eds), *Advertising Theory*, New York: Routledge, 402–416.

Gilbert, D. T. (1991), 'How mental systems believe', *American Psychologist*, 46, 2, 107–19.

Gopalakrishna, S. and Williams, J. D. (1992), 'Planning and performance assessment of industrial trade shows: an exploratory study', *International Journal of Research in Marketing*, 9, 19, 207–24.

Guth, R. A. (2005), 'New Microsoft services will rely on online ads', *The Wall Street Journal*, 2 November, B-2.

Harris, T. (1993), *The Marketer's Guide to PR: How Today's Companies are Using the New Public Relations to Gain a Competitive Edge*, New York: John Wiley and Sons.

Howard, J. A. (1977), *Consumer Behaviour: Application of Theory*, New York: McGraw-Hill.

Iezzi, T. (2010), *The Idea Writer*, New York: Palgray MacMillan.

Interbrand Group (1992), *World's Greatest Brands: An International Review*, New York: John Wiley & Sons.

Ives, N. (2010), 'App for that: magazines forge new vision of digital future', *Advertising Age*, 22 February, 44.

Kent, R. I. and Allen, C. T. (1993), 'Does competitive clutter in television advertising "interfere" with recognition and recall of brand names and ad claims?', *Marketing Letters*, 4, 2, 175–84.

Kotler, P. (2003), *Marketing Management*, 11th edn, Upper Saddle River, NJ: Prentice Hall.

Launder, W. (2013), 'Marketers seek online edge with "sponsored content"', *The Wall Street Journal*, 26 August, B4.

Lee, Y. H. and Ang, K. S. (2003), 'Brand name suggestiveness: a Chinese language perspective', *International Journal of Research in Marketing*, 23, 4, 323–58.

Levin, P. and Gaeth, G. J. (1988), 'How consumers are affected by framing attribute information before and after consuming the product', *Journal of Consumer Research*, 15, 3, 374–378.

Maloney, J. C. (1962), 'Curiosity versus disbelief in advertising', *Journal of Advertising Research*, 2, 2, 2–8.

Meenaghan, T. (1998), 'Current developments and future directions in sports sponsorship', *International Journal of Advertising*, 17, 2, 3–28.

Mela, C. F., Gupta, S., and Lehmann, D. R. (1997), 'The long-term impact of promotion and advertising on consumer brand choice', *Journal of Marketing Research*, May, 34, 2, 248–261.

Mobile Marketing Association (2005), 'What is mobile marketing', www.mmaglobal.co.uk

Needleman, S.E. (2009), 'Social Media con game', *Wall Street Journal*, 12 October, B4.

Neff, J. (2010), 'Once skeptics, brands drink the Facebook Kool-Aid', *Advertising Age*, 22 February, 20.

Neff, J. (2013), 'L'Oreal attacks fast-growing E-commerce space', *Advertising Age*, 9 September, 18.

Nelson, P. E. (1970), 'Information and consumer behavior', *Journal of Political Economy*, 78, 2, 311–29.

New Shorter Oxford English Dictionary (1990), Oxford: Clarendon Press.

Nielson Company, The (2010), 'What Americans do online: Social media and games dominate activity', Reported in Gangadhambatla (2012).

Patel, K. (2010), 'You're using social media, but just who is overseeing it all'? *Advertising Age*, 22 February, 8.

Percy, L. (2014), *Strategic Integrated Marketing Communications*, 2nd edn, Oxford: Routledge.

Percy, L. and Rosenbaum-Elliott, R. (2012), *Strategic Advertising Management*, 4th edn, Oxford: Oxford University Press.

Prentice, R. M. (1977), 'How to split your marketing funds between advertising and promotion', *Advertising Age*, January, 41.

Ries, A. (2011), Comment in *Advertising Age*, 10 January.

Rossiter, J. R. and Bellman, S. (2005), *Marketing Communication: Theory and Applications*, French Forest NSW, Australia: Pearson Education Australia.

Rossiter, J. R. and Percy, L. (1988), 'Visual communication in advertising', in R.J. Harris (ed.), *Information Processing Research in Advertising*, Hillsdale, NJ: Lawrence Erlbaum Associates.

Rossiter, J. R. and Percy, L. (1997), *Advertising Communication and Promotion Management*, New York: McGraw-Hill.

Rossiter, J. R. and Percy, L. (2000), 'The a-b-e model of benefit focus in advertising', in T. J. Reynolds and J. C. Olson (eds), *Understanding Consumer Decision Making*, Mahwah, NJ: Lawrence Erlbaum Associates.

Rossiter, J. R. and Percy, L. (2003), 'How the role of advertising merely appears to have changed', *International Journal of Advertising*, 32, 3, 391–8.

Rossiter, J. R., Percy, L., and Donovan, R. J. (1991), 'A better advertising planning grid', *Journal of Advertising Research*, 31, 5, 11–21.

Schacter, D. L. (2001), *The Seven Sins of Memory*, Boston: Houghton Mifflin Co.

Schultz, D. (2010), 'The pyrite rush', *Marketing News*, 30 September, 12.

Shipley, D. Egan, C., and Wong, K. S. (1993), 'Dimensions of trade show exhibiting management', *Journal of Marketing Management*, 9, 1.

Silberer, G. and Engelhardt, J. F. (2005), 'Streaming media: a new way of online advertising', *Advertising and Communication*, Proceedings of 4th International Conference on Research in Advertising, Saarbrucken, Germany: Saarland University, 254–9.

Sonne, P. and Miller, J. W. (2010), 'EU chews on Web cookies', *The Wall Street Journal*, 22 November, B1–B2.

Southgate, P. (1994), *Total Branding by Design*, London: Kogan Page.

Steel, E. (2006), 'Web-page clocks and other "widgets" anchor new Internet strategy', *Wall Street Journal*, 21 November, B4.

Sullivan, E. A. (2010), 'Marketing aptitude', *Marketing News*, 15 March, 6.

Vrancia, S. (2005), 'Anywhere, anytime', *Wall Street Journal*, 21 November.

Vrancia, S. (2013), 'Web companies embrace TV ads', *The Wall Street Journal*, 2 December, B1.

Warr, P., Barter, J., and Brownbride, G. (1983), 'On the independence of positive and negative affect', *Journal of Personality and Social Psychology*, 44, 8, 641–51.

Wickelgren, W. A. (1977), *Learning and Memory*, Englewood Cliffs, NJ: Prentice Hall.

Wood, W. and Quinn, J. M. (2003), 'Forewarned and forearmed: two meta-analytic syntheses of forewarnings of influence appeals', *Psychological Bulletin*, 129, 1, 119–38.

Yuan, L. and Bryan-Low, C. (2006), 'Coming soon to cell phone screens—more ads than ever', *Wall Street Journal*, 16 August, B1.

Zmuda, N. (2013), 'Pepsi uncaps bottle redesign—but that's just the beginning', *Advertising Age*, 25 March, 6.

159

 Test your understanding of this chapter and explore the subject further using our Online Resource Centre. Visit the Online Resource Centre at http://www.oxfordtextbooks.co.uk/orc/elliott-percy3e/

7 Measuring Brand Performance and Equity

Key Concepts

1 Measuring brand performance and the effectiveness of a brand's marketing communication is critical to effective brand management.

2 There is an important difference between the strength and the nature of brand equity.

3 To effectively measure brand equity one must understand how it is built and developed.

4 A brand equity audit helps to uncover the elements of a brand and its market that are likely to affect its equity.

5 Both qualitative and quantitative methods for measuring brand equity are necessary.

6 The effective measurement of brand equity leads to a better understanding of its nature and how to manage it.

7 Pre-testing marketing communication is important to ensure that the brand's communication objectives are being met.

8 Continuous tracking is the optimum method for measuring brand performance and communication effectiveness.

Introduction

Brands must conduct a wide range of research beyond measures of performance and brand equity. Issues such as brand image, target audience, new product introductions, brand or line extensions, product portfolio mix, positioning, and much, much more must be addressed. All of this is well beyond the scope of this book. But we will be addressing specific ways to measure brand equity, pre-testing a brands marketing communication, and brand tracking because of their critical importance in monitoring brand performance and the effectiveness of a brand's marketing communication.

Measuring brand equity

While 'brand equity' as such is a relatively recent addition to the marketing vocabulary, the idea of brand equity as discussed in Chapter 5 dates back to much earlier times. In fact, over a century ago Karl Marx is quoted as saying that 'the mystical value of commodities does not originate in their value'. This sounds very much like the idea of brand equity.

Given this long history, it is surprising that it was only about 30 years ago that people began in earnest to develop methods for measuring brand equity. The Marketing Science Institute (MSI) in the USA began to seriously address the issue of measuring brand equity around 1990. They remarked at the time that the response to their call for proposals had exceeded anything they could remember. They awarded six grants in two categories: two for studies in the financial area and four in what they called the 'behavioural and psychological area'. Interestingly, three of the four 'behavioural and psychological' studies looked at brand equity only in terms of brand extension. The fourth utilized supermarket scanner data in an attempt to model the residual utility of a brand after objective characteristics are accounted for, such as specific product attributes and store environment (things like price and promotion).

In this chapter we are concerned with the 'behavioural and psychological' nature of brand equity, not the financial dimension, and this will be discussed in terms of the *strength* of a brand's equity and its *nature*. In the management of a brand, the building, strengthening, and nurturing of its equity will lead to a more positive contribution to market value for the company. But from a strategic brand *management* standpoint, one is concerned with measures that will help better manage that equity. If successful, the financial value of a brand name will take care of itself.

In order to successfully manage a brand's equity, one must understand how it is built, and where it is likely to lead. It is necessary to assess the strength of the brand and to understand its nature. And because brand equity is dynamic, and subject to change, its impact over time (along with that of competitive brands) must be tracked. Too often managers are content with only assessing the strength of their brand in the market. While it is important to know where you stand, without also understanding a brand's *nature* and its equity it is impossible to develop an effective long-term strategy for the brand.

Assessing the strength of a brand's equity and understanding its nature are clearly complementary processes, and require that a number of important questions are addressed, for example:

- Which brands are seen by consumers as the most competitive?
- How prominent or salient is a brand in the consumer's mind relative to other competing brands?

- What are the key dimensions of a brand's identity and how do consumers single it out from competitors?
- How high a value do consumers place on a brand, and on the basis of what benefits (product attributes, subjective considerations, emotions) do they discriminate in the brand's favour?
- What is the level of commitment to a brand?
- To what extent is loyalty to a brand dependent upon the situation in which the product is used?
- What is the relative price sensitivity of a brand versus competitors?
- How extendable is a brand, and in what areas?

A variety of research techniques will be discussed that are available to help answer these questions. But the very first step for a manager in addressing these issues is to review everything currently known about a brand, something called a brand equity audit.

Brand equity audit

The first step in conducting a brand equity audit, before any new research is contemplated, is to carefully examine all the information currently available. What is known about the brand? One of the problems with brand research is that it is all too frequently conducted to address a particular issue, and never really looked at in relation to other research that is being, or has been, conducted for the brand. On at least an annual basis, it is important to look at reports that have previously been done for the brand, or even done for other brands in the company's product portfolio. When reviewing different research findings, from different sources, together for the first time, the result may offer significant new insights (Robinson, 1992).

In this review of available information about a brand, the primary objective is to generate hypotheses concerning the key 'assets' of the brand that are likely to mediate its equity. These hypotheses will help guide and frame the measures of brand equity that should be used in any research that is conducted. Also, depending upon the brand's marketing strategy, a manager may also want to consider the information under review in light of other potentially related issues, for example possible line or brand extensions.

The real benefit of conducting a brand equity review on a regular basis is that it helps provide a look at the current state of knowledge about a brand's equity as well as providing a fresh understanding of the brand. It will also provide the manager with a better understanding of what role advertising and other marketing communication has played and can play in maintaining the brand.

What should be reviewed? In a word, *everything*. At least, everything that is reasonably available and likely to be relevant to the brand. Obviously, this will include any recent research that has been conducted for the brand, but also studies of general market trends and other information about the category, distribution channels, competitive activity, etc. How far back a manager should go in looking at this information must be determined specifically for each brand. But, for whatever period is appropriate, everything available should be reviewed.

It is critical that this 'everything' includes all the marketing communication that surrounds the brand. A brand really only exists in and through the marketing communication about it and its competitors. It is essential, therefore, in a brand equity audit to review the marketing communication for a brand and its key competitors. An advertising content analysis should be completed for the entire category, in terms of both underlying communication strategy and the claims each brand makes; and this analysis should reach back in time.

Even though most (if not all) of the information included in a brand equity audit will have been available and studied by the manager before, the benefit comes from looking at everything *together*, at one time. In this way themes can be detected that may not have been obvious when each report was being considered in the light of a specific issue. The brand equity review is an opportunity for a complete and comprehensive look at a number of elements likely to affect a brand's equity. Generally speaking, it should be summarized in a written report that presents what is currently known about a brand in three areas: the overall market, competitive strategies, and insights into brand equity.

- *The overall market.* Given that a brand's equity is relative, that it only makes sense within a particular marketing and competitive context, it is important to understand what is known about the existing state of things in the market where the brand competes. What the manager should be particularly interested in are any external factors likely to affect a brand's equity. This will provide the context necessary for understanding brand equity in the category.

- *Competitive strategies.* The second area should provide a clear summary of current marketing and communication strategies and tactics for the brand and its key competitors. It will be in this section that an analysis of the current advertising and other marketing communications will be summarized in relation to brand equity.

- *Insights into brand equity.* Here is where the report summarizes what has been learned about the brand that helps to evaluate its strengths or weaknesses. This is where the manager should speculate on the current strength and nature of the brand's equity, and what must be done to sustain, nurture, and protect it.

With this report in hand, the manager is in a position to look into what new measures of brand equity should be considered. This decision will be guided by gaps in the current understanding of the brand (or of key competitors, especially if they have changed), as well as key ongoing measures and measures necessary for new strategic considerations.

The brand equity audit makes use of existing research and other already available information. Building upon that base of understanding, research to measure current brand equity is needed. This type of research is known as *primary* research, and is conducted among members of the brand's target market (as opposed to *secondary* research, which is published research that is generally available from various other sources).

Qualitative brand equity research

There are two fundamental ways of conducting primary research: using qualitative methods and using quantitative methods. *Qualitative* research is done either with focus groups, where 8–10 members of a target population are led by a group moderator in a discussion of a topic, or with one-to-one, individual in-depth interviews. *Quantitative* research is conducted among a larger sample of the target population (usually 100 to 1,000, depending upon the complexity of the target market and the degree of reliability desired), utilizing a structured questionnaire. In this section we will be looking at qualitative research, and in the next quantitative.

The number of focus groups or in-depth interviews conducted will be a function of any number of market considerations. How many important market segments are involved? Are brand attitudes or behaviours expected to differ among particular demographic or geographic populations? If so, it is important to ensure adequate representation in the research design.

While occasionally it may only be necessary to conduct in-depth interviews, rarely will it be sufficient to only conduct focus groups. More often both in-depth interviews *and* focus groups will be needed. When each are conducted, both the social and individual considerations involved in decision making will be accounted for. Many aspects of people's responses to brands are mediated by their interaction with others, and focus groups permit this interaction to be explored. But a great deal of what *motivates* how people think and react is deeply personal, and this requires in-depth interviews, conducted on a one-to-one basis, to explore these issues.

Too often when thinking about qualitative research, especially focus groups, managers do not see it as part of a systematic or purposeful plan. Focus groups are looked upon as a (relatively) inexpensive and easily interpreted means of gathering information about an issue, one where answers are readily and quickly forthcoming. But in point of fact, there are no 'findings' from focus groups, only *learning*. Focus groups do not provide answers. What they do is help focus our thinking by treating reality as it is understood by people, and relating it to the everyday experiences of people. This is not easy, and requires a moderator well versed in the psychology of consumer behaviour, and a moderator's guide that reflects this same understanding.

One of the important inputs from using qualitative methods as a first step towards measuring brand equity (remember there are no results as such) is the identification of the key aspects of the equity: what many people think of as emotional versus functional aspects. In reality, these terms can be misleading, because they are not necessarily independent. Brands and their equity are better understood in terms of perceived benefits, and these benefits may be either specific attributes, subjective characteristics, or emotions associated with the brand or its use as we have discussed. This will be dealt with in more detail.

There are many, many techniques that skilled moderators and interviewers may use in qualitative research; more than can be dealt with here. But in terms of laying the foundation for measuring brand equity, there are two key areas that must be covered: motivation and benefit structure (Table 7.1). Some of the techniques used to address these two areas are discussed next.

TABLE 7.1 Key qualitative measures for brand equity

Motivation	Gaining an understanding of the underlying motivation that drives behaviour in a brand's category.
Benefit structure	Determining the benefits that help inform a brand's image.

Motivation

Understanding the underlying motivation that drives behaviour in a product class is critical. Without that knowledge, it is impossible to set strategy because brand attitude is related to that motivation. In fact, back in the early days of qualitative research, it was known as 'motivation research', pioneered by the psychologist Ernest Dichter (1964). Motivation can be explored with either focus groups or in-depth interviews. But because consumers are really not introspective about their behaviour, skilled probing is necessary to ensure that you get 'under the surface' and to the real nature of the motives involved. Some useful probes for getting at motivation include questions like:

- How does thinking about the brand make you feel?
- What is the significance of the product in your life?
- How do you use the brand?
- How do you feel when you use the brand?
- What else makes you feel that way?
- What is your first memory of the product?
- What would your life be like without products like this?

Careful analysis of a series of probes such as this will provide insight into motivation. Do not simply ask: 'Why do you buy this brand?'

Another popular way is to use what are known as projective techniques. These can be especially useful in situations where someone may be reluctant to talk about personal feelings, or where the actual motives involved are ambiguous. In such cases one might ask a question like: 'Why do your friends buy these products?' There are a wide variety of projective techniques available (Semeonoff, 1976). Some popular projective techniques include using cartoon characters in various brand purchase or usage situations and asking people to fill in what they are saying in the 'balloons' over their heads, or asking people to 'become the brand' and talk about themselves. Projective techniques can provide important insight into people's motives (Levy, 1985).

What one is looking for is a sense of whether the underlying motivation is either positive or negative. Does the brand make you happy? Does it solve or avoid a problem for you? One thing to look for is to see if the responses people give are brand-focused or people-focused. Brand-focused responses tend to reflect negatively oriented motivations (the more 'functional' aspect of brand equity); people-focused responses tend to reflect positively oriented motivations (the more 'emotional' aspect of brand equity). This is not an absolute, but does generally hold.

Benefit structure

The benefit structure of a brand will help inform its image. Think about brands you know. Sometimes that image is well formed, while in other cases it may be less well defined. For example, what one word comes to mind when you think about Volvo? Most people would say 'safety'. What comes to mind when you think about Ford? Different people are likely to come up with different thoughts here because Ford does not have a well-defined and focused image like Volvo. Does this mean that Ford's brand equity is not as strong as Volvo's? Not necessarily, only that Ford's equity is not so easily defined. They could both be equally positive.

To fully understand a brand's equity it is necessary to understand the *benefit structure* that supports it. This is a critical point, and will be discussed in more detail later in this chapter. One of the most important functions of qualitative research is to uncover what constitutes this benefit structure (Bong *et al.*, 1999). Note that it is important to understand the benefit structure of a brand as well as the benefit structure of its competitors. This means that in the qualitative phase of research the benefits associated with the *product category* are explored as well as individual brands. With quantitative research the benefit structure of specific brands will be assessed, as discussed later.

There are a number of qualitative techniques that help in identifying the components of a brand's image or personality, and its benefit structure. One way is to use projective techniques such as those already discussed in the section on motivation. Another way is to ask for cognitive associations (Krishnan, 1996), that is, the first thing that comes to mind when a person thinks of the category or brand (as illustrated in the example earlier with Volvo and Ford). This technique can then be enhanced by 'laddering' the responses, asking what that word brings to mind, and then what that response brings to mind (something called means-end analysis) (Rossiter and Percy, 2001).

Laddering is a good way of getting at benefit structure. Consider this example for a building society. When asked for the first thing that comes to mind when someone thinks about saving (cognitive responses), they might respond with comments like 'security', 'children', 'retirement', or 'money'. In itself, this is important information. But with laddering, it is possible to learn even more. If someone initially said 'security' when asked for the first thing that came to mind when thinking about saving, they would then be asked: 'And what does security make you think of?' They might respond, 'family'. Then they would be asked: 'And what does family make you think of?' The answer might be 'the future'. This laddering exercise has uncovered a series of associations in the person's mind related to the product category. Fig. 7.1 shows the results of an actual laddering exercise for 'saving'.

What is really important in looking at these responses is that they are all strongly *interrelated* in people's minds. This suggests a tightly associated benefit for the category. Each of the key benefits initially associated with the category is likely to stimulate one of the other benefits. A careful analysis of this laddering exercise suggests that at the heart of saving in people's minds is the benefit of security. How a building society rates in terms of perceived security will go a long way towards determining the strength of its brand equity; and this will depend upon associations in the target market's perception of the brand in terms of the other key benefits. These interrelationships are illustrated in Fig. 7.2, and reflect something known as cognitive structure.

security	→	family	→	future
future	→	security	→	preparation
or				
future	→	retirement	→	fear
children	→	future	→	preparation
retirement	→	no children	→	freedom
money	→	security	→	retirement

FIGURE 7.1 Means-end laddering analysis of 'savings'

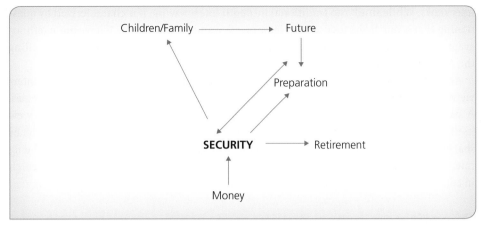

FIGURE 7.2   Cognitive structure for 'savings'

When strong interrelationships among key benefits are found, it generally means that the brand equity for all brands in the category will be constructed in basically the same manner, since the perception of one key benefit is strongly related to the other important benefits. But this is the exception rather than the rule. More often, when laddering, all the associations are not interrelated. When this occurs, it means that individual brand equities may be equally strong, but constructed in different ways, built upon different key benefits.

Consider a second example, this time fruit drinks. When asked for cognitive associations with their favourite fruit drink, people might respond with things like 'great taste', 'gives me energy', 'real fruit flavour', and 'lots of vitamins'. It is highly unlikely that when thinking of 'great taste' one of the other benefits mentioned would come to mind, or that any of these benefits would be likely to trigger another. This would mean that the equity for some brands might be built upon taste benefits, others on more health-oriented benefits. Each could have positive brand equities, but those equities would be built upon quite different benefit structures. Exactly what benefit structure defines a brand's equity must be measured in the quantitative research, as discussed in the section below on brand attitude. But the manager will have learned quite a bit about how brand equity in the category is constructed from the qualitative research.

Before leaving this subject, there is something else to be learned from these examples. The nature of the benefit structure can also aid a better understanding of motivation. Looking back at the benefit structure for savings, it is clear that it is very *functional*, suggesting the likelihood of negatively originating motives for saving. The fruit drink category is less well defined. Benefits such as 'taste' or 'flavour' suggest a more emotional association, and hence positively originating motives; benefits such as 'energy' or 'vitamins' could suggest more negatively originating motives. But remember, this is *qualitative* research, and we are not looking for answers, but direction. The answers, the actual *measures* of brand equity, will follow from the quantitative research.

Ethnography

While not normally thought about when thinking of measuring brand equity, the use of ethnographic research can be useful because of its ability to help gain insights into consumer behaviour. Beyond the generally understood use of ethnographic research in observing behaviour, good ethnographic research will also include extensive personal interviews. While similar to traditional in-depth interviewing, it is characterized by questioning that is much less focused. As Hammersley and Atkinson (1983) have put it, ethnographic interviews should be used as triggers to help stimulate the respondent into telling the researcher about a particularly broad area.

At the heart of ethnographic interviewing is a very informal approach where the interviewer does not use a structured set of questions, but a series of question-asking strategies. A strategy is picked according to the direction the discussion takes. Also, the interview itself may take place anywhere: while the subject is cooking a meal, on a shopping trip, or sharing a drink. In other words, the aim is for casual conversation where the person being interviewed is in control (Geertz, 1973). For a review of the role of ethnographic research in consumer behaviour, see Elliott and Jankel-Elliott (2003).

Quantitative brand equity research

The job of quantitative research is to assess the strength as well as understand the nature of a brand's equity relative to competitive brands. Up to this point the discussion has centred on those things it is necessary to understand before trying to quantify brand equity. Everything currently known about a brand has been reviewed and the manager has conducted qualitative research to help understand the motivations driving category and brand behaviour, and to identify the benefit structure involved. Now we will consider a number of techniques that may be used to assess the strength of brand equity, and then other techniques that should be used to gain an understanding of its nature. For a more detailed look at various quantitative research techniques, see any good marketing research text (such as Brown, Suter and Churchill 2014).

Assessing brand equity strength

The most common measures of brand equity involve measuring its strength. While this is important, such measures are really only addressing the *results* or consequences of brand equity. Managers do need to know about awareness and preference, who is buying the brand, and the effects of price. These are the practical measures that 'describe' a brand and its users, and where it stands in the market relative to competitors. But we must remember that this does *not* tell the manager *why*, or what can be done to positively affect brand equity. That will require more than descriptive measures. Nevertheless, the measures described in this section are essential because they provide managers with an assessment of their brand's performance in the market (Table 7.2).

TABLE 7.2 Assessing brand equity strength

Brand salience	The strength of a brand's awareness in relation to the awareness of other brands in the category.
Brand preference	The level of consumer preference for a brand versus others in the category.
Price elasticity	Indication of the extent to which consumers are willing to pay a higher price without switching brands.
Choice trade-offs	Identifies what product characteristics consumers are willing to trade-off before switching brands.

Brand salience

The idea of brand salience goes beyond brand awareness. Brand salience depends upon awareness, but it also reflects the relative *strength* of that awareness in relation to the target market's awareness of other brands in the category. This relationship will be reflected in the relative relationship between what is known as 'top-of-mind' awareness and all the other brands in the category of which someone is aware.

To measure brand salience one asks a representative sample of a brand's target market for 'all the brands that come to mind' in the category, and record the order in which they are mentioned. Then, one takes these responses and plots the number of first mentions for each brand versus the total number of mentions. Once this has been plotted, fit an exponential curve to the data, as seen in Fig. 7.3. These are awareness figures for brands of mineral water in France, and the plot is typical of what one usually finds. Most brands fall along the curve, indicating that the relationship between total mentions and top-of-mind is proportional.

Evian is clearly the strongest brand, most likely to come to mind first and being recalled by almost everyone. But what is of more interest are the results for Contrex, Volvic, and Badoit. Volvic and Badoit have proportionately greater top-of-mind awareness compared with total awareness, suggesting they are 'niche' brands with high brand salience. If one is aware of Volvic or Badoit, they are likely to be mentioned first, ahead of any other brand; otherwise they are much less likely to be mentioned. This suggests that only a small segment of the market is aware of them, but that those who are aware are likely to buy them. Contrex, on the other hand, is likely to be mentioned by most people, but relatively unlikely to be on the top of their mind. This suggests a low brand salience even though it has high overall brand awareness. Brand salience is important because brands that come to mind first are usually the brands we buy most often.

Another aspect of brand salience that provides insight into brand equity is the relationship between first brands mentioned and other brands mentioned by the same people.

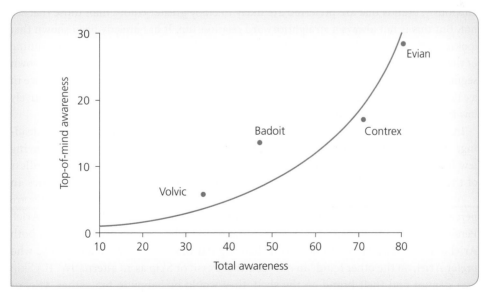

FIGURE 7.3   Relationship between top-of-mind and total brand awareness

TABLE 7.3 Contingency table of brand awareness

| Brands aware | Brand mentioned top-of-mind | | |
	Evian	Volvic	Contrex
Evian	—	75%	49%
Volvic	28%	—	62%
Contrex	55%	60%	—

Since the first brand mentioned is a good indicator of current usage (and in fact correlates highly with brand share), and other brands mentioned by the same person are potentially in their considered set for switching, comparing this relationship between brands provides a useful insight into brand equity. This can be done with a simple cross-tabulation of the awareness data gathered, as shown in the contingency table in Table 7.3.

Looking at this example, there is an asymmetrical relationship between Volvic and Evian. It suggests that it is not unusual to find that those who mention Volvic first are aware of Evian, the brand with the greatest awareness (or with Contrex, given its overall high awareness), and that those who mention Evian first are unlikely to mention Volvic because it appears to be a niche brand. On the other hand, Contrex is clearly symmetrical in structure to both Volvic and Evian. What is surprising here is that those likely to be buying Contrex are well aware of Volvic, a brand not otherwise well known. Such a finding should alert the manager to look into what is going on here. Perhaps Contrex users actually prefer Volvic, but have trouble finding it. Whatever the case, the brand manager for either Volvic or Contrex will want to get to the bottom of this.

Brand preference

Brand preference, like brand salience, can be an indicator of the strength of brand equity. Obviously, brands that are preferred are likely to enjoy greater equity than those that are not. But this is not always a straightforward relationship. It has already been shown that looking only at the level of overall brand awareness will not provide a good understanding of the strength of niche brands (which will have strong awareness only within their own segment of the market). This will also hold when looking at overall brand performance in a category. Preference for a niche brand may be high in its market segment, but relatively low in the market as a whole.

In addition, there is another aspect of overall brand preference that can be misleading, and that is the issue of perceived substitutability. Brands that are seen as having few likely substitutes are brands that are likely to have strong brand equity regardless of their share (assuming, of course, brand attitude is positive). Table 7.4 illustrates an asymmetric table of potential brand switching for washing powders. What it shows are perceived alternatives to their preferred brand, mentioned by people who use Ariel, Persil, and Skip. In this example, it is clear that people who say they prefer Skip see both Ariel and Persil as good alternatives if their regular brand is not available. Those who prefer Ariel, on the other hand, do not see either Persil or Skip as an alternative. If a Skip user cannot find their brand on the shelf, they would be happy to buy either Ariel or Persil; if an Ariel user cannot find their brand, it would not be an easy for them to find

TABLE 7.4 Asymmetric table of potential brand switching

Alternative brands considered	Brand preferred		
	Ariel	Persil	Skip
Ariel	—	60	80
Persil	25	—	60
Skip	5	30	—

Persil: Unilever © abimages / Shutterstock.com

a substitute. From these data it would be fair to assume that Ariel enjoys strong brand equity while Skip's is rather weak.

The result for Ariel and Persil is less dramatic, but it shows basically the same situation. Persil users are more open to alternatives than are Ariel users. But suppose market shares for Ariel and Persil are roughly the same. What does this say about the relationship between brand preference and brand equity? Clearly, brand share would not be a good measure of likely equity. Ariel would surely enjoy a stronger brand equity because users of Ariel (in this example) are much less likely to feel that another brand would be a good alternative.

Looking at brand preference is useful, but it is important to go beyond overall preference and examine likely switching behaviour. Questions of preference and switching are bound up with issues of brand loyalty, which will be discussed in the next section.

Price elasticity

Another important indicator of the strength of a brand's equity is price elasticity. To what extent is a consumer willing to accept a price increase without switching? Clearly one would expect a brand's core loyalty segment to be less price sensitive than switchers. But by their very nature, a brand's switchers use other brands, and price will be a key determinant of a switcher's choice. Usually this will be the result of a price promotion. But looking at price elasticity, the concern is with regular pricing policy. If a brand's price is raised relative to a switcher's brand set, how long will that brand remain in their set? This will be a function of the strength of the brand's equity.

One of the better ways of looking at price elasticity in terms of brand equity was offered some time ago by Moran (1978). He talked about a *dual* concept of upside and downside price elasticity. Upside elasticity is measured by looking at how much sales go up when the price is lowered, and downside elasticity by looking at how much sales go down when prices are increased. It is important to understand that upside and downside elasticity are *independent*. Just because sales do not drop significantly with a price increase does not guarantee (or even suggest) that sales will not rise with a price cut. The extent to which sales do or do not go up or down with a corresponding decrease or increase in price is entirely independent, they are not related.

The *relationship* between upside and downside elasticity, however, does provide a measure of brand equity strength. What one wants is a greater upside elasticity relative to downside elasticity; and the greater that difference, or the smaller the downside elasticity, the stronger the brand equity. This is because a strong upside elasticity, a significant increase in sales when prices go down, suggests increased perceived value for the brand; and weak downside elasticity, where sales do not fall off much when prices are increased, suggests a strong positive brand equity and reluctance to switch.

Choice trade-offs

A valuable (but often misused) technique that can be used to measure the strength of brand equity relative to specific product or marketing considerations likely to influence choice is a multivariate procedure called conjoint analysis (Green and Srinivasau, 1990; Lattin *et al.*, 2003). Conjoint analysis assumes that people make direct trade-offs among a set of product characteristics (e.g. package design, available flavours, promotions, etc.) when choosing among brands, and that the pattern of those trade-offs will 'predict' their preference. When a competitive set of brands is included as one of the variables, conjoint analysis will measure the extent to which brand name is a factor in choice relative to other considerations, reflecting not only the impact of brand name on choice, but also the strength of the individual brand equities.

The results of a conjoint analysis provide a summary of the importance of each variable studied to choice, as well as the 'part worth' of each level within the variables studied. An example should help make clear what is meant. In the pasta category, what is the effect of brand name, price, and promotion considerations (a coupon or free recipe book) on the choice of pasta? The results of a study looking at this found that brand name is very important. People seem willing to stick with the brand Mueller's even if Skinner is offering *both* a price-off coupon and a free recipe book (assuming both brands are at the regular price). No amount of marketing would give store brands an advantage over Mueller's without a price cut. The reason one can draw this conclusion is that conjoint analysis is what is called an 'additive' model. This means that by combining the part-worth values for any combination of variables one is able to 'predict' what the choice will be. Table 7.5 contains the part-worth values and shows, for example, that Mueller's at 0.98 is greater than Skinner with a 20¢ off coupon and free recipe book at 0.94 (0.26 + 0.34 + 0.34).

Consider another example. Suppose the brand manager for an airline wishes to measure the impact of a brand equity relative to a number of specific operational considerations: schedule, on-time performance, and ticket price. In other words, would people still

TABLE 7.5 Part-worth values for pasta choice

Brand	Price	Coupon	Incentive
Mueller's 0.98	20¢ off 0.96	20¢ 0.34	Free recipe book 0.34
Skinner 0.26	10¢ off –0.08	15¢ –0.34	No incentive –0.34
Store brand –1.20	Regular –0.88 price		

prefer to fly with an airline even if it did not have the most convenient schedule, best on-time performance, or lowest price. Fig. 7.4 shows the results of a conjoint analysis that addressed this issue.

What it shows is that in this example brand name has *no effect* on airline choice relative to schedule (the most important consideration), price (the second most important consideration), or on-time performance. In this case, any positive brand equity associated with a specific airline is not enough to overcome scheduling or price considerations. This does not, however, mean that airline brand equity plays no role at all in choice. If schedule, price, and on-time performance are all roughly the same, individual brand equities would then be likely to influence choice.

It is important to remember when using conjoint analysis that it is an additive model, assuming that people make direct trade-offs among alternative variables, but most actual decisions are not, strictly speaking, linear. So while conjoint analysis can be a useful measure of the relative extent to which brand equity may be influencing choices in a category, actual prediction of behaviour using conjoint models (unless they are non-linear) will be

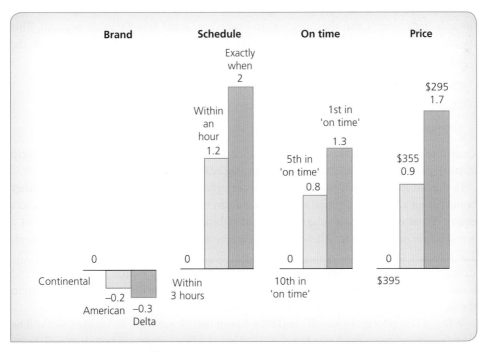

FIGURE 7.4   Brand effect on airline choice

TABLE 7.6 Measures for understanding brand users

Core loyalty	Going beyond purchase behaviour to get at the *attitudes* underlying purchase behaviour in the category.
User profiles	Comparing user images with actual user profiles and gaining an understanding of how the brand is used.

subject to the extent that people actually do make linear trade-offs in their decision making among the product or marketing considerations studied.

Understanding brand users

One of the primary functions of quantitative research is to gain an understanding of category users, and specifically users of a brand versus users of competitive brands (Table 7.6). How similar are category users to the general population? In what ways are users of a brand similar to or different from users of competitive brands? How committed are users of each brand in the category? Who are the brand's loyal users, and how do they differ from loyal users of other brands? There are two basic types of measures that are used in answering these questions. First is a measure of 'loyalty', which is a combination of brand purchase behaviour and brand attitude. Then, based upon this, one is able to 'profile' various user segments.

Core loyalty

Traditionally, researchers look at purchase behaviour and infer loyalty. They measure how often people buy a brand, repeat purchase behaviour, or share of usage occasions. But these measures do not go far enough. Brand loyalty is a function of people's *attitude* towards both brands and the category, and measures must take this into account. This means using more attitudinally based questions such as having people choose one of the following to indicate their brand behaviour:

'I prefer this brand over others in the category.'

'I buy a number of brands in the category and don't feel strongly about any of them.'

'Although this is my favourite brand, I will buy others that I like if they are on sale.'

Questions like this get at the attitudes that underlie category purchase behaviour, and help identify people who are willing to switch among brands in the category.

In the last section it was pointed out how the extent to which users of a brand see other brands as an acceptable alternative can provide an indication of the strength of a brand's equity. What one is trying to do in measuring brand loyalty is identify the extent of a brand's core commitment. All brands have users with various degrees of commitment. The stronger the commitment, generally speaking, the stronger the brand equity. The stronger the perceived brand equity, the less willing a user is to switch. Because the brand is seen as providing 'more' of what they want, purchase is more likely to continue, even in the face of things like competitive price-off promotions.

While it is important to identify and understand these loyal users, in reality there will be more 'switchers', those users who buy the brand but also buy competitor brands as well. From the manager's perspective, *strategically* these brand switchers are more important because that is where the brand's growth is most likely to come from, always remembering that brand loyals will usually provide the foundation of a brand franchise, and must never be taken for granted. As a result, marketing communication will be aimed at attracting increased usage from switchers while reinforcing positive attitudes among brand loyals. The key here is brand attitude. In order to successfully target switchers and retain brand loyals, it is critical to understand what drives brand attitude, the foundation of a brand's equity for its users.

This issue will be addressed later in the chapter, in the section on measuring the nature of brand equity. But in addition to the attitudes of a brand's users, it is also useful to have profiles of just who they are, and how they compare with the users of competitor brands.

User profiles

Determining the profile of brand users is perhaps the most common use of quantitative research. Profile measures are useful to managers because they provide an idea of who it is that uses their brand, which can be especially useful when developing marketing communication. The most common measures for profiling brand users reflect what Gerrit Antonides and W. Fred van Raaij (1998) have described in their book on consumer behaviour as *general level* characteristics of a market: demographics (e.g. age, income, geographic area), lifestyle (e.g. active in sports, like to travel), and psychographics (e.g. outgoing, conservative). Like all the assessments of brand equity strength discussed so far, profile measures reflect the results of brand equity. Some brands are seen as 'young', some as 'old', and the demographic profile of their users is likely to reflect this. Some brands are thought of as 'cutting edge' while others in a category are more 'traditional', and this is likely to be reflected in the psychographic profile of their users.

In effect, these profiles are user *images*. In the main, the image of a brand's user will reflect the profile of actual users, because the image embodies the characteristics associated with the brand. If actual user profiles do not reflect the image of the user, one of two things may be happening. Either there is a misperception of who uses the brand (unlikely) or there are strong aspirational considerations involved. In either case, such differences will reflect brand equity. A brand may be seen as used only by upscale consumers, or perhaps by those engaged in a vigorous outdoor lifestyle, when in fact the brand is actually used by a broad spectrum of people. There may be a segment of the middle class who use a brand precisely because it is known to be the brand of choice among the rich; or football fans may use a brand because it is known to be used by athletes. In each case this will be a function of the *image* of the brand. Understanding the user image profile is as instructive as knowing the actual profile of brand users (and often more instructive).

Another important aspect of profiling brand users is an understanding of *how* the brand is used. What are the actual usage occasions? Are some brands in a category seen by users as more or less appropriate for specific occasions? Think of chocolate. While Cadbury would make a good snack, Perugino is more likely to be considered only for special occasions. Some cleaners are seen as generally for everyday use, others for really tough jobs; some brands of whisky you order at a pub, others at a fine restaurant. Why a brand is purchased and how it is used reflects brand users' image of usage occasion, part of its brand equity.

The nature of brand equity

Up until this point the discussion has been about measures of brand equity strength. In this section measures of brand equity that provide insight into understanding its nature are considered. Specifically, the questions of brand image and brand attitude (Table 7.7).

TABLE 7.7 Measures for understanding the nature of brand equity

Brand attitude	Determines those benefits that drive positive brand attitude, which are the components for building brand equity.
Image ownership	Identifies those benefit claims uniquely associated with a brand versus competitors.

Structure of brand attitude

Most marketers would agree that brand equity is that 'something' attached to a brand that adds value over and above the objective characteristics of the product or service, as discussed in Chapter 5. Whatever that 'something' is, it is embodied in people's attitudes towards that brand. It is dynamic, and subject to change over time. It attaches itself to the brand name, providing a current summary of people's feelings, knowledge, and experience with that product or service. Brand equity is a result of brand attitude, and this is what provides the key to its understanding. In many ways, building and ensuring a continuing positive brand attitude is what strategic brand management is all about, because it leads to strong brand equity.

What is needed to really understand the *nature* of brand equity is a measure of the *components* that lead to it, and this means measures of how the market forms current attitudes towards the brand. To really understand a brand's equity, it is necessary to understand how it is constructed. It is this understanding that ensures an effective positioning, and the ability to adjust that positioning over time as needed to continue building and sustaining positive brand equity.

The expectancy-value model introduced in the last chapter is considered by most researchers in consumer behaviour to be the best model of attitude, and it provides one of the best ways to measure it. As we have seen, this model states that an attitude towards an object, a brand or product in our case, is the sum of everything we know about it weighted by how important those beliefs are to us (Fishbein and Ajzen, 1975). Obviously, it is impossible to study 'everything' about a brand or product, but one can and should consider everything critical to the *benefit positioning* of the brand. This will be known from the benefit structure uncovered in the qualitative research that leads to the brand's positioning.

In the last chapter we saw how the expectancy-value model is used to select the optimum benefit for positioning a brand. Here we shall see how this same type of analysis is also used to measure how a brand's equity is *structured*; what it is about a brand that contributes most to the overall attitude toward the brand and hence its equity.

Consumers hold what might be thought of as an overall summary judgement about a brand, reflecting their attitude toward it and its brand equity. 'Clarks makes great shoes' is an *attitude* about Clarks that connects the brand in the consumer's mind with what is the likely purchase motive, sensory gratification (i.e. they buy Clarks shoes to *enjoy* them). This brand attitude, however, does not just spring from nowhere, but is the result of one or more beliefs about the *specific benefits* the brand offers in support of that overall attitude. In the same way that the expectancy-value model is used to identify those benefits with the most potential leverage in positioning, it can be used to identify what it is about a brand that drives overall brand attitude.

TABLE 7.8 Comparative expectancy-value model of attitude for hard candy

	Importance weight (a_i)	Belief (b_i)	
		Taverner's Drops	Cavendish and Harvey
Lasts a long time	3	1	3
Real fruit flavour	3	3	1
Burst of fruity flavour	1	3	1
So good to share	1	1	1
Wakes up taste buds	0	1	0
All familiar flavours	1	1	3
$A_o = \sum_{i=1}^{n} a_i b_i$		17	17

What we are looking to include in measuring brand attitude are those benefits associated with the category, and the benefit claims for the brands in it, that define the positioning of those brands; and especially those related to the underlying motives driving behaviour in the category. Table 7.6 lists a number of benefits and benefit claims that have been associated with hard candy. While in reality there may be as many as 15 or 20 benefits associated with a category and its brands, these (which came from an actual study) will serve to illustrate how an expectancy-value model is used to measure brand attitude and help understand brand equity just as we saw in the Volvo and BMW example in the last chapter.

In a quantitative survey of the target market, people are first asked how *important* each of the benefits and benefit claims are to them when considering buying hard candy. Importance is measured using a three-point scale where if the benefit is essential to the target market it is weighted a '**3**', if the benefit is desirable but not essential it is weighted a '**1**', and if it is not all that important it is weighted '**0**'. Then, for the brand under study and each of its major competitors, people are asked how well that brand delivers the benefit. Here again, a three-point scale is used where if the brand is thought to definitely deliver the benefit it is weighted a '**3**', if it is thought to only do an acceptable job in delivering the benefit it is weighted a '**1**', and if it is not perceived to deliver the benefit it is weighted a '**0**'.

After conducting a study among hard candy consumers, suppose the results shown in Table 7.8 are found. What understanding does this provide about the equity of Taverner's Drops and Cavendish and Harvey? Overall, people's attitudes towards the two brands are the same (the expectancy-value weighted sum of importance times benefit delivery is the same for each). But the real insight is that the *equity* for each brand is different, even though they are both seen as equally good. Taverner's equity is built upon a perception in the market that it has a good fruit taste while Cavendish and Harvey's equity is a function of the fact that it is perceived to last a long time and offers many flavours.

Because people's attitude towards these two brands is positive and equally strong, measures of their brand equity strength are also likely to be positive and roughly the same. If the only measures available are of brand equity strength there would be no *understanding* that while both are strong brands, their positive brand equity is a result of quite different perceptions of each brand.

This is a mistake made too often by managers. Each of the measures discussed in the last section in this chapter address various aspects of brand equity, and all are useful tools in the manager's kit, but they are only measuring various consequences of brand equity. Even more comprehensive brand building and brand equity models such as Young and Rubicam's BrandAsset Valuator or Millward Brown's BrandDynamics model, while identifying relative brand strengths and weaknesses, do not address the fundamental underpinnings of brand equity. This requires gaining an understanding of the way in which attitude towards a brand is built.

This understanding is critical for the *managing* of a brand. What could the marketing manager for Taverner's Drops do to increase its brand equity and create an advantage over Cavendish and Harvey? At least three strategies are available, based upon an understanding of the market as revealed by the research. They could attack Cavendish and Harvey's strength along the 'lasts a long time' benefit, or introduce more 'favourite' flavours. Creating the perception that the brand really delivers on the 'lasts a long time' benefit, not just does an okay job, makes the most sense because it is more important to people, and they would not need to change their flavour line. If the brand could convince the market that Taverner's Drops do indeed last a long time, overall attitude towards the brand would increase significantly (applying the expectancy-value model, going from the current level of 17 to 23).

Another option open to them would be to try and raise the importance of a 'burst of fruity refreshment' in people's consideration of hard candy from desirable to essential because the brand already enjoys an advantage over Cavendish and Harvey on that benefit. If successful, it would again significantly increase favourable brand attitude, and hence brand equity.

You can see how this analysis is closely tied to benefit selection for positioning, and it should underscore how important it is to get the correct positioning for a brand. An effective positioning, through marketing communication, leads to positive brand attitude, which in its turn helps build strong brand equity. Measuring brand equity with the expectancy-value model provides managers with the opportunity to evaluate what it is that is at the heart of their brand's equity, and what it will take to further the old positive brand attitude to increase that brand equity.

Image ownership

Brand images are created by benefit claims that are made about a brand, usually through marketing communication. As we saw in the last chapter, benefits are either attributes (e.g. low in fat), subjective considerations (e.g. healthy), or emotions (e.g. look great), that are associated with a brand. Benefit *claims* are how these benefits are presented to the consumer.

In positioning a brand, benefits are selected that are important to the brand's target market and that they feel the brand can deliver (and, ideally, are uniquely associated with the brand as we saw in the previous chapter). They are then presented in marketing communication as a visual or verbal benefit *claim* (Percy and Rosenbaum-Elliott, 2012). For example, through research it may be learned that a brand is perceived to taste better than most of its competitors. This benefit of 'great taste' might be turned into a benefit claim along the lines of 'so good you will want to share it'. The type of benefit selected will suggest the orientation of the benefit claim, which may be looked at in terms of rational, emotional, relational, or value considerations. As Rossiter and Percy (1997) have pointed out, benefit claims should be designed to elicit an emotional response that will help motivate the consumer to consider the brand, and create or reinforce positive beliefs about the brand.

An important key to *understanding* brand equity is to identify those claims that 'signal' a brand's image. These 'signals' are those aspects of the brand that are most likely to come to mind or be associated with the brand. As already mentioned, benefit claims may be either visual or verbal, so brand signals too may be either visual or verbal. A good example of a visual brand signal is the one associated with Andrex toilet tissue in the UK. If you are familiar with the brand, what are you now thinking about? If you are like most people, you will be thinking about the Labrador retriever that was introduced into their advertising way back in 1972 and has been a continuing part of their advertising ever since. The retriever puppy 'signals' Andrex, and helps drive the brand's image.

In measuring a brand image, and more particularly its image relative to competitors, one is looking for something that might be thought of as 'image ownership'. This is measured by asking questions about what brands are linked to what claims, and what benefits are related to those claims. A general idea about what benefits and claims are associated with the category will come from qualitative research. What is measured quantitatively is specifically what brand or brands people associate with each benefit and claim.

Based upon what is learned from the quantitative measures of the importance of the benefits and claims, and their association with a brand, it is possible to paint a good picture of how the market 'sees' or understands the image of specific brands in a category; and with that, an understanding of brand equity. A particularly good way of looking at this is to plot the strength of claim associations in a category with the number of brands associated with each claim, as shown in Fig. 7.5. This relationship helps to clarify image ownership, and underscores the desirability of coming up with a believable claim, appropriate to the category, but unique to the brand.

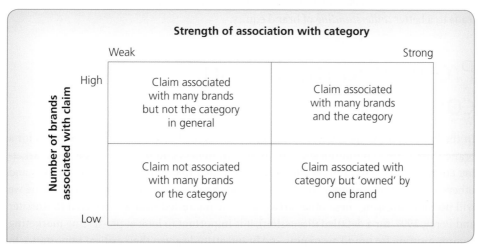

FIGURE 7.5 Relative brand image ownership

This helps the manager understand brand equity in the following way. Assuming only claims that are based upon benefits important to the target market are considered, if it is found that only one brand in the category is strongly associated in people's minds with a claim, in effect that brand 'owns' the image suggested by that claim. If people in the target market are asked which brand or brands of tea are 'a lovely cup of tea', and almost everyone says Yorkshire Tea, this suggests a strong and unique brand image for it built upon the benefit claim of 'a lovely cup of tea'. Suppose people in the market are asked for the name of an automobile which is 'for life', and while a few people mention Volvo, most people do not associate the claim with any automotive name plate. Since only one brand is associated with the claim, and only among a small segment of the market, this benefit helps define an important market *niche*. This would suggest that for that particular segment of the market, the claim 'for life' helps to define the brand equity of Volvo.

On the other hand, if the target market for private banking is asked what bank or banks 'challenge us, we'll find the solution' and a high association with the claim is found for Lloyds TSB, UBS Private Banking, Investec, and others, it would suggest that the claim is not 'owned' by any one bank, but is seen more as a *category* benefit, describing a number of private bankers. This would mean that UBS Private Banking (which used the claim) was getting *no differential advantage* from the benefit claim in building its own brand image and equity. If this same target market was asked which bank or banks are 'Out of the Ordinary', we might find that almost no one associates the claim with any bank. This would mean that the benefit implied by the claim 'Out of the Ordinary', while important to the target market (only benefit claims found to be important to the market are being measured), is not perceived as being a part of the image for any bank in the category. This means that while Invertec (which used the claim) had correctly positioned itself on an important benefit, it did not link that benefit to the brand, and as a result it is not contributing to the brand's image and equity.

There are many other ways of measuring brand image. Perhaps the most common is to simply develop a 'profile' of the brand by measuring how many people feel each of a number of attributes or benefits associated with the category describes a brand. In a sense, that is what is going on here, but the important difference is that one is also looking at what benefit *claims* 'signal' a brand's image, not just the attributes and benefits that are related to the brand. This enables a fuller understanding of image ownership, which in its turn leads to a better *understanding* of brand equity.

Pre-testing marketing communication

In the last chapter we pointed out that the two universal communication objectives for a brand's marketing communication are brand awareness and brand attitude. All marketing communication for a brand should be pre-tested to ensure that these objectives and others are being met, along with the likelihood the message will be processed. While we will not be addressing these other areas here (the interested reader is referred to Rossiter and Percy, 1997, for a detailed discussion), it is important to look at pre-testing marketing communication for brand awareness and brand attitude given their critical importance to brand success.

Before dealing with how to measure brand awareness and attitude in a pre-test, we need to address how *not* to 'measure' it. All too often focus groups are used to 'test' the effectiveness of marketing communication, but they are wholly inappropriate. They are of course useful in the development of messages, but not evaluating their effectiveness. There are two fundamental reasons why focus groups should *never* be used in pre-testing marketing communication. One, focus groups vastly overexpose the execution. In the real world, advertising and other marketing communications are only seen briefly, if at all. In a focus group attention is directed to the execution, and it is thoroughly discussed. The second problem concerns validity. By their very nature focus groups encourage interaction among group participants that militate against the individual reaction to the message and execution that occurs in the market.

Another frequently used, but also inappropriate, way of pre-testing (and also post-testing) marketing communication, especially advertising, is recall testing. While advertising recall measures may provide some very rough indication of attention to the message, that is also part of the problem. Recall tests are *advertising*-based and not brand based. What is needed are brand-associated measures of awareness, not awareness of the advertising or attitude toward the advert.

Measuring brand attitude

In measuring brand attitude in a pre-test we want to know how favourably our brand is evaluated relative to competitor brands, regardless of purchase intent. Recall from our discussion earlier in the chapter how the expectancy-value model of attitude is used to gain an understanding of the beliefs associated with a brand, and their importance, and how managers can use the model to evaluate the relative strength of their brand versus competitive brands. Additionally, the model enables the manager to access the attitude structure, those beliefs that help build positive attitude for the brand.

While this helps provide an understanding of the nature of brand attitude and brand equity, when pre-testing marketing communication we are only looking for an overall or global measure of brand attitude. The best way of measuring this is with a simple bipolar scale. As Rossiter (2011) has pointed out, too often researchers use multiple item scales in measuring brand attitude, which more often than not are addressing different types of evaluations. Because brand attitude is a quantitatively conditioned response, it should be measured with a single item numerical scale. A simple Good-Bad bipolar scale will usually suffice. The extent of the scale will vary with the complexity of the category. With 'simple' products such as most fmcgs the scale should not exceed 5-points (-2, -1, 0, $+1$, $+2$ running bad to good). But for products with complex choice decisions, where more consideration is given to the purchase, a 9-point or 11-point bipolar scale should be used.

Measuring brand awareness

You may be wondering why we are discussing brand awareness after brand attitude and not before. This is because in a pre-test brand awareness should be the very last thing to be measured. The reason for this reflects the role brand awareness plays in the purchase decision process. Recall from our discussion of brand awareness strategy in the last chapter that there are two types of awareness, recognition and recall, and that 'awareness' of a brand is not required until the actual purchase decision is being made. With recognition brand awareness this means at the point-of-purchase, and with recall when the need occurs prior-to-purchase. Awareness of the brand is not needed until then, well *after* exposure to marketing communication.

This presents a problem in trying to measure the effectiveness of creating strong brand awareness in a pre-test. You can create an artificial delay before asking about awareness by asking a series of 'filler' questions after gathering the brand attitude and other measures taken in the pre-test, such as collecting the demographic information. The point would be to encourage other neural activity that is not associated with the brand. But a better, if inconvenient and more expensive, way is to conduct a separate follow-up interview a day or even a week or more later. Yet even with a delay like this, the measure is likely to over-estimate actual brand awareness because the pre-test itself drew specific attention to the brand, significantly more attention than the marketing communication is likely to achieve on its own in the market.

Earlier we discussed how to measure brand salience, and while brand salience reflects brand awareness, what we are measuring here in connection with a brand's marketing communication is different. Here, measures of brand awareness reflect the role of recognition versus recall awareness in the decision process. With recognition brand awareness, one way to measure it is to provide people with a display of several competing brand-packages and ask which brands would satisfy a particular category need. To measure recall brand awareness, you must present the need first and then ask for all of the brands that come to mind that would satisfy that need. For example, if you ran a chain of Thai restaurants, you would ask what restaurants came to mind when someone wanted to eat out at a Thai restaurant. For both recognition and recall, the order of brand mention should be recorded.

We have now looked at a number of ways of measuring brand equity, and how to pre-test marketing communication to measure its effectiveness in building brand awareness and attitude. But it is important for managers to have an on-going understanding of brand performance and the impact of the brands marketing communication. This requires tracking studies, which we address in the next section.

Tracking brand performance

There are three basic tracking study methodologies: panel, wave, and continuous. There are advantages and disadvantages to each, but overall continuous tracking is the best (Rossiter and Percy, 1997).

Panel tracking involves interviewing the *same* people each time, from the benchmark prior to a campaign and in each successive 'wave' of interviews during the campaign. This permits causality to be established at the individual consumer or customer level. The disadvantage, however, is that panels are very expensive and difficult to maintain, and if the interviews are conducted too frequently there is the potential to sensitize the participants to be more likely to make purchases in the studied category.

With *wave* tracking, *separate samples* are interviewed each time. This enables the manager to relate steps in the chain of effects, but only at the aggregate level. It does not permit processing to be causally linked to communication effects over time.

Continuous tracking uses small random samples of consumers or customers drawn from the target audience, and interviews are conducted *daily* or *weekly*. Instead of interviewing, say, 600 people every quarter or so, as happens with panel and wave tracking,

50 people would be interviewed every week for 12 weeks. The total number of interviews over the quarter is the same, but the interviewing is continuous. The potentially large variance due to the small sample error is overcome by tabulating results with a moving average. Continuous tracking provides a good compromise between panel and wave tracking methodologies. It is sufficiently casual and reliable, and it enables the manager to take quick action because the results are available continuously and all but instantly.

To give you some idea of what can be learned about brand performance in response to marketing communication from continuous tracking, we will briefly look at some insights gained from actual studies. (These and many others are discussed in *Advertising and the Mind of the Consumer*, by M. Sutherland, 2008.)

Brand awareness versus trial

Brand awareness is critical for all brands, but especially so for new products. If people are not aware of the new brand, there is almost no chance they will try it. When introducing a new brand into the market, it is critical that not only sales are tracked, but also awareness of the brand. New products, especially low-involvement products, must generate trial quickly for a number of reasons. It is important to reach payout quickly in order to sustain marketing budgets. But it is also important to capitalize on the 'newness' of the brand. With fmcgs, there are new product introductions all the time, and without an early foothold, the brand is not likely to succeed.

Suppose a new brand is introduced, but after two months sales remain disappointingly low. Is it time to give up? It depends. If most of the target audience are aware of the brand, but have not tried, the answer is 'yes'. But what if only a few people are aware of the brand? That is the case we see illustrated in Fig. 7.6. After two months, awareness for this new brand was only 26%. This suggests that something is wrong with either the advertising itself or its media schedule. Brand awareness is the *easiest* thing to communicate about a brand, and the tracking results indicate it is not happening. If sales remain low after new advertising (or an adjustment in the media schedule) increases awareness, then it is time to pull the brand. But this decision cannot be made without a good understanding of how your advertising is working.

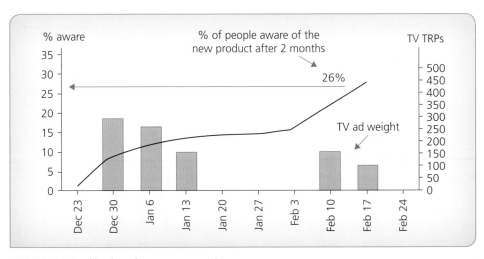

FIGURE 7.6 Tracking brand awareness over time

Building the brand–benefit link over time

In the discussion of the Rossiter–Percy grid it was pointed out that strategies for building brand attitude when dealing with positively motivated behaviour—transformational strategies—the benefit is often implied by the execution, and takes time to build. This makes it very difficult to use standard advertising 'testing' to determine if your message is working. In the 1990s a new snack brand was introduced using a musical jingle that talked about a couple of general benefits that were not very differentiating (such as 'best'). The execution itself, especially the visual components and the pacing, however, was meant to imply that this was a 'modern' brand, the brand's primary positioning.

Not surprisingly, when asked what the message said, people responded with the benefits offered in the jingle. Very few talked about it being 'modern'. But transformational brand attitude strategies take time to build, and this is just what happened. In a continuous tracking study, when people were asked 'which brand or brands do you most associate with the description "a modern, up-to-date brand?"' the new snack brand was mentioned even though people did not mention this as a part of the message. And as seen in Fig. 7.7, this benefit association with the brand built over time.

This is a good example of how effective transformational advertising builds positive brand attitude, and how continuous tracking can measure its effect. If the brand manager relied only upon a traditional advertising 'effectiveness' study that only looked at what people felt the message 'said', it is likely the advertising would have been seen as a failure. It required *indirect* measurement, over time, with something like a continuous tracking study, to learn if the emotional authenticity of the execution was effective in associating the brand in people's minds with the desired benefit.

Building brand attitude over time

In contrast, we know that for informational brand attitude strategies we must provide information, and that for high-involvement decisions the potential buyer must be *convinced* by the advertising (and other marketing communication) before making an actual commitment to purchase. And this brand purchase intention takes time to arrive at because someone is unlikely to be convinced the first time they see an advert. If managers

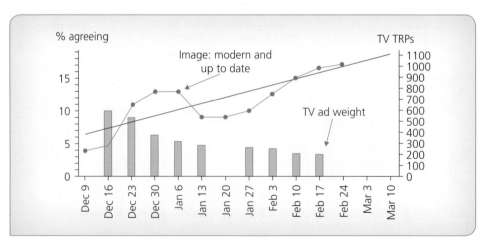

FIGURE 7.7 Building brand-benefit link over time

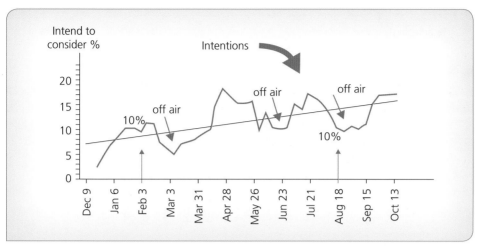

FIGURE 7.8   Building brand attitude over time

for high-involvement products are not sensitive to this need for advertising to take time in order to fully convince the target audience to take action, they may give up on the brand because sales are slow to develop.

After launching a new high-involvement durable product, a company wanted to cut out advertising after only 7 weeks because of disappointing sales results. But the company was conducting a continuous tracking study of the launch, and was convinced by the researchers that even though sales were below expectation, it was too early to give up. As can be seen in Fig. 7.8, this was a smart decision. Each time the brand was advertised, a positive increase in brand attitude and intention to buy occurred, and eventually sales did respond.

Uncovering unexpected advertising effects

There is a fascinating aspect to how our minds work that psychologists call the *mere exposure* effect (Zajonc, 1968). If someone is simply exposed to something, they are more likely to prefer it to something to which they have not been exposed. Psychologists know this from conducting studies where they show people a set of random shapes or some other stimuli. Then, at a later time, they show them a series of paired examples, one from the set they had seen earlier and one similar, but not seen, and ask which is preferred. Consistently people 'prefer' the one they have been exposed to earlier.

This same effect can occur with advertising. Fig. 7.9 illustrates how the popularity of a brand increased over time with advertising. The advertising execution reflected its 'taste and occasion suitability' positioning, but over time the number of people who felt that 'everyone seems to be drinking it' increased steadily. This increase in *popularity* for the brand was a function of mere exposure. Simply because it was seen advertised, the target audience felt the brand was more popular, even though this was not part of the creative strategy.

As just these four examples show, tracking studies (especially continuous tracking) can help managers better understand the effect their advertising and other marketing communication is having on the market, and this in turn enables the manager to make better strategic decisions for the brand. It is not enough to position the brand well and develop

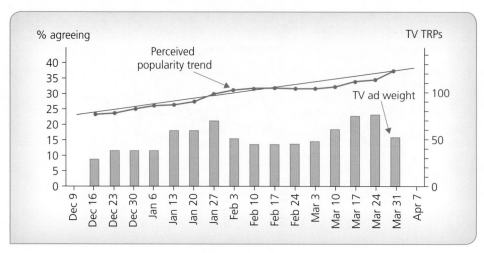

FIGURE 7.9   Brand popularity increasing over time

effective communication strategies. Managers must also monitor and evaluate how well the advertising itself, as well as another marketing communication, is contributing to a brand's success.

CHAPTER SUMMARY

The importance of not just measuring brand equity but *understanding* its nature should now be clear. While it is important to measure brand equity in order to know where a brand stands relative to others in the market, to successfully *manage* a brand, understanding brand equity is critical. In the final analysis, there is no one measure of brand equity. Rather, as we have seen, it is important to use measures of both strength and understanding. Additionally, the importance of pre-testing marketing communication to ensure the objectives for the brand are being met was discussed. Finally, the role of continuous tracking was shown to be critically important in measuring brand performance and the effectiveness of a brand's marketing communication.

DISCUSSION QUESTIONS

1 What is a benefit structure, and why is it so important to the measurement of brand equity?

2 Conduct a laddering exercise for two competing brands, and discuss what the results tell you about the image and positioning of the two brands.

3 What are the essential measures of a brand's equity strength and how does each contribute to a better understanding of the brand equity?

4 What is the benefit of profiling a brand's users?

5 Discuss how price elasticity can indicate the strength of a brand's equity.

6 What does it mean to 'own' an image, and how does that help build strong brand equity?

7 Discuss how the expectancy-value model is used to uncover the components of brand attitude, and what that means for understanding the nature of brand equity.

8 Why should focus groups not be used in pre-testing marketing communications?

9 How does measuring the nature of brand equity differ from measuring brand attitude resulting from marketing communication?

10 Why is continuous tracking the best way to measure the effectiveness of a brand's marketing communication?

CASE STUDY

Nike women's dance campaign 2006: 'Tell me I'm not an athlete'

Nike is a popular and leading brand name in the world of sportswear. Today, nearly four decades have passed since its foundation and Nike has never ceased to stop becoming a chief resonating brand name in the world's major global markets. The globally recognized 'Just do it' slogan and swoosh logo stand as marketing evidence to Nike's universal brand recognition.

Nike has long established its grounds as the popular choice for major, serious athletes. Using high profile athletes in major sports categories in its marketing communications, Nike gained a foothold among fans of such athletes and became the preferred brand choice among such groups. Not so surprisingly, Nike's campaigns with their focus on predominantly male sports have largely attracted the young male consumer to its brand, as opposed to the female.

In an attempt to expand its target market, Nike sought to attract athletes of the opposite sex. This, however, is not a mere replication and adaptation of existing campaigns to incorporate a feminine perspective. Rather, much work is needed. To attract young women, Nike recognized that it needed to understand the nature of those sports activities that sparked a passion in the young active female.

Being a successful brand at targeting young men, Nike aspired to achieve similar success with targeting young women. Specifically, their major objective was to become the number one choice of sportswear for women by the summer of 2006. Aiming to target women between 17 and 24 years old, Nike sought to understand what made these women unique athlete-wise. Through market research, it was determined that Nike's target woman believes (and prefers) dancing to be her ultimate athlete training method. Specifically, Nike's target group was comprised of 'Dance Crazy Girls', as their campaign focus entailed.

The 'Dance Crazy Girl' is young, extrovert, and confident with herself. She believes dancing to be the greatest sport because of its ability to merge athleticism with sexiness, or in other words, sweat with beauty. Learning new dance moves and seeing how great her dance moves are inspire the 'Dance Crazy Girl' to dance even more. She pushes herself further each day, developing her dance moves, to aim for an imagined moment of fame under her illusionary spotlight. Basically, dance and music are the key definitions of the personality of Nike's 'Dance Crazy Girls'.

In order to expand Nike's insight into its new female target segment, Nike sought to further understand the 'Dance Crazy Girls' outlook, attitude, and perception of sports, which, at first glance proved to provide a sharp contrast to the perceptions of many others outside the arena of dance. Nike found that although those young women feel a strong passion for dance, they were equally disappointed with the fact that dance has not received widespread recognition as a form of sport. This lack of recognition inspired Nike to bring this issue forward, not just to create an appreciation of dance, but also to create a need for the recognition of all women.

The core of Nike's creative women's dance campaign strategy was focused on a specific message. Playing on the fact that the world does not recognize dancing as a form of sport, Nike (with its serious, athlete brand reputation) enjoyed an advantageous position to change that conception. In their campaign, Nike's dancers dance with an obvious athletic ability which removes any doubts about dancing's athletic 'Just do it' attitude. This creative attempt on the part of Nike, sought to bring forward the salient aspect of the 'Just do it' attitude through the promotion of athletic dancers. As a result, Nike was telling the world to see dance as a 'real sport'.

The concept developed for Nike's campaign centred on a challenging statement: 'Tell me I'm not an athlete'. This concept was promoted through the athletes themselves, and sought to set out Nike's point of view of dancing through the athletes. In other words, the communication flowed from one athlete to another, with Nike's athletes debunking the conventional view of sports and athleticism. As such, the concept was predicted to be successfully inspirational to the target of female dancers. Furthermore, the message was also designed to attract the attention of all women by echoing their struggles of fighting to be heard and taken seriously in today's prejudicial and egotistical world.

The women's dance campaign was aimed at the major European markets of Germany, Portugal, Spain, and The Netherlands. Roughly, the total commercial communications expenditure of the campaign was between €10 and €20 million, running for the three consecutive months of February, March, and April during 2006.

Nike set out clear communication objectives for their campaign. These objectives naturally lend themselves to each other, as opposed to being distinct from one another. First of all, in an attempt to target as many women as possible, Nike set an objective of reaching at least 40 million women across Europe. Secondly, since exposure increases awareness, Nike sought to increase their brand awareness by 10%—a measure that would help the company verify the results of its exposure goals. Thirdly, above mere brand awareness, Nike wants to increase its perception as the coolest brand in its category by another 10%. Fourthly, being perceived as the coolest brand is not beneficial to the company if it does not lead to sales. Therefore, Nike's last objective was to increase sales by 5% and hence, be 'the most recent brand purchased'.

Nike's women's dance campaign made use of various media strategies across Europe, including: broadcast, print, outdoor, interactive, online, events, and public relations. TV was utilized as a primary medium for exposure, building awareness, excitement, and engagement with the brand message. Print and outdoor media were also used as a secondary medium to support the brand message and highlight Nike's new target market.

Furthermore, Nike made use of over 500 gyms to hold special events to communicate its campaign in its perceived natural environment. These events played a key part in the campaign and encouraged the participation of over 60,000 women. The events were held by and connected with 'Dance Crazy Girls' to further prove Nike's commitment to its new target market. Nike also made use of internet media, developing Nikewomen.com and allowing women to directly participate in the campaign. Retail stores were utilized to take the brand message in-store and provide a connection between the 'Dance Crazy Girls' and Nike's women's sportswear collection.

Most importantly, the public relations aspect of the campaign played a fundamental part in leveraging the concept of 'Tell me I'm not an athlete'. This concept in particular, increased the success of the women's dance campaign, helping Nike to gain an extra target market reach of

15 million through non-paid-for media placements on national TV stations. Furthermore, the concept also got a foothold in over 800 free press placements.

Due to the success of the women's dance campaign, Nike attained a huge triumph in attracting the female segment. As evidence of their success, Nike has exceeded the objectives set prior to the campaign. As opposed to their goal of reaching 40 million women, they managed to gain the attention of 60 million women across Europe with 25% less budget. Furthermore, unaided brand awareness amongst women increased beyond the aimed-for 10%. Due to that, key competitors in the athlete segment suffered drastically.

Furthermore, Nike's awareness grew more than mere unaided recall into being perceived as the 'coolest brand' in major markets. As mentioned earlier, being cool is only beneficial if it leads to actual sales. Nike managed to increase its sales in excess of 10% (recall they were aiming for only 5%!) and hence became the 'most recent brand purchased'. Overall, the success of Nike's women's dance campaign led to a huge increase in sales (21%) of Nike's women's collections during the campaign.

In summary, Nike started with an ultimate goal and new objective to fulfil: to be the number one choice of sportswear for women by the summer of 2006. In an attempt to achieve their objective, Nike aimed to create an inspiration for all women to feel like athletes through the feminine sport of dancing. This inspirational message was communicated through major forms of commercial media, to ensure widespread target market coverage. Through the creation of such a powerful brand campaign, Nike successfully became number one in the female athlete segment.

Source: WARC, Euro-Effies, Grand Prix/Gold winner 2007, Nike—Women's Dance Campaign 2006: Tell me I'm not an athlete. Edited by Fajer Saleh Al-Mutawa.

189

DISCUSSION QUESTIONS

1 How has Nike utilized its strong reputation in the male athlete segment to enter the female market?

2 What is the risk to Nike's existing brand equity in the professional athlete segment when they claim that dance is a 'real sport'?

3 What are the most suitable methods for measuring Nike's brand equity pre and post the Women's Dance Campaign? Suggest qualitative and quantitative methods.

4 How can Nike further extend its brand in the market place to reach different segments?

FURTHER READING

- An important contribution to measurement theory has been made by John Rossiter's 2002 C-OAR-SE procedure, 'The C-OAR-SE Procedure for Scale Development in Marketing' found in *Measurement for the Social Sciences*, New York: Springer (2010), and it should be read and understood by anyone doing brand or advertising research.

REFERENCES

Antonides, G. and van Raaij, W. F. (1998), *Consumer Behaviour: A European Perspective*, Chichester, England: John Wiley & Sons.

Bong, N. W., Marshall, R., and Keller, K. L. (1999), 'Measuring brand power validating a model for optimizing brand equity', *Journal of Product and Brand Management*, 8, 3, 170–84.

Brown, T. J., Suter, G., and Churchill, G. (2014), *Basic Marketing Research*, 8th Edition, Boston, MA: Cengage Learning.

Dichter, E. (1964), *Handbook of Consumer Motivation*, New York: McGraw-Hill.

Elliott, R. and Jankel-Elliott, N. (2003), 'Using ethnography in strategic consumer research', *Qualitative Market Research*, 6, 4, 215–23.

Fishbein, M. and Ajzen, I. (1975), *Belief, Attitude, Intention, and Behaviour*, Reading, MA: Addison-Wesley Publishing Co.

Geertz, C. (1973), *The Interpretation of Culture*, London: Fountain Press.

Green, P. E. and Srinivasau, V. (1990), 'Conjoint analysis in marketing: New developments with implications for research and practice', *Journal of Marketing*, 54, 3–19.

Hammersley, M. and Atkinson, P. (1983), *Ethnography: Principles and Practices*, London: Routledge.

Krishnan, H. S. (1996), 'Characteristics of memory associations: A consumer-based brand equity perspective', *International Journal of Research in Marketing*, October, 13, 4, 389–405.

Lattin, J. M., Green, P. E., and Carroll, D. (2003), *Analyzing Multivariate Data*, Pacific Grove, CA: Thomson Brooks/Cole.

Levy, S. J. (1985), 'Dreams, fairy tales, animals, and cars', *Psychology and Marketing*, 2, 2, 67–81.

Moran, W. T. (1978), 'The advertising-promotion balance', paper presented at the Association of National Advertisers' Workshop, New York.

Percy, L. and Rosenbaum-Elliott, R. (2012), *Strategic Advertising Management*, 4th edn, Oxford: Oxford University Press.

Robinson, I. (1992), 'Brand strength means more than market share', *ARF Fourth Annual Advertising and Promotion Workshop*.

Rossiter, J. R. and Percy, L. (1997), *Advertising Communication and Promotion Management*, New York: McGraw-Hill.

Rossiter, J. R. and Percy, L. (2001), 'The a-b-e model of benefit focus in advertising', in T. J. Reynolds and J. C. Olsen(eds), *Understanding Consumer Decision Making: The Means-End Approach to Marketing and Advertising Strategy*, Mahwah, NJ: Lawrence Erlbaum Associates Publishers.

Rossiter, J. R. (2011), *Measurement for Social Science*, New York: Springer.

Semeonoff, B. (1976), *Projective Technique*, London: John Wiley & Sons.

Sutherland, M. (2008), *Advertising and the Mind of the Consumer*, St. Leonard's, Australia: Allen & Unwin.

Zajonc, R. B. (1968), 'Attitudinal effects of mere exposure', *Journal of Personality and Social Psychology Monographs*, 9, 213, 1–27.

Test your understanding of this chapter and explore the subject further using our Online Resource Centre. Visit the Online Resource Centre at http://www.oxfordtextbooks.co.uk/orc/elliott-percy3e/

Managing Brands

This section uses a combination of consumer involvement and symbolic meaning to differentiate between two approaches to brand strategy, symbolic brands and functional brands. The unique contexts of high tech and corporate brands are also considered.

Brand Strategies 1—Symbolic Brands

8

Key Concepts

1 An integrative model of brand building in mindspace.

2 Advertising builds strong and profitable brands.

3 Brand strategies based on personal meanings.

4 Brand strategies based on social differentiation.

5 Brand strategies based on social integration.

6 The importance of understanding brand ecology.

7 Innovation and strategic cannibalization.

Introduction

In this and the following chapter we bring together the concepts and models discussed in earlier chapters and derive actionable insights into how managers might develop strategic plans for brands. In Chapter 1 we separated the functional realm from the emotional realm as requiring differing brand attributes and consumer benefits (see Fig. 1.1). Additionally, we will now use the two dimensions of consumer involvement and cognition-emotion to identify two basic strategic alternatives, as illustrated in Fig. 8.1.

Managing brand strategies in mindspace

In constructing a model of how brands can be built in the market place we can turn to two large-scale commercial projects, the BrandAsset Valuator (Young and Rubicam Group, 2010) and BrandDynamics (Millward Brown, 2010) models which have used data from hundreds of brands across many markets over many years to derive some essential insights into how brands develop. The BrandAsset Valuator model has involved over 500,000 consumer interviews conducted in 46 countries measuring more than 55 different consumer perceptions with regard to over 35,000 brands. The model explores the mindspace of the market and how it develops over time as the brand builds a relationship with its customers. The BrandDynamics model is also derived empirically, from brand tracking data collected by Millward Brown covering 17,000 brands in 35 countries. Common between these models is the term 'relevance' to the customer and while different constructs are otherwise used, there are a number of similarities; for example, with the BrandDynamics model indicated in parentheses, the need for knowledge (presence) and energized differentiation (advantage). We have melded these findings into a model of how a brand can be built within our minds, that is, mindspace (Fig. 8.2).

The starting point for all brands is developing brand awareness. For all markets awareness is a necessary requirement, first because it reduces perceptions of purchase risk, but

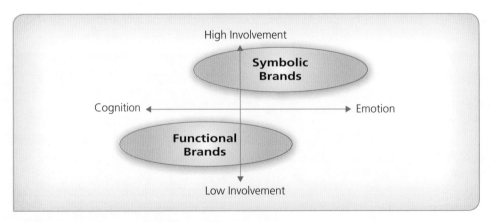

FIGURE 8.1 Brand strategy alternatives

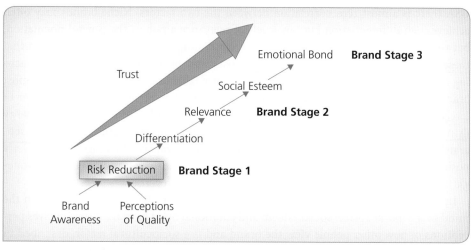

FIGURE 8.2 Building a brand in mindspace

also in many low-involvement markets it may be sufficient for purchase to ensue. It is also necessary that consumers develop perceptions about the quality of the brand's performance, and these perceptions are conditioned by the product's category and the standards set by the competition. It is about a generic perception of the product acceptability (Dyson *et al.*, 1996). Together these two perceptions reduce the consumer's perceived risk of purchase and we can say that a brand that achieves reasonable levels of both factors has reached Brand Stage 1. Millward Brown's data suggest that for many brands, a substantial proportion of customers do not develop a relationship beyond this point. Red Bull, famous for its variety of energy drinks, was founded in Austria in 1987. Partly due to the many sponsorships and marketing events undertaken by Red Bull, it is now one of the most recognized international brands. The target market for Red Bull views their products as low-risk, low-involvement, but as we shall see, the brand also has progressed to other stages.

In order for a brand to progress to Brand Stage 2, two vital elements are required, perceptions of differentiation and of personal relevance. To be perceived by consumers as truly differentiated from the competition, three beliefs must be developed; that the brand is different from other brands (either positively or negatively), that this point of difference is unique to the brand, and distinctive in that it is worth paying more for. Young and Rubicam's huge dataset points to differentiation being critical for brand success, not just in building the brand in the first place, but also it continues to be vital as a fall in perceptions of difference is often the first sign that a mature successful brand is starting to decline. So a key insight for managing a mature brand is to ensure that it maintains perceptions of differentiation.

Relevance reflects perceptions that the brand has something that is personally relevant or appropriate to the consumer. Data shows that relevance is the key to household penetration and the size of franchise and is thus about the market segment or segments that the brand has connected with. Successful new brands on a growth trajectory show higher differentiation than relevance, indicating that consumers see the brand as standing out from the competition so the first objective is to be noticed. However, this then has to be turned into promising a benefit that is relevant to the consumer's particular lifestyle. Young and Rubicam's data show that relevance is not a natural outgrowth of differentiation: in the

USA there is almost zero correlation between the two factors. Niche brands may often achieve high differentiation but low levels of relevance amongst the general population, but very high levels amongst a specific segment. Young and Rubicam's data suggest that these niche brands tend to be amongst the most profitable in the market place. So, reaching Brand Stage 2 can mean a sustainable and profitable brand, and it is likely that most brands do not progress beyond this point. Red Bull differentiates itself on a number of levels: special ingredients like alpine spring water in a can half the size of other energy drinks, store acceptance of special display cases that prominently feature the product separately from competing brands, and a premium pricing strategy. Their logo is also cleverly positioned via multiple extreme sports sponsorships and also by way of their other strategic business units such as Red Bull Mobile and Red Bull Records.

In order to reach Brand Stage 3 two further perceptions have to be developed in the mind of the market place: social esteem and emotional bond. Social esteem involves perceptions of how other people view the brand and is a sociocultural factor, described in Chapter 4 as implying either social integration or social differentiation. So as we have both personal and social experience with a brand, the wide range of possible subtleties of perceptions become rich areas for study and management action. Emotional bonding involves the development of a consumer-brand relationship based largely on personal experience with the brand and this has been discussed in detail as aspects of the personal meanings of a brand in Chapter 4. As a brand is built over time, consumers gradually develop familiarity, confidence, and trust in it, as described in Chapter 2, such that if through personal experience and perceptions of other people's opinions of the brand they develop an emotional bond with the brand, we would expect that they will eventually also invest high levels of trust in the brand. Note that before trust can be developed, consumers need repeated experiences with the brand in order to build beliefs about its predictability and dependability. Thus consistency in all aspects of the brand is essential to any brand strategy. Red Bull has established a unique position in the mindspace of young and multicultural customers. It has developed a brand personality upon traits such as speed, power, and recklessness (Brasel & Gips, 2011) through some clever advertising—these have long featured cartoon characters and the slogan 'Red Bull gives you wings'—coupled with a reputation for contributing to high performance and a well publicized company ethos. These aspects of the brand are regularly reinforced within the mindspace of consumers through multiple brand touchpoints, which we will discuss further in Chapter 12.

**TOO TIRED FOR THE AFTER-PARTY
AFTER THE AFTER-PARTY?**

RED BULL GIVES YOU WIIINGS.

Brand building in mindspace

How does one build a brand in a mindspace? What we mean by this is that we hold different associations in our minds (you could visualize this as different places in your mind) as we become more committed to a brand. The model in Fig. 8.2 is presented as hierarchy, so a customer will go through each of the steps in a sequence. It is desirable that your customers are further up the chain because they are then likely to be more committed to you. The reality is that most brands have customer groups at each of these stages. It is the brand manager's task to move them up but also to be aware that some customers will move down, for example, if a crisis event occurs with the product or a new entrant manages to gain share of that mindspace. So, although presented as a sequence, the process is often iterative and brand managers must closely monitor the market to counter the competition to maintain customer positions at the top as well as move others up.

Symbolic brand strategies

We will now concentrate on how a symbolic brand can offer to transform the consumer's experience of the world and how the social language of the brand can help a consumer enhance their perceptions and communication of self, and manage their social positioning. In most cases, brand strategy will involve advertising as the primary conveyor of meaning, although in some instances, particularly in the areas of neo-tribes and sub-cultures, word-of-mouth may be the primary communication channel. Fifteen approaches to brand strategy are discussed below, organized into three categories. They build on the symbolic meaning of brands discussed in Chapter 3 and cultural meaning systems discussed in Chapter 4.

- Strategies based on personal meanings:
  - brand-as-a-person;
  - brand-as-a-friend;
  - brands and romance;
  - nostalgia;
  - instant heritage;
  - experience brand;
  - brand as underdog.
- Strategies based on social differentiation:
  - fashionization;
  - cool and cultural capital;
  - strategic cannibalization;
  - gender identity.

- Strategies based on social integration:
  - brand community;
  - neo-tribes;
  - sub-cultures;
  - brand mythologies.

KEY CONCEPT

Advertising builds strong and profitable brands

Despite the proliferation (and potential) of social media facilitated by the internet, advertising remains a primary mechanism for communicating the meaning of a brand. As a promotional tool, advertising is a macro term and even though you may see it alongside other tools such as sponsorship, sales promotion, and direct selling, it is often through advertising that these strategies are implemented. In our frequently cluttered, mature markets few consumer brands can survive without substantial advertising spend. Even those who have an emotional bond with the brand need to be reassured.

Personal meaning strategies

Brand-as-a-person

The core idea is to create a personality for the brand so that it takes on human characteristics in the perceptions of the consumer. The brand does not have personality because of its own behaviour and beliefs: rather this is generated through the contact the consumer has with the brand (Aaker, 1997, p. 348). The personality traits that appear to be most robust across developed cultures are those of sincerity, excitement, and sophistication, so these are the basic building blocks of a brand's personality. The theory of *animism* has been used to describe attempts to humanize brands (Sweeney and Brandon, 2006). This is done to encourage a relationship that will then generate brand personality. These perceptions can be built into the brand through its communications strategy. For example, in 2010 VCCP won a Gold British Television Advertising Award for best 10–20 second commercial with **compare**the**market**.com. The ad depicts a wealthy Russian Meerkat called Aleksandr, who wears a smoking jacket and lives in a mansion. Aleksandr complains that he is receiving a lot of unwanted traffic from **compare**the**market**.com to his site **compare**the**meerkat**.com. Whilst the ad is humorous it also taps into the goodwill felt towards these animals generated by popular television shows such as *Meerkat Manor*. The clever execution, part of an ongoing series, serves to bring the insurance website to life.

But consumers also draw inferences about the personality of the brand through its market place actions. For example, a brand that is highly visible and advertises frequently has the inferred personality trait of being friendly and popular, a brand that is repositioned and changes its marketing programme constantly is seen as flighty and schizophrenic, while a brand sold through selective outlets at a high price is seen as snobbish and sophisticated (Fournier, 1998).

comparethemarket.com

Social media has allowed some brands to engage with their customers in what appears to be a more organic process of personality development. The 'Smell Like a Man' campaign developed for Old Spice deodorant is a standout example of this. Launched by Wieden + Kennedy Portland in 2010, the agency quickly realized the potential in the character played by Isaiah Mustafa a heavily muscled 'perfect' man labelled the 'Old Spice Guy' (D&AD 2011). Viewers of the ad (you can see it at: http://oldspice.com/en/videos/videos) wanted more, so they developed a Response Campaign leveraging social media to amplify the buzz around the character and build the brand's personality in real time. They did this by having the character post message and video responses to consumer questions on Facebook, Twitter, and other social media platforms. The video responses were uploaded incredibly quickly—sometimes within half an hour—with over 180 videos produced in total. The effect was impressive, with in excess of 65 million views of the campaign (D&AD 2011).

A brand's personality can also develop independent of the firm on the internet. For example, trappedinspace.com uses the Yahoo search engine to capture the percentage of hits on websites where fashion brand names and a predetermined set of attributes are used together. With over 100 matched attributes, visitors to this site can check which brands will make them look exciting, confident, powerful, arrogant, even wicked.

Brand-as-a-friend

The core idea is to build an emotional attachment to a brand through implicating the brand in important areas of consumers' lives and to offer a degree of comfort and security similar to that people find in their human relationships. An example of this strategy is that used by the largest beer brewer in Australia, Foster's Group, to revitalize the main holding of their portfolio, Carlton & United Breweries. In an effort to distance the company from undesirable connections between alcohol and violence, during July 2011 Foster's implemented a new brand logo and a corporate slogan that showcased beer as the centrepiece of responsible family and community celebrations. They repositioned their product as being

'Raised in Friendship' to emphasize the central belief held by their CEO that '. . . if a whole lot more people raised a beer in friendship, the world would be a better place'. Despite intensifying competition and an influx of foreign beers, Carlton & United Breweries continues to retain approximately half of the entire market share for Australian beer sales, which indicates that their positioning strategy has proved to be effective.

An example from the beauty industry shows how valuable the communication of reassurance can be. The 'Dove Campaign for Real Beauty' is a worldwide marketing campaign launched by Unilever that has been running since 2004. The programme has made use of many themes and media channels, but in 2014 Dove partnered with digital greeting card company 'Open Me' to re-engage the audience in a discussion of what beauty is by placing the focus upon friendship. Through leveraging the influence of their 22 million Facebook fans, Dove sought to extend reach and amplify the effect of their message without acting invasively. The brand used promoted posts that encouraged their followers to send a complimentary e-card to friends—which included the saying 'Beauty is Friendship' on the cover—as a way to inspire people to feel confident and appreciated. Not only does this approach increase brand awareness, but it also allows the brand to establish an emotional link with the intended audience, which is very valuable, bearing in mind that each message is actually individually tailored to the recipients by a personal friend.

KEY CONCEPT

Brand strategies based on personal meanings

We connect with brands that signify personal meaning because they help us to determine or reinforce our purpose in life. This is important to us. Empirical evidence shows that people with a strong sense of personal meaning have improved immune capabilities, are less prone to depression, and generally have better mental and physical well-being (Harris and Standard 2001). Personal meaning develops in what Janoff-Bulman & Berg (1998) call an 'assumptive world' in which taken-for-granted senses of security, predictability, trust, and optimism exist. Brands that can best signify those 'taken-for-granteds' will resonate with consumers.

A key focus in developing strategies to connect with consumers is on understanding the *brand ecology* (Percy and Elliott, 2009), that is, to consider not just the attitudinal, emotional, and behavioural aspects of brand consumption, but to explore how this brand-related behaviour integrates with wider social and cultural experience in the life-world of the active consumer and in particular their media consumption. You might like to watch The X Factor with friends over a glass of wine; read Vogue magazine on your own on the porch, or the business news on your commute to work. We may switch from low-involvement consumption of US comedies, to high-involvement consumption of a documentary programme or football match, all on the same evening. We also have media imperatives, such as a 'must-view' appointment with an episode of a soap opera, or a 'must-read' appointment with a heavyweight Sunday newspaper. In short, we consume a range of media, often in a different mind-set at different times of the day or week. In order to match brand attitude strategy with media consumption we need to know how and why customers are consuming the media, not just that they are in the same room as the TV. The relationship with a medium may involve high levels of trust, respect, affection, personal, and family history. Alternatively it may involve distrust, lack of respect, an absence of any emotional connection, and little history. The close relationship between a consumer and his/her personal media architecture is at least as important as any brand–consumer relationship, because it is from our trusted media that we construct our view of the world, gain enjoyment, and entertainment, stimulation, and information. By understanding and leveraging the brand ecology, we can build into the brand communications the key attribute of *intimacy*, and support it by customer intimacy actions in the market place (Hansen, 2003).

KEY CONCEPT

The importance of understanding brand ecology.

How much influence does a friend's response to the brand have in comparison to the advertised positioning of the brand? Ecology is the study of how organisms interact with their environment. By thinking of the brand as the organism, we can consider how it interacts with other organisms like customers and their friends. By studying the ecology of the brand we gain insight to how they are encountered by customers and how they affect customer experiences. This means more than just considering the direct impact of the marketing communication for the brand. We cannot assume there will be direct impact anyway. What if the customer is distracted, or not interested? Or if their first encounter with the brand is through seeing a friend use it? It is useful for a brand manager to think about all of the ways that a brand is encountered as this enables a much deeper understanding of a customer's response to it.

Brands and romance

Romantic love is widely used in brand communications reflecting its universality and importance in consumers' lives, as evidenced by the worldwide consumption of romantic novels and other forms of popular culture. Although it is often subsumed under sexual appeal, there is evidence that non-sexual forms of love may be very powerful motivators. In particular, spiritual companionate love has a separate influence on consumer attitudes than sexual passionate love, particularly for adult consumers as opposed to teenagers (Huang, 2004). This implies that brand communications emphasizing romantic love may be more effective if they depict love as part of a meaningful relationship rather than one based primarily on sexual attraction. The power of romance is demonstrated in the entrepreneurial exploitation of the Rolo brand strategy discussed above. Memorisethis.com suggests 'Show your love with a hall-marked gold-plated Rolo in a beautiful branded gift box finished with a silky red ribbon'.

Nostalgia

The evidence suggests that for some people, particularly those who need to belong, nostalgia for early experience can determine consumer preferences later in life via a process of nostalgic bonding (Loveland *et al.*, 2010). This seems to occur primarily for products for which a preference is formed at age 16–20, when it is accompanied by intense positive emotional experiences. The implications of this are that brands may utilize designs and styles for which consumers formed an emotional preference in their teenage years in order to motivate brand preferences later in life. Holbrook and Schindler (2003) identified ten nostalgia-related themes listed in Table 8.1.

A reflection on your own nostalgic memories will no doubt trigger a number of brand associations under these themes. Hovis is a brand which has actively pursued a strategy based on nostalgia with its hugely successful 'Go on Lad' campaign which repositioned the brand in 2008 as a source of security during times of upheaval and change in Britain. Television advertising used to support the brand's position show a young boy, with a Hovis loaf tucked under his arm, scampering home through different parallel worlds depicting events which led to momentous change in Britain like protests from the British Suffragette Movement, war-torn London, and the coal miners' strike.

In Germany, many former eastern bloc brands are experiencing a revival as consumers become nostalgic for the former communist homeland. Rotkaeppchen sparkling wine, once the drink of choice for party leaders in East Germany, sold 15 million bottles a year at its height during the communist regime, but that fell to just 2.9 million in 1991 (Hall, 2009). It now sells 149 million bottles a year, claiming a 47% share of the German sparkling wine market. Whilst this is, in large part, due to a widening brand portfolio and effective marketing strategy, Hall considers the nostalgic power of the brand to be an important factor in its re-emergence.

TABLE 8.1 Nostalgia related themes

Nostalgia theme	Possessions . . .
Sensory experiences	. . . such as profound scents or fragrances.
Homeland brands	. . . reminders of our distant homes.
Rites of passage	. . . which signify an important moment or achievement.
Friendships and loved ones	. . . that remind us of special times with others.
Gifts of love	. . . like those received from loved others like grandparents, partners.
Feeling of security	. . . which bring comfort during troubled or stressful times.
Breaking away	. . . which help us to remove ourselves from situations representing the norm.
Art and entertainment	. . . like the first inspiring novel you read or the concert ticket of the first live act you saw.
Performance and competence	. . . relating to our own perfected skills like a DJ's favourite brand of deck or writer's notebook computer.
Creativity	. . . relating particularly to artistic creativity.

Sourced from the findings of Holbrook and Schindler (2003).

Other resurgent brands include the American snack food Hostess Twinkies and Zeha trainers. Hostess Twinkies are a long-standing and iconic American brand, but when the company fell into bankruptcy during 2012, production came to a grinding halt. Given the opportunity to capitalize upon the nostalgic value of Twinkies and other famed Hostess brands, the company was bought out of bankruptcy, immediately downsized, and the Twinkies brand was reintroduced to store shelves under the marketing tagline of 'The sweetest comeback in the history of ever'. By drawing attention to the nostalgia of the brand, the marketing campaign generated significant buzz on social media and the brand was revitalized.

Instant heritage

However, it is possible for brands to construct their own historical connections or 'bolt-on provenance' with outstanding success in the market place. The launch of Caffrey's Irish Ale was a deliberate use of semiotics to build a new brand of high tech nitrogen-flushed beer 'through the cunning use of our own symbolism, language and imagery' Vallance (1995). 'In assembling Caffrey's personality we were faced with an embarrassment of riches, such is the power of Irish provenance . . . old Ireland stood for lyricism, softness, and tranquillity, new Ireland stood for a tougher, harder, more gritty reality'. The result was the positioning of Caffrey's as an expression of the two natures of Ireland captured in the end-line 'Strong Words Softly Spoken' wrapped in such beguiling and seductive imagery, no one for a moment questioned the product's claim to greatness or its status as a nitrogenated keg beer. The semiotic alibi was complete. The results were astounding as Caffrey's grew from nothing to 500,000 barrels in 32 months, maintained a price premium against established opposition and became the UK brand leader.

Experience brand

It has been argued that we are moving into a new economic era based on experience, where competition is less about product or service but about how well companies can

Twinkies: Nostalgic revival © Catherine Lane / istockphoto.com

stage experiences (Pine and Gilmore, 1998). This represents a move from tangible products through intangible services to memorable experiences, and a brand plays a key role in promising an experience. The creation and staging of a compelling personal memorable experience that can be a major part of the brand strategy can be guided by five experience design principles. *Theme the experience*, to make it cohesive and easily remembered. *Imbue the experience with impressions*, which are 'takeways' that affirm the nature of the experience. *Eliminate all negative cues*, even minor negatives can spoil the experience. *Mix in memorabilia*; as discussed in Chapters 3 and 4, special possessions play a major role in helping people construct their identity through the memories they symbolize. *Engage all five senses*; the more senses an experience engages the more memorable it will be.

You may have experienced the slick lighting, design, and product placement of a Nike concept store, or been buzzed by low-flying balloons, planes, and helicopters at Hamley's toy store in London or perhaps gazed in wonder at the Galeries Lafayette shopping centre in Paris, all are excellent examples of experience brands. However, perhaps the oldest of experience brands are the seemingly mundane, direct selling companies like Avon and Tupperware who for many years have relied on 'entertaining' community gatherings in the form of parties or barbecues, legitimized by a sales force who are typically part of the social group invited. Ironically these companies are again at the forefront of building experience into their brand, this time via social media. Both use Twitter and Facebook to announce brand events, establish dialogue with customers and allow them to communicate with one another and in doing are helping to re-stimulate one of the oldest sales models in the business (Canning, 2010).

Brand as underdog

When faced with a very large and powerful competitor, there is an opportunity to position a brand as a valiant underdog, using their very strength to harness support from consumers, a version of the Aikido brands discussed in Chapter 4. This strategy has been used very successfully by Richard Branson, first by positioning Virgin Atlantic against the monolithic British Airways, and then by positioning Virgin Money against the huge, grey financial services establishment. In both cases, 'against the big institutions' carries the very valuable connotation of 'being on the side of the small guy', and takes advantage of the common feeling that somehow we are being exploited by big business.

Social differentiation strategies
Fashionization

Nokia took the mobile phone market by storm when it repositioned its phones as fashion items with a huge range of alternative covers, rather than as functional products. Similarly, no matter how much the company keeps denying it, Nike's key promise is one of fashion leadership rather than function (Goldman and Papson, 1998). Even teeth braces are now fashion items:

> Braces are becoming a girl's best friend. What was once a teenage turnoff has turned into a high fashion accessory. Rather than hide the tramlines designed to straighten their teeth, Scots youngsters are demanding multi-colours on their molars.
>
> (*Glasgow Evening Times*)

Car manufacturers are also replacing a traditional focus on function with an emphasis on fashion and style. For example, the launch of the Ford Ka was a deliberate decision to by-pass investment in new engineering and instead design a fashionable body. It has been a great success in many parts of the world: 'Ka owners rate aesthetics above mechanics . . . it's not a car, it's a consumer durable, it's much more like a Walkman than it is a Ferrari' (BBC News online). A key part of the Ford Ka marketing strategy was to target opinion leaders whose aesthetic tastes might be followed by others and this has been found to be viable in many fashion markets, following the trickle-down theory. There is evidence that opinion leaders can be identified and targeted through the subtle use of media with whom they have a special relationship (Vernette, 2004), and that this can then lead to word-of-mouth spreading to fashion followers. But in considering fashionization as a brand strategy, it is vital to remember Oscar Wilde's warning: 'Nothing is so dangerous as being too modern; one is apt to grow old-fashioned quite suddenly.'

Cool and cultural capital

Closely linked to fashionization is the concept of cool, the leading edge of fashion usually appealing to the youth market; it includes terms like 'street', 'hip', 'authentic', and 'real'. Research by the Coolbrands identified Apple as the UK's coolest brand, followed by Aston Martin, Nike, and Chanel (theguardian 2014). What they seem to have in common is a mix of aesthetics and attitude that capture the spirit of the moment ahead of the mass of brands. In a Superbrands (2002) study, 40% of the 18–30-year-olds interviewed said that they were prepared to pay more for a cool brand. The findings established that 72% of respondents believe the personality of the brand is the most vital factor when determining whether that brand is cool. Just below half, 44%, of respondents believe that their friends' opinion or use of a brand has an influence on their decision on whether that brand is cool, while only 11% take into account a celebrity's use or opinion of a brand. Nearly a third, 31%, deemed press coverage to be an influencing factor: 'The nature of cool is always a fickle thing but it fascinates us all. It is difficult to manage people's perception of cool but it can make the difference between success or failure for many brands, people, and places.'

An important concept in using cool as a strategy is that of the *Sacrifice Group*. In order to be perceived as authentically cool by one group, a brand has to be rejected or at least not be liked by the majority. In deciding who the brand wants, it also needs to decide who it does not want, who are the group it will sacrifice in order to maintain the interest of its targets. South African brewer Garagista ran a campaign in which the consumers of its Pale Ale are positioned against another group, hipsters. In the example their desired consumer is positioned, like the beer, as authentic, i.e., an authentic alternative music lover, in this case through reference to the American New Wave/Punk scene (Ramones) and not just a selfie-taking fashionista. While the use of a profanity may be an attempt to appeal to or amuse the target audience, research also indicates that shocking the reader leads to heightened awareness and improved attention, recall, and recognition (Dahl *et al.*, 2003).

Rather than manage perceptions of cool, many marketers seek out leading-edge consumers by using specialist research agencies as 'cool hunters' in order to identify style leaders who are 12–18 months ahead of the mainstream. Nancarrow *et al.* (2002)

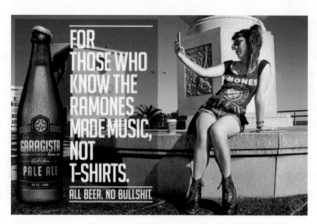

Garagista Pale Ale

demonstrate that it is possible to identify and interview 'cultural intermediaries' whose occupations involve symbolic goods and services and who interpret what they see and hear at work and what they read in the 'hip' media, both adopting and adapting the innovations of others. They devote considerable time and effort to acquiring cultural capital, seeking out the new and then moving on, ever fearful of being caught up by the mainstream. This study led to a realization of the importance of black culture to cool and resulted in a very successful campaign for Morgan's Spiced Rum, featuring black artists, writers, actors, and musicians, groups who were identified as particularly cool and crucially relevant to the Caribbean roots of the product. 'The connection was a natural one, not forced, and therefore the advertising itself was considered "Authentic;" it was cool.'

Strategic cannibalization

As more and more markets become driven by fashion, style, and aesthetics, the demand for innovation becomes ever more intense. But rather than view this trend as a problem, it can be turned into a successful strategy of deliberately limiting supply and replacing products well before their sales decline. Zara, the Spanish clothing retailer, has developed a supply chain revolution that enables it to design, produce, and deliver a garment in 15 days. Zara produces 10,000 new designs annually, but each one in only a limited supply; this drives the consumer perception 'If I don't buy it now, I'll lose my chance'. This strategy of strategic cannibalization with limited supplies of new designs available for only a short space of time has led to brand-specific buyer behaviour, as in central London, consumers visit the average clothing store four times per annum but they visit Zara 17 times a year. This creates word-of-mouth communications that allow Zara to spend 0.3% of sales on advertising versus the 4% spent by its competitors (Ferdows *et al.*, 2004).

The importance of stimulating a sense of excitement in a market defined by low degrees of consumer loyalty is recognized by The Sanctuary brand of mass-market body care products in the UK. Management has recognized that constant new product launches are the key to keeping the brand 'talked about' and to keeping consumer promiscuity 'within the brand' (Edwards, 2004).

> ## KEY CONCEPT
>
> ### Innovation and strategic cannibalization.
>
> The term strategic cannibalization refers to scenarios where consumers are offered new products despite this being within a time frame in which the sales potential for old or current products or services is yet to be exhausted. This may seem counterproductive, but what it achieves is a sense of renewal and vitality that is appealing to shoppers. It can also be a necessity, particularly in highly competitive and dynamic markets. Think about the demise of major book chains around the world who delayed selling online while sites like Amazon went from strength to strength. Strategic cannibalization is a legitimate growth strategy. Major brands like Zara, Top Shop, Coke, and Flight Centre all release products and services that may in part cannibalize their current offerings but long term make them more competitively robust.

Gender identity

Children as young as four develop behaviour consistent with gender roles (Bakir and Palin, 2010). Women make or influence the purchase of as much as 80% of all consumer goods and there are a number of factors that must be borne in mind if they are to be targeted as a brand strategy. Women's roles in society have changed dramatically over the last 50 years as more and more women go out to work regardless of whether they are married or have children, and women for whom work is a career versus those for whom it is 'just a job' exhibit attitudes, buying motivations, and buying behaviour which differ markedly. Along with the move into work has come the progressive breakdown of the traditional family with rising divorce rates and children born outside marriage, so women are not only juggling home and work responsibilities but also increasingly having to raise children alone (White, 2002). Compared with men, women are more sensitive to details of relevant information and tend to favour objective over subjective claims, but are better able to integrate emotional and rational factors; women take a broader view of life, bringing more factors into play when making decisions (Evans *et al.*, 2000). Learned (2004) offers some valuable insights into how brands can connect with women through developing an accessible human face. Emotional connections are built through elements like stories and testimonials from customers; visual images of employees and customers add a human face to the brand; social cause partnerships can also help humanize the brand.

Japan has been at the forefront of gender-based brand building. In a report for the brand architect group, Seireeni and Chen (2010) explain how the DoCoMo group was first to develop small and stylish mobile phones which fit more easily in a woman's hand and purse, in recognition that women used these devices far more often than men. They also highlight the development of a brand called WiLL which has been created around gender rather than a product. WiLL has partnered with a number of prominent brands to produce products specifically for women including a car with Toyota, a computer with Panasonic, and a beer with Asahi. Even Japanese insurance companies are getting involved with packages including child care and husband care, the latter in light of the fact that women typically live longer.

Contrary to many men's self-perceptions, men are more likely to make emotional buying decisions based on partially digested evidence than women, and are less well disposed to pictures as opposed to words. There is also some suggestion that they are likely to be more brand loyal than women (Evans *et al.*, 2000). As women's roles in society have become broader, men have begun to experience role turmoil and to resent that women are in control of many areas of men's lives (Langer and Carroll, 1998). Men remain characterized by competitiveness, aggression and the desire to be, and to be seen to be, in control. Young men are highly susceptible to anything that can be seen to offer an adrenaline rush. This is perceived partly as an attempt to escape the pressures of modern life. Men at all life stages tend to see life as linear; the drive to be moving forward, progressing, building is a strong one. Status anxiety is prevalent and 'offers fertile ground for brands to provide men with reassurance' (Conway, 2004).

Tag Heuer's recent 'Knights of Time' campaign appeals directly to young men's desire to achieve by depicting their product with high achievers like Lewis Hamilton, Leonardo Di Caprio, and Tiger Woods. Tag positions its brand by association with each of the stars discussing how they share Tag Heuer's values. Advertising for the campaign features the tag line 'What are you made of?'

An interesting example of a brand which repositioned itself from children to adult men is the Nintendo Game Boy. The problem was how to make a toy acceptable to adults, and research indicated that there was a group of men whose lives were very different, but who shared a need for entertainment that absorbed and stimulated them. The key to making Game Boy relevant was to provide permission to buy a toy because it was mental stimulation or a way to exercise the mind: 'If your mind is being challenged you are not wasting your time' (Bioletti, 1995). The play element was vital, but as a support, not the main platform; the position that 'Game Boy taxes your brain' managed to banish childish associations. Nintendo have had great success with this and have gone on to develop appeals for women and the elderly with brain training, recipes, and of course Wii Sport.

Some brands which have attempted to use both genders in a brand positioning strategy have used an approach of 'gender rancour', which appears to signal contemporary relationships in which 'women give as good as they get', for example, Smirnoff Ice. Research indicates that where the relationship between genders is depicted as playful and interactive then the response is positive; if it involves deceit, especially where a woman is showing the worst (masculine) behaviour, responses are negative for all but the youngest female respondents (Fuller and Sommerville, 2002). What seems to be most successful is a tone of celebration, males and females enjoying themselves together, which conveys a relaxed, positive brand.

Social integration strategies
Brand community

The major issue here is the extent to which marketers can construct and manage brand community and thereby enhance brand loyalty. The DaimlerChrysler Jeep brand is an exciting example of how through marketer-organized 'brandfests', including Jeep Jamborees, Camp Jeep, and Jeep 101, the characteristics of a consumer-led brand community were consciously fostered by sponsorship of 2–3-day events (McAlexander *et al.*, 2002). Participation in brandfests led to a more positive relationship with the Jeep brand

and with other Jeep owners and these relationships proved to be long-lasting and to prolong brand loyalty by erecting social exit barriers. Community-integrated customers serve as brand missionaries, carrying the marketing message into other communities. A key point is the importance of designing events with a focus on socializing new and intending brand owners while offering special recognition to those who are already most integrated into the brand community.

Neo-tribes

The essence of *tribal marketing* is not to follow tribes but to inspire them and earn their respect by understanding their values and standing back and letting them make most of the running (McDonald, 2001). Sony PlayStation used the time-honoured premise that to children in the target audience anything forbidden becomes immediately attractive. TV commercials run throughout Europe featured a spoof society, SAPS (Society Against PlayStation), and later moved on to more enigmatic communications derived from studies of skateboarders about competition, self-actualization, and mastery. Using the concept of the sacrifice group, Sony PlayStation positioning is all about only the tribe really understanding what the brand communications actually mean.

Red Bull energy drink also uses elements of tribal marketing. Its communications are also enigmatic, but it puts much more effort into creating and supporting 'brand evangelists', students who are recruited to be 'student brand managers' and then provided with free drinks to distribute on campus and to educate users about the product and its benefits. This grass-roots effect is enhanced by the organization of free extreme sports events and 'consumer educators' who drive Red Bull jeeps and distribute free cans.

An unusual product category to target neo-tribes is that of pain relievers. Tylenol is attempting to form 'pain partner' relationships by funding events such as skateboarding, breakdancing, and snowboarding; items in an event goodie bag carry the word 'Ouch!'. 'In this target market pain is cool, they wear it as a badge' (Grapentine, 2004).

KEY CONCEPT

Brand strategies based on social differentiation and social integration.

Some brands enable us to be told apart from a group (social differentiation) while others help us to assign ourselves to a group (social integration). In truth, few brands differentiate us from everyone. Indeed if you want to be seen as different then you are likely to be in the 'group' of those who want to be seen as different. The same can be said for integration, if you want to be like a certain group then you need another group to 'not be like'. As such there is a continuum along which some brands are positioned as differentiators and others integrators.

Sub-cultures

An opportunity for co-creation of brand meanings using gender as a sub-cultural brand strategy lies with the gay market. Recently described as an untapped goldmine

(Burnett, 2000), a handful of brands have achieved legitimacy with this group through gay-friendly actions like supporting Lesbian and Gay Pride days and advertising in gay media (Kates, 2004). Since 2004, VW have actively targeted the gay market and are consistently rated as a favourite brand within the gay community. A travel agency in Nepal recently announced that it will be targeting the gay community for tours. The company, named Pink Mountain, has the support of the Nepal's Tourism Ministry (Agence France-Presse, 2010). The brand Grindr offers an iPhone or iPod touch app which allows gay men to identify like others using GPS technology. Despite the promise in this market, a potential problem is that homosexual consumers dislike and distrust advertising, and thus direct marketing attempts to court them can be difficult (Burnett, 2000).

Brand mythologies

The concept of developing a brand mythology is based on a brand representing an idea or set of ideas that people can live by, and embody and legitimize a new way of living in a rapidly changing society (Grant, 1999). For example Calvin Klein with CK One celebrated androgyny; Clarks shoes redefined adult shoes as things to romp around in: 'Act your shoe size not your age.' Opportunities to develop brand mythologies are legion, but many reside in social changes such as attitudes to gender, to old age and maturity, to friends versus family, to not having children, to class mobility, to the nature of relationships. Many of these themes are at the core of popular cultural forms such as the global success of *Modern Family* and *Sex in the City*, and via association brands can play a role in showing people possible ways to live. For instance when, in 2014, Malaysia's Mulpha International undertook a multi-million dollar refurbishment of their Hayman Island resort in Queensland, Australia, they contracted *Modern Family* to film a segment of the show's Australian vacation episode at the resort. This included a visit to the Great Barrier Reef—one of the primary reason visitors, often families, come to the area. The subsequent launch party was well attended by prominent and celebrity guests generating tens of millions of dollars' worth of press (Neubauer 2014). Most fans will recall vividly the character Carrie Bradshaw opening her Apple laptop in her apartment to write her column and thus narrate each episode of *Sex in the City*. This product placement is regarded as one of Apple's most iconic and lucrative brand building exercises (Elliott, 2010). It was perhaps unsurprising Hewlett Packard signed, for an undisclosed sum, a deal to have their PCs and notebook computers in scenes in the movie sequel *Sex and the City 2* (Elliot, 2010).

CHAPTER SUMMARY

In this chapter we have proposed a basic model of how brands are built in mindspace over time. The evidence suggests that advertising plays a key role in the process. We have discussed brand strategies based on personal meanings, on social differentiation, and on social integration. We have emphasized that the social language of the brand (see Chapter 1) can provide a wide range of benefits to the consumer and help transform their experience of the brand.

DISCUSSION QUESTIONS

1 What is the relationship between brand relevance differentiation and what implications does this have for brand building?

2 Why is brand awareness the starting point for building a brand?

3 What is the role of perceptions of differentiation and relevance?

4 What is the relationship between relative advertising expenditure and share of the market?

5 Think about your personal media architecture, choose a favourite brand and describe how it might best communicate with you.

6 When might word-of-mouth be the primary communication channel?

7 Provide an example of a brand pursuing a nostalgic brand strategy and analyse it in terms of Holbrook and Schindler's (2004) nostalgia themes.

8 Would the positioning tactic of 'brand as underdog' work in your country? Explain.

9 What are the five design principles for building an experience brand?

CASE STUDY

Crumpler bags

Chumpy, Industry Disgrace, The Sherpa, Albert Stash, Barney Rustle Blanket, Toshi Squirts, Dreadful Embarassment, 8 Million Dollar Home. To most, these phrases may seem like random gibberish, but believe it or not, they have one thing in common: They are all names of Crumpler merchandise. Crumpler, a world-renowned bag company is known not only for its quirky merchandize names but also for its practical designs, unique patterns, high quality fabric, durable workmanship, bright colours and of course, its QuickFlick buckle.

The origins of Crumpler can be traced back to the world of bicycle couriers and messenger bags. The year is 1992. The place: Ballarat, Australia. Hunched over his grandmother's sewing machine, Stuart Crumpler, a sculptor-come-furniture maker was sewing a bag. But not just any bag. A bag that was strong enough to carry a slab of beer home on his bike. It just so happened that Crumpler was also a bike messenger for Will Miller's and David Roper's Melbourne based courier company, MinuteMan. Drawing on Crumplers' creative talents, Miller and Roper commissioned Crumpler to design and sew messenger bags for their MinuteMan couriers. The brief: bags that were roomy, strong and durable enough to carry documents and packages in; bags that were practical, had easy access and were comfortable such that it distributed weight evenly and would not move during the ride; and bags that were fashionable and distinctive so that MinuteMan couriers, already decked out in pink lycra, stood out even more from the crowd. The prototype bags were so successful that riders from competing courier services started to put orders in for Crumpler's bags. Over time, the messenger bags were spotted all over town. Demand had soared, and in 1995, Crumpler, Miller, and Roper decided to go into business together to commercially manufacture these bags. The Crumpler brand was born.

Given their limited resources for marketing and building the brand, Crumpler, Miller, and Roper relied on word-of-mouth and had to devise rather creative and unique ways of building brand awareness. For example, in the early days, the three Aussie blokes would drive around in a campervan and spray-paint the memorable Crumpler logo on bicycle paths around the Melbourne CBD. Over time, people started to notice the Crumpler logo. Having no idea what the logos meant, given that the graffiti consisted of just a simple doodle of a stick man with crazy hair (as did the signage on the first Crumpler retail shop in Fitzroy, an inner-city suburb of Melbourne), people were encouraged to explore the brand. The boys would also sponsor nude foot races, where the Crumpler logo was stencilled on participants' naked bodies, and pay local apple farmers to put the Crumpler logo on their stickers. Drawing on and fostering creative local talent, they also collaborated with young local filmmakers to create edgy home-made advertisements for the brand. They would also support the local community, in particular the Big Issue initiative, by supplying bags to homeless Big Issue vendors.

It didn't take long for the bag designs and quirky approach to marketing and branding to resonate strongly and gain huge traction within the cycling and the broader creative community. Yet, they continued to rely on their creative resourcefulness to spread the word. In 2002, Crumpler developed the now infamous 'Beers for Bags' promotion. The idea behind the promotion was simple: Consumers use beer as currency to purchase Crumpler bags. They are exposed to Crumpler's high quality merchandize. Hopefully, in future, these customers will consider the Crumpler brand and purchase Crumpler merchandize with real currency. The promotional campaign was a hit and is now an annual event, attracting boozy bag-lovers and plenty of PR attention. Given that each year, Crumpler would donate a majority of the beer from the promotional campaign to student art events and opening nights, the Beers for Bags campaign also resonated with a key target market, university students.

Today, Crumplers' classic messenger bags no longer appeal only to bike couriers. They have become a 'must have' fashion accessory for the urban cool. With the rise of casual workforce dressing, Crumpler's messenger bags can be seen hanging off the shoulders of advertising types, architects, and lawyers in place of the formal briefcase. Crumplers' bag collection has also greatly expanded. The brand now offers a wide variety of merchandize, ranging from small accessories, camera straps and bags, laptop bags, travel and luggage. As the brand expanded, so too did its range of target market. Maintaining its urban cool positioning, Crumpler has won the hearts and minds of many young city dwellers including photographers, travel lovers, and the fashion elite—worldwide.

To connect with its growing international fan base, Crumpler maintains an active presence across a variety of social media platforms, including Twitter, Youtube and Facebook. Recently, the company launched 'Crumpler Films' on Vimeo, a series of short films showcasing Crumpler products across a range of contexts, and the people that use the brand.

In less than 20 years, the Crumpler brand has undergone a transformation–from niche bicycle brand to a major player in the lucrative streetware market. Despite their success, Crumpler, Miller and Roper continued to stay away from mass media, preferring instead to advertise on public radio stations and sponsor local community initiatives, such as bike events and photography competitions. They continue to devise fun, unique, and ingenious ways to promote the Crumpler brand. Their latest: the TP project, in which 100,000 rolls of Crumpler branded toilet paper were distributed and placed in bathrooms, internationally. In Las Vegas, 3000 Crumpler rolls were placed in the bathrooms at the Sands Expo and Convention Centre during the Interbike International Bicycle Expo. This student-level humour approach to brand building very much reflects the personalities and spirits of the Aussie founders—laid back, always having fun and a good laugh.

Where to from here? In 2011, Crumpler hired former Apple creative director, Sam Davy to help the brand move to the next level. Only time will tell what novel brand building campaigns and strategies the boys will come up with next.

Case Written by Dr Jo En Yap | Lecturer, Marketing

Faculty of Business and Law, Swinburne Business School | Department of Marketing, Tourism and Social Impact

Swinburne University of Technology

CASE QUESTIONS

1. Based on your understanding of three stages of brand building in mindspace, discuss the effectiveness of Crumplers' brand building efforts.

2. Brand building in mindspace entails maintaining consistency across all aspects about the brand. What is the consistent message coming across Crumpler's brand touch points? Draw on examples from the case study to support your response.

3. What symbolic brand strategy(ies) have Crumpler employed? Draw on examples from the case study to support your response.

4. Will Crumpler's move from niche bicycle brand to mainstream street ware alienate its initial supporters? How can they maintain appeal to this group?

FURTHER READING

- A thoughtful approach to brand strategy which integrates theory with practice is taken in H. Edwards and D. Day (2005), *Passionbrands*, London: Kogan Page.

- A practitioner approach is taken in M. Gobe (2001), *Emotional Branding*, Oxford: Windsor Books.

- An historical US approach to brand myths is D. Holt (2004), *How Brands Become Icons*, Cambridge, MA: Harvard Business School Press.

REFERENCES

Aaker, J. L. (1997), 'Dimensions of brand personality', *Journal of Marketing Research*, August, 34, 347–56.

Agence France-Presse (2010), 'Nepal taps gay market to develop tourism', *Sydney Morning Herald*, 25 January, http://www.smh.com.au/travel. Last accessed 22 July 2010.

Bakir, A. and Palin K. M. (2010), 'How are children's attitudes towards ads and brands affected by gender-related content in advertising?', *Journal of Advertising*, 39, 1, 35–48.

Bioletti, F. (1995), *Creative Planning Awards: Big Boys' Toys—Making Game Boy Something to do with your Brain,* London: Account Planning Group.

Brasel, S. A. and Gips, J. (2011) 'Red Bull "Gives You Wings" for better or worse: A double-edged impact of brand exposure on consumer performance', *Journal of Consumer Psychology*, 21, 1, 57–64.

Burnett, J. (2000), 'Gays: Feelings about advertising and media used', *Journal of Advertising Research*, 40, 1/2, 75–85.

Canning, S. (2010), 'Social networking sites lure direct sellers', *Business with the Wall Street Journal, The Australian*, 3May 2010, http://www.theaustralian.com.au/business/ Last accessed 22 July 2010.

Conway, J. (2004), 'Men: What are they really thinking?', *Admap*, November, 455, 12–17.

D&AD (2011), 'Case study: Old Spice response campaign', http://www.dandad.org/en/old-spice-response-campaign/ Last accessed 17 November 2014.

Dahl, D. W., Frankenberger, K. D., and Manchanda, R. V. (2003). 'Does it pay to shock? Reactions to shocking and non-shocking ad content among university students', *Journal of Advertising Research*, 43, 3, 268–80.

Dyson, P., Farr, A. and Hollis, N. (1996), 'Understanding, measuring, and using brand equity', *Journal of Advertising Research*, November/December, 36, 9–21.

Edwards, H. (2004), Presentation to the MBA *Brand Strategy* elective, Saïd Business School, University of Oxford, 8 May.

Elliot, S. (2010), 'What next, the official salad dressing of "Sex and the City 2"?', *The New York Times*, 20 April, http://mediadecoder. blogs.nytimes.com. Last accessed 1 August 2010.

Evans, M., Nairn, A., and Maltby, A. (2000), 'The hidden sex life of the male (& female) shot', *International Journal of Advertising*, 19, 1, 32–41.

Ferdows, K., Lewis, M., and Machuca, J. (2004), 'Rapid-fire fulfillment', *Harvard Business Review*, 82, 11.

Fournier, S. (1998), 'Consumers and their brands: Developing relationship theory in consumer research', *Journal of Consumer Research*, 24, 4, 343–73.

Fuller, K. and Sommerville, A. (2002), 'Trouble in paradise: Getting to grips with the gender game', *Admap*, January, 36, 15–23.

Goldman, R. and Papson, S. (1998), *Nike Culture*, London: Sage Publications.

Grant, J. (1999), *The New Marketing Manifesto*, London: Orion.

Grapentine, T. (2004), 'No pain, no pain reliever', *Marketing Research*, Winter, 16, 4.

Hall, E. (2009), 'East German brands see nostalgia 20 years after the wall's fall' *Advertising Age*, http://adage.com/globalnews Last accessed 1 August 2010.

Hansen, H. (2003), 'Antecedents to consumers' disclosing intimacy with service employees', *Journal of Services Marketing*, 17, 6/7, 573–89.

Harris, A. H. S., and Standard, S. (2001), 'Psychometric properties of the life regard index: A validation study of a measure of personal meaning', *Psychological Reports*, 89, 759–73

Holbrook, M. and Schindler, R.M. (2003), 'Nostalgic bonding: Exploring the role of nostalgia in the consumption experience', *Journal of Consumer Behaviour*, 3, 2, 107–27.

Huang, M. (2004), 'Romantic love and sex: Their relationship and impacts on ad attitudes', *Psychology and Marketing*, 21, 1, 53–73.

Janoff-Bulman, R., and Berg, M. (1998). Disillusionment and the creation of value: From traumatic losses to existential gains, in J. Harvey (ed.), *Perspectives on Loss: A Sourcebook*, Philadelphia: Brunner/Mazel, 35–47.

Kates, S. (2004), 'The dynamics of brand legitimacy: An interpretive study in the gay men's community', *Journal of Consumer Research*, 31, 2, 455–65.

Langer, J. and Carroll, T. (1998), *Mantrack: A case study in qualitative trend detection*, ARF *Workshop*, New York: Advertising Research Foundation.

Learned, A. (2004), 'How to market to women by humanising your brand', *Admap*, December, 456, 31–7.

Loveland, K.E., Smeesters, D., and Mandel, N. (2010), 'Still preoccupied with 1995: The need to belong and preference for nostalgic products', *Journal of Consumer Research*, October, 37, (published online at http://www.journals. uchicago.edu). Last accessed 2 August 2010.

McAlexander, J., Schouten, J., and Koenig, H. (2002), 'Building brand community', *Journal of Marketing*, 66, 38–54.

McDonald, N. (2001), 'Tribe talking—tribal trends in post-cool Britannia', *Admap*, April, 17–19.

Millward Brown (2010), 'Brand dynamics', http://www.millwardbrown.com/Solutions/ProprietaryTools/BrandDynamics.aspx Last accessed 29 July 2010.

Nancarrow, C., Nancarrow, P., and Page, J. (2002), 'An analysis of the concept of cool and its marketing implications', *Journal of Consumer Behaviour*, 1, 4, 311–22.

Neubauer, I. L. (2014), "The meteoric rise of One&Only Resorts" Marketing Magazine, 8th August, Last accessed 1st December, http://www.marketingmag.com.au/tags/product-placement/#.VIoBP3tBGu8

Percy, L. and Elliott, R. (2009), *Strategic Advertising Management*, 3rd edn, Oxford: Oxford University Press.

Pine, J. and Gilmore, J. (1998), 'Welcome to the experience economy', *Harvard Business Review*, July/August, 97–105.

Seireeni, R. and Chen, S. (2010) 'A case of gender branding: How it's done in Japan', *the brand architect group*, 16 May, http://www.brandarchitect.com/ Last accessed 24 July 2010.

Sweeney, J. C. and Brandon C. (2006), 'Brand personality: Exploring the potential to move

from factor analytical to circumplex models', *Psychology & Marketing*, 23, 8, 639–63.

Superbrands (2002), *Cool Brand Leaders*, London: The Superbrands Organisation.

theguardian (2014), 'Apple voted United Kingdom's coolest brand as Twitter slumps', *theguardian*, 22 September, http://www.theguardian.com/technology/2014/sep/22/coolbrands-apple-twitter-stella-mccartney-chanel-uk Last accessed 20 November 2014.

Vallance, C. (1995), *Creative Planning Awards. Caffrey's: Re-Inventing Keg Beer*, London: Account Planning Group.

Vernette, E. (2004), 'Targeting women's clothing fashion opinion leaders in media planning: An application for magazines', *Journal of Advertising Research*, 44, 1.

White, R. (2002), 'Best practice: Advertising to women', *Admap*, November, 433, 23–8.

Young and Rubicam Group (2010), 'BrandAsset Consulting', http://www.brandassetconsulting.com/ Last accessed 22 July 2010.

215

 Test your understanding of this chapter and explore the subject further using our Online Resource Centre. Visit the Online Resource Centre at http://www.oxfordtextbooks.co.uk/orc/elliott-percy3e/

9

Brand Strategies 2—Low-Involvement Brands

Key Concepts

1 Top-of-mind brand awareness and brand salience are critical to a brand's success.

2 Pre-conscious processes of mere exposure and classical conditioning work well where there are no salient competitors.

3 Brand associations are built through all elements of communication over time and by laying down somatic markers.

4 The implications of consumers buying within brand repertoires.

5 Deciding between an emphasis on increasing penetration or purchase frequency.

6 Managing consumer perceptions over time.

Introduction

If symbolic brands are metaphorically the world heritage cities of Bath and Florence then functional brands are the industrial cities of Newcastle and Ruhr. To readers not familiar with these destinations, Bath and Florence are world heritage listed cities with astounding architectural beauty, while Newcastle and Ruhr, both fine cities in their own right, are traditional industrial powerhouses for England and Germany respectively. To continue the metaphor, they are as important to the economy (market place) as each other and, despite lacking the glitz, managing the latter is equally complex and rewarding.

As discussed in Chapter 1, the cognitive choice processes for functional low-involvement brands varies from very low levels of pre-conscious processing and habit, to a combination of minimal cognitive processes using a range of short cuts or heuristics. Brand salience is a key objective of strategy as it drives much purchase behaviour and we will examine a number of approaches to building awareness and salience. It is also important to understand the buying behaviour tendencies of different market segments and we will consider pre-conscious, cognitive, and behavioural processes and how market segmentation by customer buying behaviour can be the focus of brand strategy. We will then review approaches to managing consumer perceptions and influencing consumer purchasing behaviour including choice, usage quantity, and loyalty.

Brand awareness and brand salience

Brand salience, often called top-of-mind awareness (i.e. the first brand mentioned in response to a spontaneous awareness question), is probably the most important characteristic any low-involvement brand can possess. Ehrenberg *et al.* (2002) argue that salience also includes how many people have it in their active brand repertoire or in their consideration set, and maintain that it represents the 'size' of the brand in consumers' mindspace. From work on the double jeopardy effect in static fmcg markets, where brands with small market shares attract fewer customers but also experience less customer loyalty than more popular brands, Ehrenberg *et al.* (1997) claim that empirically there is very little difference between what brand users feel about their brands. However, the number of people for whom a brand is salient does differ greatly from brand to brand. It is salience that divides big brands from little brands and this effect is related to market dominance, as we have seen when we discussed brand equity in Chapter 5. Big brands have much greater levels of salience than do small brands because salience increases exponentially in relation to total spontaneous awareness, that is, if a brand is twice as big as the next two brands, its salience will be four times as great (Morgan, 1999).

Building and maintaining brand salience

Salience is a consequence as well as a cause of many aspects of brand strategy. A salient brand is likely to have wider distribution, more shelf-space and display, more promotions, more advertising, more word-of-mouth, and more media mentions (Ehrenberg *et al.*, 1997). This is why one of the critical steps in positioning a brand is to establish the link between a category need and the brand. We want the brand to be immediately associated with the need for the product when that need occurs.

For brands purchased largely out of habit, what John Howard (1977), one of the fathers of consumer behaviour theory, has called routinized response behaviour, Ehrenberg and his colleagues (1997) have suggested that brand salience can be built effectively by 'Here I am' advertising that focuses largely on the brand name and package and which leaves long-term memory traces for the brand, but does not try to communicate a persuasive message to change attitudes. This assumes that, for whatever reason, a positive brand attitude already exists, and needs only to be nurtured by reminding the user of the brand. The benefits associated with the brand are already in memory, even if these 'feelings' are consciously a result of the notion that 'I use it therefore I like it' (Ehrenberg *et al.*, 1997).

How brand salience is built is critical. It must take into account the way in which the link between the category need and the brand is triggered at the time a purchase decision is made. That is when the brand must be 'salient', and this may be triggered either by *recognizing* the package at the point-of-purchase, or *recalling* the brand name when the need to make a choice occurs. In the first case, marketing communication must feature the package as it will be seen at the point-of-purchase. The user sees the package, it triggers a need, and is purchased. On the other hand, when a choice is made prior to purchase (e.g. where to go for lunch) or at the point-of-purchase, but where packages are not visible (e.g. when a waiter asks you what beer you would like), the brand must be recalled. Marketing communication here must actively seek to connect the need with the brand.

Brand salience is critical to a brand's success, but it is not enough. Without the formation of a positive brand attitude, as discussed in Chapter 5, the development of strong brand equity is unlikely. Romaniuk (2003) suggests that since many brands seem to compete on the same basic attribute, the key seems to be to go for quantity rather than quality of associations, concentrating on linking the brand to a wide range of attributes and thus to 'obtain a wide mental distribution' for the brand. But the mind does not work like that. It makes much more sense to position a brand on one or two benefits the target market believes (or can be persuaded to believe) the brand can deliver; and ideally, can deliver better than competitors (Percy and Elliott, 2009).

We now turn our attention to some important buying behaviour tendencies towards functional brands including pre-conscious, cognitive, and behavioural processes.

KEY CONCEPT

Top-of-mind brand awareness and brand salience are critical to a brand's success

There may be oil in your back yard or you may have walked past an enormous nugget of gold on your last hiking trip. Unless you know about it the value is unrealised. The same goes for brands. You may have produced a brand with features perfect for a target audience that is finely tuned and superior on every key attribute your research has identified. If the target market does not know the brand name it will not succeed. As a brand manager, achieving brand awareness is critical, a hurdle requirement. It's also important for you to know whether your brand needs to be just recognised or recalled by consumers.

Brands and pre-conscious processes

Mere exposure

A host of experimental studies have demonstrated that low levels of preference can be obtained by merely exposing people to a stimulus a number of times, without their conscious awareness being necessary. This 'exposure effect' has been called mere exposure, and results from the unconscious priming of a stimulus (a brand in our case). The findings of these studies suggest that people do not remember seeing the brand, but they will be more likely to 'prefer' it to other unknown brands to which they have not been exposed. Importantly for brand marketing, the preference will only occur in the *absence* of brands with which someone is already familiar. Clearly this is not often the case, nevertheless generating an unconscious positive emotional congruence with the brand through repetition of a brand name or logo is a sound strategy. The goal of brand management is to positively affect higher-order cognitive processing, while encouraging unconscious positive emotional congruence with the brand. Before discussing cognitive processing, a brief digression into classical conditioning lends further precision to pre-conscious processing.

Classical conditioning

This approach requires not just exposure of the brand or logo but also pairing with a pleasant emotional stimulus, and eventually the brand alone will automatically evoke the pleasant emotional response as the link is established in non-declarative emotional memory. An example is insurance company Direct Line's practice of pairing their red telephone with frequent repetition of a musical car horn; over time the two become fixed in memory. In 2008 Sennheiser launched a sound logo competition in which consumers were invited to submit a new sound motif. The winner received 5,000 euros, with an additional 30,000 euros (over 43,000 US dollars!) if Sennheiser acquired unlimited rights to the winning logo (Sweetwater, 2008).

Both mere exposure and classical conditioning seem to work well when there is low involvement and no salient competitors, as pointed out above. Evidence suggests that mere exposure can be as successful as classical conditioning and is easier to execute, but will not be successful against known, well-established competitors (Baker, 1999). The key strategy is to maximize the prominence of both brand name and package in communications to take advantage of any potential pre-conscious processing that will positively influence choice among unknown competitors.

> ### KEY CONCEPT
>
> **Pre-conscious processes of mere exposure and classical conditioning**
>
> Findings that pre-conscious processing can have an important and positive effects on brand evaluations could mean many brand managers sleep a little easier at night. In the absence of strong recall or recognition results, many campaigns are questioned or cancelled. However, this research gives credence to the notion that continually having a presence using well-targeted media is enough in itself to benefit the brand.

Minimal cognitive processes

Shallow processing

A large proportion of our daily activities operate at semi-conscious levels of awareness, which leads to implicit rather than active learning of information. Unfortunately, with the exception of emotion, implicit memory is not likely to have any impact upon the evaluation or choice of brands (Percy, 2005). If we are motivated to do so, we can find complexity in the most mundane and low-risk product categories like soap powder and toothpaste, but typically we don't have the time or inclination to engage in higher-order cognitive elaboration. Damasio (1994) has talked about the ability of secondary emotion to aid in decision making in terms of something he calls *somatic markers*. He defined somatic markers as 'a special instance of feelings generated from secondary emotions', and stated that these emotions and feelings have been 'connected, by training, to predicted future outcomes of certain scenarios'. As he put it, somatic markers do not deliberate for us, but assist the deliberation. With soap powder the secondary emotion triggering the somatic marker may be elicited by the design and colour of the package or even the shape of the product.

The key here is to build associations through repetition of all elements of communications, not just advertising, and over time to build up connections between a brand and positive feelings, through the laying down of somatic markers, which can be triggered by a choice situation and give us simple guides to action without much, or indeed any, thought being necessary for purchase to ensue. We can plan to lay down as many somatic markers as possible by using a combination of associations and meanings to differentiate the product in some way. Let us now take a look at some brand tactics in relation to these.

KEY CONCEPT

Laying down somatic markers

The concept of somatic markers seems complex—and in theoretical terms it is. From a brand management perspective we can simplify its application. The theory suggests that it may be advantageous to elicit positive emotions in relation to the brand, which are in addition to the unique selling proposition of the product. It may be the shape, the design, the colour, or a celebrity or musical association that generates the emotion. This then leads to a feeling (physiological response) that is identified as the somatic marker, which we hope will bias favourably our thoughts (cognition) about the brand.

Building brand associations and meanings

Taste, shape, and texture

The taste of Marmite, the shape of Toilet Duck, the feel of Dove soap, and the texture of Cadbury's Flake are unique associations which define the brand for many consumers (Heath, 2001).

Colours

Red means passionate and exciting, blue means dependable and reliable, green means security (Hynes, 2009), and all can be learned without any conscious effort being required. But a manager must be certain the colour associated with the brand in memory is consistent with the desired *long-term* positioning of the brand. For example, colours towards the red end of the spectrum (as well as more intense colours) tend to increase arousal (Osgood *et al.*, 1957). This makes sense for Coke, but it would not make sense for a brand that wanted to be associated with a sense of calm and serenity.

In an interesting study of the synesthesic effects (i.e. where one sense evokes another) of colour on taste, Percy (1973) found that the colour of a sauce (condiments such as ketchup, steak sauce, and salad dressing) is directly and consistently related to the colour spectrum. Running from orange through dark brown to black, it was found that people perceived orange sauces to be milder than red, and so forth through dark brown and black, which were perceived to be the spiciest. This can have important implications for condiment brands.

At the time of this study, both Heinz 57 Sauce and A-1 Sauce (steak sauce brands) were basically the same reddish-brown colour. But Heinz 57 Sauce was packaged in a clear bottle while A-1 Sauce was packaged in a black-tinted bottle. Because people could see the reddish-brown colouring of Heinz 57 Sauce, they perceived it to have a milder taste than A-1 Sauce, which was perceived as spicier because of the dark bottle. Unfortunately, 'spiciness' was the most important attribute of a steak sauce.

More recent research by Miller and Kahn (2005) indicates that care should be taken if colours are to be named as well as shown. They found that, despite seeing the colour first, consumers preferred atypical but descriptive colour names like Coke red and Florida orange to ambiguously named colours like antique red and millennium orange.

In 2014, budget US airline Spirit rebadged its aircraft in bright yellow livery. As one aviation branding commentator reflected 'I can't help but be reminded of the plain yellow packages of the No Name generic brand found in Loblaws grocery stores. Much of Spirit's recent advertising has been aimed at setting consumer expectations: you won't get much on Spirit, but you won't pay much, either. The yellow planes aren't elegant, and they aren't beautiful, but they are very well-suited to communicating the kind of airline Spirit wants to be' (Fly the Branded Skies, 2014).

Music

We can add additional associations to the brand by adding sound to visual elements so doubling the modalities of association, for example Hamlet cigars and Bach, British Airways and Delibes, Intel and their reassuring four notes. This is known as sound or audio branding,

Sound is also used effectively in a retail setting. There are three main variables that mediate the effect of music on brand purchase behaviour: tempo, type, and how it is presented (Rossiter and Percy, 1997). Tempo seems to operate emotionally. Slow music has been found to have a positive effect upon sales. In Milliman's (1982) primary study of tempo, he found that when slower instrumental music was played in a retail store, customers spent 17% more time shopping and 35% more money compared with when faster music was played (60 beats per minute versus 108 beats per minute).

The type of music heard appears to operate more upon cognitive processes. In a study of musical types Areni and Kim (1993) found that when classical background music was played in a wine store versus Top 40 pop music, the amount of money customers spent was three times greater (US$7.43 versus US$2.18). In another study conducted in the wine section of a UK supermarket, it was found that when French music was played, French wine was four times more likely to be purchased than German wine. But when German music was played, German wines outsold French wines two-to-one (North *et al.*, 1999).

What is also likely to be operating upon cognitive interpretation is how the music is presented. In an experiment where music was played on a clearly visible tape player in a shopping setting, younger customers were likely to spend significantly more than if the music was played in the background as part of the store's audio system. With older adults, it was just the opposite. With background music, significantly more was spent than with music played in the foreground. These results were not related to either a person's mood at the time or whether they liked the music being played or not (Yalch and Spangenburg, 1993).

Brand name suggestiveness

Research has shown that a brand name that explicitly conveys a product benefit leads to higher recall of advertising than a non-suggestive name and thus builds positive associations more effectively (Keller *et al.*, 1998). A brand name that explicitly conveys a product benefit (e.g. PicturePerfect televisions) leads to higher recall of an advertised benefit claim compared with non-suggestive brand names (e.g. Emporium televisions).

Celebrities

A short-cut to associating meaning with a brand is to use the ready-made meanings of a celebrity endorser, for example. Cristiano Ronaldo and Castrol Oil, Roger Federer and Gillette. The influence of sports celebrities is particularly strong on teenagers of both genders, increasing both positive word-of-mouth and brand loyalty (Bush *et al.*, 2004). But the primary benefit of using a celebrity endorser is heightened awareness for a brand. As Holman and Hecken (1983) have shown, a celebrity presenter will almost always increase recall for a brand. Of course, the presenter must be seen as a celebrity in the eye of the brand's target market. Also, brand recall, as opposed to brand recognition, should be the primary brand awareness objective.

But in using a celebrity endorser the manager must be careful. As Percy and Elliott (2009) have pointed out, while a celebrity presenter may raise a brand's visibility, one must be equally concerned with the likely effect specific characteristics of the celebrity will have in relation to the underlying nature of the decision involved in choosing brands within a category. For example, with symbolic brands where the underlying purchase decision is positively motivated, for sensory gratification or social approval, the celebrity presented must be seen as likeable; and the more highly involving the decision, the more the presenter must be seen by the target market as similar to an 'ideal user'. In other words, with symbolic brands, not only must purchasers like and identify with the celebrity, they must also feel their social circle will also identify with the celebrity as positively representing the brand.

And of course, the use of a celebrity endorser for a brand must be carefully evaluated in relation to the generally high cost of securing the endorsement. Also, the risk of possible negative publicity associated with the celebrity must be weighed. Recent examples include Lance Armstrong's drug cheat allegations and the conviction of Oscar Pistorius for culpable homicide. Just how much damage the celebrity will do to a brand may depend on their cultural meaning and their match up with the brand's own meaning. For instance, Kate Moss's publicized use of cocaine did little to affect her cachet or that of high street brand

Cristiano Ronaldo: the ready-made meanings of a celebrity endorser

Topshop, arguably because the incident was not completely incongruent with the world of fashion. By contrast, Armstrong's supposed drug use ended his endorsement of multiple high profile brands including Nike and Anheuser-Busch (Pearson, 2012) because he was no longer perceived as the epitome of performance and success following the stripping of his Tour de France crowns.

Choice heuristics

Studies have shown that consumers often make choices between brands based on simple rules-of-thumb, or choice heuristics, which short-circuit the process into an almost instantaneous decision. Heuristics such as 'buy the cheapest brand' and 'buy the brand I feel warm about' are the most common for fmcgs (Hoyer, 1984), while for leisure activities 'buy the brand my friends buy' is most common (Elliott and Hamilton, 1991). In some product categories, pictographic thinking is very common, where consumers rely on package illustrations to infer attributes (Viswanathan *et al.*, 2005). Therefore, before focusing on any particular heuristic, it needs to be identified through research as being frequently used by consumers in the product category of interest. But once identified, communications can focus on providing the relevant information, preferably visually.

Surrogate indicators

Consumers often use surrogate indicators to simplify their choice processes, where hidden dimensions of a product are inferred from some visible attribute. A common surrogate in purchasing grocery products is small size = low price; however the implications of this for strategy are complicated by the use by some consumers of a large size = low price inference (Viswanathan *et al.*, 2005). Again, specific research must be carried out before making decisions about pack sizes.

Market beliefs

As well as using heuristics based on aspects of the product, consumers also use more generalized beliefs about companies, advertising, and shops to guide their decisions. Some widely-held market beliefs include 'when in doubt, a well-known brand is a safe choice',

223

'bad brands just don't survive', 'hard-sell advertising is associated with low-quality products', 'larger shops offer better prices than small shops' (Duncan, 1990).

Meaningful differentiation from meaningless differences

As discussed in the previous chapter, the BrandAsset Valuator studies identify differentiation and relevance as the core elements in building brand strength. However, for low-involvement brands in highly competitive markets, having a real source of differentiation in the product's functional attributes is very difficult to achieve and sustain. However, an intriguing study has demonstrated that it may be possible to differentiate a brand on the basis of irrelevant attributes (Carpenter *et al.*, 1994). Esso famously told us to 'put a tiger in our tank' to promote its petrol stations. Alberto Natural Silk Shampoo is differentiated by including silk in the shampoo and advertised as 'We put silk in a bottle'. This suggests that the consumer's hair will be silky, but there is no known benefit of adding silk to a shampoo. Experimental studies have shown that consumers will use a meaningless difference to aid decision making, but most importantly it seems that a premium price increases the differentiating effect as consumers infer from the price that the (meaningless) differentiation is in fact valuable.

Behavioural processes

Brand repertoires

Using data from large-scale consumer panel studies, Ehrenberg and his associates have shown that in many fmcg markets, rather than buying only one brand—solus brand loyalty—consumers regularly buy from within a small number of competing brands: their brand repertoire. Within this set of brands they seem to buy at random and the brands usually share some physical characteristics. Interestingly, when asked about their buying behaviour consumers frequently over-estimated their loyalty when compared with their recorded actual purchases (Table 9.1).

The implications of this are that the pursuit of solus brand loyalty may be fruitless in many fmcg markets, and the aim should be to build the number of consumers who have the brand in their repertoire. This why brand salience is such an important objective.

TABLE 9.1 Brand repertoires: Average frequencies of purchase of cereals in a year

Brand	Average purchases by buyers of stated brand	
	Stated brand	Other brands
Nabisco Shredded Wheat (USA)	4	37
Nabisco Shredded Wheat (UK)	7	33
Kellogg's Corn Flakes (USA)	5	29
Kellogg's Corn Flakes (UK)	10	23

Source: Ehrenberg and Goodhardt (1979)

> **KEY CONCEPT**
>
> **The implications of consumers buying within brand repertoires**
>
> Many brand managers need not seek absolute brand loyalty from their customers. Evidence from the fmcg market suggests that it is more important to be in the group of brands that consumers would consider purchasing. This suggests that consumers like to seek variety within safe boundaries. Key to this is brand salience, the share of mind-space the brand has. Companies achieve this through consistent and well-targeted promotion often focusing more on having a presence in the marketplace while sacrificing more expensive and creative communication. Companies like Mars have been very successful at this and, as they have expanded, have developed multiple high profile brands in a single category strategically cannibalising one another but nevertheless dominating the mindspace of consumers e.g., M&M's®, SNICKERS®, DOVE®/GALAXY®, MARS®/MILKY WAY® and TWIX®

Penetration and purchase frequency

A major issue in deciding on strategy in fmcg markets is whether to focus on increasing penetration (new users) or increasing frequency of purchase (by current users). The large-scale IRI study in the USA (1,251 brands, 14 fmcg categories, 82,000 households, over a two-year period) demonstrated that for brands which grew in the period, brand growth came largely from increased penetration, accounting for 75% or more of all growth (McQueen *et al.*, 1998). However, purchase frequency increases were important too, playing some role in growth for 76% of brands and being the predominant source of growth for 25% of brands. A further study has found convergent results, penetration being the primary growth driver, especially for brands that showed dramatic growth (Baldinger *et al.*, 2002).

If we look at the differences between large and small brands, we find that the larger the brand, the more likely it is to grow through purchase frequency, although penetration still contributes most. However, small brands with low penetration make up a sizeable proportion of many fmcg categories, and these brands grew almost exclusively through penetration (Table 9.2).

The IRI study also classified the consumer panel data according to patterns of purchasing, resulting in five types of purchasing behaviour (Fig. 9.1).

These buyer segments contribute to brand growth differentially, and brands have different profiles of the various buyer types. Brands dominated by 'loyals' gain most growth from increased frequency of purchasing; they also tend to be the biggest brands. At the other extreme, brands with a lot of 'light users' get most of their growth from penetration gains and are extremely vulnerable as the 'light users' are likely to buy a different brand every time they enter the market (Stockdale, 1999) (Table 9.3).

The implications for strategy are that all brands should attempt to increase penetration, but that large brands have less room to grow through this strategy and must also concentrate on increasing purchase frequency. It is also vital to understand the profile of consumer segments for any specific brand in order to target appropriate efforts towards major segments.

TABLE 9.2 The effect of brand size on growth mechanics

Brand Year 1 Penetration (%)	Percentage contribution to growth		
	Penetration	Frequency	Percentage of brands
0–5	92	8	23
6–10	77	23	34
11–30	68	33	32
30 +	54	46	11

Source: Adapted from McQueen *et al.*, (1998)

Five types of buying behaviour:

- Long-term brand loyals
- Deal selectives
  - Who buy brand leadars on offer
- Rotators
  - Heavy users with large brand repertoire
- Price driven
  - Buy cheap brands and anything on offer
- Light users

FIGURE 9.1 All customers are not equal

Source: Adapted from Stockdale (1999)

TABLE 9.3 Deconstruction of brand growth

Brands by buyer types	Contribution to growth		% of brands
	Penetration (%)	Frequency (%)	
Loyals	15	85	15
Deal selectives	50	50	17
Rotators	68	32	20
Price driven	75	25	29
Light users	100	0	19

Source: Adapted from Stockdale (1999)

Managing consumer perceptions

A consumer's perceptions of a brand are based on their history with the brand, including advertising, packaging, actual usage experiences, etc., and these perceptions can be refreshed and reinforced by associating the brand with new goals and usage situations or by encouraging category substitution (Wansink and Huffman, 2001).

Refreshing favourable perceptions

New information is most easily learned when it is related to what is already known, and it can be quicker and less expensive to re-activate existing associations than to create new ones (Deighton, 1984). An excellent example of going back to what differentiated the brand originally and bringing it up to date is Nestlé's Yorkie bar, which was originally launched in the UK in 1976 at a time when Cadbury had been reducing the thickness of their brand leader Dairy Milk bar in response to raw material cost rises, rather than increasing the retail price. Nestlé took advantage of this opportunity by launching a bar that was a much thicker shape and associating the brand with a large muscular truck driver biting down on the bar. The same truck driver image was used in TV advertising for many years. The brand was refreshed by a return to the male-oriented position with a more contemporary feel: 'It's not for girls'; 'Not for handbags'; 'Not available in pink'. This was carried through to the packaging and created much word-of-mouth through media attention.

Extending favourable perceptions

The creative use of product development can be instrumental in extending a brand's current perceptions into a new space. Virgin Money's expansion into retail banking reflects the positive perceptions the Virgin brand brings to its range of lifestyle products. Virgin loyalists have grown up with the brand for over 25 years and are now in a stage of the life cycle, with a family and mortgage, where money matters. Virgin has recently acquired a UK banking licence and looks likely to bid for a major retail bank in the near future (Kowsmann, 2010).

New usage situations

There is clear evidence that associating a brand with new usage situations can increase sales, sometimes dramatically. Corsodyl mouthwash made a successful move from the dentist's surgery to the family home, capitalizing on its authenticity as a brand preferred by professionals. More recently, National Geographic released an updated edition of their entire collection of magazines (all issues from 1888 through 2010) on DVD-ROM that enables it to be used as a research and education tool. Readers are able to reference and rediscover all pages ever printed. The package includes features that enable new uses of this archived content. For example, Geobrowse—a visual geographic search tool—makes it possible to easily find articles, maps, and photographs that are specific to the chosen location.

Sometimes new usage situations are not entirely driven by the firm. An example of this is Microsoft's belated move onto the Cloud in response to a growing trend for consumers wanting mobility in their access to applications. Google Docs had capitalized on the consumer trend for web-based applications, ushering in a new world of cloud-computing where 'software roams free on the computer, phone, tablet and television' (Chan, 2010).

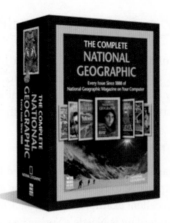

National Geographic made a successful move from bookshelves to desktop computers

Encouraging category substitution

A related strategy is to promote a brand as a substitute for products in other categories. For example, Danone yogurt was promoted as a substitute for high-fat eggs and oil in baking. Kellogg's Special K breakfast cereal was promoted for use not just at breakfast but as an afternoon or evening snack. This was later followed by new product development to create Special K bars, which resulted in greatly increased sales without damage to the core cereal product.

KEY CONCEPT

Managing consumer perceptions over time

Consumers need to be reminded about the benefits of the brand, whether this is rein-forcement of the current position or an announcement of something new. Wrigley's gum is a brand that has had to continually reposition itself despite the product being essentially the same. Initially it was positioned as fun, tasty and refreshing. As com-petition increased and the benefit was less differentiating, a campaign was launched announcing it as an important social facilitator because it reduced bad breath. This was followed by a health positioning whereby chewing gum after meals facilitated the breakdown of food by encouraging the production of important enzymes in the body. The health based positioning has been maintained although it has been tweaked a lit-tle. Chewing Wrigley's gum is currently promoted as facilitating oral health and helping weight gain management.

Real users

A new approach to managing perceptions of fmcg brands has been the use of 'real people' in advertising. The established brand of soap Lever Fabergé's Dove 'received significant publicity when it asked real women to strip down to their underwear to advertise its Body Firming range of products. Using the strapline 'As tested on real curves' the poster version proclaimed 'It wouldn't be much of a challenge to firm up the thighs of size 8 supermodels, would it?' (Mediaweek, 2003). Conspicuously, the women in the Dove campaign were not impossibly beautiful, unattainably perfect models, and as a consequence the communication was more believable. Lever Fabergé reported that sales doubled after the campaign.

Cause-related marketing

A very powerful way to influence consumers' perceptions of fmcgs is to associate a brand with a 'good cause'. A study by Cone Inc. (2004) indicated that 86% of respondents would switch to an otherwise similar brand which supports a social cause.

In 2011, Coca-Cola joined forces with the largest independent international conservation group, the World Wildlife Fund (WWF), to help protect the polar bear and its arctic habitat. The Arctic Home campaign, which is still running, was launched in Canada and the U.S. but it expanded into 17 European countries during winter 2013. It prominently features visual imagery (thus transcending language barriers), and in particular, those of the polar bear, which has served an iconic role during Coca-Cola's seasonal promotions for over 90 years. Despite causing consumer confusion by changing the colour of cans from red to white for the initial promotional launch, the campaign has proved to be highly successful. During its first year, $2 million in donations were raised, and in 2014 Coca-Cola offered to match all donations made across Europe up to €1 million. While this campaign raises awareness of the need to protect polar bear habitats, it also is a cause-related marketing campaign that improves consumer perception of the brand and ultimately drives up sales. The affective messages associated with the cause are featured across multiple mediums and they appeal to the senses, which strengthens existing relationships with the brand and thereby increases brand loyalty.

Coca-Cola: associating a brand with a good cause

Managing choice situations

New distribution outlets

Snapple and Lipton's Iced Tea have extended their reach by accessing vending machines, as have video rental firms, and Taco Bell and Pizza Hut have been successful with their mini-stores inside supermarkets and convenience stores (Wansink and Huffman, 2001). The internet has extended the reach of most brands and in some cases has transformed industries, like travel, music and books. It has also shortened the distance between manufacturer and consumer allowing some brands to deliver customized products. In most cases, this involves variation from a base offering—be it designing your own pizza topping at Pizza Hut or personalizing your stationary at Zazzle, an online retailer which specializes in the design of unique products.

New packaging

Heinz introduced child-friendly containers and revolutionary colours ('Blastin' Green' and 'Awesome Orange') in its EZ Squirt ketchup, which revitalized a dormant category. Individual-servings packages have increased demand for a variety of products such as crisps, fruit drinks, coffee, and cheeses. Small packets of crisps purchased in multi bags have proved particularly popular, with a large part of the appeal thought to be a reduced impact on the waistline. Ironically, a recent study has shown that, when concerns about weight were highlighted, consumers were twice as likely to start consuming crisps in small packets compared with those who were offered crisps in a larger packet but, when they did, they consumed them nearly twice as much (Coelho Do Vale, 2008). It appears that when the temptations seem small consumers are not as vigilant in maintaining self-control.

The toothpaste market has seen an explosion in design and packaging innovation. Pump dispensers and aerosols have been available for some time and now cartons are being used to attract consumers with the use of bright colours and textures such as embossing and even holographic printing (Clarke, 2010). In addition, the detergent market has seen positive consumer response to 'liquitab' gel sachets, and 'powerball' tablets have been well received in the dishwashing market, both adding some new appeal to markets very low on consumer interest.

Packaging can be extremely important to some consumers. The phenomenon of 'unboxing' has recently emerged through sites like YouTube. Unboxing is an 'opening event' whereby the consumer records and shares the revealing of the contents of the package. This is conducted with great precision and care and described in detail, often with tremulous excitement. Research conducted by Google indicates that one in five consumers have watched at least one unboxing video on YouTube and, as of mid-November 2014, there were more than 20 million search results on YouTube for the keyword 'unboxing' (The National 2014). Unboxers say it heightens the connection between the brand and the company and can occur with anything from Happy Meals to iPhones.

Multiple shelf placements

Consumers often settle into a 'shopping script' that only includes a limited number of aisles in the supermarket (Hoyer, 1984). By placing pasta, Bolognese sauces, and Parmesan cheese not only in their respective product categories but also together in a 'tonight's meal' section, supermarkets can make it easy for consumers to put a meal together. Similarly, consumers with allergy problems can find a whole range of products free from gluten, wheat, or dairy products in the 'Free From' section in Sainsbury's supermarkets.

For online retailers, research suggests that reducing the click count to buy or to find related items significantly enhances the user experience in term of customer goodwill and repeat visits (Chiang and Nunez, 2007). Amazon.com, currently holds a US Patent Office-certification on one-click online shopping.

Increasing purchase quantities

Studies have shown that it is possible to increase the actual amount a customer buys of a product either through effects on the desired quantity or through reducing the perceived price (Wansink *et al.*, 1998).

Quantity limits

Paradoxically, limiting the amount of a product that a customer can buy increases the number purchased; for example specifying that customers can only buy 12 cans of soup per person leads to a larger quantity being purchased than without the quantity limit.

Quantity cues

Giving a cue as to how many to buy, for example 'buy ten for the weekend' or 'buy five for the family', can also result in increased purchase quantities.

Price perceptions

Larger packages can reduce consumers' perceptions of unit price. This is often the operation of a market belief that 'larger package means lower price per unit'.

The shortened distribution channels on the internet as well as the absence of time consuming face to face negotiations has allowed consumers to interact directly with manufacturers and as a result created the opportunity to implement variable pricing strategies. This is of course not a phenomenon of the online world but is made easier in this environment. Traditional brick and mortar stores have all but removed the option for haggling because the process requires extensive training, is time consuming and as such takes frontline staff away from other customers, and therefore often requires the hiring of additional staff (Terwiesch, Hann, and Savin, 2005). Variable pricing allows retailers to target consumers who otherwise may not buy, can help to manage demand and supply imbalance, and is empowering to the consumer.

Implementation of this strategy is currently not widespread as those in the supply chain wish to secure their margins, however, there is evidence it is gaining traction. At the extreme end variable pricing represents a leap of faith in the consumer's interpretation of value. For example when international act Radiohead ended their deal with EMI they launched their next album independently allowing consumer to 'name their price' based on what they felt the track or album was worth. What appears a more feasible strategy, however, is the setting of a base and a listed price between which there is room to move. In 2014, Amazon announced it will allow a variable pricing option for a number of its sellers whereby consumers can negotiate prices with sellers on individual items. Labelled 'Make an Offer' it is available on approximately 150,000 items where value is difficult to set, for example Amazon's

Sports and Entertainment Collectibles, Collectible Coins, and Fine Art listings, however, plans are being made to expand this to 'hundreds of thousands of items' (Claburn 2014)

Increasing usage quantities

Promotion effects

Promotion can help increase purchase quantity with what is known as a loading device. Such promotions are aimed at changing the minimal purchasing pattern by encouraging the consumer to 'load up' on the brand by purchasing more than usual. This can be done with price-offs at the point-of-purchase, or with special 'price packs' where a reduced price is printed as part of the brand's label. Additionally, special bonus packaging may be used where more of the product is offered at the regular price.

Loading promotions are an effective strategy when it is known that a competitor is about to enter the market with a new product or new version of an existing product because it effectively removes people from the market, discouraging them from trying the new offering.

Increasing the amount a customer buys can also result in increased usage of a product.

Stockpiling

Studies show that household stockpiling can increase usage frequency, particularly in the categories of snacks and beverages (Wansink and Deshpande, 1994). This effect is most pronounced if the products are visible in the house.

Packaging effects

Possibly as a result of reducing price perceptions, larger pack sizes can also increase usage rate.

Increasing the size of the opening is one way to increase usage quantity. For example changing to 'big-mouth' bottles resulted in increased consumption of Mountain Dew. This has become a widely used strategy in many food and drink categories.

Advertising effects

Advertising can help increase usage quantity in two ways: it can encourage new use situations or it can make the brand and category salient through tactical media scheduling.

Usage expansion advertising is most effective when it frames the new use as a complement to existing behaviour, for example many baby gates have been repositioned as safety gates, to include the safety of pets by excluding them from high risk areas.

Scheduling can also have an impact on consumption by making the brand top-of-mind when the consumption decision is being made. For example, Campbell's soup runs its radio ads just before lunch and dinner times, and also has standing instructions for radio stations to run specially developed 'Storm Spot' ads during bad weather (Wansink and Huffman, 2001).

Building brand loyalty

With symbolic brands, loyalty is based on the meaning of the brand and the strength of its emotional connection with the consumer. By contrast, with functional brands with low consumer involvement, loyalty is usually seen as being a factor that can be increased through reward schemes.

Loyalty programmes

There has been a proliferation of loyalty programmes in which consumers are offered incentives in exchange for repeat business, and there is some evidence that they can be successful with low-involvement products and services, particularly if the incentives overlap with brand meanings (Roehm *et al.*, 2002). It is likely that a programme that tries to restrict the operation of double-jeopardy behaviours like buying from within a brand repertoire will be inefficient (Dowling and Uncles, 1997). However, low and moderate reward programmes which target light users may generate cost-effective incremental sales (Wansink, 2003).

Raising consumer involvement

However, it may be possible to create some degree of loyalty in fmcg markets through raising consumer involvement. An example is the development by Lever Fabergé's Ponds skin-care brand of a membership programme around the 'Pond's Institute'. Originally an 'advertising fiction', the Pond's Institute aims to build bonds with customers by providing the reassurance required by consumers in this category. It has been developed into a vehicle for relationship marketing as customers have access to a range of services including email access to a qualified skin-care consultant (Miller, 2001).

Ferrero established a brand community for its chocolate cream spread Nutella named 'my Nutella The Community'. Members log on to talk about the brand and engage with each other, including discussion about family, recipes, and even the arrangement of Nutella parties (Cova and Pace, 2006). This has proved hugely successful and there are also many independently run fan sites including the World Nutella Day site, launched in 2007, which can be found on Twitter and Facebook.

CHAPTER SUMMARY

In this chapter we have emphasized the vital importance of top-of-mind awareness and brand salience to a functional brand. We have discussed a range of ways in which brand associations can be built up through pre-conscious and minimal cognitive processes using all elements of communication. We went on to consider behavioural processes to increase penetration and/or frequency of purchase, and then discussed ways of managing consumer perceptions. We ended with a consideration of how the choice situation can be managed, and approaches to building brand loyalty.

DISCUSSION QUESTIONS

1 Why is brand salience so important for functional brands?

2 Explain how classical conditioning can be used to manage a brand.

3 What are somatic markers and how does their use by consumers inform brand management?

4 Provide two examples of brand tactics which may help functional brands to build a combination of associations and meanings to differentiate the product.

5 What issues need to be considered when brand building around a celebrity?

6 When should brand strategy favour increasing purchase frequency?

7 How can existing favourable consumer perceptions be refreshed?

8 How can advertising be used to increase usage quantities?

CASE STUDY

Clorox Bleach: Bleach it away

As Clorox entered its centennial year in 2013, it was clear that many of today's younger consumers were not reaching for the bleach when the time came to clean up life's messiest moments. With the baby-boomer generation ageing out, Clorox took the initiative to get a new and younger generation, dubbed 'newly responsibles', to grab for the iconic bottle to clean up their mess. Enter Bleachable Moments, a frank and funny campaign that sought to engage these newly responsibles with informative and authentic content worthy of sharing on social media websites.

This programme was different from the typical Clorox campaign because the primary focus was not on cleaning. Instead, the spotlight was on legitimately humorous content that was paired with the influential endorsements of sources that had 'street cred'. With bleach use dropping, Clorox wanted to increase sales by reaching new users. However, marketing insight revealed that this younger audience is wary of marketing in general—only 6% of millennials (those between the ages of 25–35) consider online advertising to be credible—and newly responsibles are not as familiar with or as accepting of bleach. Thus, the team sought out to educate this segment of new users on when to reach for the bleach and how bleach could be relevant in their lives. In order to achieve this goal, it was determined that Clorox should not market *to* them, but rather *with* them.

To show the target how easily bleach fits into their lives and helps with cleaning, the marketing approach was based upon leveraging partners and online platforms that the audience already trust. Of any generation, social networking penetration is highest amongst millennials, and because they grew up in a completely digital age, social media is embedded into the fabric of their lives. Thus, to create a consistent connection between Clorox bleach and messy moments, it was crucial for the team to leverage these platforms and engage with them using content that actually gets them talking. To breakthrough and effectively reach the audience online, Clorox partnered with SomeEcards, the maker of humorous e-cards that appeal to youthful, tech-savvy and social media consumers, to create bleach themed e-cards. The cards illustrated the ways in which bleach is helpful while highlighting the humour of those events that people wish they could literally make disappear. The partnership proved to be a success; on the SomeEcards Facebook page, one card garnered the second highest level of interaction for a sponsored card and another became the most popular in the 'wine' category. In conjunction, the team boosted visibility of the Bleachable Moments campaign on Twitter using promoted tweets from the @Clorox handle; the tweets resulted in over 1,534,000 impressions.

Although the campaign lived online, the Clorox team also took it to the Las Vegas Strip to make a bigger splash and to give newly responsibles even more to talk about online. With Las Vegas being the spot to have fun, go a little crazy and make some mess, it was the perfect place to bring the Bleachable Moments story to life. The team partnered with award-winning actress and active Twitter user Angela Kinsey to intercept consumers on the Vegas Strip to talk about their messy moments. Set within a backdrop of interactive, social-enabled Bleachable Moments advertising, including billboards and themed cab toppers, the unexpected placement of Clorox bleach created the 'perfect storm' for buzz. The edgy tone and setting resonated with consumers, most notably with the younger target, and it generated over 143,554,000 total media impressions.

The team also conjoined forces with established online influencers, particularly those already popular with newly responsibles, to maintain the momentum online, engage consumers, and encourage social sharing throughout the entirety of the campaign. Lala Anthony, Danielle Jonas and Rosie Pope—celebrities and Twitter fanatics—drove conversation about Bleachable Moments with tweets to their followers. A Twitter party—an online event that usually last 1–2 hours which allows Twitter users to interact with the host via a specific hashtag—was run by an influential blogger to increase reach, and as a result, #BleachItAway momentarily became the top trending topic in the United States. On the platform known as reddit, where the median user is male (59%) and 25–34 years of age, Clorox's 'Dr. Laundry' addressed bleach-use questions. Clorox also had influencers promote unexpected uses for bleach on Pinterest, the first of which secured more than 700 entries while generating online chatter about atypical laundry and disinfecting uses.

In terms of both social effects and business effects, the five-month campaign surpassed all of its objectives. Across its entire duration improvements to all indicators were made. And by the conclusion of the campaign, online conversation volume about Bleachable Moments had tripled and online connections between Clorox and messes had doubled. In addition, the BleachItAway.com website received over 20,000 visits from the promoted tweets and nearly 10,000 from the celebrity tweets. In accordance, by increasing the connection between Clorox and messes amongst newly responsibles, significant business effects were also observed. For example, a 10% increase in brand favourability was achieved, and in comparison to those who have not visited BleachItAway.com, purchase intention was 17% higher amongst visitors.

Despite the difficulty in reaching a young audience and making bleach relevant to their lives, Clorox rose to the challenge by leveraging strategic insights and tactically planning how to move the needle on the ways that the target audience viewed the product. The combination of online and on-site activity didn't merely get people talking, it created a surround-sound effect that maximized engagement, which consequentially created a deeper connection to the brand. Overall, this campaign revealed the following key lessons:

- Partnering with key influencers enhances the authenticity of the messages.
- There is more engagement when sharable content is provided and that content is authentic enough to resonate with the target audience.
- On-ground activation can help bring added attention and energy to an online programme.
- Focusing on reaching millennials online where they are already spending their time is more effective than reaching them through other channels.

Source: WARC, Warc Prize for Social Strategy 2014, Clorox Bleach: Bleach It Away. Edited by Suni J. Mydock III

DISCUSSION QUESTIONS

1 What brand associations and meanings did Clorox build through its 'Bleachable Moments' campaign?

2 How can Clorox maintain top-of-mind brand awareness and brand salience with the younger generation?

3 Did Clorox focus more upon increasing penetration or purchase frequency?

4 How significant of a role did classical conditioning strategies have to the 'Bleachable Moments' campaign?

FURTHER READING

- The classic text based on analysis of over 20 years of panel data is A.S.C. Ehrenberg (1988), *Repeat-Buying: Facts, Theory and Applications*, Oxford: Oxford University Press.

- A useful discussion of how to utilize a wide range of physical stimuli is M. Lindstrom (2005), *Brand Sense: How to Build Powerful Brands Through Touch, Taste, Smell, Sight and Sound*, London: Kogan Page.

- An account of P&G's success in inventing and sustaining a vast range of functional brands in markets around the world is D. Dyer *et al.* (2004), *Rising Tide: Lessons from 165 Years of Brand Building at Procter and Gamble*, Boston: Harvard Business School Press.

REFERENCES

Areni, C. S. and Kim, D. (1993), 'The influence of background music on shopping behavior: classical versus top-forty music in a wine store', in L. McAlister and M.C. Rothschild (eds), *Advances in Consumer Research*, Vol. 20, Provo, UT: Association for Consumer Research, 336–40.

Baker, W. (1999), 'When can affective conditioning and mere exposure directly influence brand choice?', *Journal of Advertising*, 28, 4, 31–46.

Baldinger, A., Blair, E., and Echambadi, R. (2002), 'Why brands grow', *Journal of Advertising Research*, January/February, 42, 1, 7–14.

Bush, A., Martin, C., and Bush, V. (2004), 'Sports celebrity influence on the behavioral intentions of generation Y', *Journal of Advertising Research*, March/April, 44, 1, 108–18.

Carpenter, G., Glazer, R., and Nakamoto, N. (1994), 'Meaningful brands from meaningless differentiation: The dependence on irrelevant attributes', *Journal of Marketing Research*, August, XXXI, 339–50.

Chan, S. P. (2010), 'Big leap: Microsoft makes free version of Office, its cash cow', *The Seattle Times*, 9 May, http://seattletimes.nwsource.com/ Last accessed 5 August 2010.

Chiang, I. R. and Nunez M. A. (2007), 'Improving Web-Catalog Design for Easy Product Search', *INFORMS Journal on Computing*, Fall, 19, 4, 510–19.

Claburn, T. (2014), 'Amazon invites haggling over some prices', *InformationWeek*, 12 September, http://www.informationweek.com/mobile/mobile-business/amazon-invites-haggling-over-some-prices/d/d-id/1318011 Last accessed 1 December 2014

Clarke, S. (2010), 'Markets: Toothpaste seeks fresh ideas', *packagingnews.co.uk*, 5 March, http://packagingnews.co.uk/ Last accessed 5 August 2010.

Coelho Do Vale, R., Pieters, R., and Zeelenberg, M. (2008), 'Flying under the radar: Perverse package size effects on consumption self-regulation', *Journal of Consumer Research*, October, 35, 380–90.

Cone Inc (2004), *Cone Corporate Citizenship Study*, Boston. MA: Cone.

Cova, B. and Pace, S. (2006), 'Brand community of convenience products: New forms of customer empowerment—the case "my Nutella The Community"', *European Journal of Marketing*, 40, 9/10, 1087–105.

Damasio, A. (1994), *Descartes' Error: Emotion, Reason and the Human Brain*, New York: Quill.

Deighton, J. (1984), 'The interaction of advertising and evidence', *Journal of Consumer Research*, 11, 763–70.

Dowling, G. and Uncles, M. (1997), 'Do customer loyalty programs really work?', *Sloan Management Review*, 38, 4, 71–82.

Duncan, C. (1990), 'Consumer market beliefs: A review of the literature and an agenda for future research', *Advances in Consumer Research*, 17, 729–35.

Ehrenberg, A. and Goodhardt, G. (1979), *Essays on Understanding Buyer Behavior*, New York: J. W. Thompson.

Ehrenberg, A., Barnard, N., and Scriven, J. (1997), 'Differentiation or salience', *Journal of Advertising Research*, 37(6), November, 7–14.

Ehrenberg, A., Barnard, N., Kennedy, R., and Bloom, H. (2002), 'Brand advertising as creative publicity', *Journal of Advertising Research*, July/August, 42, 4, 7–18.

Elliott, R. and Hamilton, E. (1991), 'Consumer choice tactics and leisure activities', *International Journal of Advertising*, 10, 4, 325–33.

Fly the Branded Skies (2014), 'Two airlines go back to their roots', http://brandedskies.com/2014/09/two-airlines-go-back-to-their-roots/ Last accessed 3rd December 2014.

Heath, R. (2001), *The Hidden Power of Advertising: How Low Involvement Processing Influences the Way We Choose Brands*, Henley-on-Thames: Admap Publications.

Holman, R. H. and Hecker, S. (1983), 'Advertising impact: Creative elements affecting brand recall', *Current Issues in Research and Advertising*, 157–72.

Howard, J. A. (1977), *Consumer Behavior: Application of Theory*, New York: McGraw-Hill.

Hoyer, W. (1984), 'An examination of consumer decision making for a common repeat purchase product', *Journal of Consumer Research*, 11, 822–9.

Hynes, N. (2009), 'Colour and meaning in corporate logos: An empirical study', *Journal of Brand Management*, 16, 8, 545–55.

Keller, K., Heckler, S., and Houston, M. (1998), 'The effects of brand name suggestiveness on advertising', *Journal of Marketing*, 62, 1, 42–52.

Kowsmann, P. (2010), 'Ross boosts Branson's RBS dream', *Wall Street Journal (Eastern Edition)*, 7 April, C3.

McQueen, J., Sylvester, A., and Moore, S. (1998), 'Brand growth', in J. P. Jones (ed.), *How Advertising Works*, London: Sage.

Mediaweek (2003), *Strategic Review: Getting Real to Boost a Brand*, http://www.mediaweek.co.uk/ Last accessed 5 August 2010.

Miller, J. (2001), 'Building bonds with packaged-goods consumers', *Admap*, November, 36, 22–5.

Miller, E. G. and Kahn B. E. (2005), 'Shades of meaning: The effect of color and flavor names on consumer choice', *Journal of Consumer Research*, June, 32, 86–92.

Milliman, R. E. (1982), 'Using background music to affect the behavior of supermarket shoppers', *Journal of Marketing*, 40, 3, 86–91.

Morgan, A. (1999), *Eating the Big Fish*, Chichester: John Wiley.

North, A. C., Hargreaver, D. T., and McKendrick, J. (1999), 'The influence of in-store music on wine selection', *Journal of Applied Psychology*, 85, 2, 271–6.

Osgood, C. E., Suci, G., and Tannenbaum, R. H. (1957), *The Measurement of Measuring*, Champaign: University of Illinois Press.

Percy, L. (1973), 'Determining the influence of color on a product cognitive structure: A multidimensional scaling application', in S. Ward and P. Wright (eds), *Advances in Consumer Research*, Vol. 1, Provo, UT: Association for Consumer Research, 218–27.

Percy, L. (2005), 'Unconscious processing of advertising and its effects upon attitude and behaviour', in S. Diehl, R. Terlutter, and P. Weinberg (eds), *Advertising Communication*, Proceedings of the Fifth International Conference on Research in Advertising, Saarland University, Saarbrücken, Germany.

Percy, L. and Elliott, R. (2009), *Strategic Advertising Management*, 3rd edn, Oxford: Oxford University Press.

Pearson, P. (2012), 'Doping scandal costs Lance Armstrong sponsors, charity role', *CNN*, 22 October 2012, http://edition.cnn.com/2012/10/17/us/lance-armstrong-doping/ Last accessed 3 December 2014.

Roehm, M., Pullins, E., and Roehm, H. (2002), 'Designing loyalty-building programs for packaged goods brands', *Journal of Marketing Research*, May, XXXIX, 202–13.

Romaniuk, J. (2003), 'Brand attributes: "distribution outlets" in the mind', *Journal of Marketing Communications*, 9, 73–92.

Rossiter, J. R. and Percy, L. (1997), *Advertising Communication and Promotion Management*, New York: McGraw-Hill.

Stockdale, M. (1999), 'Are all consumers equal?' in J.P. Jones (ed.), *How to Use Advertising to Build Strong Brands*, London: Sage.

Sweetwater (2008), 'Sennheiser launches sound logo competition', *inSync*, http://www.sweetwater.com/insync/sennheiser-launches-sound-logo-competition/ Last accessed 1 December 2014.

Terwiesch, C., Hann, I-H., and Savin, S. (2005), 'Online haggling at a name-your-own-price retailer: theory and application', *Management Science*, 51, 3, 339–51.

The National (2014), 'Why the phenomena of unboxing is so popular online', *The National: Arts and Life Style,* http://www.thenational.ae/arts-lifestyle/why-the-phenomena-of-unboxing-is-so-popular-online Last Accessed 1 December 2014.

Viswanathan, M., Rosa, J., and Harris, J. (2005), 'Decision making and coping by functionally illiterate consumers and some implications for marketing management', *Journal of Marketing*, January, 69, 15–23.

Wansink, B. (2003), 'Developing a cost-effective brand loyalty program', *Journal of Advertising Research*, September, 301–9.

Wansink, B., and Deshpande, R. (1994), '"Out of sight out of mind": The impact of household stock-piling on usage rates', *Marketing Letters*, January, 5, 1, 99–100.

Wansink, B., and Gilmore, J. (1999), 'New uses that revitalize old brands', *Journal of Advertising Research*, March/April, 39, 2, 90–8.

Wansink, B., and Huffman, C. (2001), 'Revitalizing mature packaged goods', *Journal of Product and Brand Management*, 10, 4, 228–42.

Wansink, B., and Ray, M. (1996), 'Advertising strategies to increase usage frequency', *Journal of Marketing*, January, 60, 3, 31–46.

Wansink, B., Kent, R., and Hoch, S. (1998), 'An anchoring and adjustment model of purchase quantity decisions', *Journal of Marketing Research*, February, 35, 1, 71–81.

Yalch, R. F. and Spangenburg, E. (1993), 'Using store music for retail zoning: A field experiment', in L. McAlister and M. C. Rothschild (eds), *Advances in Consumer Research*, Vol. 20, Provo, UT: Association for Consumer Research, 632–6.

Test your understanding of this chapter and explore the subject further using our Online Resource Centre. Visit the Online Resource Centre at http://www.oxfordtextbooks.co.uk/orc/elliott-percy3e/

Brands, Innovation, and High Technology

10

Key Concepts

1 The benefits of branding innovations.

2 Crossing the chasm.

3 Paradoxes of technology.

4 Innovation and the active consumer.

5 Sociocultural factors in the adoption of innovations.

6 Sociocultural brand management.

7 Customer relationship management in high-tech markets.

Introduction

Investment in branding may be more important than being at the leading edge of technology according to the National Bureau of Economic Research in the USA. A large-scale study of the PC market concluded that 'Having a brand name conferred a large advantage in the sense of shifting out the demand function, whereas being early at the technological frontier did not' (Bresnahan *et al.*, 1996). In this chapter we discuss the relationship between brands and innovation. First we highlight the importance of branding innovations before exploring how individual, personal, and sociocultural factors impact on the adoption of new offerings. We then discuss the strategic brand management implications for a particularly dynamic innovation environment, the high-tech market.

The vital importance of branding an innovation is captured by the mantra 'Innovation: Brand it or lose it' in a seminal paper by Aaker (2007) who maintains that branding can enhance the potential of an innovation in four main ways. It aids differentiation and allows ownership of an innovation, adds credibility, improves visibility, and enhances communication. As we discuss in Chapter 12, branding also helps drive the organizational culture and builds corporate reputation (Fig. 10.1).

Owning the innovation

Although a competitor may soon be able to match the objective benefits of an innovation, if it is branded effectively then there will only be one authentic product, the one that carries the brand name. This protects the branded product/service from the competition by adding credibility/legitimacy, helping to build corporate reputation, enabling employees to live the brand, improving visibility, and enhancing communication. A strong brand may even be given the credit for innovations made by other organizations.

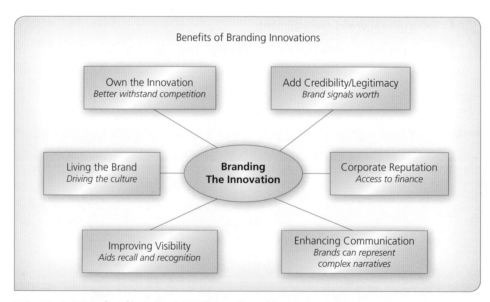

FIGURE 10.1 Benefits of branding innovations. Adapted from Aaker (2007)

Sony Bravia X8500B: The power of meaningful brands

KEY CONCEPT

The benefits of branding innovations

Being the innovator rather than the follower allows companies to establish a brand as the authentic offering in the product category. While this is often not sustainable in the long-term, it does provide an initial advantage that firms can capitalize on. Major competitors will inevitably copy or develop comparable products. However, for a short period, the innovator has the opportunity to capture the minds and hearts of consumers. Swiss manufacturers famously developed the first digital watches, but did not develop the culture within their firms to capitalize, with many employees simply viewing it as a novelty. In contrast, Nissan's development of electric car technology has seen it dominate the electric vehicle market with its Nissan Leaf. Nissan's early push into this non-traditional market for automobiles has resulted in its position as market leader, with analysts and customers benchmarking the competition against their brand.

Adding credibility/legitimacy

The very fact of being branded may signal a worthwhile innovation. You may be thinking about purchasing a 4K television. Would you consider a Bravia X8500B? This is an unfamiliar brand and the chances are you would not. However, you may well change your mind when told it is a Sony Bravia X8500B. As discussed in Chapter 9, branded attributes that added no objective benefit can nonetheless dramatically affect customer preferences, even when the attribute is seemingly irrelevant to choice (Carpenter *et al.*, 1994).

Audi branded their innovative use of four-wheel drive for a mainstream production car in 1980 and has managed to dominate the consumer mindspace with the quattro brand despite the fact that many other maufacturers now offer four-wheel drive vehicles (see http://www.pistonheads.com/doc.asp?c=52&i=10065).

Building corporate reputation

There is a strong relationship between good corporate reputation and superior financial performance (Roberts and Dowling, 2002), and perceptions of market leadership and innovativeness are important aspects of building reputation (see Chapter 12). Good reputation can help raise capital on the equity market (Dowling, 2001). For example, the market capitalization value of Apple—an exemplar of innovation and good corporate reputation in recent years—recently surpassed $700 billion, which represents a figure higher that the gross domestic product of all but 19 of the world's countries (Huddleston, 2014).

Living the brand

Branding can help mobilize employees to deliver the brand promise, turning each member of the organization into a brand champion. Transformational leaders like Marissa Mayer, Google's former Vice-President of Search Product and User Experience, have been credited with creating a 'geek machismo' at Google instilling the confidence in employees to consistently develop, launch, and champion new product ideas like its now famous desktop search function (Elgin, 2005). We describe how this can be achieved in Chapter 12.

Improving visibility

A brand name provides an aid to recognition and recall and can make an innovation more visible in a crowded market place. In a survey by PCWorld.com, visitors to the site could choose from ten different laptop brands, 11 desktop brands, and 17 high definition television brands (Null, 2010).

Enhancing communication

An innovation may not be high-involvement to customers, so they will make little effort to process detailed information (see Chapter 1). A brand name can help summarize complex information and make it easier to categorize and remember. Google Drive, launched in April 2012, is a new web-based file storage and synchronization service, tied to Gmail, which enables user file sharing and collaborative editing, via cloud storage. It is difficult to comprehend all of the functional features of Google Drive by reading about it alone but, like so many high-tech products, its realized value comes through use. The application has been hugely successful, with 120 million users adopting it within the first 18 months from release and 240 million by October 2014. This is in large part due to the fact that people have been willing to try the service given the Google brand and its reputation for web innovation.

We now turn our attention to individual, personal, and social factors which impact the adoption of innovations.

Individual factors in the adoption of innovations

The technology adoption life cycle

It has often been assumed that the adoption of innovative technologies follows the well-known bell-curve model of the diffusion of innovation developed by Rogers (1962). Rogers

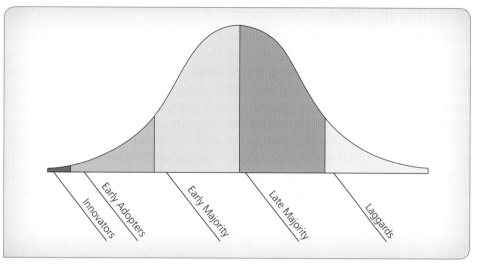

FIGURE 10.2 Technology and adoption life cycle
Adapted from Moore (1999)

demonstrated that adopters of any new innovation or idea can be categorized as innovators (2.5%), early adopters (13.5%), early majority (34%), late majority (34%), and laggards (16%). These categories, based on standard deviations from the mean of the normal curve, when graphed show a cumulative percentage of adopters over time—slow at the start, more rapid as adoption increases, then levelling off until only a small percentage of laggards have not adopted (Fig. 10.2).

However, in a ground-breaking book based on the IT industry, Moore (1991) pointed out that when using the adoption curve to the guide marketing of disruptive or discontinuous innovations, companies very often fell victim to the Chasm Effect, where a chasm opens up between the early adopters and the early majority (Fig. 10.3).

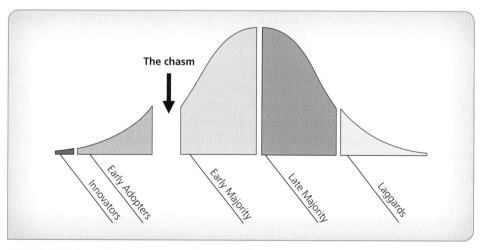

FIGURE 10.3 The revised technology and adoption life cycle
Adapted from Moore (1999)

Crossing the chasm

Moore (1999) points to a fundamental difference in customer motivation between Visionaries (early adopters) and Pragmatists (early majority). Visionaries are seeking technological performance, Pragmatists want solutions and convenience. The challenge for the marketing of high-technology innovations is to cross the chasm between the small market of Technology enthusiasts and Visionaries and reach the mainstream market of Pragmatists, and then later to win over the price-sensitive Conservatives. The key target is the Early majority, because once they are converted to users, the Late majority and eventually the Laggards will follow over time. Let us return to Google by way of example.

We have highlighted the success of Google Drive from 2012 and onward, however, Google has also had its share of failure. For example, Google Wave, which was launched in 2009. This web-based application allows groups to be formed around particular ideas, work projects, family networks, etc., where participants contribute via video, images, files, and text. New participants can be invited at any time and they can view the entire discussion history to understand context and then contribute to and edit the contribution at any point in the 'wave'. Google suggest that this makes the application truly flexible and dynamic and considered that it would be very useful to group projects in many different settings. The brand was launched after a much-hyped, invitation-only period to 'tech insiders'—innovators and early adopters (visionaries)—many of whom were lauding the product on their websites based only on a very polished demonstration by Apple. However, very soon after the product faltered. Why? Because pragmatists didn't perceive that the brand had delivered. Word of mouth began about an 'over hyping' of the product, the application was prone to spamming, the real-time chat allowed others to actually see typing, including spelling mistakes, all additional applications made the waves slow to load, and the product itself did not seem to contain any real new technology—just a mesh of the old.

Branding and the chasm

One important factor about the early majority is that they tend to be 'vertically oriented'; that is, they communicate more with others like themselves within their own industry than do early adopters and technology enthusiasts, who are more likely to communicate 'horizontally' across industry boundaries. This suggests that attention to the development of brand community may be particularly important in building usership among the early majority.

A second important factor about pragmatists is that they are rational, high-involvement buyers who will invest time and effort to ensure that their purchase is likely to last in the long term, as opposed to visionaries who are likely to be planning to move on quickly to new technological developments. So pragmatists are not just buying the innovation, they are buying a relationship with the company and are therefore liable to use corporate reputation as a key indicator of quality.

Paradoxes of technology

It is clear that paradoxically technology does not just bring benefits but can also bring problems. Mick and Fournier (1998) develop a model of the key paradoxes that consumers experience in their everyday life when buying and using new technological products. They argue that as well as a range of powerful benefits obtained from using new technologies,

FIGURE 10.4 Paradoxes of technology

> ## KEY CONCEPT
>
> ### Crossing the chasm
>
> A lesson learnt by many technology visionaries is to not believe their own hype or those of their fans. The key to technological innovation is to realize value amongst day-to-day consumers of the product—the users. Google Glass is one example. Lauded by the tech press as the next big thing in portable devices, the product has failed to convince consumers. While the potential to view information similarly to a smart phone in a hands-free format remains compelling, the reality is consumers have not yet found them functional or, perhaps more importantly, fashionable.

consumers can experience strong emotional conflict and anxiety that requires the development and use of coping strategies (Fig. 10.4).

Some of the key paradoxes of technology include:

- *Control versus chaos*—technology can facilitate order but can also lead to upheaval or disorder.
- *Freedom versus enslavement*—technology can facilitate independence or fewer restrictions but can lead to dependence or more restrictions.
- *Competence versus incompetence*—technology can facilitate feelings of intelligence or efficacy but can lead to feelings of ignorance or ineptitude.
- *Fulfils needs versus creates needs*—technology can facilitate the fulfilment of needs or desires but can lead to the development or awareness of needs and desires previously unrealized,
- *Assimilation versus isolation*—technology can facilitate human togetherness but can lead to separation.

Consumers use a wide range of behavioural coping strategies to manage the conflict and stress both before and after purchase:

- *Pre-acquisition avoidance strategies*—ignore information about benefits and availability, postpone but eventually purchase. We all have friends and relatives initially dismissive of social media sites like Facebook and Twitter who are now permanently camped on these sites.
- *Pre-acquisition confrontative strategies*—pre-test by using someone else's product, use a buying heuristic based on brand awareness/reputation, use an extended

decision-making process based on information gathering, buying additional insurance contracts.

- *Consumption avoidance strategies*—neglect the product, develop restrictive rules for how the product will be used. Your parents or grandparents might still have the mobile phone locked in the glove box, only to be used in emergencies.
- *Consumption confrontative strategies*—changing preferences and routines to accommodate the technology, establish a close committed relationship with a product. How many of you checked work or personal emails or surfed the web in a cafe before you had your wireless netbook or laptop?

Paradoxes and the adoption of innovations

The behaviour of the late majority and laggards may be the result of the coping strategies used by consumers to manage the anxiety and stress of buying and using innovations. Indeed, Mick and Fournier (1998) suggest that it should be possible to segment markets by determining the linkages among technology paradoxes and coping strategies over the course of the diffusion curve.

Branding plays a key role in the adoption of new technology by reducing perceptions of risk and just as important, by helping the consumer make emotional attachments to a product by providing narratives that allow them to incorporate it into their lives.

KEY CONCEPT

Paradoxes of technology

Many years ago when modern technology developed portable well-digging machines that could dig quickly with minimal labour and could do so much deeper than the local tribes could, whole societies lost a very important part of their complex castes systems. Those at the top of the hierarchy were traditionally based closest to the well, where the water was clean; those further down the hill were lower caste and received water used many times over. The technology, however, allowed wells to be dug easily all over a village and clean water to be received by all. Thus this 'good' technology was also disruptive, often leading to conflict. This is the paradox of technology.

Modern day examples include Skype and other VOIPs that enable you to communicate with friends, so diminishing the problem of time and distance but potentially reducing the amount of face-to-face time you make for some people. Or video games, which provide hours of entertainment to children (and adults), but have been associated with the rising problem of obesity in many societies.

Narrative processing and branding innovative products

There is evidence that narratives or stories are important in helping consumers to organize their experiences, create order and make evaluations and may underlie the development of a self-brand connection (Escalas, 2004). The role of narratives in helping consumers understand the world around them and their own lives may be particularly important when dealing with innovative technologies, where consumers are faced with novel information and experiences. Narrative processing can be evoked by advertising and integrates information into a framework of meaning over time. This suggests that brand strategies for innovations that implement a narrative structure in their communications may help consumers to link the new information to their sense of self and build a connection to the brand (Escalas, 2004). For example BT wireless broadband has used the longest-running TV campaign in the UK to feature a romantic drama between 'Adam and Jane' (see: http://www.guardian.co.uk/media/2010/jul/12/bt-ad-family). When viewers were given the chance to vote on the next plot move, 1.6 million people voted (see: http://www.vote. bt.com/?s_cid=con_FURL_calls_vote).

Time and perceptions of quality

Time is, of course, a fundamental element in the diffusion of innovations, but it plays an important role in consumers' perceptions of quality. By studying the relationship between objective and perceived quality for 241 products in 46 product categories over a period of 12 years, Mitra and Golder (2006) showed on average the effect of a change in objective quality is not fully reflected in consumer perceptions until after six years (Fig. 10.5).

What is particularly interesting from this study is the fact that brand reputation had a double advantage: high reputation brands are rewarded three years quicker for an increase in quality and punished one year slower for a decrease in quality compared with low-reputation brands. This implies that a brand with a high reputation does not have to respond immediately to competitor innovations: 'companies like Cisco, Intel and Microsoft do not need to be first or best anymore, it's enough to be observant and nimble' (*Wall Street Journal*, 2003).

Brand reputation and the adoption of innovations

There is considerable evidence that a positive brand reputation can aid the rapid adoption of new products (Robertson and Gatignon, 1986) and, not surprisingly, that corporate image associations of innovativeness and trustworthiness can have a particularly strong effect (Gurham-Canli and Batra, 2007). What associations come to your mind when you think of the brand Dyson? Dyson initially built its brand around its now famous bagless vacuum cleaner. However, now, and more importantly, it has a reputation for quality and

---

Perceptions of Quality

Time taken for consumer perceptions of quality to 'catch-up'
with actual quality changes:

Disposable nappy	3.1 years
Personal computer	3.3 years
Vacuum cleaner	4.6 years
Automobile	9.5 years

FIGURE 10.5 Perceptions of quality

Adapted from Mitra and Golder (2006)

Dyson Air Multiplier: Corporate image associations of innovativeness and trustworthiness

ingenuity. This has enabled it to launch new products like the Airblade (hand dryer) and, most recently, the Air Multiplier (bladeless fan).

The key factor appears to be the reduction in perceptions of the risk in purchasing. But it is emotive rather than factual associations that have been shown to be the most important elements within a corporate brand reputation in its positive influence on the adoption of an innovative service (Corkindale and Belder, 2009). Image, credibility, and trust have more influence than factual elements of awareness and knowledge.

So clearly it is important to understand how the customer responds to branding innovations and the value the brand represents to them. In recent times much has been made of the importance of the co-creation of value between customer and firm, a market place in which the customer is very much an active participant (Vargo and Lusch, 2004).

The evolution of the active consumer

Largely as a result of the internet, consumers are fundamentally changing the dynamics of the market place and are becoming a new source of competence for the company (Prahalad and Ramaswamy, 2000). The competence that customers bring is a function of the knowledge and skills they possess, their willingness to learn, and their ability to engage in active dialogue (Table 10.1).

Innovation and the active consumer

The concept of 'community sourcing' (related terms include crowd sourcing and citizen science) which uses innovative customers as a resource is widely used in the open-source software industry by brands such as eBay, Nokia, and DoCoMo (Linder *et al.*, 2003). Empirical studies on the sources of innovation in the fields of both industrial and consumer goods has revealed that users are often the initial developers of products, prototypes, and processes which later gain commercial significance (Prugl and Schreier, 2006).

An example of the active consumer creating value by innovation is through the process of 'toolkits' (Thomke and von Hippel, 2002) which allows the customer to take an active

TABLE 10.1 The evolution and transformation of customers

	Customers as a passive audience		Customers as active players	
Nature of business	Persuading predetermined groups of buyers	Transacting with individual buyers	Lifetime bonds with individual customers	Customers as co-creators of value
Managerial mind-set	Customer is an average statistic	Customer is an individual statistic in a transaction	Customer is a person, cultivate trust and relationships	Customer is not only an individual but also part of an emergent social and cultural fabric
Company's interactions with customers	Traditional market research, little feedback	Shift from selling to helping customers via call centres	Providing for customers through observation of users	Customers are co-developers of personalized experiences
Purpose and flow of communication	Gain access to and target predetermined groups of buyers. One-way communication	Database marketing, two-way communication	Relationship marketing	Active dialogue with customers to shape expectations and create buzz

Adapted from Prahalad and Ramaswamy (2000)

part in product development. A toolkit for user innovation is a technology that allows users to design a novel product by trial-and-error experimentation and delivers immediate (simulated) feedback on the potential outcome of their design ideas. One application of toolkits in the watch industry demonstrated that customers were willing to pay a 100% price premium for a watch that they had designed with the aid of a simple design toolkit (Franke and Piller, 2004). In addition, many software and web-based companies ask or allow prospective users to 'beta test' their products before they are fully launched. For example, the Apple Developer Program allows users to join for a fee, starting at US$99/year, to beta test pre-release products as well as contribute to the development of new applications.

Although virtual products such as home videos on 'YouTube' are common examples of co-production between the organization and the consumer, some novel commercial concepts have emerged. The Build-A-Bear Workshop international chain involves children in building their own stuffed toys: they choose the materials, they stuff the toys, and then they stitch them in the shop (Etgar, 2008).

KEY CONCEPT

Innovation and the active consumer

Technology has enabled firms to engage customers in a deeper and more interactive manner, in processes such as product development and feedback. It has also allowed customers to initiate dialogue and change. Many organizations use crowd sourcing or citizen science to come up with new product ideas for products and communication as well as test prototypes. For example, Anheuser-Busch asked customers to upload ideas for its range of ale as well as inviting videographers to contribute to its marketing campaigns. Dell runs a social innovation challenge to supports its CSR program in which students are encouraged to submit product ideas that are beneficial to society.

Sociocultural factors in the adoption of innovations

Brand communities

Brand communities are composed of people who share a social identification with others who share their interest in a particular brand, and this has been shown to influence word-of-mouth behaviour and purchase intentions (Algesheimer *et al.*, 2005). Consumers rely on the brand community as an important source of product information and experience normative pressures to remain loyal to the brand and the community (Muniz and O'Guinn, 2001).

There is evidence that higher levels of participation and longer-term membership of a brand community not only increases the likelihood of adopting a new product from the preferred brand and accelerates the time to adoption, but also decreases the likelihood of adopting new products from opposing brands and decelerates the time to adoption (Thompson and Sinha, 2008). But this oppositional brand loyalty is contingent on whether a competitor's new product is first to market. The evidence suggests that in markets with large brand communities, first movers realize significant advantages in the form of higher adoption rates and shorter time to adoption among rival communities as well as among their own communities.

As discussed in Chapter 4, the ways that brand communities can create value have been modelled as a range of social practices consisting of four categories that support and enhance the sense of membership and identity which develops over time (Schau *et al.*, 2009) (Fig. 10.6).

Social networking practices include both welcoming new members and assisting their brand learning, lending emotional and/or physical support, and articulating the behavioural expectations within the community. Community engagement practices centre on creating and sharing the brand story and significant milestones and translating them into symbols. Brand use practices include modifying the brand to suit both individual or group needs and developing systematic optimal use patterns. Impression management involves sharing the brand 'good news' and inspiring others to use; it may approach a level of 'missionary' zeal.

The implications are that companies should provide customers with the opportunities and materials to engage in the various practices through a process of 'seeding'. A key point

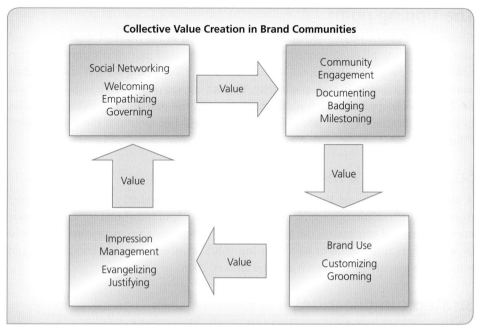

FIGURE 10.6 Collective value creation in brand communities

Adapted from Schau *et al.* (2009)

is that although practices are emergent and become self-perpetuating in some organic brand communities, systematic actions by management can broaden the range of practices and lead to higher levels of engagement.

Innovation can be stimulated by studying the details of emergent practices as they indicate un-met needs and desires which can lead to a form of co-creation or co-production between company and consumers. However, it seems that the relationship between innovation and members of brand communities is not straightforward, as rather than just high engagement with the brand, it depends on an individual's interest in innovation activities and a creative personality that leads to actual innovative behaviour (Fuller *et al.*, 2008).

KEY CONCEPT

Sociocultural factors in the adoption of innovations

Brand communities can evolve around all sorts of products; for example PowerAde, Chrysler Crossfire, Sprite, and Ford Fiesta all have company run and independent communities of support from customers. Facebook has become a popular social media platform for customers to discuss and review new product innovations. Here customers review new products, encourage purchase, reassure those waiting for delivery, daydream about past experiences, and reminisce about previous offerings. The benefit for new innovations is that it immediately integrates the offering into the brand's pantheon creating a reassurance based on past experiences as well as amplifying value in the new.

The tipping point

Gladstone (2000) maintains in his 'law of the few' that at the heart of most trends and new styles are a small number of particularly well-networked individuals whose adoption of a new trend is gradually adopted by the majority until a tipping point is reached when some trends tip into wide-scale popularity. This is a version of 'influentials theory', which has been widely applied in both marketing academic and practitioner circles and relates to the identification of style leaders as triggers for word-of-mouth in the market place. (Thompson, 2008).

Social network theory

A different perspective on the relationship between the individual and the group comes from social network theory, which de-emphasizes the role of individual consumer preferences, but instead emphasizes the power of social influence: 'when people are influenced by what others think or do or buy, their individual choices interact in complicated and inherently unpredictable ways' (Watts and Hasker, 2006).

Strategic implications

A major implication of this perspective is that companies should focus on creating portfolios of products than can be marketed using real-time measurement of and rapid response to consumer feedback.

Increase the number of innovations brought to market and decrease their size

If one acknowledges that it is impossible to predict consumer preferences then companies should plan relatively modest product development and launch programmes.

Focus on detection, measurement, and feedback

Tracking demand and satisfaction indicators through online communities, chat rooms, blogs, and search engines combined with separately available sales data allows companies to tailor their marketing to a rapidly evolving and unpredictable market.

Exploit naturally emerging social influence

Once a particular product has built up a following, companies can amplify the corresponding social influence signals by directing the attention of a much wider audience towards individuals or groups that are already enthusiastic.

Branding and the psychology of inter-group bias

There is persuasive evidence that social groups use a number of stereotypes to guide their behaviour towards other groups. Two dimensions that have particular importance for developing brand personality are perceptions of *warmth* and *competence,* and these can influence decisions about whether to trust a brand (Cuddy, 2009). It seems that people tend to see warmth and competence as inversely related, if there is an apparent surplus of one trait, they infer a deficit of the other.

This can be captured in: *Nice = Dumb; Nasty = Capable.* So when developing a brand personality for a high-tech innovation, companies should be careful that they do not err on the side of being perceived as a very warm and friendly brand, which may also be seen as being incompetent.

Let us now consider the strategic brand management implications for the particularly dynamic environment of the high-technology market place.

Managing high-technology brand strategy
Strategies for branding in high-tech markets

A fundamental element of brand strategy in high-technology environments is the need to brand the company and not just a product. Further strategies are shown in Table 10.2.

Corporate brands

A strong corporate brand is vital in the high-technology industry as it can help provide stability and longevity in a rapidly changing and ultra-competitive market (Tickle *et al.*, 2003). Since product innovations often provide the growth drivers for technology companies, it is critical not to neglect to build brand equity in the corporate brand and not just in the product name.

This is particularly important in B2B (business-to-business) markets where corporate customers buy companies first, products second. Customers seek an established firm that can provide safe, secure, and stable products and services and require the trust engendered by a strong corporate brand.

It is also possible to go beyond the company's tangible products, and brand the idea behind them, such as 'Intel Inside' and Apple's 'Think Different' (Winkler, 1999). Tangible products change over time while the intangible brand essence can be virtually unchanging.

Creating a steady stream of innovations

As a minimum, customers expect companies not to just deliver a one-off innovation, but to maintain a steady stream of innovations with strong value propositions. It is important

TABLE 10.2 Strategies for branding in high-tech markets

- Brand the company, platform, or idea
- Create a steady stream of innovations with strong value propositions
- Media advertising and PR
- Influence the influencers and stimulate word-of-mouth
- Rely on symbols or imagery to create brand personality
- Manage all brand touch points
- Work with partners: co-branding and ingredient branding
- Make effective use of the internet and social media

Adapted from Mohr, Sengupta, and Slater (2005)

in building a strong brand that it delivers the value it promises, and that the price/performance ratio is perceived as equitable.

Media advertising and PR

Media and online advertising with a strong brand message focused on benefits rather than just price is an important element in brand building, and the world's top brands continue to support their brands even through recession (Seddon, 2009). Brands that outspend their competitors with a share of voice higher than their market share are likely to increase their share (Millward Brown, 2006) even in difficult economic conditions. Public relations takes advantage of the value of the media as a news and information dissemination vehicle with greater credibility than paid advertising (Winkler, 1999).

Influence the influencers and stimulate word of mouth

Many high-tech companies rely on an 'influence the influencers programme to generate publicity and favourable word-of-mouth endorsements' (Winkler, 1999). Journalists who specialize in reviewing technology products are a key influence on adoption and a vital target for brand communications of all forms. Word of mouth is really more likely to be conveyed electronically via the internet and social media, and the evidence suggests that it is the volume of word of mouth that impacts on awareness and that has the greatest effect on sales, and not its positive/negative content (Liu, 2006).

Rely on symbols or imagery to create brand personality

Associations related to brand personality or other imagery can help establish a brand identity, particularly in near-parity products. In particular, the CEO may often be a key component of the brand, building corporate credibility and as an advocate of the technology involved (Keller, 2003).

As argued in Chapter 8, social differentiation strategies such as Fashionization and Gender Identity have been used successfully in the mobile telephone market and the car market.

Beats Electronics was co-founded by rapper and hip hop producer Dr. Dre and Interscope-Geffen-A&M Records chairman Jimmy Iovine. The company is now owned by Apple. The headphones and speakers branded as Beats by Dr. Dre have been hugely successful in no small measure due to the charisma and authenticity, as a successful musician, conveyed on the brand by the rap artist.

Manage all brand touch points

As will be argued in Chapter 12 a brand is co-created by its customers and the organization's employees and meaning is created across all contacts the customer has with the company and these meanings must be managed to ensure a great customer experience. A study of B2B customers found that while 56% of companies rate themselves as 'extremely customer-centric' only 12% of customers agreed (Solman, 2007). One suggested approach is to improve customer affinity by facilitating engagement and intimacy through online communities and interactive programmes, face-to-face conferences, and dialogues.

Brand personality: Beats by Dr Dre © 360b / Shutterstock.com

Work with partners: Co-branding and ingredient branding

Co-branding can reduce the costs of product introduction through leveraging brand equity to create distinctive points of difference, to increase access points, and broaden brand meaning. Ingredient branding involves creating brand equity for components or parts that are included within other branded products, and are often seen by consumers as a sign of quality (Keller, 2003). Examples include Intel, Dolby noise reduction, Gore-Tex fibres, Nutrasweet.

Make effective use of the internet and social media

Consumers now spend more time online than on television viewing, as image, music, and video sharing sites abound. Two new models of advertising have evolved from studies of the internet: On-demand and Engagement (Rappaport, 2007). On-demand relates to the consumer's growing ability to actively control when and how they consume media content, and their growing demand for content personalization.

Engagement centres on two key ideas: the high relevance of brands to consumers and the development of an emotional connection between the consumer and the brand. The emphasis is on supplying compelling brand experiences through multiple communication channels and touchpoints. In its ideal form it is about bonding, shared meaning, and identification.

Sociocultural brand management

In a prize-winning paper, Beverland and Reynolds (2010) set out some principles for brand management derived from consumer culture theory and interviews with mangers of cultural brands (e.g. Morgan cars) and made a strong case for the value of an emergent approach to brand meaning which applies just as much to high-tech brands. They suggest that companies should focus on basic benefits and allow consumers to ascribe higher-order meanings to the brand. They identify three supportive brand practices which can reinforce the brand's emerging meaning: locating, interaction, and experimentation.

Locating

This is the practice of embedding the brand within networks, immersing it in the relevant sub-cultural space, getting close to the consumer, and building credibility and gaining information useful for innovation.

Interaction

Companies should encourage interactivity with customers and staff and other members of the sub-culture. The emphasis is on listening and adapting rather than marketing communication, demonstrating that the firms recognize that the consumers own the brand meaning. This also builds credibility and encourages consumer buy-in and innovation opportunities.

Experimentation

By experimenting by taking the brand into new areas, companies can keep it relevant, generate excitement, and prompt discussion among consumer sub-cultures.

Strategies for customer relationship management in high-tech markets

A number of information-intensive strategies based on the use of information technology to manage customer relationships in turbulent market environments have been identified by Glazer (1999).

Capture the customer

Using data from past interactions—from captured customers—allows future offers to be designed to maximize lifetime customer value. Using interactive communications, a company can use information gained during previous transactions to cross-sell and up-sell products appropriate to individual customers.

Event-oriented prospecting

Based on information about customers that might trigger a purchase, marketing is tailored to a particular life cycle event, such as a first job which could be an opportunity to sell a laptop to the parents as a gift. Also known as 'magic-moment marketing', the goal is to anticipate the customer's situational needs so that the company appears with a solution just when the problem arises.

Extended organization

This involves going beyond traditional EDI processes to dissolve functional boundaries between firms, and to create high switching costs for customers. For example, a steel company differentiated itself in a mature category by helping customers manage their own operations after installing and operating an interactive computer network.

Mass customization

Mass customization requires flexible manufacturing that tailors products to individual customer needs at little additional marginal cost:

> Mini Cooper customers can choose from among hundreds of options for many of the car's components, as BMW is able to manufacture all cars on demand according to each buyer's individual order. My Virtual Model Inc., based in Montreal, is changing the very nature of the buying experience. The software enables consumers to build virtual models, or 'avatars', of themselves that allow them to evaluate (by virtually trying on or using) products from retailers like Adidas, Best Buy, Levi's, and Sears. More than 10 million users have already signed up for the service, and the early results are impressive: Land's End Inc. reports an increase in average order value of 15% and a jump in conversion rate of 45%.
>
> (Salvador *et al.*, 2009)

Yield management

This involves tailoring prices to different customers' price sensitivities, particularly in relation to time, in order to maximize the total return to a fixed asset. Yield management has been practised in a sophisticated form by airlines.

CHAPTER SUMMARY

In this chapter we have explored how branding can impact on the development, evaluation, and success of new innovations. Brands are very important to new innovation as they can confer credibility and legitimacy to the consumer as well as help employees to deliver the brand promise. When planning the launch of new high-tech innovations, firms must be aware that the challenge is to cross the chasm between the small market of Technology enthusiasts and Visionaries and reach the mainstream market of Pragmatists. Further, consumers are now much more involved with idea generation and new product development both at an individual and social level. The strategic implications are that customers expect a steady stream of customized brands which in many instances are co-created in development and use.

DISCUSSION QUESTIONS

1 How can a brand add authenticity to a new innovation?

2 What is the chasm effect in relation to new product adoption?

3 Provide three new examples of how consumers cope with the paradoxes of technology.

4 Identify a beta testing website and explain how consumers co-create value with the firm.

5 Provide an example of how one of Schau *et al.*'s, (2009) social practices for creating value would aid in the development and release of new idea for a firm.

6 Why is it so important to build the corporate brand in high-tech markets?

CASE STUDY

Argos: Name our baby

Argos was founded in 1972 and is one of the largest high-street retailers in the UK. The company offers a range of more than 30,000 products across multiple categories, but with the emergence of online players, such as Amazon, contributing to the decline of number of traditional bricks-and-mortar retailers, Argos has worked towards repositioning itself as a leading digital online retailer. One vital competitive advantage that Argos has over many of their online competitors is that customers can order products online and pick them up straight away in store without having to wait days for a delivery.

The overall commercial strategy of Argos is premised upon boosting sales within key categories through undertaking additional marketing activity in these areas. Nursery is one such category. However market share is fiercely competed for by other retailers such as John Lewis, Asda, Mothercare, Tesco, etc. These companies regularly promote nursery and baby events to showcase their product ranges and discounted prices. With the birth of the royal baby, George in the UK, it was anticipated that most retailers would see the occurrence as an opportunity to take advantage of the national hype. To truly capitalize upon the conversation surrounding the arrival of George, Argos recognized the need to gain an unequal share of voice versus competitors over a sustained period. Consequently, the marketing team crafted a campaign with specific objectives that could be used to evaluate its success before taking part in the big event.

The central goal of the campaign was to increase brand relevancy and engagement with their very broad target audience. To achieve this, the team focused upon driving home the message that Argos 'is the place to buy all your nursery products' primarily because of their uniquely convenient shopping solution, which is brilliant for busy families looking for seamless easy shopping experiences. Based upon data showing that 75% of people watch TV with a second device to hand and that 48% of those use social networks, it was decided that the Twitter chatter and warmth surrounding the little blue alien family (featured in their TV advertisements since 2011) could be leveraged to deepen engagement by inviting viewers and users to get involved in shaping the story of the Argos alien family in a truly dynamic way.

Argos chose to present a comical tale where the alien family learns they are expecting a new baby and of course, in true alien style, it is the dad who is pregnant. The experiences of the alien pregnancy were played out over the course of one week in the lead up to the birth of the royal baby. With the intention of bringing TV and social media together to build real-time engagement, Argos invited the audience to help name the little one via Twitter using #NameOurBaby. This was a complete first from a UK retail brand, as customer votes were sourced through Twitter and the result was played out on TV in the same week. This created a sense of time relevance and a need to view subsequent ads to find out the winning name.

Engaging new mothers was determined to be pivotal to the success of the campaign as a report published by the BabyCentre (UK Media Mum, 2012) showed that after becoming mums, women increase their internet and mobile usage by 45% and 28%, respectively. They also have high usage levels of social media, with 81% stating that they use social media regularly, and 19% using Twitter daily. To gain the greatest level of awareness and engagement, the campaign was launched on TV and brought to life using a phased approach.

In the first TV spot (Tuesday) Argos shared the happy news with the nation, the dad is seen having an ultrasound, inspecting his swollen 'cankles', struggling with his emotions and craving pickles. A second spot aired on Thursday encouraging people to vote for names that had been crowd-sourced on Twitter over the previous two days. A Twitter feed dedicated to the family (@ArgosAliens) was launched at this time to allow fans to follow the aliens' adventures off TV, to provide a platform to actively respond to name suggestions, and to build followers fast with the use of promoted tweets. Other social channels such as the Argos Facebook page and YouTube channel encouraged fans to get involved by hosting the ads. The final shortlist of names was selected—Jessie, Blue, and Phizzy—before broadcasting the third TV spot on Saturday, for one day only, which revealed the winning name: Blue. The promotion revolved around humour, but it also gave Argos the perfect opportunity to showcase their baby and nursery range.

When the royal birth occurred about three weeks later, Argos aired a congratulations message precisely 85 minutes after the 8:13 PM announcement—immediately after the end of the ITV news coverage. This ad was amplified across all Argos social channels but it wasn't just a congratulatory message to the Duke and Duchess; Argos offered congratulations to all new parents, which further drove positive social effects and retweets in appreciation of the broader sentiment. The last TV ad of the mini-campaign featured the aliens getting used to life with a new baby in the house. A surprisingly fleet of foot Baby Blue gives Dad the run-around—thank goodness he could purchase a baby playpen from home, and ask Mum to pick it up straight away on her way home. This final spot emphasized how swift, easy, and seamless the Argos shopping experience is, presenting it as a godsend for busy shoppers (none more so than new parents).

Given the short time length of the programme, the simple mechanic that underpinned the campaign resulted in high levels of engagement. Twitter itself proclaimed that the hashtag was 'really strong' and that it was '. . . to the point but also timely, neatly and legitimately capturing some of the buzz surrounding the royal baby'. In terms of measurable social effects there were 21,300 mentions of #NameOurBaby, with 80% positive sentiment. In addition, there was immense engagement (3.04% versus 1–2% retail norms) and engagement levels were sustained, sometimes as high as 18.5%. Plus, the @ArgosAliens Twitter handle, which has acquired more than 12,000 followers, now serves as another touchpoint that the brand can use to interact with customers.

Source: WARC, Warc Prize for Social Strategy 2014, Argos: Name Our Baby. Edited by Suni J. Mydock III

DISCUSSION QUESTIONS

1 In what ways did Argos manage its brand's touchpoints?

2 Discuss the significance of using bonding, shared meaning, and identification strategies to interact with customers upon one key campaign message.

3 Apart from focusing upon the seamless online purchasing experience offered by Argos, how else could the brand have attracted customers during the lead-up to the birth of the royal baby?

4 In the future, how can Argos maintain its perception as a leading innovative high-street and online retailer?

5 As to shaping the story, what role did viewer empowerment play in driving engagement?

REFERENCES

Aaker, D. (2007), 'Innovation: Brand it or lose it', *California Management Review*, 50, 1, 8–24.

Algesheimer, R., Dholakia, U., and Hermann, A. (2005), 'The social influence of brand community', *Journal of Marketing*, 69, 19–34.

Beverland, M. and Reynolds, S. (2010), 'Sociocultural brand management: Exploring branding practices in the postmodern age,' 6th Thought Leaders in Brand Management Conference, Università della Svizzera Italiana, Lugano, Switzerland.

Bresnahan, T., Stern, S., and Trjtenberg, M. (1996), 'Market segmentation and the sources of rents from innovation: Personal computers in the late 1980s', Working Paper 5726, Cambridge, MA: National Bureau of Economic Research.

Carpenter, G., Glazer, R., and Nakamoto, N. (1994), 'Meaningful brands from meaningless differentiation: The dependence on irrelevant attributes', *Journal of Marketing Research*, August, XXXI, 339–50.

Corkindale, D. and Belder, M. (2009), 'Corporate brand reputation and the adoption of innovations', *Journal of Product and Brand Management*, 18, 4, 242–50.

Cuddy, A. (2009), 'Just because I'm nice, don't assume I'm dumb', *Harvard Business Review*, February, 87, 24–5.

Dowling, G. (2001), *Creating Corporate Reputations*, Oxford: Oxford University Press.

Elgin, B. (2005), 'Managing Google's idea factory: Marissa Mayer helps the search giant out think its rivals', *Business Week*, 3 October, http://www.businessweek.com/ Last accessed 27 August 2010.

Escalas, J. (2004), 'Narrative processing: Building consumer connections to brands', *Journal of Consumer Psychology*, 14, 168–80.

Etgar, M. (2008), 'A model of the consumer co-production process', *Journal of the Academy of Marketing Science*, 36, 97–198.

Franke, N. and Piller, F. (2004), 'Value creation by toolkits for user innovation and design: The case of the watch market', *Journal of Product Innovation Management*, 21, 401–15.

Frost, V. (2007), 'La Vie en Rose', *Guardian*, 8 June.

Fuller, J., Matzler, K., and Hoppe, M. (2008), 'Brand community members as a source of innovation', *Journal of Product Innovation Management*, 25, 608–19.

Gladstone, M. (2000), *The Tipping Point: How Little Things Can Make a Big Difference*, London: Little Brown.

Glazer, R. (1999), 'Winning in smart markets', *MIT Sloan Management Review*, Summer, 40, 4, 59–69.

Gurham-Canli, Z. and Batra, R. (2007), 'When corporate image effects product evaluations: The moderating role of perceived risk', *Journal of Marketing Research*, 41, 2, 197–205.

Huddleston, T., Jr. (2014), 'Apple's market cap just hit $700 billion for the first time', 25 November, http://www.fortune.com/2014/11/25/apple-700-billion/ Last accessed 1 December 2014.

Keller, K. (2003), *Strategic Brand Management*, Upper Saddle River, NJ: Pearson Education.

Linder, J., Jarvena, S., and Davenport, T. (2003), 'Toward an innovation sourcing strategy', *MIT Sloan Management Review*, 44, 4, 43–9.

Liu, Y. (2006), 'Word of mouth for movies: Its dynamics and impact on box office revenue', *Journal of Marketing*, 70, 74–89.

Mick, D. and Fournier, S. (1998), 'Paradoxes of technology: Consumer cognizance, emotions and coping strategies', *Journal of Consumer Research*, 25, 123–43.

Millward Brown (2006), '*Five Steps to Brand Growth*', Millward Brown Knowledge Points, www.millwardbrown.com Last accessed 27 August 2010.

Mitra, D. and Golder, P. N. (2006), 'How does objective quality affect perceived quality? Short-term effects, long-term effects, and asymmetries', *Marketing Science*, 25, 3, 230–47.

Mohr, J., Sengupta, S., and Slater, S. (2005), *Marketing of High-Technology Products and Innovations,* Upper Saddle River, NJ: Pearson Prentice Hall.

Moore, G. (1999), *Crossing the Chasm*, New York: HarperPerennial.

Muñiz, A. and O'Guinn, T. (2001), 'Brand community', *Journal of Consumer Research*, 27, 4, 412–32.

Null, C. (2010), 'Technology's most (and least) reliable brands', *PCWorld.com*, March, 78–86.

Prahalad, C. and Ramaswamy, V. (2000), 'Co-opting customer competence', *Harvard Business Review*, 78(1), Jan-Feb, 79–87.

Prugl, R. and Schreier, M. (2006), 'Learning from leading-edge customers at *The Sims:* Opening up the innovation process using toolkits', *R & D Management*, 36, 3, 237–50.

Rappaport, S. (2007), 'Lessons from online practice: New advertising models', *Journal of Advertising Research*, 47, 2, 180–86.

Roberts, P. and Dowling, G. (2002), 'Corporate reputation and sustained superior financial performance', *Strategic Management Journal*, 23, 12, 1077–93.

Robertson, T. and Gatignon, H. (1986), 'Competitive effects on technology diffusion, ' *Journal of Marketing*, 50, 3, 1–12.

Rogers, E. (1962), *The Diffusion of Innovations*, New York: The Free Press.

Salvador, F., Holen, P., and Piller, F. (2009), 'Cracking the code of mass customization', *MIT Sloan Management Review*, 50, 3, 1–10.

Schau, H., Muniz, A., and Arnould, J. (2009), 'How brand community practices create value, ' *Journal of Marketing*, 73, 30–51.

Schouten, J.W. and McAlexander, J.H. (1995), 'Subcultures of consumption: an ethnography of the new bikers', *Journal of Consumer Research*, 22, 1, 43–61.

Seddon, J. (2009), 'Firms that build brand value will be recession survivors', *Admap*, 505, 16–22.

Solman, G. (2007), 'Leading tech brands face customer power outage, ' *Brandweek*, 48, 46, 10–11.

Thomke, S. and von Hippel, E. (2002), 'Customers as innovators: A new way to create value', *Harvard Business Review*, 80, 4, 74–81.

Thompson, C. (2008), 'Is the tipping point toast?' *Fast Company*, location: www.fastcompany.com/magazine/122/is-the-tipping-point-toast.html. Last accessed 29 August 2010.

Thompson, S. and Sinha, R. (2008), 'Brand communities and new product adoption: The influence and limits of oppositional brand loyalty', *Journal of Marketing*, 72, 65–80.

Tickle, P., Keller, K., and Richey, K. (2003), 'Ten guidelines for branding in high-tech markets', *Market Leader*, 22, 1–5.

Vargo, S.L. and Lusch, R.F. (2004), 'Evolving to a new dominant logic for marketing', *Journal of Marketing*, 68(1) (January), 1–17.

Wall Street Journal (2003), 'How Titans swallowed Wi-Fi', 8 August.

Watts, D. and Hasker, S. (2006), 'Marketing in an unpredictable world', *Harvard Business Review*, 84(9) September, 25–27.

Winkler, A.M. (1999). *Warp-Speed Branding*, New York: John Wiley & Sons, Inc.

WEB LINKS

Build-A-Bear Workshop: http://www.buildabear.co.uk/

SAP: Building a Leading Technology Brand (2006): http://www4.gsb.columbia.edu/null/download?&exclusive=filemgr.download&file_id=10149

SAP Design Guild branding resources: http://www.sapdesignguild.org/editions/edition6/links.asp

Philips Sense & Simplicity brand strategy: http://www.simplicityhub.philips.com/

VeryPC environmental & ethical IT solutions: http://www.very-pc.co.uk/

'Blue ocean' thinking can create waves: http://www.guardian.co.uk/media/2009/feb/02/advertising-industry-news

Audi Quattro: http://www.pistonheads.com/doc.asp?c=52&i=10065

BT Wireless Broadband: http://www.guardian.co.uk/media/2010/jul/12/bt-ad-family and http://www.vote.bt.com/?s_cid=con_FURL_calls_vote)

261

Test your understanding of this chapter and explore the subject further using our Online Resource Centre. Visit the Online Resource Centre at http://www.oxfordtextbooks.co.uk/orc/elliott-percy3e/

11 Brand Stretching and Retrenching

Key Concepts

1 Product and brand portfolio management strategy guide, brand stretching and retrenching strategy.

2 Portfolio strategies inform corporate merger and acquisition strategy.

3 The brand hierarchy comprises company brands, group brands, and single brands.

4 Category development index and brand development index help inform brand stretching and retrenching strategy.

5 Master brands have led to significant changes in product and brand portfolio management.

6 When to use source versus endorser branding strategies.

7 Brand extensions are different from line extensions.

8 Postmodern notions have been associated with brand strategy.

Introduction

When talking about brand stretching and retrenching, one is dealing with a *branding strategy*, one that considers a number of elements related to the existing brands in a company's product portfolio (or sometimes just a single brand) and the best way to use those brands (or an individual brand) in order to maximize the overall potential of the company. This can involve quite complex branding strategies, utilizing multiple brand names and positionings over an entire product portfolio; or simply a brand strategy dealing with one brand. In the end, a brand stretching strategy is part of the overall strategy for developing and nurturing a strong overall equity for the brand, building upon a brand's equity to strengthen the overall product portfolio; and a retrenchment strategy looks to the elimination of brand extensions or the retirement of a brand, again to strengthen the overall product portfolio.

Before discussing the various ways one can think about brand stretching and retrenching strategies, it would be a good idea to consider just what is meant by such things as product and brand portfolios, and how they are related to one another. This is important because it provides the framework for understanding brand stretching and retrenchment strategies.

KEY CONCEPT

Product and brand portfolio management strategy guide brand stretching and retrenching strategy.

In effect, brand stretching and retrenching strategies are an extension of product and brand portfolio management. Brand stretching strategy addresses how the portfolio can profitably be expanded, and brand retrenching strategy looks at the overall portfolio for brands or products that can be dropped or sold off to improve the overall health of the company.

Product and brand portfolios

Everyone knows what a product is. A company's *product portfolio* is how marketers often describe the collection of different products they market in a category, and this will include individual products as well as product lines. A *product line* is a group of products within a single product category that are closely related to each other in some way, usually because they are seen as being used for the same thing. Brands too may be described in terms of portfolios and lines. A *brand portfolio* reflects the various brands marketed by a company, again within a particular product category; and a *brand line* is all of the products marketed under a single brand name.

One way to think about the interrelationships implied here (as Keller has) is in terms of a grid, with all of the products a company markets running along the top and the brands for each product listed below (Keller, 2008). Fig. 11.1 illustrates this for products marketed by Levi-Strauss. Looking along the rows reflects the product portfolio, and looking down the columns, the brand portfolio.

It is important to think about products and brands in this way, because looking along a row is really looking at the current *brand extension* strategy of the company. What this partial example for Levi-Strauss shows is that when they made the decision to market cotton trousers, they decided *against* marketing them as Levi's. While they did initially introduce them under a Levi's umbrella (Levi's Dockers) in order to borrow and build upon the existing equity in the Levi's brand, now the brand stands alone, and in fact has spawned its own line extensions.

Looking at the brands for each product in the grid, one gets a feel for the branding strategy used by a company for the products it markets. In our example Levi-Strauss has chosen to use the Levi's brand name as a group brand (which will be discussed below), providing an umbrella for all their jeans, and trading upon the original equity in the brand.

Fig. 11.2 illustrates part of Volkswagen's product portfolio. Most people are likely to know that Audi is part of Volkswagen, but not that such diverse brands as Bugatti, Lamborghini, and Bentley are also a part of Volkswagen. They have laid their product portfolio out with the various types of vehicles in the category across the top (the products) and the market segments in the category down the side, with their various brands inserted in the grid where appropriate. As it shows, Volkswagen as a corporation has deep penetration with several brands in a number of segments; and at the same time, there are a number of vehicle types where they only offer one brand, and two segments (mini and upper) where there is limited coverage. Perhaps the primary reason for having multiple brands within a category is to satisfy different market segments. Barwise and Robertson (1992) discuss several other reasons for doing so.

A look at this product portfolio suggests any number of areas where Volkswagen as a corporation could consider brand extensions via either line extensions for a particular brand for other vehicle types or an extension to additional segments. But it should be clear that not all their brands would be appropriate for extending into just any area. Would it make sense to extend Bentley into the mini segment, or Lamborghini into off-road? Hardly. The brand image and equity must fit, something that will be dealt with at length later.

PRODUCT PORTFOLIO

	Denim pants	Non-denim pants	Shirts	Jackets	Other
	Levi's	Dockers	Dockers	Levi-Strauss Signature	
	Levi's 501	Levi-Strauss Signature	Levi-Strauss Signature		
	Levi's Engineered Jeans				
	Other				

BRAND PORTFOLIO

FIGURE 11.1 Levi-Strauss partial product and brand portfolio grid

	Hatch	Notch	Sports coupe	Roadster	Pickup	Off-road
Luxury		Bentley, Lamborghini, Bugatti	Lamborghini			
Upper		Audi				
Upper middle		Audi				Audi
Middle		VW,SEAT				
Compact	Audi VW,SEAT	VW,SEAT Škoda	Audi			
Small	VW,SEAT Škoda	VW,SEAT Škoda			VW,SEAT Škoda	
Mini	VW,SEAT					

FIGURE 11.2 Volkswagen partial product portfolio

Product and brand portfolio strategy may also inform corporate acquisition strategy. Kraft Foods provides a very good example of this. In the early 2000's Kraft was the largest packaged-foods company in the USA, in large part a result of its merger with General Foods a number of years ago, with a strong portfolio of well-known, longstanding brands such as Ritz crackers, Oscar Mayer, Mirical Whip, Oreo, Philadelphia Cream Cheese, Kool-Aid, Maxwell House, Grey Poupon, Jell-O, Carte Noire—and the list goes on.

In recent years Kraft have been very active in adjusting their product and brand portfolios, buying Groupe Danone's global biscuits business in 2007, selling the Post Cereal business in 2008, and selling their frozen pizza business in 2010. In September of 2009 Kraft began a hostile takeover bid for Cadbury plc. Kraft was keen on Cadbury in part because of their access to the fast-growing developing markets around the globe, but primarily because it would move them competitively into the confectionery business. Cadbury, following their purchase of Adams in 2003 had become the world's largest confectionery brand. Cadbury's brand portfolio then included such brands as Dairy Milk chocolate, Crème Eggs, Dentyne chewing gum, and Halls cough drops.

Cadbury attempted to block the takeover by opening discussions with Hershey, seen as being a better cultural and operational fit. However, at about half the size of Cadbury, the financial strain was considered too much by Hershey, and in January of 2010 a deal was completed with Kraft for £11.9 billion (Lublin and Cordeiro, 2010).

The acquisition of Cadbury by Kraft significantly altered the confection category, and placed competitors with the challenge of competing with two confection giants: the new Kraft-Cadbury and Mars Inc., which itself had acquired the leading chewing gum brands to broaden its product portfolio with the acquisition of Wrigley in 2008. In the wake of the Kraft–Cadbury deal, speculation began that Hershey would try to sell itself to the number three confectioner, Nestlé, which found itself in an even more distant third place in the category. Interestingly, Cadbury is now a part of Mondelez International following a demerger in 2012 of Kraft from Kraft Foods, Inc., which was then re-named Mondelez International. Mondelez retained the snack and confectionery brands, and markets them internationally.

As this discussion makes clear, mergers and acquisitions can play a significant role in product and brand portfolio strategy. From a brand management perspective, of course, managers are unlikely to be involved in such strategic decisions. But, from a competitive standpoint, they will certainly have to deal with the consequences of such decisions. In addition, there are other situations where a brand's portfolio could be affected by circumstances beyond the manager's control.

Jack Daniel's was acquired by Brown-Forman in 1956, nearly 100 years after Jack Daniel distilled his first bottle of Tennessee Whiskey. But what exactly is a Tennessee Whiskey? As it happens, in 2013 at the urging of Brown-Forman (which interestingly is headquartered in Kentucky) the Tennessee state legislature passed a law defining anything labelled 'Tennessee Whiskey' to not only be made in the state, but also to be made from at least 51% corn, filtered through maple charcoal, and aged in new, charred oak barrels. No surprise, but that just happens to be the recipe for Jack Daniel's.

George Dickel, the distant number two selling Tennessee Whiskey (Jack Daniels sells more than 90% of the state's whisky) is fighting the law (as we write), not because it does not comply with it, but because they felt it inhibited innovation and should not be the only way to make high quality Tennessee Whiskey. As a spokesman for Dickel's UK-based parent company Diageo plc (the world's largest liquor company) put it, 'We're in favour of flexibility that lets all distillers, large and small, make Tennessee Whiskey the way their family recipes tell them,' a sentiment echoed by a number of smaller distillers in the state (Ester, 2014). The issue was tabled by a divided legislature until 2015 at the earliest, if at all.

> ### KEY CONCEPT
>
> **Portfolio strategies inform corporate merger and acquisition strategy**
>
> Portfolio strategies consider the best mix of products and brands for the long-term strength of the company. An important element in this consideration is the value of adding products or brands through merger or acquisition to the correct mix.

Brand hierarchy

Brand names may be used in many ways, depending upon the branding strategy. As already seen in the brief Levi-Strauss example, Levi's is used alone as a brand name for jeans and to help introduce a new product (Levi's Dockers); and it is also used in combination with sub-brands of jeans (Levi's 501). This suggests, as many people have pointed out, that brands may be thought about in terms of a hierarchy. We will be looking at this hierarchy in terms of company or parent brands, group brands, and single brands. A *company brand* identifies the parent company, brands like Daimler-Benz or Unilever. A *group brand* is a brand name that is used in more than one category, brands like Yamaha that are used to market such diverse products as pianos and motorcycles. At the bottom of the hierarchy are single brands, where the brand name is restricted to a single product category.

In practice, this hierarchy is not always so clear cut. When you think about Nestlé what comes to mind? Was it chocolate, or perhaps coffee? That is what most people are familiar with. In fact, one of Nestlé's very earliest advertising slogans was 'Nestlé makes the very best, chocolate'. Obviously, Nestlé is a chocolate brand, but is there such a thing as Nestlé coffee? No, but of course they are well known for such soluble coffee brands as Nescafé, Taster's Choice, and Gold Blend. Returning to chocolate, most people are probably also familiar with Nestlé Crunch bars. Consider this for a minute. What is the brand name? Nestlé, Crunch, Nestlé Crunch? And what does this say about the business they are in? If Nestlé is a brand of chocolate, what are Nestlé Crunch ice cream bars? Taking this further, how does one deal with the fact that Nestlé is, or has been, in a lot of other businesses, such as wine, non-dairy creamers, and frozen foods (under such brands as Berringer, Carnation, and Findus)? And what about the more intangible aspects of a company's image (cf. Barich and Kutter, 1991; Hatch and Schultz, 2001)? This is really the focus of this chapter: branding strategies that help managers determine when and how a brand should be stretched or retrenched.

Thinking about branding strategies within a brand hierarchy helps make sense out of how brand names can be used, and this is essential before one can begin to consider how to stretch or retrench a brand. Does it help understand Nestlé's brand strategy? Not if one is looking to place Nestlé as a brand into one of the hierarchical classifications. But it does help to see the various ways in which Nestlé *use* their name. They use it as a single brand in the chocolate confection category; they use it as a group brand in chocolate confection and coffee (as well as other categories); and they use it as a company brand. The reasons *why* it is used in various ways, why the Nestlé brand name has been stretched in different ways over the years, is all about (or should be) how the brand equity of the name Nestlé contributes to building the brand equity of each brand name with which it is associated in the company's product and brand portfolio.

One of the authors of this book worked with Nestlé on a project where they were looking into ways to expand their overall product portfolio. They wanted to know into what additional product categories consumers felt a number of Nestlé single and group brands could believably be stretched. They were looking along the rows of the product-brand grid to see if any current categories in the product portfolio could benefit from a new product introduction under another Nestlé brand (broadening it as a group brand), or if it made sense to stretch one of these brands to an entirely new product category for Nestlé, thus expanding the overall product portfolio. For example, would a line of Taster's Choice coffee-flavoured confections make sense to consumers (moving Taster's Choice into the confections category where Nestlé already markets several brands); or what about a line of Taster's Choice baking products, moving the brand into a new category for Nestlé?

At issue is whether or not the images of one of these brands is compatible in people's minds with a different product category. In other words, does the current equity of the brand easily transfer to another product? While this will be dealt with in more detail throughout the chapter, at this point it is important to see how the idea of hierarchies and product and brand portfolios helps frame stretching (and retrenchment) branding strategies.

Levels of branding

A critical consideration in developing brand stretching strategies is the level at which a brand chooses to be positioned. At its most basic, considerations of level reflect brand hierarchies, but the question goes much deeper than this. What is the optimum level at which a brand should be positioned in order to optimize value to the consumer as well as profit for the company? This is a fundamental *strategic* issue that must be continuously revisited as a company looks for competitive advantage. Depending upon where a brand is now, any number of strategic questions might be raised. Does it stay where it is seen as the 'leader', or move the brand into new categories? Should it 'brand' a product or service that it provides, but has not marketed as a brand? In many areas of technology consumers are often not aware of the company behind a product or service, for example the broadband source of their high-speed internet connection or the satellite company providing their television signals.

This is often the case too with so-called 'ingredient' products, which may or may not be branded. Most people with computers are familiar with Intel and its Pentium processor. But are they aware of who makes other components in the computer? Would it, or could it make a difference to the manufacturer if these components were 'branded'? Would it make sense for Intel to change its brand level and introduce a line of Intel computers? Or to stretch even further and market a line of Intel cellular phones or perhaps hi-fi components? All these questions are dealing with brand level, and as Kapferer (2001) has pointed out, the problem of choosing a level, especially when considering brand life cycle, is addressed in terms of brand stretching, even though it is not always understood by managers as such.

Answers to all these questions should be considered in terms of long-term strategic concerns such as how long any change in positioning level for a brand will sustain a competitive advantage, and how profit may migrate with changes in customer base (as Slywotzky (1998) has discussed).

Product portfolio management

This leads directly to the question of managing a product portfolio. The key to managing a product portfolio is taking a *long-term* view. Markets are dynamic, changing over time, and a company's product portfolio must take this into account. This means that top management must carefully consider the role of different brands, and the relationship among these different brands in the portfolio *over time*.

Anticipating changes in markets and assessing gaps in the company's current portfolio can suggest possible areas for different branding strategies. How are brands likely to change over time? As consumer needs change, how likely is it that they will switch to other brands in an existing product portfolio (something Keller (2008) called 'migration' strategies)? And as they change, does the company already market products for these new needs?

The development of the Anheuser-Busch product portfolio (before being acquired by InBev) offers a good example of effective product portfolio management as markets grew and changed. Originally, there was Budweiser. With the growth of imported beer in the US market, Michelob was added to the portfolio and positioned against the imports. As the brewery's production capacity increased, Busch Beer was added to attract 'regular beer' drinkers.

With the success of Miller Lite in the 1970s, the beer market in the USA was significantly altered. There had been many, many attempts in earlier years to introduce lower calorie (and lower carbohydrate) beers, but none of them had been successful. Owing to all the previous failures by other brewers, Anheuser-Busch was very cautious about entering the market. They began by introducing something they called Anheuser-Busch Natural Light, with the emphasis on the company brand. But when they learned that the 'bar call' for the brand (the way people ask for a brand when ordering) was 'Busch Light' or even 'Bud Light', a decision was made to drop the Anheuser-Busch from the name, and focus on the word 'natural'. They dropped the emphasis on the company brand because there was still the concern, even though Miller Lite looked like a real success, that there could be *negative* associations from a lower calorie beer that could impact their regular Busch brand and the premium, flagship brand, Budweiser.

They were correct to be concerned, because research has shown that unsuccessful extensions tend only to hurt the parent brand when there is a strong perceived 'fit' between them. An unsuccessful extension into a different product category is much less likely to negatively affect the parent (Roedder John *et al.*, 1998). It was not until some time later that the Budweiser and then Michelob brands were extended with Bud Light and Michelob Light. At that point Natural Light was repositioned as a price brand with no marketing support.

This is a good example of an adjustment to a product portfolio to meet competitive change in a market place, while withholding brand extensions within existing product lines until the company is certain there will be no problems for the equity of their established brands. Beginning in the 1990s and continuing today, with the popularity of 'micro-breweries' AB-InBev continues to adjust their product portfolio, adding new single brands such as Killian's Red *outside* the umbrella of the parent family of brands.

Changes in fashion and taste will also drive changes in product portfolios. A good example may be seen with another Jack Daniel's case. Lagging spirits sales received a boost, beginning in 2011, with the introduction of various flavoured vodkas, rums, and whiskeys that appealed to a younger, 21–29 year old demographic. While remaining the best-selling whisky in the US, as well as being popular around the world, Jack Daniel's saw this trend as an opportunity to attract new drinkers to the brand, including non-whisky drinkers. They did this by blending a honey liquor with Jack Daniel's Tennessee Whiskey. Capitalizing on the brand's incredibly high awareness and positive brand attitude (even among non-users), a source branding strategy was used, branding the new flavoured whisky as Jack Daniel's Tennessee Honey. The heavy emphasis on the Jack Daniel's name is evident in the packaging label. Given the younger target audience, the introduction and subsequent marketing relied heavily upon a more digitally oriented, socially intense media. Jack Honey (it's 'bar call') was the first official spirit advertiser on the Twitter platform (Birkner, 2013).

Projected and actual changes in the market may also lead to retrenchment branding strategies. Product obsolescence, a glut of brands in a category, a new corporate focus, or changes in a market's dynamics may suggest it is time to eliminate certain brands or brand extensions from the portfolio. In some cases, a brand's equity may no longer provide potential growth because the market is now looking for different things. In extreme cases a brand's existing equity may in fact have a negative impact upon the product portfolio because of changing attitudes in the market. In such cases it will be necessary to retrench, and retire the brand.

The short-lived introduction of the New Coke brand in the 1980s provides an example of where the introduction of a new product to the portfolio was meant to lead to the eventual retirement of the existing Coke product, with the new version eventually taking over the Coke brand name. It never happened because the market reacted in a strongly negative way, and New Coke was hastily withdrawn. What happened? The original reason for considering stretching the brand in this way came from research that suggested Coke was losing share to its main competitor Pepsi among younger cola drinkers. Pepsi was a somewhat sweeter product, so the decision was made to develop a product that was sweeter than the existing Coke, and preferred to Pepsi. As we have discussed, this could seem to be an appropriate response to a change in the market.

But it did not work. In all their product development and taste testing for New Coke, the company never considered the strength of the equity in the existing Coke brand. While New Coke was indeed preferred to regular Coke in all the taste tests, and to Pepsi, these were all *blind* taste tests where people did not know what brands were involved. When New Coke was introduced, it was now being compared with a Coke brand that came with 100 years of positive brand equity attached. People preferred the original Coke brand *because*—because it *was* Coke.

There can be no better example of the power of brand equity. In *any* consideration of brand stretching or retrenchment, it is essential that the effect a brand's current equity will have in that branding strategy is understood. Original Coke was re-branded Classic Coke, and for a brief period of time was marketed with New Coke. In the end, however, it was New Coke that was retired. Classic Coke remained in the portfolio, and eventually returned to its original brand name, Coke.

Brand involvement

The importance of involvement with brands and its relationship with how they are seen in terms of product portfolio management and potential brand extensions has been considered in a rather interesting way by Kunde (2000) in something he talks about as 'corporate religion'. He looks at brands in terms of a hierarchy, much as we have been discussing it, but with more of an emphasis on involvement. At its most basic level, some consumers are thought to see a brand as nothing more than a product: washing powder is washing powder, whether Persil or some other brand. Other consumers, however, may invest a certain level of emotional value with a brand, involving them with the brand in such a way that it provides a competitive advantage, even when the brand is basically a commodity (very much along the lines of how brand equity is defined).

Next up the scale for Kunde is where a brand has actually achieved such a superior position in the market that it quite literally *becomes* the product category: this would include brands such as Kleenex, Hoover, and Xerox. In effect, consumers have replaced the function of the product with the brand. It is brands like this that may use a centrally positioned strategy, as discussed in Chapter 6. Finally, the ultimate goal for a brand in this scheme is to achieve what he calls 'brand religion', where a brand has extended its brand culture to a point where it becomes *essential* to the consumer. Kunde estimates that only about 10% of brands reach this level, and offers The Body Shop and Harley-Davidson as examples. The Body Shop sells a 'religion' based upon natural ingredients and environmental concerns; Harley-Davidson 'freedom'.

When to consider brand stretching or retrenching

In the earlier discussion of product portfolio management the subject of when to consider brand stretching strategies was introduced briefly, and examples of when to consider stretching (as in the case of Anheuser-Busch) or retrenching (the initial decision to replace Coke with New Coke) were described. But many branding strategies also result from opportunities that present themselves outside the traditional notions of product portfolio management: such things as co-branding, ingredient branding, or even how brands are distributed.

In the next section we will be looking at a number of ways one might look at and consider opportunities for brand stretching or retrenching. But before getting into specific strategies, we would like to talk about the idea of category and brand development indexes. While this is an old idea in marketing that does not seem to be discussed much any more, it remains a very useful tool offering the manager a measure of the overall dynamic of the market, and where their brand 'fits'.

A category development index (CDI) reflects the size of penetration into a product category. A low CDI indicates that the category does not enjoy widespread usage in the market. This will almost always be the case with new product categories; and often with older categories where new technology is leading to product obsolescence. But in some cases, CDIs are low simply because the market itself is small. A high CDI indicates that the product category enjoys strong penetration among most, if not all, of its potential market. Brand development indexes (BDIs) reflect the same thing, only in relation to competitive brands in a category. A low BDI indicates that a brand has a low share relative to others in the category; a high BDI indicates a large share of the target market.

This is important when considering brand stretching strategies, because when brand managers look at their brand portfolio for a given category, there are a number of strategic questions to address related to the development of the category and the brand's share of that category. These questions follow from the four possible combinations of CDIs and BDIs. A brand may find itself with a low BDI in a category with either a low or high CDI; or it may enjoy a high BDI in a category with either a low or high CDI. (These are, of course, not dichotomies in actual practice. A brand or category might fall anywhere along a continuum from high to low, but for the purposes of discussion, we need only concern ourselves with high versus low.)

Suppose a brand has a low BDI in an established category. If the brand has been around for a long time and has not been able to capture a larger share of the market, this very definitely opens up the possibility of stretching the brand in some way (even introducing a new brand rather than brand extension) in order to drive up overall share in the market

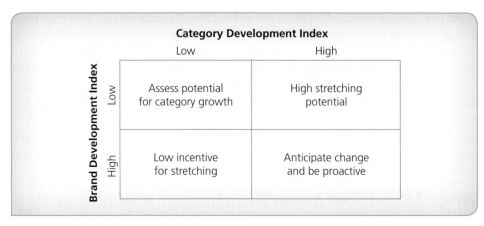

FIGURE 11.3 Brand stretching opportunities relative to brand and category development

for the company. This would certainly make sense in a category with a high CDI. But what if it has a low CDI? Would it be worth the effort to try and capture a larger share of a small market unlikely to grow? Would a new product innovation be likely to drive up the CDI? What if a brand enjoyed a strong BDI in a category with a low CDI? There would probably be very little incentive to stretch the brand, because it already enjoys a large share.

Newer product categories with low CDIs may have the potential for growth. Brand stretching strategies must then take into account *how* the category is likely to grow. With high CDIs, opportunities are obviously greater for brand stretching. If the category is not established, things change. Even with established product categories, managers must be looking at how their market is likely to change. This means they must *anticipate* change in their market and become proactive with their brand stretching strategy (Fig. 11.3).

As should be evident, what is going on in the category will influence how the managers should approach brand stretching (and retrenchment) strategies. Whether or not one thinks in terms of CDIs and BDIs, brand stretching strategies will be influenced by how well developed the category is where a brand is marketed, and where that brand stands relative to its competitors in that category.

KEY CONCEPT

CDI and BDIs help inform brand stretching and retrenching strategy.

An old idea in marketing provides a useful way of looking at brands and markets: category development index (CDI) and brand development index (BDI). A CDI reflects the penetration of a product category into the market at large; and a BDI reflects brand share in the category. They can help inform brand stretching and retrenching decisions by asking such questions as: Do we want to be a big brand (high BDI) in a small market (low CDI) or a smaller brand (low BDI) in a larger market (high CDI)? They could be equally profitable. If you are already in a small market, is there any hope of category growth, or of your brand gaining share if the market remains small?

Evaluating stretching (and retrenching) opportunities

There are three fundamental questions that must be asked when evaluating opportunities for a change in branding strategy. First of all, does it make sense *strategically* for the brand and company in terms of its product and brand portfolio? Secondly, if it makes sense strategically, will the change '*fit*' in terms of the parent brand's equity? And finally, if the change makes sense strategically, and the extension fits logically into the new market, will it be *profitable*?

Strategically, there are many reasons why a company might want to consider stretching a brand; or to retrench. They may wish to exploit a competitive weakness in the category by introducing sub-brands; fill a gap in the category or in new product categories for the brand; or position the brand for expected changes in either market structure (e.g. technological advances in the category) or in the target market (e.g. an ageing population that could create more, or less, demand for a product).

Kraft has been a major parent brand in its own right for many years, as we saw earlier. And in spite of its mergers and acquisitions, it provides a good example of a company that did not respond to some important changes in their key markets during the early 2000s (Ellison, 2003). For years, they were a master of brand extension, offering a never-ending line of 'new and improved' versions of their well-known brands. But they failed to develop new products that private labels could not easily copy. By endlessly extending existing established brands they missed out on one of the most important changes in grocery store food dynamics in the late 1990s, the rising importance of 'healthy' foods such as cereal bars and foods with organic ingredients (to name just two). As a result, they fell behind in the race to adjust their product portfolio, with a significant impact upon profit and share prices.

Regardless of the market issues involved, there are other strategic questions dealing with potential changes in the meaning of a brand that must be asked. If a brand is stretched into a new category, what is the potential for a change in the image or meaning of the brand? If it retrenches, and the brand is no longer associated with a particular product (especially if that product is the one with which the brand was originally associated), how might that affect the image of the brand for those products that remain associated with the parent brand? Also, how recently has a brand been extended? And into what areas? If a brand is seen as moving into several new areas within a short time, it could lead to brand identity confusion; whereas, if the brand is extended into the same categories, but over time, consumers might more easily assimilate the extensions.

In terms of 'fit', suppose a brand enjoys a strong image or equity for a particular benefit that on the surface seems logically transferable to another product category. With a strong reputation for killing germs, a hand and face soap manufacturer might consider stretching the brand into the household cleanser market. With a strong brand equity built upon killing germs, this should easily transfer to, say, a kitchen or bathroom cleanser. On the other hand, a household cleanser brand with the same strong image for killing germs in the kitchen or bathroom might not be a good fit for stretching into the hand and face soap market. If it works for a soap-to-household cleanser extension, why might it not work for a household cleanser-to-soap extension? While the key benefit is the same, there might very well be a perceptual problem in transferring the germ-killing equity from a product used on hard surfaces in the kitchen or bath to a soap that will be used on your face. Consumers must accept that an equity transfer makes sense, or the brand extension is likely to fail.

Interestingly, consumers may *not* feel an extension makes sense simply because they cannot imagine the parent brand in any other way. This is often the case with strong category leaders (Farquhar and Herr, 1993).

Even if the equity of a brand would seem to transfer well, much more could be involved. Juan Valdes offers a good example of this. Long a well-known brand representing Columbian coffee for the Columbian Coffee Growers Federation, through Procafecol SA in the mid-2000s they attempted to build up their successful brand of packaged coffee by introducing a global Coffee Café chain. Unfortunately, the effort failed financially. But in 2013 a second effort was made, this time with a shift in business strategy. Procafecol used franchises to avoid the need for heavy up-front capital. Internationally, this new effort met with more success (Muñoz, 2013). Still, there is always a risk using a franchise model rather than company store model because of potential problems with individual franchises, problems which could damage the present packaged coffee brand.

If there is a good strategic reason to consider brand stretching or retrenching, and a proposed extension 'fits' in terms of brand image and equity, it only remains to determine if the extension or retrenching will lead to better long-term profitability for the company.

Can any brand be stretched?

Abercrombie & Fitch provides an interesting example of the importance of brand equity in brand stretching. The company was once the legendary outfitter of Theodore Roosevelt (the famous 'Rough Rider' and later US President almost a century ago) and such luminaries as Ernest Hemingway. After passing through a number of changes in ownership, it was acquired by Limited Brands in 1988. They tried unsuccessfully to reposition the chain as a preppy, button-down-collar men's store. In 1992 they gave up and invited a veteran of the fashion industry to take over the company and it became independent with a public shares offering in 1996.

Up to this point in its history, the company had turned from its original positioning as an outfitter for adventurers, with a successful brand extension into exotic location travel bookings, to a preppy apparel store for men. Under their new CEO, the company pursued yet another positioning, entering the volatile world of youth fashion, utilizing on-the-edge, often homoerotic, sexual imagery. Promotions featured partially clad young men, often in provocative poses. Initially successful, the imagery was pushed further and further out, offering thong underwear for girls with words such as 'eye candy' on the front, and a feature on group sex, heterosexual as well as homosexual, in their quarterly 'magalog' (this last proved too much and led to it being discontinued at the end of 2003). Men defected from the brand in droves.

In an effort to stretch the brand and reach younger consumers, a group of 'abercrombie' stores was launched for children, and Hollister stores for younger teens. The brand extension for kids utilized a rather clever device, creating the extension by simply utilizing a lower case 'a' in the name. For the so-called 'tweens' market, a completely new brand, Hollister, was created. Unfortunately, these brand stretching efforts did not help the overall bottom line. The parent brand had itself become too narrowly focused, and along with the controversy over its marketing communication, the company was experiencing its fourth consecutive significant drop in same-store sales in early 2004.

What does this case suggest? To begin with, it illustrates the potential problems that a complete repositioning of a brand can bring, abandoning its established equity. Establishing a new position without any positive carry-over from a brand's equity in effect is the same as introducing a new brand, but with the burden of possible confusion in the market *because* of the brand's established equity. In terms of brand stretching, it shows that stretching a brand to reach a broader market does not always work, even with a well-known brand. The problem for Abercrombie & Fitch was, even though the name was well known, the parent brand was seriously weakened by its ever-more confrontational and unconventional sexual imagery. To the extent that it was building an equity, that equity hardly made sense in providing credibility to its sub-brands: group sex and homoerotic images for pre-teens? Add to this the fact that such equity was itself subject to the vagaries of youthful fancy and fashion, and one can understand the difficulties.

As one analyst put it, by pushing the edge of fashion the brand also pushed many of its customers out of the brand. But the CEO was unmoved: 'If I exclude people—absolutely. Delighted to do so' (Branch, 2003). With a parent brand in trouble because of its narrowly focused positioning, it becomes almost impossible to successfully stretch the brand. And in the case of Abercrombie & Fitch, add the fact that they were spending only about 2% of revenue on marketing and advertising compared with an average of 10% among other youth-oriented marketers, and it becomes very difficult to build and sustain a successful brand, let alone stretch it.

Retrenching strategies

Just as brand stretching decisions centre on considerations of long-term profitability for the company, so do retrenching strategies. As market dynamics change, with the growth of strong competitors or the introduction of new products, a brand may simply no longer be able to compete. Situations where a manager might want to consider retrenching were discussed earlier, and examples offered where it made sense to eliminate a brand. But in addition to the normal attrition of brands owing to market conditions, many companies have begun to incorporate retrenching strategies as a part of their overall marketing strategy.

In recent years many large consumer marketers have taken a serious look at their brand portfolios and retrenching strategies, eliminating many marginal brands. This trend has been particularly evident among large multinational marketers as they not only eliminate marginal brands from their portfolios, but eliminate many local and regional brands as well, concentrating on consolidating their strongest brands.

While retrenching at the local level by global marketers may undermine a firm's ability to satisfy particular market segments and cater to individual market differences, there can be significant cost savings. Ongoing shareholder pressure for cost reduction and such things as the changing retail environment (e.g. consolidated distribution) have all contributed to the loss of marginal and local brands.

Another way of retrenching, of course, is to sell off under-performing brands and in 2013 Nestlé SA, after a review of their huge portfolio, identified a group of products to sell. This represented a relatively new strategy for Nestlé, who traditionally would hang on to brands and businesses, adjusting strategies in an effort to improve performance.

Juicy Juice, acquired in the mid-1980s is an example. Once the top-selling natural juice in the category, over the last few years its share of a shrinking market had been falling, and it was not making any money. Nestle' revived the brand to an acceptable level of profitability, but rather than reinvest that profit in the brand, it was channelled into faster-growing areas of their beverage business, and the brand was sold (Dezember and Gasparro, 2014).

Disposing of under-performing brands is one way to increase the return on invested capital. A number of companies employ this strategy. In 2013 Unilever too was selling off food businesses, but in their case it was to re-focus their product-portfolio mix, concentrating on household and personal care businesses (Revill, 2013).

Master brands

One result of this retrenching has been the rise of something known as *master brands*; or perhaps the rise of master brands has led to these retrenching strategies. Regardless of which came first, there is no question that the creation of master brands has led to significant changes in product and brand portfolio management. The trend to master brands has included everything from consumer durable manufacturers like Philips to fmcg marketers like Cadbury. In the late 1990s, Unilever embarked upon a course to retrench, trimming its global brand portfolio of some 1,400 brands by 75% to 400. Even ingredient brands like DuPont's Teflon have undertaken a master brand strategy, refocusing on marketing and promoting the technology as a single, core, non-stick brand worldwide; and then extending into new categories like apparel, upholstery, and carpeting.

In many ways, a master brand is just another way of thinking about sub-branding and brand hierarchy. For example, Unilever's Bestfoods division took one of its more formidable brands, Hellman's mayonnaise, and positioned it as a master brand in 2003. They then extended it, using the brand as an umbrella for their Wish Bone salad dressings, as well as several new categories. This push for master brands at the cost of eliminating marginal brands, and sub-branding others, leads to significant downsizing, with corresponding cost savings. In one of many retrenchings as they eliminated more and more brands while creating new master brands, Unilever cut some 8% of its Bestfoods staff, eliminating 130 marketing, sales, and finance positions in 2003 (Thompson, 2003).

Along with downsizing of staff, another consequence of this trend towards master brands has been a radical rethinking and realignment of marketing communication strategies, budgets, and advertising agency affiliations. In 2003, Unilever North America's President announced that only 200 of the surviving 400 brands in their brand portfolio were likely to receive advertising support. In fact, it was reported that the real goal for the company was to identify as few as 50 'power brands' that would receive heavy advertising levels (Thompson, 2003).

Beyond the strategic issues involved in the creation of a master brand, when considering a retrenching strategy there are very real organizational issues that must be considered. With the wrong corporate culture, the likelihood of successfully developing a master brand is low. Where do brand issues fall on top management's priority list? Is attention paid to branding by senior management outside marketing departments? Are there communication channels within the organization that encourage interdivisional or interdepartmental cooperation? How will decisions for a master brand be made? Are there procedures in place that enable the optimization of marketing funds between the master brand as parent and sub-brands? These are just a few of the questions that must be satisfactorily addressed if a company is considering the creation of a master brand (Upshaw and Taylor, 2000).

Creating master brands is more and more common today as a retrenching strategy. However, it must be carefully considered, not only in terms of a company's product and brand portfolio but, as just discussed, also in terms of the company's organizational structure and its ability to effectively manage a master brand.

Before leaving the subject of master brands, we should point out that in the marketing literature a master brand has sometimes been defined as an established brand that holds a central position within a product category, dominating associations in memory with all of the important brand and category benefits. This notion follows from work in the early 1990s by Farquhar and his colleagues dealing with indirect brand extensions (Farquhar *et al.*, 1992). Interesting as this idea may be, that is not what we have been talking about here.

KEY CONCEPT

Master brands have led to significant changes in product and brand portfolio management

Master brands are in many was just another way of thinking about sub-branding and brand hierarchy. You want to create a master brand by using a strong brand, and one with strong brand equity, that is extended over the brands in the portfolio, as a parent brand. This will mean the elimination of marginal brand names, and as a result should be considered within a company's retrenching strategy.

Brand extensions

Earlier the idea of hierarchy in branding strategy was introduced, and it was noted that it is not always so clear-cut as one would like. Before talking more specifically about brand extensions, it would be well to take a closer look at this idea. As suggested, at the top of the hierarchy are company brands, which may or may not be a part of the positioning for all the brands marketed by that company (as evident in the Nestlé case). Next come group brands, which may be used in a wide variety of ways. In some cases they may be subsumed under a company brand (e.g. in the case of something like Kellogg's Frosties), or on their own they could be used to cover a wide variety of products. Last are single brands, used within a single category, and often used to cover a number of different products within a category, for example with L'Oréal, which markets such items as hair products, perfumes, and cosmetics under the L'Oréal brand name.

But as with most things discussed in this chapter, it is never quite so straightforward. Consider the case of L'Oréal. While it acts as a single brand in the personal care category, it is also a group brand as part of Elsève and other sub-brands, and also a 'hidden' company brand behind Lancôme, another of its brands. It is also the parent company of Giorgio Armani and Diesel. So when considering a brand extension, just what is the 'brand' being extended? The key, of course, is to remember that branding policy is a *strategic* decision aimed at optimizing the promotion and marketing of a product.

Although brand extensions have been mentioned several times in this chapter, what exactly is a brand extension? The idea of brand extensions in marketing is certainly not new (cf. Gamble, 1967), even if research into brand extensions is relatively recent. Basically, it is nothing more than adding an existing brand name to a new item in a line, or perhaps a new or revised version of a product. Consumer packaged goods companies use brand extensions, retail stores extend their 'brands' to other types of outlets, and services or other businesses extend their names to cover a variety of different products or activities under the same 'brand' name. Brand extensions may be accomplished using a single brand name, a group brand, or a company brand. Perhaps the most important reason for considering adding a brand extension is to capitalize on existing strong brand awareness and positive brand equity, but there are other reasons as well:

- Brand extensions can create excitement in the market, for the consumer as well as the trade.
- Brand extensions can offer the appearance if not the actual consequences of positive change.
- Brand extensions can help meet new market demand, and they can also provide new competitive advantages.

Brand extensions can be close, logical extensions of the original product, or they can mark a complete change. When Gucci extends its brand from high-fashion clothing and accessories to sunglasses, it is a logical extension; when it moves into cosmetics, it is moving further from its origin. Other high-fashion houses such as Armani and Hugo Boss extended their high-priced brands downwards by extending vertically to more mid-priced boutiques, Emporio Armani and Boss. One must be careful with such vertical extensions, however, so as not to dilute the equity of the higher-priced parent (Kirmani *et al.*, 1999). Even a traditional brand like Harley-Davidson, founded in 1903 and for many years in the mid-twentieth century the only manufacturer of motorcycles in the USA, found it useful to maximize its strong brand image and introduce a number of brand extensions, including a line of Motor Clothes and licensed products!

Obviously, brand extensions, brand stretching, can occur anywhere along the brand hierarchy. At issue is where and how a brand extension makes the most sense within the product and brand portfolio. For example, will it improve overall brand image or reduce risk for consumers (Milewicz and Herbig, 1994)? Will it produce economies of scale in terms of more efficient use of marketing expenses, versus the value of a new brand name (Sullivan, 1992)? This is tied tightly to how the brand extension will be *positioned*. In our definition of brand hierarchy, we have identified three rather general and straightforward brand levels. Others have taken a more detailed view of branding strategies. Kapferer (1997), for example, offers six different levels of possible branding strategies. While he makes some very useful distinctions, for most purposes this is probably more than we need to be concerned with. However, the distinction he makes between what he calls 'source' brands and 'endorser' brands is worth noting.

Briefly, Kapferer describes a *source brand* as one where products are directly named, while a company brand acts as a guarantee of the product's quality. An example would be Tommy Hilfiger's Freedom line of perfume. The brand extension is Freedom, but the source assuring the customer of the brand's quality is Tommy Hilfiger. On the other hand, an *endorser brand* is one that acts as a guarantee of quality for a wide range of products, possibly ranging over a variety of lines as was noted with Yamaha. What makes this distinction so important for brand stretching strategies is that the benefit structure driving the brand equity of the source or endorser brand, and the benefit structure underlying the potential brand extension, should be considered in terms of which of these two potential branding strategies makes the most sense for the individual product. The choice, of course, will depend (primarily) upon the product or brand portfolio strategy, as well as the perceived strength of the potential equity in the brand extension's positioning. It will be this equity trade-off that should drive the choice.

> ## KEY CONCEPT
>
> ### When to use source versus endorser branding strategies
>
> A source branding strategy in brand extension is where the product is directly named, with the company acting as a guarantee of the product quality, providing a direct parent-product link. An endorser branding strategy is where the brand acts as an overall guarantor of quality. When involvement with a category is high, an endorser strategy makes the most sense because people are looking for specific benefits associated with the brand. With low category involvement, a source strategy should be used because it offers more general reassurances of quality.

This distinction reflects a critical difference in brand architecture, which is important for how a brand is marketed (Kapferer, 1997). A source branding strategy provides a *direct* parent–product link: source brand name plus brand extension. An *endorser* branding strategy projects greater independence between the parent-endorser and the extension: brand extension from the endorser brand. The higher the level of someone's involvement with a product, the more likely they are to have a strong focused idea of what benefit they want from that product. This means they are more responsive to a single, stand-alone brand or an *endorser* brand, where the specific positioning is more likely to be unique and reflective of the specific benefit(s) for which they are looking. Those with lower levels of involvement with the category tend to be looking for more general benefits, and are more likely to look for the reassurance that comes with a strong *source* brand (assuming the source parent brand is indeed seen as the guarantor of quality or value related to the brand extensions).

These brand extension opportunities may be found in either a line extension of the existing product, an extension within the category where the brand is currently marketed, or a new category altogether. Brand extensions offer the opportunity to reach or better serve specific segments within a market in the case of product *line extensions* or *category extensions*; or to reach new markets with extensions into new categories. The key to success in either case is the compatibility of the equity in the parent brand name with the proposed brand extension.

Line extension

Brand extensions may be introduced as either a line extension or category extension (Farquhar, 1989). If considering a line extension for a brand, both brand stretching and retrenching strategies for the line as a whole must be considered. As a result, adding items to a line will increase market penetration, but it will also increase costs. Even if the proposed line extensions can be produced using the same manufacturing facility, it adds to the burden of overall production; and there will always be additional marketing costs. The projected increase in overall sales for the brand must more than cover its costs; it should also increase overall profitability. While there may be tactical considerations that might excuse lower profitability in the short term (e.g. to meet a competitive threat), long-term strategy should aim for increased profitability for the brand from the line extension.

Another issue to be concerned with when considering line extensions is the possibility of a change in a brand's image as the line expands. One must be very careful here. Recall the discussion earlier of Anheuser-Busch's concern for their flagship brand Budweiser if they were to introduce a Bud Light, deciding first to introduce a new brand (Natural Light) into the category.

One does not normally think about premium versions of ordinary household products, but in 2013 and 2014 Proctor & Gamble introduced high-end versions of many of their mundane household products such as paper towels and dishwasher soap. Their Bounty brand paper towels was extended as Bounty DuraTowel, launched with embossing that resembled that of a dishcloth, and at a price point 20% higher than regular Bounty, already considered a premium paper towel compared with many other brands. Cascade Platinum, a higher-end version of their Cascade dishwasher soap, was also introduced at about the same time. They were not alone. Both Kimberly-Clark and Colgate-Palmolive introduced more premium versions of their products (Ng, 2013).

Yet at the same time, Proctor & Gamble was also adding products in what they called their 'mid-tier' as well as low end extensions such as Tide Simple Clean and Flash for more cost conscious buyers. Their aim was to create more vertical portfolios.

More is not always better. In fact, with brand extensions within a product line it is often a good idea to consider a retrenching strategy as well, retiring some existing items from the line, as new extensions are added. A good example of this is with lines of prepared food products. Because of something the industry refers to as 'flavour fatigue' most prepared food companies will regularly extend their line offerings, while at the same time eliminating some items from the line. Aside from issues of overall profitability if the line is too long, there is also the very practical issue of distribution to be considered. Just because a brand offers a long line of items does not mean that the trade will stock all the items. Brand stretching within a product line often must be coupled with retrenching.

KEY CONCEPT

Brand extensions are different from line extensions

Line extensions should not be confused with brand extensions because line extensions are a specific type of brand extension where new items or varieties are added to an existing brand or brand set. In addition to a line extension, a brand may be extended into a new category, a category extension.

Category extensions

Category brand extensions may occur either within the product category where a brand is already marketed, or in an entirely new category for the brand. In terms of brand hierarchy, if the extension is within a product category where the brand currently has a presence, the existing brand will become a parent or company brand (if it is not already one), and the new introduction a sub-brand, either as part of a source or endorser brand strategy. If the extension is outside the category where the brand is currently marketed, it may also become a sub-brand in the same way, or simply a group brand.

As discussed earlier, a company or product brand is one where the brand identifies the parent company, such as L'Oréal or Nestlé, and is associated with one or more sub-brands. Group brands are those where the same brand name is used in more than one product category, such as Harley-Davidson or Yamaha. And as was also discussed, while this hierarchy (including single brands) provides a good way to look at brand stretching strategies, in reality there are many variations and permutations possible (and likely).

The number of brands or sub-brands offered by a company within a product category is often referred to as the *depth* of a company's brand strategy. The obvious reason for offering different brands within the same product category is to address the needs of different segments within the market (as we saw with Volkswagen). In terms of brand stretching, the issue is whether to extend an existing brand from another category or to introduce a sub-brand of an existing brand in the category. Of course, there is always the option of creating an entirely new brand. The decision will be based upon the broader considerations of the company's branding strategy.

Co-branding

Co-branding, briefly introduced in the last chapter, is another aspect of brand extension. While co-branding has long been used in marketing, in recent years it has become more common. In just the first five months of 2014 (as we write this) 6% of all products launched in the U.S. used co-branding, double-trade marking or licensing, up from 3.5% in the previous two years (Schultz, 2014).

The advantage of co-branding is that it allows for faster new product launches, but the downside is that you give up complete control when you are relying upon another brand's equity in addition to your own. An example of co-branding was Kellogg's decision to introduce a peanut butter breakfast cereal in 2014. Rather than relying only upon their own strong brand equity in the cereal category, they entered into a licensing agreement with Smuckers to use their well-known Jif peanut butter brand. The resulting Kellogg's Jif Peanut Butter cereal emphasized the Jif name, and the package featured the familiar red, blue, and green stripes from the Jif peanut butter jar.

Advantages of brand extensions

Almost all companies at one time or another will be actively involved in brand stretching. It is in the nature of markets to evolve, and this requires ongoing evaluation of the product and brand portfolios. Inevitably, this will lead to brand stretching (or retrenching). Brand stretching with extensions makes sense, primarily because of the advantages associated with being able to transfer a brand's existing equity to an extension. While there can be risk here, as we have already seen, when there is a positive fit there is the potential for real advantages (Fig. 11.4).

Building positive brand attitude from scratch for a new brand introduction takes time, and a great deal of marketing resources. Introducing a brand extension rather than a new brand significantly reduces the cost of a new product introduction from a marketing

- Reduces the cost of new product introduction through easier distribution, building brand awareness faster, creating positive brand attitude faster
- Reduces risk of trial
- Increases customer base
- Stronger overall brand attitude for parent brand
- Increased extension opportunities

FIGURE 11.4   Advantages of brand extensions

standpoint. It is the existing brand awareness and brand attitude that facilitates the introduction. Because the brand name is a known entity, gaining distribution is easier. Because the brand name is known, building awareness for the new product is easier. Existing brand attitude means there is an equity base already established to form the foundation for positive attitudes towards the new product, significantly reducing marketing communication costs for advertising and promotion.

This is especially true when the parent brand is seen as high quality, and this has been shown to hold cross-culturally (Bottomly and Holder, 2001). Also, when consumers see an extension as a particularly good fit with the product category, it is easier for them to transfer positively held affect for the parent brand to the new brand extension (Roedder John and Loken, 1993). In the end, the more successful a brand is in building positive brand equity, the easier it will be to expand into more diverse product categories (Rangaswamy *et al.*, 1993).

In addition to these marketing efficiencies, there are a number of other benefits to brand extensions. Because the brand name is familiar, it facilitates the acceptance of the new product by reducing perceived risk in trying it on the part of the consumer. Because the new product is likely to address a new customer segment, the customer base for the brand is likely to increase, along with the potential for trial of the parent brand by these new customers. And when successfully implemented, there is the opportunity to build an even stronger overall brand attitude for the parent brand. Finally, by extending the brand to a new product, it opens up the opportunity for additional extension from that new product.

Disadvantages of brand extension

For the most part, if a brand extension is carefully considered, along the lines discussed, there are no significant *dis*advantages. However, if the extension has not been carefully considered, there is a real potential for problems. In fact, what are advantages when brand extensions are well considered can often become disadvantages with a bad brand stretching strategy (Fig. 11.5).

- Potential consumer confusion
- Cannibalization of parent brand sales
- Limited extension opportunities

FIGURE 11.5   Disadvantages of brand extensions

It has been noted how existing brand knowledge can help facilitate building brand awareness and brand attitude for an extension, but when not well considered, that same positive understanding of the parent brand could lead to confusion over just what the brand is all about. This can really be a problem when consumers do not readily see the congruence between the equity of the parent brand and the new product. If a high-fashion line like Chanel were to extend its brand into the active participation sportswear category, it could very well cause confusion with the haute couture image of the brand. This would be especially true if they were to extend as a group brand, using only the Chanel brand name, and even if they were to extend with a sub-brand using a source strategy, for example, 'Chanel Sport'. While the potential for confusion might be less with an endorser sub-branding strategy, something along the lines of 'Excell, active sportswear from Chanel', people are not likely to see any logical association with Chanel's long-established high-fashion brand equity. High fashion is simply not likely to be an important benefit for the active sportswear worn by someone running a marathon or working out in a gym, with the possible exception of a very small segment of the market.

But even if a small segment of the market was interested in wearing high-fashion active sportswear, one must consider what the overall impact would be upon the existing market for Chanel. Would someone spending thousands of euros for a Chanel dress want to see the brand associated with people perspiring in a heavy workout? Not very likely! This example should underscore how important it is to consider the 'fit' of any brand extension.

Helmut Panke, chief executive of BMW (in 2004) put this in an interesting way. When asked in an interview 'For you, as a CEO, are there any special responsibilities you have for maintaining or building your brand image?' he replied: 'As provocative as it sounds, the biggest task is to be able to say 'No'. Because in the end, authentic brand management boils down to understanding that a brand is a promise that has to be fulfilled everywhere, at any time. So when something doesn't *fit* [our emphasis], you must make sure that that is not done' (Boudette, 2003). He went on in that interview to illustrate the point by talking about an internal debate on their product portfolio. 'There is a segment in the market which BMW is not catering to and that is the minivan or the MPV segment. We don't have a van because a van as it is in the market today does not fulfil any of the BMW group brand values. We all as a team said no. We will not bring a van.'

There are other advantages that might become disadvantages if a brand extension strategy is not well considered. For example, while a known brand can often help secure distribution for a new product, if a brand already has a strong presence in a market, it could meet with resistance from the trade, particularly if there are numerous or particularly strong brands already in the category. While this is especially true for line extensions (particularly with fmcgs where, with different sizes and variations, a brand could easily market 20 or more items in a line), it can also be a problem for brand extensions within a category. If you are a brand like Nivea, with an extensive line of skin-care products in the beauty aid category, and decide to stretch the brand into the already crowded cosmetic market with a line of lipsticks and fingernail polish, you could very well meet with resistance from the trade.

The trade, especially retailers, is constantly dealing with trade-offs among the space available for products, the available alternatives to offer, and what combination will maximize profit. Agreeing to carry a new brand extension will almost always mean dropping an item. Adding to the pressure on retailers to optimize the best mix of brands and varieties in a category is industry research suggesting that profitability might actually be increased by stocking *fewer* items from a category (Boatwright and Nunes, 2001).

While carefully planned brand extensions should increase the customer base, there is the possibility that a new product introduction will actually reduce the overall customer base, either through a negative effect upon overall brand attitude for the parent brand (as above) or through cannibalization of the existing brand franchise. Cannibalization occurs if a new product is seen as a preferred alternative to the parent brand by those who currently buy it. Even if the extension attracts new customers to the brand, if it cannibalizes the existing base, the dynamics of the brand will change significantly. This may not be a bad thing if the new configuration increases profitability overall for the brand, but it will require a new overall brand strategy and marketing plan. In effect, the brand extension becomes the parent brand, and the original brand the sub-brand, and this new situation would need to be carefully evaluated in terms of the company's product and brand portfolio strategies.

Finally, if a new product is introduced as a brand extension, this means it will not have the potential for its own unique identity, and it will have limited opportunities for extensions in its own right. In many situations, this is not a problem. But it is something that should be carefully considered. It is important to think well beyond the short term when considering a brand extension. The company may be sacrificing future opportunities by limiting a new product to the umbrella of a parent brand. There are many advantages to well-considered brand extensions, but managers must always be aware of the fact that these same advantages could become disadvantages.

Considering options for a brand extension

To help put all this into perspective, consider a situation that confronted Nestlé in the 1980s (and with which one of the authors was involved). At the time their Findus division (now no longer a Nestle' company but the Findus Group), marketed frozen prepared foods under that brand name and was considering the introduction of a new line of frozen prepared foods specifically positioned for lunch. With the introduction of refrigerators and microwaves for employee use in many offices, this seemed like a natural expansion for them. But how should it be positioned in terms of branding strategy?

Nestlé was considering using another of their brand names, Lean Cuisine, in some way. It was a line of lower calorie prepared frozen food products. But would it make more sense to introduce it as a line extension of Findus, and not consider Lean Cuisine at all? Or would it be better to introduce a stand-alone single brand called Lunch Express? What would you recommend? They were initially keen on a sub-branding strategy using an endorser strategy with Lean Cuisine as the parent: Lunch Express from Lean Cuisine. They wanted to trade upon the strong market position of Lean Cuisine with its already high levels of brand awareness and brand attitude. But consider Lean Cuisine's brand equity. It centres on good-tasting products that are calorie-controlled for people watching their weight. This would limit the market for Lunch Express, as well as *significantly* limiting the potential for any future Lunch Express brand extensions.

Using an endorser or source brand strategy with Findus would have made more sense because it would not be limited to calorie-controlled products, but its brand equity in the market was not as strong as Lean Cuisine. We argued for Lunch Express to be a new single brand from Nestlé because it opened the opportunity for addressing both those looking for calorie-controlled products and those not concerned with watching their weight, with product lines oriented to both markets. Also, it would open the opportunity for brand extensions into a number of other areas. Importantly, this would enable the brand to expand into non-frozen foods, everything from snacks to beverages. In the end, Nestlé decided against introducing the new product, opting instead for advertising their existing Findus and Lean Cuisine product lines as 'great for lunch', and promoting the idea with a portable freezer pack so you could carry them to the office.

As this case illustrates, branding strategy requires a great deal of strategic thought and planning. The matter must be looked at from many aspects, not just short-term profitability. Where would such a move fit within the company's overall product and brand portfolio strategy? Does it make strategic sense for the brand? Will the proposed extension 'fit' in terms of brand equity congruence? What are the advantages of such an extension; and what disadvantages might there be? Carefully considered, brand extensions will strengthen the overall brand position; when not well considered there is the potential for serious long-term problems.

Brand stretching: postmodernism to metamodernism

In the 1970s the beginning of what came to be known as postmodernism 'magically appeared' according to Kim Levin (2012) 'dedicated to saving architecture and art from the doctrinaire constraints of Modernism'. By the end of the 1980s Postmodernism had gone retro, and terms were multiplying: there was post-Postmodernism, Supermodernism, Hypermodernism, New-modernism, Anti-modernism, Altermodernism, and more. While there may have been a surfeit of 'modernisms', they all assumed a major role for irony and pastiche (Levin, 2012).

It was during this period that a group of marketing academics, led by Steven Brown, began to link the idea of Postmodernism with marketing. As Brown (1995) put it at the time, postmodernism provides a way of looking at the dramatic changes that are taking place in the marketing arena, and that it is very much in tune with contemporary marketing sentiment. We are not so sure of that, but certainly Baudrillard's suggestion (in Brown, 1995) that 'image is all', and more important than reality (in fact *is* reality), is consistent with the importance of understanding a brand's equity in making brand stretching decisions. Recall that brand equity reflects that which attains to a brand over and above its intrinsic qualities. In other words, its 'image'.

KEY CONCEPT

Postmodern notions have been associated with brand stretching

Not long after the ideas of postmodernism were introduced into the world of art and architecture they found their way into marketing and branding strategy. The notion that brands can provide an anchor in an increasingly frantic and uncertain postmodern world would suggest that extending an existing brand with strong brand equity could provide an advantage over introducing a new brand. Additionally postmodernism encouraged 'retrospective' thinking, which lead to 'retro' marketing, again an application of brand extension.

One of the arguments made in discussions of postmodernism and marketing is that owing to the frantic, uncertain nature of life in a postmodern world, brands can provide an anchor, especially long-established brands. In a world increasingly taken up with hyperreality (the postmodernist would argue), the stability offered by brands with a positive equity and history can provide a bit of stability. In terms of brand stretching strategy, this would suggest that extending existing, well-established brands could have an advantage over the introduction of a new brand name.

Beyond this, the reality, such as it is, of a postmodern world (again the postmodernist would argue), creates an ideal environment for 'retrospection', the recycling of fashion. This notion is perhaps best typified by postmodernism in the arts, and most especially in architecture. Nowhere do we see the idea of postmodernism on firmer ground. Postmodern architecture uses traditional materials and styles, but combines them in unique, innovative ways. Usually informed by classical or neoclassical styles, various elements of these traditions are combined to provide a new but familiar look. The results may not be pleasing to the traditionalist's eye, 'Hepplewhite and Chippendale in drag' (Hepplewhite and Chippendale were two leading eighteenth-century English cabinetmakers who defined the taste and style of the period), as quoted in Jencks (1989), but reflect the idea that there can be no one style, no 'correct' style, in a postmodern world.

In looking for brand stretching opportunities, this idea of recycling earlier fashions must go beyond a simple revival of an earlier product or brand. In Stephen Brown's (1995) words, it should reflect 'a retrospective inclination to appropriate and recycle past styles in an ironic or parodic manner'. The new brand extension will be informed by the old, but with a twist; the world of retro marketing. In the late 1990s, and continuing into the early 2000s, there was an ongoing stretching of established brands with extensions reflecting earlier versions of the brand: Parker pens, Hobbs coffee percolators, Vimto, Converse All Stars, Ovaltine, the list goes on and on.

This 'look back' has been especially prevalent in the automotive market. Chevrolet revived its old Impala name plate, but as a 'sportier' model rather than a staid family saloon; Daimler-Chrysler introduced the PT Cruiser, a small-scale reproduction of a 1940s-like estate wagon, with a raked look reminiscent of a 1950s 'hot rod'; and the Mini Cooper was revived. In each case, the companies are reaching back to find a brand extension, yet the resulting product does not duplicate the original. This is especially true for the Mini Cooper. While it may resemble that old much-loved vehicle, the new version carries a hefty price tag. The same is true of the retro Ford Thunderbird. One senses the 1955 original, it has the mesh-like grille and hood scoop reminiscent of the original, and it uses the original T-bird logo. But side-by-side, they are very different vehicles. And like the Mini Cooper, this is one expensive automobile. With the Mini Cooper and the T-bird, the search for a sense of stability in nostalgic brands is anything but cheap.

Consider one more example. Levi's are almost synonymous with jeans, and we have used them as an example several times in this chapter. Yet their share of the market plunged significantly during the 1990s. The company, long the dominant brand in the market, had lost its focus. It had stretched itself into every conceivable niche for jeans, and was no longer seen as unique. The many brand extensions had begun to erode the original brand equity. Among other attempts to reverse declining sales and revive the brand, it looked back to its heritage (Sanderson, 2002). The company reacquired an original pair of their jeans from the 1880s that had been found in a coal mine, and reproduced it as a limited edition extension at US$400 a pair! In addition, they significantly retrenched, eliminating many extensions. Those retained, along with new brand extensions (such as the limited edition Nevada jeans described above), were positioned more consistently with the brand's original equity. The results arrested the slide in sales, and have made the company more competitive.

Once seen as a radical concept in Western culture, today it can be argued that postmodernism has run its course and is now nothing more than another style trend, as reflected in the 2011 Victoria & Albert Museum's retrospective in London: 'Postmodernism: Style and Subversion 1970–1990'. So, is there still a place in marketing today for brand strategy and positioning within a postmodern framework?

While the idea of postmodernism may have run its course, a new post-postmodernism movement known as metamodernism has recently emerged in Europe. In 2009, cultural theorists Timotheus Vermeulen and Robin van den Akker founded the webzine *Notes on Metamodernism*. They talk about metamodernism as negotiating the built-in confusion and contradictions between Modernism and Postmodernism, and replacing the culture of Postmodernism with a post-ideological condition that stresses engagement, affect, and storytelling (as discussed in Levin, 2012). Just as Postmodernism found its way into marketing, perhaps we shall some day be hearing from marketing Metamodernists. The *Notes on Metamodernism* webzine already has a section on Economics.

CHAPTER SUMMARY

In this chapter we have looked at brand stretching and retrenching within a strategic context, placing them within the broader framework of product and brand portfolio management. We looked at how an evaluation of both category and brand development can help suggest how a manager approaches brand stretching and retrenching. Next, we addressed the fundamental questions that must be asked when considering a change in branding strategy: does it make strategic sense; does it 'fit' in terms of a brand's equity; and will it be profitable? Then we looked at what is involved in brand extensions, and discussed different ways of dealing with a brand extension strategy. Various advantages and disadvantages associated with brand stretching and retrenching were presented, and the fact that what begins as an advantage may end up a disadvantage. Finally, we looked at branding strategy in light of postmodern thinking and the emergence of metamodernism.

DISCUSSION QUESTIONS

1 How do product and brand portfolio management influence the development of brand stretching and retrenching strategy?

2 Identify a recent merger or acquisition and discuss how it influenced the company's portfolio strategy.

3 Discuss the idea of brand hierarchy and its role in branding strategy.

4 What criteria are important when making a brand stretching or brand retrenching decision? Are some of these criteria more important than others?

5 Think of two or three brands you feel are likely candidates for brand stretching, and discuss why and in what direction you think it would make sense for them to 'stretch'.

6 Pick two or three brands that you feel could not or should not be stretched, and discuss why.

7 How does the concept of a master brand fit with retrenching?

8 Discuss the difference between a brand extension and a line extension.

9 When does it make more sense to use a source rather than endorser branding strategy, and when an endorser rather than source?

10 When can a brand extension advantage become a disadvantage?

11 How can postmodern theory influence brand stretching strategy?

12 Contrast metamodernism and postmodernism and indicate how it could influence branding strategy.

CASE STUDY

The White Stuff: How advertising helped stretch Hovis without breaking it

Hovis, a brand owned by British Bakeries, moved into the white bread sector in 1991. This movement would have threatened Hovis' original values and the reputation for homely brown bread; yet, it successfully transferred Hovis from a brown bread specialist to a bread leader. This case demonstrates how British Bakeries capitalized on its Hovis brand by guiding it safely into uncharted territory: the white bread market.

In 1886 Hovis started its life as 'Smiths Patent Germ Bread'. This was soon changed to Hovis from the Latin 'hominis vis' (strength of man) which was used to symbolize wheatgerm bread, bread that was related to Hovis' original idea of nutrition and health. Advertising played a strong role in the growth of the brand and many famous campaigns have been associated with Hovis over the years. In 1916 *'Don't say brown, say Hovis'*; in 1936 *'Have you had your Hovis today?'*; in 1954 *'Hovis is the slice of life'*. All in all, perhaps the most famous advertising of all for Hovis started in 1973 (and lasted for 20 years thereafter) when the 'Boy on the Bike' campaign first appeared executing the thought and the line: *'Hovis. As good for you today as it's always been.'*

No other food is as integral to the British diet as a loaf of bread. It was a massive market worth just under £2 billion, or 60 million loaves a week. The problem was that bread is not something consumers think about very much because it is taken for granted. With the notable exception of the small speciality bread sector (£100m) it is a habitual purchase and little time is spent at the bread fixture. 60% of the total market was own label and branding appeared to be pretty unimportant, especially in the huge standard white sliced sector which was very close to being a classic commodity market. There was, however, an exception to this general rule within white bread—which represents 70% of the total market. This was the white premium sector, which is worth about £200 million, about 18% of total white bread value. It was created in the late 1980s with the launch of Allied Bakeries' Kingsmill brand. British Bakeries followed with Mother's Pride Premium, but they failed to gain sufficient distribution to challenge Kingsmill. In addition, against a background of decline in the natural environment of brown bread, the Hovis brand was capitalized on by British Bakeries as an opportunity for corporate growth. The company decided to use the strength of the Hovis brand to attack this important sub-market. In 1991, British Bakeries launched Hovis White—using the renowned brand to support a non-brown product for the first time.

Yet Hovis' entry to the white bread segment stimulated some concerns. These concerns were clear and significant: could a premium brand still remembered for '*Don't say brown, say Hovis*' take a step into territory seen as the very antithesis of all of Hovis' homely, nutritious, and wholesome values without weakening its own character and strength? And would the white bread buyer see a Hovis White as a credible product? However, a number of factors conspired towards a Hovis White launch. First, research indicated that people lacked a meaningful grammar for understanding the bread-related terms, such as fibre, wheatgerm, and granary. Faced with such insecurity and a plethora of own-label products, consumers looked on Hovis as a trusted signpost, shorthand for good, reliable baking. Secondly, research also confirmed the new topography of the bread market, where discrete segregation was becoming a thing of the past as products like softgrain and mildbake blurred the traditional brown/white boundary. Thirdly, for British Bakeries it was imperative to secure the Mother's Pride Premium listings and support *one* brand effectively against Kingsmill. The strongest brand to fight that battle (it was felt) was Hovis, which had potentially a more attractive franchise than Kingsmill. And finally, an AGB Repertoire Analysis confirmed that 85% of Hovis buyers were already buying white bread and over a quarter were purchasing Mother's Pride. Following this thread, British Bakeries saw a huge growth opportunity available to turn Hovis into the definitive bread brand. Hovis' first task, therefore, was to launch Hovis White as a credible product in its own right at the same time as reassuring existing Hovis (brown) consumers that their brand had not changed for the worse.

Hovis White was launched in July 1991. The launch was supported by a new execution in the 'Boy on the Bike' advertising style called 'Stages In Life', featuring an elderly Hovis enthusiast reminiscing about how he was brought up on Hovis from boy to man. Set in the present day it captured his memories of Hovis in his past life (using flashbacks); he says that Hovis has always been part of his life, so he will probably get used to the idea of a new Hovis white bread. The music, voice over, and filmic style were the same as the core 'Boy on the Bike' campaign.

The initial burst of advertising lasted six weeks from 1 September until mid-October 1991. The advertising was not only very visible in itself, but contributed to a high degree of spontaneous awareness of the brand. More importantly, though, a range of evidence, qualitative and quantitative, suggested that the advertising, in communicating the historical antecedents of Hovis White, gave the new product a credible legitimacy—in the words of the qualitative debrief, it was a 'contemporary reaffirmation of a traditional ideal'.

> It was about the little boy who has grown up with Hovis brown bread, he was going into his desk to nick a bite of this sandwich, then again when he's sitting on a stone wall, then again when he's an old man, I think he's with his wife and he's now eating Hovis white bread. That Hovis can change with the times. That they are willing to try new things.
>
> 24, DE/Millward Brown

> They were advertising white Hovis. This old boy said he had had Hovis all his life and was amazed to find they were producing white Hovis; he thought he might get used to it. That they were up to date and white Hovis is as good as brown.
>
> 61, AB/Millward Brown

> Hovis now makes a white loaf that is made with all the quality and goodness that Hovis has always had.
>
> MI Qualitative Research

Within a market that was essentially flat, Hovis White made an immediate sales impact. It not only recovered the Mother's Pride Premium sales base, but rapidly exceeded it. Despite being massively outspent by its chief rival in the premium white sector, the Hovis White commercial succeeded in announcing a new, unexpected Hovis variant at the same time as representing essential Hovis characteristics in a more modern and universally relevant tone. Within three months Hovis White achieved a 3% share of the market and was approaching Kingsmill on 5% (the gap might have been eroded more quickly were it not for Kingsmill's barrage of advertising throughout the Hovis White's launch period). Within eight months, Hovis stood as the biggest single brand in the bread market. Moreover, the brand reached its proposed positioning, having bona fide (premium) white credentials based on popularity and family acceptability alongside the inherited (brown) values. A subsidiary benefit was that the Hovis Brown image also showed a positive response to the Hovis White advertising.

The ideal brand is one where the link between brand values and product values is seamless. That Hovis has succeeded as the strongest, most durable brand in the market is a direct result of the way in which advertising has built a formidable bridge between brand and product values. It has been argued that, as well as retaining endangered distribution from its British Bakeries stablemate, the Hovis White advertising has successfully announced a new and unexpected Hovis variant at the same time as representing essential Hovis values in a more modern and universally relevant tone. Nevertheless, it achieved this balancing act without jeopardizing its heritage or credibility. More than this, it reinforced and rejuvenated its past in a way that only hindsight could consider straightforward—and this while being spectacularly outspent by its main competitor. The brand's business base now caught up with the power of its imagery and identity.

Sources: WARC, IPA Effectiveness Awards 1992, The White Stuff: How Advertising Helped Stretch Hovis Without Breaking It, by Anthony Tasgal (Historical information is referenced from WARC, Relaunching the white loaf from the brown bread company, 1996, by Mo Fisher. Edited by Hazel H. Huang.

DISCUSSION QUESTIONS

1 What were the possible reasons for British Bakeries' launch of Mother's Pride Premium before Hovis White?

2 What were the advantages and disadvantages of British Bakeries' determination to launch Hovis White?

3 How did the advertising help Hovis gain credentials in the white bread sector and reinforce its inherited values in the brown bread sector?

4 What is the difference between Hovis positioning itself as a brown bread specialist and then as a bread expert? How did the change in position help Hovis to break through its concerns regarding launching Hovis White?

FURTHER READING

- For a good overview of product and brand portfolio management see D.A. Aaker (2004), *Brand Portfolio Strategy*, New York: Free Press.

- Aaker and Keller provide evidence for a two-step consumer evaluation of brand extensions when they first determine the 'fit' between the parent brand and the extension before then deciding whether or not to apply their attitudes towards the parent brand to the extension in their January 1990 *Journal of Marketing* article 'Consumer evaluations of brand extensions', 84, 27–41.

- Tony Apéria and Rolf Back provide a brand overview of models appropriate for use when considering brand extensions (among other brand management issues) in their book 0000 *Brand Relations Management*, Copenhagen: Copenhagen Business School Press.

REFERENCES

Barich, H. and Kutter, P. (1991), 'A framework for image management', *Sloan Management Review*, Winter, 94–104.

Barwise, P. and Robertson, T. (1992), 'Brand portfolios', *European Management Journal*, September, 3, 277–85.

Birkner, C. (2013), '10 minutes with Casey Nelson and Wade Devas' *Marketing News*, September, 46–52.

Boatwright, P. and Nunes, J. C. (2001), 'Reducing assortment: An attribute-based approach', *Journal of Marketing*, 65, 50–63.

Bottomly, P. A. and Holder, S. (2001), 'The formation of attitudes towards brand extensions: Empirical generalizations based on secondary analysis of eight studies', *Journal of Marketing Research*, November, 494.

Boudette, N. E. (2003), 'BMW's CEO just says "no" to protect brand', *The Wall Street Journal*, 26 November, B1.

Branch, S. (2003), 'Maybe sex doesn't sell, A&F is discovering', *The Wall Street Journal*, 12 December, B1.

Brown, S. (1995), *Postmodern Marketing*, London: Routledge.

Dezember, R. and Gasparro, A. (2014), 'Nestle's Juicy juice sold to buyout firm as brand struggles', *The Wall Street Journal*, 2 July, B8.

Ellison, S. (2003), 'Kraft's state strategy', *The Wall Street Journal*, 18 December, B1.

Ester, M. (2014), 'Whiskey label dispute is put on ice', *The Wall Street Journal*, 26 March, B2.

Farquhar, P. H. (1989), 'Managing brand equity', *Marketing Research*, 1 September, 24–33.

Farquhar, P. H., and Herr, P. M. (1993), 'The dual structure of brand associations', in D. A. Aaker and A. L. Biel (eds), *Brand Equity and Advertising: Advertising's Role in Building Strong Brands*, Hillsdale, NJ: Lawrence Erlbaum, 263–77.

Farquhar, P. H., Han, J. Y., Herr, P. M., and Ijiri, Y. (1992), 'Strategies for leveraging master brands', *Marketing Research*, September, 32–43.

Gamble, T. (1967). 'Brand extension', in L. Adler, (ed.), *Plotting Marketing Strategy*, New York: Interpublic Press Book.

Hatch, M. J. and Schultz, M. (2001), 'Are the strategic stars aligned for your corporate brand?', *Harvard Business Review*, February, 129–34.

Jencks, C. (1989), *What is Postmodernism?* 3rd edn, London: Academy Editions.

Kapferer, J. N. (1997), *Strategic Brand Management*, 2nd edn, London: Kogan Page.

Kapferer, J. N. (2001), *Reinventing the Brand*, London: Kogan Page.

Keller, K. L. (2008), *Strategic Brand Management*, 3rd edn, Upper Saddle River, NJ: Prentice Hall.

Kirmani, A., Sood, S., and Bridges, S. (1999), 'The ownership effect in consumer responses to brand line stretches', *Journal of Marketing*, 63, 1, 88–101.

Kunde, J. (2000), *Corporate Religion*, London: Financial Times, Prentice Hall.

Levin, K. (2012), 'How PoMo can you go?', *ARTnews*, October, 80–5.

Lublin, J. S. and Cordeiro, A. (2010), 'Kraft's CEO put on the defense with Cadbury', *Wall Street Journal*, 7 January, B1.

Milewicz, J. and Herbig, P. (1994), 'Evaluating the brand extension decision using a model of reputation building', *Journal of Product and Brand Management*, 3, 1, 39–47.

Muñoz, S. S. (2013), 'Juan Valdez's latest travels', *The Wall Street Journal*, 20 December, B5.

Ng, S. (2013), 'Basics get luxury treatment', *The Wall Street Journal*, 5 September, B1.

Rangaswany, A., Burke, R., and Oliva, T. A. (1993), 'Brand equity and the extendibility of brand names', *International Journal of Research in Marketing*, 10, 61–75.

Revill, J. (2013), 'Nestle' to sell off underperformers', *The Wall Street Journal*, 2 October, B3.

Roedder John, D., Loken, J. B., and Joiner, C. (1998), 'The negative impact of extensions: Can flagship products be diluted?' *Journal of Marketing*, 62, 19–32.

Roedder John, D., Loken, J. B. (1993), 'Diluting brand equity: The impact of brand extensions', *Journal of Marketing*, July, 71–84.

Sanderson, C. (2002), 'New old Levi's', *Esquire*, September, 46–5.

Schultz, E. J. (2014), 'Why one brand name might not cut it anymore', *Advertising Age*, 23 June, 37.

Slywotzky, A. (1998), *Value Migration*, Paris: Village Mondial.

Sullivan, J. L. (1992), 'Brand extensions: When to use them', *Management Science*, 38, June, 793–806.

Thompson, S. (2003), 'Best foods strategy results in shakeup', *Advertising Age*, 7 July, 3.

Upshaw, L. B. and Taylor, E. L. (2000), *The Masterbrand Mandate*, New York: John Wiley & Sons.

 Test your understanding of this chapter and explore the subject further using our Online Resource Centre. Visit the Online Resource Centre at http://www.oxfordtextbooks.co.uk/orc/elliott-percy3e/

Managing Corporate Reputation

Key Concepts

1 Products and services can be placed on a tangibility spectrum which emphasizes positioning by a focus on either evidence or image.

2 The importance of managing brand touchpoints through the touchpoint chain.

3 The vital role of employees in influencing customer perceptions.

4 The vision–culture–image gap analysis model.

5 Understanding an organization's stakeholders and their orientation.

6 The role of corporate stories in building a culture and motivating employees.

7 Developing corporate brand strategy appropriate to different stakeholder groups.

8 Developing emotional connections to stakeholders through corporate stories, symbols, and sponsorship.

9 Internal brand communications and living the brand.

Introduction

When you consider chocolate at the supermarket it is probably not relevant to your purchase decision that a brand like Cadbury has a proud history in the UK and is now owned by a US firm, Kraft Foods, because you are more likely to be interested in the product itself, perhaps your experience of the taste and texture. However, when you make a decision to enter a Cadbury Cocoa House the corporate brand will matter. It is Cadbury's task to associate the nuanced customer service expected by café-goers with their brand because they cannot rely simply on the taste of their chocolate; we can already get that in the supermarket. The point being made here is that, although the range of brand strategies detailed in Chapters 8 and 9 apply equally to service and corporate brands, there are some special considerations due to the intangibility and person-dependence of a service. Of particular importance is the customer perception of the corporate brand (Berry, 2000) and, as a consequence, the need to manage the corporate reputation perceived by stakeholders, especially employees who manage the brand touchpoints between firm and customer. We will discuss these special considerations and the implications for creating a bond between the employees and the brand as well as the role of corporate culture and strategic vision. Before going on, some clarification is required of the terms 'corporate brand' and 'corporate reputation'. Whereas many writers have moved from talking about B2B brands to using corporate reputation as a portmanteau term, in theory we would like to make a distinction between a corporate brand, where the major focus is on customers and employees, and corporate reputation, where the major focus is on a wide range of stakeholders, particularly the media, government, and financial markets. However, in practice this distinction is hard to maintain so here we will use both terms interchangeably. Before we discuss the management of corporate reputation let us first explore services as a market offering.

The nature of services

If we place goods and services along a continuum from pure good to pure service, we can see that the customer's ability to make rational, evidence-based choices declines the more service elements are involved (Fig. 12.1).

A pure good has *search qualities*, which means potential buyers can evaluate the quality of the good before purchase using product and market knowledge. Many goods include service elements and have *experience qualities*, which mean they can only be effectively evaluated

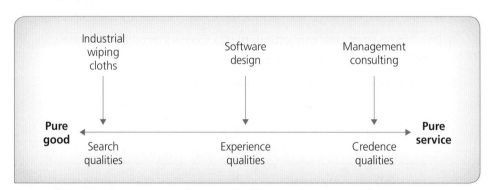

FIGURE 12.1 Product characteristics and ease of evaluation

295

after purchase and during use, and this leads to consumers using brands to reduce risk. For example, they may do this by favouring national brands over private label brands when the product category is perceived to be high in experience qualities (Batra and Sinha, 2000). But a pure service only has *credence qualities*, which means that even after purchase and use customers cannot make clear judgements based on evidence but have to believe in the quality of the service. Think about your visits to the doctor, are you always sure the procedures are thorough and the advice offered appropriate? What about the lecturer on strategic brand management you may be listening to very soon, is he or she giving you what you need? So services can be very high in perceptions of risk, and coupled with their intangibility, inseparability, and heterogeneity (Zeithaml, 1981), they are replete with problems for both customers making choices and managers delivering consistent quality. This is particularly true for labour-intensive services, as the greater the involvement of human beings in the production of a service the greater the variability in quality. The intangibility of services refers to the fact that they cannot be touched or inspected or tried out in advance. This means that customers are generally forced to depend on surrogates to assess what they are likely to get; they rely on promises of satisfaction and the marketing effort must provide metaphorical reassurance in advance. Promises, being intangible, have to be 'tangibilized' in their presentation; metaphors and symbols become surrogates for the tangibility that cannot be provided or experienced in advance (Levitt, 1981). For example, insurance companies pictorially offer to put you 'under an umbrella' or place you 'in good hands'. Products can be analysed by the degree of intangibility and positioned on a product tangibility spectrum from products that are tangible dominant, like salt, to those that are intangible dominant, like education (Fig. 12.2.)

When a product is largely a physical reality and tangible dominant then the emphasis in market positioning should be on presenting evidence, but when a product involves many service elements and is intangible dominant then the focus shifts to a market positioning focusing on intangible abstractions or image (Shostack, 1977). The more intangible elements there are, the more companies must search for all forms of evidence, no matter how trivial, that might be used to tangibilize the offer and influence customer perceptions. This is illustrated in Fig. 12.3.

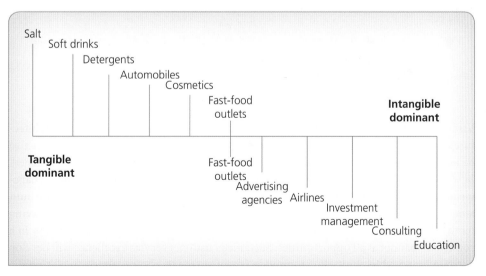

FIGURE 12.2 The product tangibility spectrum

Adapted from Shostack (1977)

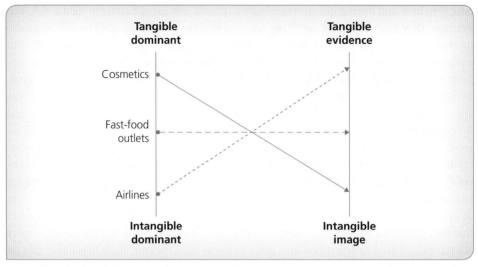

FIGURE 12.3 Tangible evidence and intangible image

Adapted from Shostack (1977)

KEY CONCEPT

The tangibility spectrum

The tangibility spectrum is relatively easily interpreted, so let's take a slightly differ-ent look at this concept. Most products are part physical good and part service. A service dominant logic (SDL) (Vargo and Lusch, 2004) goes further, suggesting that all products can be seen as services. Salt provides the service of bringing out the flavour in food. An air conditioner provides the service of cooling air. Examined this way, SDL proponents suggest that firms can better realize product improvements and, therefore, customer value because it puts the provider outside of the mindset of a physical offer-ing. For example, firms who see themselves as suppliers of a level of air temperature might use innovative air flow techniques and insulation instead of a conditioning unit.

Visible elements often have a strong influence on perceptions: colour, logos, and architec-ture can all be utilized to help a customer evaluate an intangible service. People can also be used as evidence, lawyers are 'packaged' in dark, pin-stripe suits, doctors 'packaged' in white coats, UPS drivers in brown uniforms. However, there is more to the manage-ment of people than dressing them appropriately. Fundamentally, service brands are built around interpersonal exchange, labelled here as brand touchpoints. This includes having motivated and well-trained employees who are willing to champion the corporation in a consistent manner at all opportunities. Sustained customer service excellence will develop a strong brand which in itself can provide potent surrogate choice criteria, replacing the intangibility with perceptions of a cohesive compelling brand story reinforced through multiple *touchpoints* (Berry and Lampo, 2004).

Managing brand touchpoints

A touchpoint is all the different ways that a brand interacts with and makes an impression on customers and other stakeholders, in particular on employees (Davis and Longoria, 2003). Brand touchpoints can be categorized into the pre-purchase experience, the purchase experience, and the post-purchase experience, and sum to the total experience of a customer with a brand. These touchpoints can be identified and located in a touchpoint chain that can be managed over time to deliver dynamic customer experience programmes guided by market data to focus on those interactions that have maximum impact on customer perceptions (Hogan *et al.*, 2005).

Employee behaviour has been identified as the most influential factor in shaping consumers' perceptions of their most- and least-preferred service brands, and as services are just as intangible for employees as they are for customers (Davis and Longoria, 2003) this underscores the vital importance of directing brand-building communications at employees as much as at customers.

KEY CONCEPT

Managing brand touchpoints and the vital role of employees

In a service context, brand touchpoints occur inevitably with frontline staff. The vision for the brand must therefore be communicated clearly to staff. There is nothing more damaging than a salesperson who cannot communicate the value a brand potentially presents to the customer. In a service setting that value is embodied in the way the employee delivers or supports an offering. Research shows that customers reward a firm indirectly through loyalty to frontline staff (Bove *et al.*, 2009). Digital brand touchpoints are relatively new phenomena. These are online services, like product information apps, designed to enhance the in-store experience and thus bridge the gaps between online and traditional retail. For example, high-street retailers like Oasis, Warehouse, and Coast have installed iPads in store to help shoppers browse.

Radisson BLU is Europe's largest upscale hotel brand with 170 hotels and a total of 38,079 rooms across the continent (Reiter and Snehi, 2010). Owned by Carlson Companies and managed by The Rezidor Hotel Group, the brand has a strong commitment to customer service launching its 'Yes I Can!' service philosophy in 1995. In conjunction with its broader Diversity programme, the group has won a number of awards including 100 Best Companies for Working Mothers awarded by *Working Mother* magazine in 2001–4, 2006, 2007, and 2009 as well as Best Places to Work for Gay and Lesbian Equality awarded by Human Rights Campaign, 2006–8. A great deal of effort is devoted to brand enactments within the company, including the launch of a management school to deliver 'Leading Yes I Can!' training courses for managers, 'Yes I Can!' activity packages and tool boxes made available to all staff to encourage the spirit of the

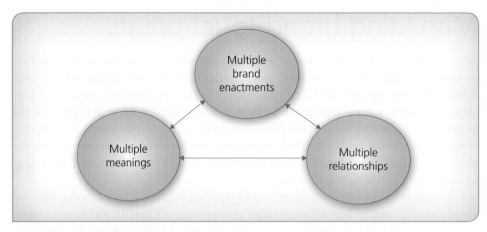

FIGURE 12.4 A semiotic model of corporate branding

programme, and a 'Gold and Diamond Anniversary Pin Program' where one diamond is earned for every five years of involvement. The programme is clearly aimed at motivating staff and does so through multiple brand touchpoints to create for employees a lived experience with the brand. The aim is to translate words into practice and help Radisson BLU achieve its stated goal of 100% Guest Satisfaction (http://www.radisson.com). As we argued in Chapter 3, brand communications are about the production of meaning as opposed to the transmission of messages, and this has been developed into a semiotic model of multiple corporate brand enactments that occur each and every time an organization interacts with its employees and its customers (Leitch and Richardson, 2003). This is illustrated in Fig. 12.4.

The key point here is that the brand is co-created by its customers and the organization's employees as a service is produced and consumed and that this process is continuously evolving and can be a rather unpredictable process. Think of all the touchpoints in a Radisson BLU hotel experience, for example booking, front desk, room service, concierge, gym, restaurant, etc. So managing brand touchpoints is actually about managing meaning and this is a very complex process. We will discuss this further when we return to the idea of living the brand.

Digital brand touchpoints

Digital brand touchpoints are attempts to close the gap between the online and the traditional retail experience using e-technology. Brands such as FlightCentre, who still have significant fixed costs in an increasingly online travel market, have invested in 'Shops of the Future'. They have opened stores on the high street with LCD screens with rotating destination imagery and in-store customer terminals for client research. Boots have an app which allows customers to search for further information about brands in-store, including other customer's reviews. A survey by Deloitte's (Digital Divide survey) revealed that more than a third of in-store purchases are influenced by digital touchpoints, with one in four shoppers spending more as a result (Pedrazolli 2014).

Digital brand touchpoints: 'The Shop of the Future' Flight Centre
Reproduced with kind permission of Flight Centre Travel Group

Corporate reputation: vision, culture, and image

In order to understand the relationship between the organization and its employees we need to utilize concepts from organizational behaviour, in particular, the concepts of strategic vision and corporate culture. These concepts have been added to the familiar concept of corporate brand image and proposed as the foundations of corporate branding by Hatch and Schultz (2003), who articulate the need to manage all three simultaneously.

Strategic vision expresses top management's aspirations for the company, while corporate culture involves the internal values, beliefs, and basic assumptions that embody the heritage of the company and the way that employees feel about the organization. Corporate image is the set of perceptions held by a range of stakeholders including customers, employees, stockholders, and the media. Together all three can be seen as components of corporate reputation: see Fig. 12.5.

The major influences on corporate image are employees, who in turn are influenced by management, but management may also have a direct influence on image through corporate communications.

Vision–Culture–Image gap analysis

Hatch and Schultz (2001) propose an alignment analysis model which identifies key problem areas where gaps arise between the component parts. They frame their Vision–Culture–Image gap analysis toolkit as a series of questions (Fig. 12.6).

A key issue in this analysis is understanding who are the organization's stakeholders and what are their relative needs.

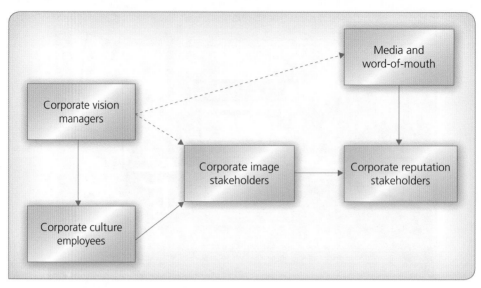

FIGURE 12.5 Corporate reputation

- **Vision-Culture Gap**

  – Do employees know the vision?
  – Does the company practise what it preaches?
  – Does the vision inspire all the sub-culture?

- **Image-Culture Gap**

  – What images do stakeholders hold of the organization?
  – How do employees and stakeholders interact?
  – What are the toughpoints?
  – Do employees care what stakeholders think?

- **Image-Vision Gap**

  – Who are the most important stakeholders?
  – What do they want?
  – Are you communicating effectively with them?

FIGURE 12.6 Vision–Culture–Image gap analysis

Stakeholder groups

A useful four-groups typology has been proposed by Dowling (2001) of groups that may all have different functional and emotional relationships with an organization and therefore hold different perceptions of it.

Customer groups: Customers analysed by their needs into different needs-based segments.

Functional groups: Employees, trade unions, suppliers, distributors, service providers.

Normative groups: Government, regulatory agencies, stockholders, board of directors, trade associations.

Diffuse groups: The media, special interest groups, community members.

KEY CONCEPT

Understanding an organization's stakeholders

It is critical for the firm to understand the importance of stakeholders beyond the customer. Qantas, Australia's flagship airline, suffered significant brand damage in 2011 when it underestimated the response of an important employee group. Pilots protested at the decision to privatize some services and move key functions offshore, threatening to strike for the first time since 1966.

Stakeholder orientations

Not only are there many stakeholders, but each stakeholder group may be looking for very different things from the organization. Customers' major interest may be service quality and reliability, whereas employees may be most interested in being able to trust the organization. Investors may be focused on credibility whilst community groups may be concerned about responsible behaviour. Analysing where to concentrate efforts can be helped by mapping stakeholders on a power/interest matrix (Johnson and Scholes, 2001) (Fig. 12.7).

Whilst the Vision–Culture–Image gap analysis approach is a very useful way to understand issues that require attention, we will discuss some other approaches to corporate reputation management later.

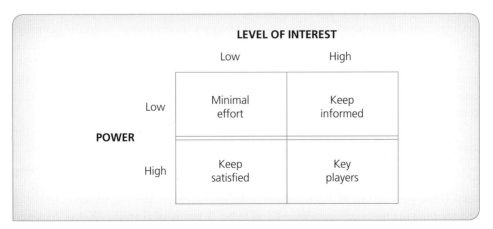

FIGURE 12.7 Stakeholder mapping

Adapted from Johnson and Scholes (2001)

Corporate culture and the corporate brand

A seminal distinction between espoused values (what organizations may claim in mission statements) and values-in-use (how organizations actually behave) was made by Schein (1992) and underlines the idea that if the values underlying a corporate brand are to be 'more than romanticism' (Hatch and Schultz, 2003) they must be rooted in the lived experience of the employees. It is not sufficient simply to articulate the brand values to employees, but requires them to be involved in the development of the corporate brand values (de Chernatony, 2002). This means that to manage the corporate brand we also need to understand how employees make sense of their world and the role which symbols and stories play in this sense-making process (Czarniawska, 1997). It may be a comprehensive training programme or diamond anniversary lapel pins, as is part of Radisson BLU's strategy that instils the right sense of corporate culture in an employee. However, seeing the boss on the factory floor, an open door policy from senior management, charismatic speeches from the CEO, or even free food and bean bags in a 'creative room' may be just as effective.

Organizational theorists argue that corporate stories are effective in motivating employees by achieving two fundamental outcomes: credibility and novelty (Barry and Elmes, 1997). Van Riel (2000, p. 164) maintains that credibility can best be achieved by corporate stories that are perceived by both internal and external stakeholders as 'illustrations of the centrality and continuity of the organization' while novelty has to express 'distinctiveness compared with players in the same or a comparable league'.

A further element in corporate culture which becomes important for the brand is the area of symbolic management, for example what does it mean to work for a certified B Corporation such as Ben & Jerry's or Patagonia? A certified B corporation has met rigorous standards of social and environmental performance, accountability, and transparency. These 'post-industrial organizations create emotional bonds and messages attracting and maintaining managers, employees, and network partners' (Larsen, 2000, p. 203); and the corporate identity is symbolized by artefacts such as logo, name, style, and other emergent cultural symbols (Hatch and Schultz, 2000). Both of these corporations have used stories (e.g. Ben & Jerry's once had a policy that no executive's rate of pay could be in excess of five times an entry level employee's) and symbols (e.g. the diary cow or the flying fish) as a part of developing the corporate brand. However, they also pride themselves upon setting the corporate standard for social and environmental performance and this permeates all aspects of the brand.

Developing corporate brand strategy

In developing a corporate brand strategy, organizations have the same two basic alternatives of functional versus symbolic strategies. Different strategies may be appropriate for different stakeholder groups, for example customers may be most concerned about corporate ability to deliver quality products and services and thus a functional strategy is most appropriate; while employees and community groups may be most interested in socially responsible behaviour and thus a symbolic strategy may be most appropriate.

Functional strategy

The objective here is to build associations in the minds of stakeholders about the company's expertise in products and services: such factors as superiority of internal research and development and the resulting technological innovation, manufacturing expertise, and customer orientation. For example, UPS makes claims about its supply-chain expertise and responsiveness, while Airbus emphasizes its non-stop innovation. Santander Bank, like many financial and consulting firms, uses the expertise of their employees. In particular, perceptions about an organization's innovativeness and trustworthiness have a marked effect when the purchase is considered to be of high risk, for example in expensive or high-technology markets (Gurhan-Canli and Batra, 2004).

Basic factors important in the functional strategies discussed in Chapter 9 are also relevant to corporate brand strategies, with salience and differentiation being key.

Brand salience
Dominating the mindspace of the market is vital for many corporate brands, and advertising and promotions play an important role here, as do word-of-mouth, media mentions, and, increasingly, the internet and blogs. Sponsorship of sports and cultural activities can play a part in building and maintaining brand awareness with stakeholders, but perhaps its greatest role is with employees (Hickman *et al.*, 2005) and we will discuss this later.

Differentiation
Perceptions of differentiation are just as important for corporate brands as for product brands, and the same factors discussed in Chapter 8 are vital here: that the brand is different from other brands, that this point of difference is unique to the brand and distinctive in that it is worth paying for. Increasingly, it appears that symbolic strategies that focus on emotional aspects may offer the most scope for differentiation.

Symbolic strategy

Although the fifteen approaches to symbolic brand strategy discussed in Chapter 8 can all be applied to corporate brands, particularly brand mythologies, we want to focus on developing emotional connections to stakeholders through corporate stories and symbols and through sponsorship.

Stories

Boje (1991) argues that organizations are essentially storytelling systems, in which stories are 'the preferred sense-making currency of human relationships among internal and external stakeholders'. Based on narrative theory, Barry and Elmes (1997) argue that successful stories can obtain credibility by the use of materiality, that is they become effective if conveyed in physical modes, for example video, PowerPoint; however they also suggest that the most significant organizational discourse is communicated verbally, as is also argued by Boje (1991). A further aspect of credibility through materiality is by reference to the everyday life of the CEOs as human beings. There is evidence to suggest that senior management associate past organizational performance with a CEO's charisma (Agle *et al.*, 2006; Rule and Ambady, 2008). Those who are both willing and able to use themselves in publicity for the organization allow stakeholders to identify more closely with the company; for example Richard Branson of Virgin, or Jill Sander of Jill Sander fashion house enabled the companies to take on a human face. It is suggested that over time as organizations become more interdependent, corporate stories may shift away from a focus on the company in isolation towards a more communitarian focus on relationships with others. When building a corporate story, the question of authenticity becomes an important factor. Its basis must be in real past experiences.

KEY CONCEPT

Corporate stories

Stories are powerful ways to communicate a set of ideas or values about a brand. The best are simply understood and can evoke emotional responses. Their impact resides not only in the content, but also in the way the story is told. In Chapter 3 we discussed emotion-based decision making and the importance of symbolism as an expression of something that cannot be fully articulated. Corporate stories can also be symbolic and are ways of expressing something about the brand that cannot be produced in a company document. Furthermore, they hold an authenticity born out of past experiences at the firm. Importantly, they can also be retold again and again as well as by others.

Authenticity and credibility

Beyond basing the story on the realities of the organizations and simply telling the truth, what is required is to communicate transparency and integrity to stakeholders (Ind, 2003). Moore (2003, p. 116) argues that authenticity can be achieved by under-promise and describes the TV documentary series Airline, which features the everyday problems of ground staff handling easyJet customers and their problems: 'With no investment in CRM and frequent-flyer pseudo-loyalty, they seem to have created a more realistic relationship with customers.' There is evidence that credibility for a wide range of organizations in different markets can be enhanced through emotional perceptions of *openness* (Maathuis *et al.*, 2003). In an industry study, conducted by Opinion Research Corporation, employees were twice as likely to engage in extra role behaviour for the company and four times as likely to recommend it to others when difficult decisions were communicated transparently (Princeton, 2009).

Symbols

Symbols 'have the power to encapsulate the senses . . . the symbol can in a magical way summarize the idea of an entire corporation', and a corporate brand and visual identity can become a rallying point for staff: 'Employees, wherever they lived and worked, whatever their social, cultural, or religious background, could identify with the whole enterprise' (Olins, 1989, pp. 73, 82). Microsoft's Blue Monster is one such symbol. It was started by Hugh MacLeod, a blogger, who liked Microsoft and drew the blue monster sending it to one of his contacts in the company, Steve Clayton, a chief technical officer at an affiliate in the UK. The image, shown here, is dramatic and grabs attention and according to Clayton is used to say Microsoft does cool stuff, things that change the world with a tag line reading 'Microsoft—change the world or go home'. The story around Blue Monster was developed by Clayton via touchpoints like presentations, business cards, and emails, all of which contain the image. He has generated further buzz by auctioning some of the lithographs on eBay, setting up a Facebook site 'Friends of the Blue Monster', and speaking about it on his blog (http://blogs.msdn.com/stevecla01/), which in turn has encouraged discussion from colleagues and contacts on other sites. There has even been a limited run of Blue Monster Reserve Label wine produced, available only to Microsoft employees and affiliates (Woollard, 2007). As Clayton says on his blog, the essence of the Blue Monster is that Microsoft needs to speak loudly and go out and talk about the 'great things that we do'. This is not a fully sanctioned corporate strategy, rather one employee's organizational citizenship behaviour. The idea took off with the Facebook site having nearly 2,000 friends and one former employee reportedly going as far as to get a Blue Monster tattoo.

Blue Monster: Symbols have the power to encapsulate the senses

Clearly symbols are not just visual devices which represent the corporate identity, they also include symbolic behaviour by management and employees. The old idea of 'walking the talk' (Peters and Waterman, 1982) is still a vital factor in building the corporate brand inside the organization, as is also attested to by Collins and Porras (1998) in their study of visionary companies driven by a core ideology that also had to be performed symbolically. Leadership behaviour matters and we will come back to this when discussing living the brand.

Sponsorship

Despite the huge amount of money spent by organizations in sponsoring sports and cultural events, there is little research that demonstrates that it has a long-term effect on the corporate brand. However, studies of sports sponsorship point to its potential role in building positive perceptions in both customers and other stakeholders, but particularly employees. Customers can form positive attitudes towards a brand, more likely to occur as identification with the sponsored team increases (Madrigal, 2000). Employee morale can be improved by sports sponsorship and it works as a form of internal communication, altering and enhancing a company's culture at different levels of the organization, helping management to communicate company values of 'strength' and 'winning' to employees, and creating a bond between frontline employees and customers (Hickman *et al.*, 2005).

Living the brand

Building a corporate brand demands that major attention be paid to employees, bringing them along with the brand strategy so that they understand it, believe in it, and also practise it in their behaviour towards customers and other stakeholders. 'Living the brand' (Ind, 2001) means transforming every member of the organization into a brand champion. This is not an easy task. A survey of US employees found that they believed that 'only 66% of company leaders are trying to do what is best for their customers, and even fewer, only 44%, believed corporate leaders are trying to do what is best for their employees' and 19% are 'actively disengaged' from their employer (Gallup, 2002). As mentioned in our discussion of symbols, leadership behaviour is very important. Evidence suggests that a transformational approach, whereby employees' values and goals are aligned with the organization's, is more effective than a transactional approach, where contingent rewards are specified and employees are rewarded for achieving particular organizational goals (Morhart *et al.*, 2009). Internal branding communications are also part of the answer, and Mitchell (2002) outlines some key principles. He suggests that people have limited tolerance for branding and visioning initiatives, but at certain 'turning points' when the company is facing challenge or change, employees are seeking direction and an internal branding campaign 'can direct people's energy in a positive direction by clearly and vividly articulating what makes the company special'.

Internal and external messages have to be linked in 'two-way branding' that harmonizes the employees' experience of the brand with what customers are being told. An example is IBM's e-business campaign, which was not aimed just at potential customers and other external stakeholders but was just as much aimed at bringing employees to the idea of the internet as the future of technology. He points out that employees have brand 'touchpoints' too and that their everyday experiences with the company must be managed to ensure that the brand strategy, and the research behind it, informs their actions. Here symbolic management practices play an important role, as does the company policy. For example, the award-winning US convenience store chain QuickTrip's customer service appraisal system and the reward structure emphasizes the team performance in satisfying and delighting customers. 'If a mystery shopper is especially impressed with a particular employee, everyone on staff at the store during the shift receives a bonus, because the company believes that individual rewards would undermine the message that all employees contribute to the customer's experience' (Bendapundi and Bendapundi, 2005).

KEY CONCEPT

Internal brand communications and living the brand

Employees live the brand when its values align with their own and they are able to embrace its raison d'être. This means more than implementing the correct communication strategy. It informs how they think about new ideas and how they communicate informally about their work to others. It is an internalised notion of what the brand means—allowing people to story-tell, understand, and communicate its relevance to different situations.

The employer brand

An organization that has a strong brand can use the brand to attract and retain employees: 'Developing an "employer brand" is increasingly seen as a winning strategy for managing all aspects of employee relationships' (Economist, 2001). It can reduce the costs of employee acquisition, improve the relationship between employees and employer, extend the average length of employee retention, and allow companies to attract high-calibre staff at lower salaries than competitors with weaker employer brands (Ritson, 2002). McKinsey Consulting, itself a formidable employer brand, advocates that employers must think of recruits as customers and use sophisticated market analysis techniques to identify key rivals and what corporate attributes matter most to specific types of recruits (Hieronimus *et al.*, 2005). Similarly, Philips, the giant electronics company, is actively engaged in a battle to attract talent using both internal and external research to uncover attraction and retention factors and then building these into an employer brand strategy of 'touch lives everyday', which was piloted in China and is now being rolled out around the world (Leeuwen and Pieters, 2005). The key point is that the strategy highlights the actual employee experience at touchpoints through the employment life cycle.

Managing the corporate brand image/reputation

A critical approach to measuring and managing corporate brand image/reputation is proposed by Dowling (2001, p. 212), who recommends going beyond the 'scorecard' approach of the Fortune Most Admired Companies survey, or its equivalents, to collect as much information as the budget will allow on detailed measures of the images and reputations held by various stakeholder groups of the organization and its competitors, and 'an indication of the characteristics of an ideal organization' in the relevant industry. From here, the management process is to close any identified gaps through managerial action and then use communication to change the perceptions of the stakeholder groups.

The process of detailed measurement, monitoring, and management has been developed into a commercial product by MORI, whose Reputation Centre offers a research-based approach to understanding the views of key stakeholder groups, and the measurement and monitoring of perceptions over time. They have particular expertise at accessing the perceptions of government at both national and European level, which is a key issue for many multinational corporate brands.

CHAPTER SUMMARY

In this chapter we have focused on the issue of tangibility, which is such a feature of service brands and how brand touchpoints can be managed. We have emphasized the importance of employees in influencing customer perceptions of the brand, and how organizational culture can be developed. We have shown that corporate brand strategy must be appropriate for different stakeholder groups, and discussed the role of corporate stories, symbols, and sponsorship.

DISCUSSION QUESTIONS

1 Why is the corporate brand so important to services?

2 What is a credence-based service and what implications does it have for brand-building?

3 How can we overcome the issues of intangibility, inseparability, and heterogeneity when building a service brand?

4 Why must brand-building communications be directed at employees?

5 Why must brand touchpoints be more than the transmission of messages?

6 How can brand salience be built for a corporate brand?

7 How can authenticity be communicated to stakeholders?

8 Why must the values underlying a corporate brand be rooted in the lived experience of the employees?

9 How can an organization become an employer brand?

CASE STUDY

Creating a culture of brand engagement from scratch

Over the years, a lot has been talked about the 'democratization of wealth' in the UK. The statistics tell us that one in every 12 adults in Britain has £50,000 or more in liquid financial assets. An ideal market for the diverse providers of financial services to target? Yet, until recently little effort had been made to address the requirements of this substantial sector of the population. Why? Because those requirements are phenomenally diverse. The 'mass affluent' are anything but a mass market and the response of much of the financial services industry to this market has been to adopt a lowest-common-denominator approach: 'What do all these people have in common? Money. So let's offer them more.' But such an approach overlooks a key feature of the mass affluent—they do not value their wealth *as* wealth. Financial services should be about providing opportunities to manipulate that money in a whole range of ways—however individuals choose—in a fashion that sits comfortably with their lifestyle choices. So—unusually for the financial services industry— we set about building distinctive brand values into the very heart of our business. The picture of our target customers informed every decision at every stage of the development of Inscape.

They're all around us

The first thing we had to realize about the mass affluent was that these are the people we see every day. They come from a wide range of social backgrounds: 34% are C1, 14% C2 and 50% A/B. They include a lot of women and people from ethnic minority backgrounds. The source of their wealth also varies, although in 40% of cases it has been built up through a salary. At present approximately two-thirds are men, 50% are aged between 45 and 65 and 44% are retired or working part-time. In addition, and as a result of the diversity of their experiences, these people's aspirations, desires, and behaviour are also quite distinct, as are their attitudes to financial services. Their only consistent and distinctive characteristic is their attitude to their wealth. Wealth for the mass affluent is a means to an end—it is about opportunity.

Representation for the 'mass affluent'

In terms of financial services, what the 'mass affluent' segment requires is a service provider who understands this fundamental driver and is capable of responding to it.

These individuals have three options for their financial services: red carpet retailing in the high street, elitist banks, or independent financial advisers. A retail bank cannot effectively address the needs of this market. Generic products are inappropriate for people with very specific, highly individual requirements. And high-street banks do not offer the high-quality investment expertise demanded by these people. By contrast, the elitist banks, which are familiar with and proficient at managing substantial wealth, are perceived as the preserve of 'old money', offering a particular kind of service to a particular class of people with whom the mass affluent simply do not identify. In theory, a middle ground does already exist, in the shape of the independent financial adviser (IFA), but many IFAs have no brand equity to call on to act as guarantor of their proficiency.

Something new, something different

Looking at the market, it was clear to us that there was a need for a new approach. We knew the kind of services our customers would respond to: high-quality investment strategies that control risk while producing attractive rates of return, expert management, good, astute advice, technical accuracy and appropriateness, and a high standard of communication through a unique customer experience. To deliver financial services expertise, we recruited from the very best fund managers in retail banking—Abbey National. But for us, their skills alone were not enough to develop the kind of company we were looking for. The whole customer experience had to be different. So to achieve such a radical transformation of business processes meant that we had to build a new culture of brand engagement from scratch.

Brand-building from the inside out

The first stage in the development of the Inscape brand was the creation of the core concept of 'True Wealth, Open Minds', which is at once a promise of a different kind of financial advice and a commitment to a different kind of customer. 'True Wealth' describes our customers' pursuit of goals through their financial arrangements other than simply swelling their bank balance. 'Open Minds' refers to the many and varied approaches they have to living their lives. While for us at Inscape, 'True Wealth, Open Minds' expresses our commitment to making the most of our customers' assets. As for 'Open Minds', that simply means that, whether a customer is a 22-year-old pop star wanting to put money away for their children's education, or a septuagenarian surfer saving for a trip to Australia, we won't bat an eyelid.

However, to realize this brand strategy, we needed to look at how the 'True Wealth, Open Minds' concept would manifest itself in the real world. First, Inscape will democratize investment management opportunities, by opening up an unrivalled range of investment management opportunities based on customers' needs for the 'mass affluent' sector. Secondly, we aim to demystify investment by providing customers with accessible, intelligible information so that they can make up their own minds about our performance. Thirdly, we are committed to delivering on standards of service through the comprehensive implementation of a brand strategy that enables customers to engage with the brand and make the promise a reality. That, of course, is a challenge, as in the past differentiation in the financial services sector has been almost exclusively on price.

Rolling out the brand

With a brand strategy in place, we looked to Circus to help us execute it. Circus adopted an all-round approach with the objective of ensuring consistent and comprehensive implementation. As an example, let us look at the physical environment of our Client Centres. We had to break away from the traditional aesthetics of either impersonal, plasticky booths or oak panelling and dark green leather upholstery. Our Centres had to defy pigeon-holing by prospective customers and indicate a serious, business-like attitude. Our first six advice centres were situated just off main streets in major towns. Din Associates were brought in to design the interiors, which are professional, modern, and informal. Staff feel the environments are well suited to their style of working and they engender a strong feeling of pride—it is clear that the offices have been designed especially for their working needs and have not simply been bought off the shelf. Initial client responses were encouraging—they find the offices bright and welcoming, different from and more professional than the standard high-street bank, yet not at all intimidating.

Our marketing included national advertising and direct mail. We needed to ensure that the promises we made to customers—'Wealth management for the privileged many'—were precisely what we, and importantly our staff, understood we would be offering. The diverse range of people represented in the posters and print ads was an accurate reflection of the initial research on which we had based the business.

Fundamental to the practical implementation of our brand strategy are our people. Ultimately it is our staff, through their encounters with prospective customers, who are the primary agents of the Inscape brand. Many of the team we brought together to create the company have been involved since the inception of the Inscape brand. They have helped build and sustain an excitement and a commitment to Inscape that would have been hard to achieve any other way. To ensure that all new staff have the skills to act as representatives of the Inscape brand, they are selected for their communication and listening abilities, as well as their financial expertise.

Getting engaged

Circus created a range of customized tools to facilitate the process of engagement within the new business, both prior to launch and as we grow in the future. The main focus of these tools was to introduce a true one-to-one customer service ethic aligned with customers' needs, not with the products we wanted to sell. We used a Brand Tool Kit to introduce staff to the brand. The kit is used by a small group and a facilitator to explain the brand's principles and values, and then to invite participation to promote active understanding and appropriate application in various circumstances. There is also an interactive CD-ROM that introduces staff to the potential range of customers, including vox-pops from a broad section of our target group. A Q&A section assesses each user's understanding of the brand and, in turn, their ability to engage the customer. Lastly, there is a further 'brand aide' in the form of a pack of postcard-sized cards, featuring references to the brand's values, some relevant quotes and inspirational sayings, and the imagery that represents the brand, in order to help the brand stay top-of-mind.

Source: WARC, Market Leader, Issue 13, 2001, Creating a Culture of Brand Engagement from Scratch. Edited by Natalia Yannopoulou.

DISCUSSION QUESTIONS

1 How did Inscape build its brand identity?

2 How did Inscape respond to the challenge of intangibility?

3 What are the key factors that contributed to the creation of Inscape's Brand Engagement culture?

4 What challenges will Inscape face in the future and how can they be addressed?

FURTHER READING

- The nature of services and the special challenges posed for their marketing is discussed by C. Gronroos (2000), *Service Management and Marketing*, 2nd edn, Chichester: John Wiley.

- A comprehensive text about corporate reputation is G. Dowling (2001), *Creating Corporate Reputations*, Oxford: Oxford University Press.

- A US approach to corporate reputation is given by C. Fombrun (1996), *Reputation: Realizing Value from the Corporate Image*: Cambridge: Harvard Business School Press.

REFERENCES

Agle, B. R., Nagarajan, N. J., and Srinivasan, J. (2006), 'Does CEO charisma matter? An empirical analysis of the relationships among organisational performance, environmental uncertainty and top management perceptions of CEO charisma', *Academy of Management Journal*, 49, 1, 161–74.

Barry, D. and Elmes, M. (1997), 'Strategy retold: Toward a narrative view of strategic discourse', *Academy of Management Review*, 22, 2, 429–52.

Batra, R. and Sinha, I. (2000), 'Consumer-level factors moderating the success of private label brands', *Journal of Retailing*, 76, 2, 175–91.

Bendapundi, N. and Bendapundi, V. (2005), 'Creating the living brand', *Harvard Business Review*, May, 83, 5, 124–32.

Berry, L. L. (2000), 'Cultivating service brand equity', *Journal of the Academy of Marketing Science*, 28, 1, 128–37.

Berry, L. L. and Lampo, S. (2004), 'Branding labor-intensive services', *Business Strategy Review*, Spring, 15, 1, 18–25.

Boje, D. (1991), 'The storytelling organization', *Administrative Science Quarterly*, 36, 106–26.

Collins, J. and Porras, J. (1998), *Built to Last: Successful Habits of Visionary Companies*, London: Random House.

Czarniawska, B. (1997), *Narrating the Organization: Dramas of Institutional Identity*, Chicago: University of Chicago Press.

Davis, S. and Longoria, T. (2003), 'Harmonizing your touchpoints', *Brand Packaging*, January/February, 17–23.

De Chernatony, L. (2002), 'Would a brand smell any sweeter by a corporate name?' *Corporate Reputation Review*, 5, 2/3, 114–32.

Dowling, G. (2001), *Creating Corporate Reputations*, Oxford: Oxford University Press.

Gurhan-Canli, Z. and Batra, R. (2004), 'When corporate image affects product evaluations: The moderating role of perceived risk', *Journal of Marketing Research*, XLI, 197–205.

Hatch, M. and Schultz, M. (2000), 'Scaling the Towers of Babel: Relational differences between identity, image and culture in organizations', in M. Schultz, M. Hatch, and M. Larsen (eds), *The Expressive Organization*, Oxford: Oxford University Press.

Hatch, M. and Schultz, M. (2001), 'Are the strategic stars aligned for your corporate brand?', *Harvard Business Review*, February, 129–34.

Hatch, M. and Schultz, M. (2003), 'Bringing the corporation into corporate branding', *European Journal of Marketing*, 37, 7/8, 1041–64.

Hickman, T., Lawrence, K., and Ward, J. (2005), 'A social identities perspective on the effects of corporate sports sponsorship on employees', *Sports Marketing Quarterly*, 14, 3, 148–57.

Hieronimus, F., Schaefer, K., and Schröder, J. (2005), 'Using branding to attract talent', *McKinsey Quarterly*, 3, 12–14.

Hogan, S., Almquist, E., and Glynn, S. (2005), 'Brand building: Finding the touchpoints that count', *Journal of Business Strategy*, 21, 11–18.

Ind, N. (2001), *Living the Brand*, 2nd edn, London: Kogan Page.

Ind, N. (2003), 'A brand of enlightenment', in N. Ind, (ed.), *Beyond Branding*, London: Kogan Page.

Johnson, G. and Scholes, K. (2001), *Exploring Corporate Strategy*, London: Prentice Hall.

Larsen, M. (2000), 'Managing the corporate story', in M. Schultz, M. Hatch, and M. Larsen (eds), *The Expressive Organization*, Oxford: Oxford University Press.

Leeuwen, B. and Pieters, J. (2005), 'Building Philips' employer brand from the inside out', *Strategic HR Review*, 4, 4, 16–19.

Leitch, S. and Richardson, N. (2003), 'Corporate branding in the new economy', *European Journal of Marketing*, 37, 7/8, 1065–79.

Levitt, T. (1981), 'Marketing intangible products and product intangibles', *Harvard Business Review*, May-June, 59, 94–102.

Maathuis, O., Rodenberg, J., and Sikkei, D. (2003), 'Credibility, emotion or reason?' *Corporate Reputation Review*, 6, 4, 333–45.

Madrigal, R. (2000), 'The influence of social alliances with sports teams on intentions to purchase corporate sponsors' products', *Journal of Advertising*, XXIX, 4, 13–24.

Mitchell, C. (2002), 'Selling the brand inside', *Harvard Business Review*, January, 80, 1, 99–105.

Moore, J. (2003), 'Authenticity', in N. Ind (ed.), *Beyond Branding*, London: Kogan Page.

Morhart, F. M., Herzog, W., and Tomczak, T. (2009), 'Brand specific leadership: Turning employees into brand champions', *Journal of Marketing*, September, 73, 122–42.

Pedrazolli, P. (2014), 'Connecting touchpoints: how multi-touch technology improves customer engagement', *Market Leader*, 4, 15–16.

Princeton, N. J. (2009), 'Effective communication positively impacts employee motivation levels, employee advocacy latest Ouch Point Survey from Opinion Research Corporation suggests', *Business Wire*, 9 March, http://www.businesswire.com/portal/site/google/?ndmViewId=news_view&newsId=20090309005073&newsLang=en Last accessed 17 July 2010.

Olins, W. (1989), *Corporate Identity*, London: Thames & Hudson.

Peters, T. and Waterman, R. (1982), *In Search of Excellence*, New York: Harper and Row.

Reiter, C and Snehi, R. (2010) 'Radisson is Europe's largest upscale hotel brand', *Press Release: The Rezidor Hotel Group*, 29 March, http://www.investor.rezidor.com/ Last accessed 17 July 2010.

Ritson, M. (2002), 'Marketing and HR collaborate to harness employer brand power', *Marketing*, 24 October, 18–21.

Rule, N. O. and Ambady, N. (2008), 'The face of success: Inferences from Chief Executive Officers' appearance predict company profits', *Psychological Science*, 19, 2, 109–11.

Schein, E. (1992), *Organizational Culture and Leadership*, 2nd edn, San Francisco: Jossey-ass.

Shostack, L. (1977), 'Breaking free from product marketing', *Journal of Marketing*, 41, 73–80.

Van Riel, C. (2000), 'Corporate communication orchestrated by a sustainable corporate story', in M. Schultz, M. Hatch, and M. Larsen (eds), *The Expressive Organization*, Oxford: Oxford University Press.

Vargo, S. L., Lusch, R. F. (2004), 'Evolving to a new service dominant logic for marketing', *Journal of Marketing*, 68, 1, 1–17.

Woollard, D. (2007), 'Blue Monster Reserve: A wine just for Microsoft', http://www.luxist.com Last accessed 15 July 2010.

Zeithaml, V. (1981), 'How consumer evaluation processes differ between goods and services', in H. Donnelly and W. George (eds), *Marketing of Services*, Chicago, IL: American Marketing Association.

Test your understanding of this chapter and explore the subject further using our Online Resource Centre. Visit the Online Resource Centre at http://www.oxfordtextbooks.co.uk/orc/elliott-percy3e/

Index